BRITTANY & NORMANDY

OLIVER BERRY
PETER DRAGICEVICH

BRITTANY & NORMANDY

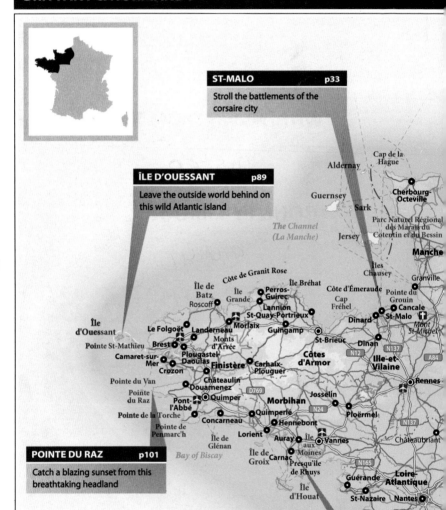

ST-MALO p33

Stroll the battlements of the corsaire city

ÎLE D'OUESSANT p89

Leave the outside world behind on this wild Atlantic island

POINTE DU RAZ p101

Catch a blazing sunset from this breathtaking headland

ALIGNEMENTS DE CARNAC p122

Marvel at the world's largest prehistoric structure

Cap de la Hague

Aldernay

Guernsey

Sark

Jersey

Cherbourg-Octeville

Parc Naturel Régional des Marais du Cotentin et du Bessin

Manche

The Channel
(La Manche)

Îles Chausey

Granville

Côte de Granit Rose

Île Bréhat

Côte d'Émeraude

Pointe du Grouin

Île de Batz

Roscoff

Île Grande

Perros-Guirec

Lannion

Cap Fréhel

Cancale

St-Malo

Île d'Ouessant

Le Folgoët

Landerneau

Morlaix

St-Quay-Portrieux

Guingamp

St-Brieuc

Dinard

Dinan

Mont St-Michel

Pointe St-Mathieu

Brest

Monts d'Arrée

N12

N137

A84

Camaret-sur-Mer

Plougastel-Daoulas

Crozon

Finistère

Carhaix-Plouguer

Côtes d'Armor

Ille-et-Vilaine

Pointe du Van

Châteaulin

Douarnenez

Pointe du Raz

Pont-l'Abbé

Quimper

D769

Morbihan

Josselin

Rennes

N137

Pointe de la Torche

Concarneau

Quimperlé

N24

Ploërmel

Pointe de Penmarc'h

Île de Glénan

Lorient

Hennebont

Auray

Île aux Moines

Vannes

Châteaubriant

Bay of Biscay

Île de Groix

Carnac

Presqu'île de Rhuys

N165

Guérande

Loire-Atlantique

Île d'Houat

St-Nazaire

Nantes

ATLANTIC OCEAN

Lac de Grand Lieu

LEGEND

- ═══ Freeway
- —— Primary Road
- —— Secondary Road
- --- Tertiary Road
- +—+ Railway line
- ✈ Airport

ELEVATION

- 300m
- 200m
- 100m
- 0

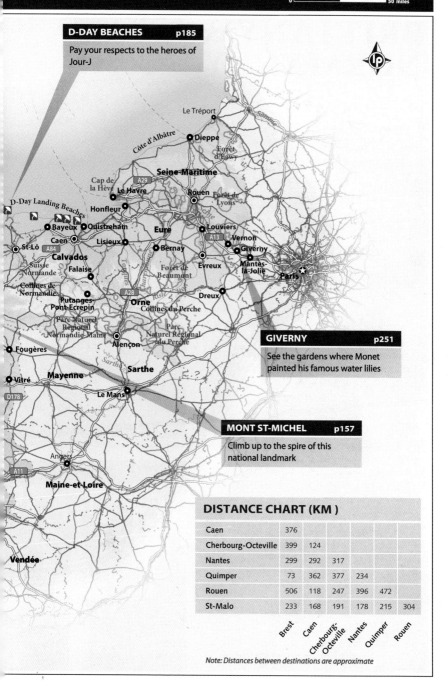

D-DAY BEACHES p185

Pay your respects to the heroes of Jour-J

GIVERNY p251

See the gardens where Monet painted his famous water lilies

MONT ST-MICHEL p157

Climb up to the spire of this national landmark

0 — 100 km
0 — 50 miles

Le Tréport

Côte d'Albâtre Dieppe

Forêt d'Eawy

Seine-Maritime

Cap de la Hève Le Havre Rouen

Forêt de Lyons

D-Day Landing Beaches

Honfleur

Bayeux Ouistreham **Eure** Louviers

St-Lô Caen Lisieux Bernay Vernon Giverny

Calvados Évreux Mantes-la-Jolie **Paris**

Suisse Normande Falaise Forêt de Beaumont

Collines de Normandie

Putanges-Pont-Ecrepin **Orne** Dreux

Collines du Perche

Parc Naturel Régional Normandie-Maine

Parc Naturel Régional du Perche

Fougères Alençon

Mayenne Sarthe

Vitré Le Mans

Angers

Maine-et-Loire

Vendée

DISTANCE CHART (KM)

	Brest	Caen	Cherbourg-Octeville	Nantes	Quimper	Rouen
Caen	376					
Cherbourg-Octeville	399	124				
Nantes	299	292	317			
Quimper	73	362	377	234		
Rouen	506	118	247	396	472	
St-Malo	233	168	191	178	215	304

Note: Distances between destinations are approximate

INTRODUCING
BRITTANY & NORMANDY

THEY MIGHT BE NEXT-DOOR NEIGHBOURS, BUT BRITTANY AND NORMANDY EACH HAVE A KALEIDOSCOPIC CHARACTER ALL OF THEIR OWN.

On one side, there's Normandy, where the relative merits of three of the nation's favourite 'c's – Calvados, cider and Camembert – are still the subject of impassioned debate. On the other, there's Brittany: wild and windswept, once an independent kingdom that has always stood one step removed from the rest of the nation, governed by its own distinctively Celtic culture and language. Put the two together and you've got one of France's most fascinating regions – a heady blend of cliffs and countryside, smugglers' ports and medieval cities, ramshackle fishing towns and stately chateaux, with a history stretching back over 6000 years.

It's certainly a region for those with a penchant for the past, but life in this corner of France is very much for the living. Whether it's browsing the day's catch at a noisy fish market, dancing to the sound of *binious* and *bombardes* at a traditional *fest-noz* or striking out across the cliff tops in search of inspiration and escape, one thing's for certain – these twin Gallic gems will stay with you long after you leave for home.

MONT ST-MICHEL

D-DAY BEACHES

TOP Mont St-Michel (p157) rises majestically above the landscape **BOTTOM LEFT** The American Military Cemetery (p187) overlooking Omaha Beach **BOTTOM RIGHT** A walking trail passes a secluded cove in Finistère (p77).

JOHN ELK III

DENNIS JOHNSON

FINISTÈRE

ST-MALO

JEAN-BERNARD CARILLET

ALIGNEMENTS DE CARNAC

DINAN

GIVERNY

TOP LEFT The walled city of St-Malo (p33) **TOP RIGHT** An old stone house in Dinan (p59) **BOTTOM LEFT** The *alignements* in Carnac (p122) cover a vast area **BOTTOM CENTRE** Monet's garden (p251) in Giverny was a major source of inspiration for the artist **BOTTOM RIGHT** Intricate workmanship on Rouen's Cathédrale Notre Dame (p238)

ROUEN

JOHN ELK III

DAVID TOMLINSON

CHRISTOPHER WOOD

GETTING STARTED

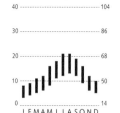

WHAT'S NEW?

* A brand new causeway to the tidal island of Mont St Michel (p163)

* A newly revamped Musée des Impressionismes in Giverny (p252)

* France's newest marine park, the Parc Marin d'Iroise (p90)

* New *voies vertes* (green ways) in Brittany and Normandy (p23)

* A new Térénez Bridge has been built just south of Landévennec (p97)

CLIMATE: ST-MALO

Average Max/Min

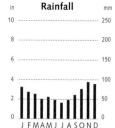

Temp

°C		°F
40		104
30		86
20		68
10		50
0		14

J F M A M J J A S O N D

Rainfall

in		mm
10		250
8		200
6		150
4		100
2		50
0		0

J F M A M J J A S O N D

PRICE GUIDE

	BUDGET	MIDRANGE	TOP END
SLEEPING	<€70	€70-150	>€150
MEALS	<€25	€25-35	>€35

TOP LEFT A traditional Breton headdress **BOTTOM LEFT** A snack of Camembert, Livarot and Pont l'Évêque **BOTTOM CENTRE** An island lighthouse in Finistère (p77) **FAR RIGHT** Window-shoppers in Rouen (p234)

ACCOMMODATION

Whether you're looking to camp under the stars, take a room by the sea or live the high life in your very own château, you'll find something to suit in Brittany and Normandy. Both are chock-full of lovely hotels and campsites, but if you really want to get under the region's skin, *chambres d'hôtes* (B&Bs) are worth considering; staying with a local family is a great way of immersing yourself in the culture, and the owners are generally mines of useful information. For more on accommodation, see p287.

MAIN POINTS OF ENTRY

ST-MALO FERRYPORT (☎ 02 99 40 64 41; Gare Maritime du Naye) Main Breton stop for ferries from Portsmouth, Poole, Weymouth and the Channel Islands.

CHERBOURG FERRYPORT (☎ 02 33 88 44 88; quai de Normandie) Normandy's busiest Channel gateway docks ferries from Portsmouth and Poole in the UK and Rosslare in Ireland.

RENNES AIRPORT (RNS; ☎ 02 99 29 60 00; www.rennes.aeroport.fr) Flights to French cities plus budget connections to the UK, Ireland and continental Europe.

THINGS TO TAKE

* Good manners. *La politesse* goes a long way in France; say *bonjour* and *au revoir* when entering and leaving shops

* A pocket dictionary with a good food section

* Beach gear but also take a waterproof raincoat

* A corkscrew for country or park picnics

* Comfy shoes for exploring old cities and coastal trails

HANNAH LEVY

WEBLINKS

BRITTANY TOURISM (www.brittanytourism.com) Online portal for the Brittany tourist board.

LE MÉTÉO (www.meteo.fr) Catch the latest weather forecast.

NORMANDY TOURISM (www.normandy-tourism.org) Plan your own Norman invasion.

VOYAGES-SNCF.COM (www.voyages-sncf.com) Train times and online bookings with France's national carrier.

FESTIVALS & EVENTS

MARCH

FÊTE DES MARINS

HONFLEUR

Local fishing boats decked out in nautical finery congregate in the Vieux Bassin (p213) for a Whit Sunday blessing.

APRIL

FÊTE DE LA COQUILLE ST-JACQUES

Scallops take centre stage at this foodie festival to mark the end of the fishing season in April. Held alternately in Erquy, St-Quay-Portrieux and Loguivy (see p67).

CARNAVAL DE GRANVILLE

GRANVILLE

One of Normandy's biggest street carnivals is held on the Sunday before Shrove Tuesday. Floats, fireworks and street parades are enjoyed by 120,000 revellers; for more see p164. www.carnaval-de-granville.fr

MAY

FÊTE DE JEANNE D'ARC

France's favourite saint met her end in Rouen on 30 May 1431. This lively national festival on the last weekend of May marks the occasion. www.fetesjeannedarc.fr

JAZZ SOUS LES POMMIERS

COUTANCES

Jazz Under The Apple Trees – sounds good already, doesn't it? Music fans congregate here (p166) in mid-May for outdoor concerts and jam sessions. www.jazzsouslespommiers.com

JULY

FÊTES MÉDIÉVALES DE BAYEUX

BAYEUX

The town (p177) goes all medieval on the first weekend in July. Jesters, jugglers, wenches and knights errant parade through the town's cobbled streets.

FESTIVAL DES VIELLES CHARRUES

CARHAIX-PLOUGUER

This major mid-July music fest held in the eastern edge of Finistère is a biggie – previous acts include Lenny Kravitz, The Killers and Bruce Springsteen. www.vieillescharrues.asso.fr.

TOP LEFT Celebrations for a *pardon* **RIGHT** The boardwalk at the seaside resort of Deauville (p208) pays homage to the stars of the silver screen

FESTIVAL DE CORNOUAILLE

QUIMPER

The region's largest celebration of Breton culture occurs in mid-July. So get your *bombardes* and bagpipes at the ready (p105).

LA PETITE TROMENIE

LOCRONAN

Pardons (religious festivals) are held all over Brittany during the summer months, but this one is among the most traditional (p102).

AUGUST

FESTIVAL INTERCELTIQUE

LORIENT

Scottish pipers, Irish bands, Welsh singers and Breton street artists come together for one great Celtic extravaganza in mid-August (p121).

SEPTEMBER

AMERICAN FILM FESTIVAL

DEAUVILLE

It's not quite Cannes, but this annual celebration of American cinema still attracts high-profile premieres and big names from the silver screen (p208).

OCTOBER

FESTIVAL DU FILM BRITANNIQUE

DINARD

Cross-Channel connections come to the fore in this early October film festival, showcasing the year's best new British films (p48).

DAVID JONES / ALAMY

CULTURE

CHRISTOPHER WOOD

ARTISTIC SITES

BAYEUX (p177) Where embroidery becomes an artform.

BELLE-ÎLE (p127) Many of the leading artists of the 19th century spent time on this idyllic island.

CÔTE D'ALBÂTRE (p217) Stroll the coastline that inspired a generation of Impressionists.

GIVERNY (p251) Claude Monet painted his water lilies here and changed the art world forever.

HONFLEUR (p211) Monet's mentor, Eugène Boudin, was born in Honfleur and the town has a museum dedicated to his work.

PONT-AVEN (p111) Paul Gauguin founded a community of painters in this town and dreamt up a new artistic movement.

CLAUDE CONNECTIONS

During the 18th and 19th centuries, Brittany and Normandy attracted a swathe of young artists including Claude Monet (1840–1926), who studied at the Le Havre School of Arts, and later under the tutelage of Honfleur painter, Eugène Boudin. Monet felt an affinity for Normandy's rolling countryside, gentle coastline and big, open skies, but as his artistic eye developed it was the shifting colours and subtle play of light across the landscape that fascinated him most – an obsession that developed into a new artistic style that became known as Impressionism. Norman locations feature in some of Monet's famous works, including Deauville, Étretat and Rouen Cathedral, but it was his quasi-abstract studies of his own Giverny gardens that have proved the most enduring. For more on the area's artistic connections, see p270; for more on Monet, see p252.

PETER BARRITT

TOP LEFT Monet's house (p251) in Giverny **BOTTOM LEFT** Monet's painting *Water-Lily Pond, Symphony in Green* **RIGHT** Josselin castle (p136) and the Oust River **FAR RIGHT** A cobbled street in Dinan (p59)

TOP MUSEUMS

MÉMORIAL DE CAEN This cutting-edge WWII museum is overwhelming in every sense (p191).

MAISONS SATIE Ponder a winged pear and a pedal-powered instrument at the house of eccentric composer Eric Satie (p214).

MUSÉE DÉPARTEMENTAL BRETON Brush up on your Celtic culture and see some historic Quimper *faïence* (p104).

MUSÉE DES BEAUX ARTS, ROUEN The region's leading fine-arts museum (p240).

DON'T MISS EXPERIENCES

- ★ The Carnac *alignements* – prepare to be dumbfounded by this megalithic marvel (p122)
- ★ Rouen's old town – delve into the half-timbered heart of this exciting city (p236)
- ★ St-Malo – get lost along the cobbled alleys of the *Cité des Corsaires* (p33)
- ★ Dinan – wander the ramparts of this medieval river town (p59)
- ★ Festival de Cornouaille – join the party for Quimper's Celtic hoedown (p105)
- ★ *Pardons* – nearly every Breton town holds its own colourful procession dedicated to its patron saint
- ★ Bayeux – savour the city's medieval festival (p10)

TOP PARDONS

TRÉGUIER (May) For St-Yves, Brittany's patron saint.

PLOUGUERNEAU (June) To St Peter and St Paul.

QUIMPER (July) Honours the House of the Mother of God.

ROSCOFF (July) To St Barbara, patron saint of artillerymen.

LOCRONAN (July) Hosts the Petite or Grand Troménie.

STE-ANNE D'AURAY (July) One of Brittany's most spectacular *pardons*.

CAROLE MARTIN

CULTURE

FILMS

CONTE D'ÉTÉ (Eric Rohmer, 1996) Summer love story set in Dinard.

JEANNE D'ARC (Luc Besson, 1999) The story of France's national icon.

THE LONGEST DAY (Ken Annakin, 1962) Big-budget D-Day epic.

PARAPLUIES DE CHERBOURG (Jacques Demy, 1964) If only Cherbourg were this pretty.

SAVING PRIVATE RYAN (Steven Spielberg, 1998) Spielberg's take on Jour-J.

FAMOUS WRITERS

AUGUSTE RÉNÉ DE CHATEAUBRIAND (1768–1848) The nation's foremost Romantic novelist grew up, wrote stories and died at Combourg (p49).

GUSTAVE FLAUBERT (1821–80) The author of *Madame Bovary* (based on real-life events that took place in the town of Ry) was a Rouen native (p234).

GUY DE MAUPASSANT (1850–93) France's most famous short-story writer, was born in Fécamp (p225) and wrote many of his short stories in Étretat.

JULES VERNE (1828–1905) Born in Nantes, he ran off to be a cabin boy as a child and later became a prolific sci-fi pioneer who penned 63 classic novels (p144).

PARDONS & FESTOU-NOZ

For many Breton villages, the biggest event of the year is the *pardon,* a traditional religious festival that can trace its roots back to the Middle Ages, when villagers were given a once-yearly opportunity to expiate their sins (hence the name). *Pardons* later developed into days of worship for the local parish saint. Once a year, the whole village turns out in all their finery to follow the organised procession behind the saintly banner, before joining in with traditional dances and *festou-noz* (night-time musical concerts), customarily accompanied by Breton instruments such as the *bombarde* (an oboe-like instrument) and the *biniou* (Breton bagpipes).

TOP LEFT Village folkloric dancers and musicians in Finistére **RIGHT** The imposing castle of Josselin (p136) is one of the finest in the region

BRITTANY'S ANCIENT MONUMENTS

Brittany has more megalithic menhirs, tombs, cairns and burial chambers than anywhere else on earth. Most of Brittany's sites date after around 3500 BC. The most frequent structure to look out for is the dolmen, a covered burial chamber consisting of vertical menhirs topped by a flat capstone. Peculiarly, Brittany's ancient architects had different architectural tastes from their European neighbours – rather than the cromlechs (stone circles) commonly found throughout Britain, Germany, Spain and Ireland, they were much keener on constructing arrow-straight rows of menhirs, known as *alignements* – one of which, the monumental Alignements de Carnac, is the world's largest known prehistoric structure and makes Stonehenge look like child's play.

TOP CHÂTEAUX

* ⋆ Fairy-tale towers and lavish interiors make for Brittany's finest at Josselin (p136)
---
* ⋆ Fougères is the picture of a medieval stronghold – moats, turrets and all (p56)
---
* ⋆ See Chateaubriand's writing desk and death bed at his baronial home in Combourg (p49)
---
* ⋆ Sumptuous Beaumesnil features a fabulous 80-hectare park designed by Versailles' landscape gardener, Le Nôtre (p248)
---
* ⋆ Admire the stunning medieval floor at Suscinio, a family manor on the Presqu'ile de Rhuys (p134)

RICHARD MILLS

FOOD & DRINK

GREG ELMS

COOKING COURSES

CUISINE CORSAIRE (www .cuisine-corsaire.fr) Roellinger-trained chefs supervise this sophisticated seafood school in Cancale.

LIBRE COURS (www.resto librecours.fr) This innovative bistro-cum-cookery school in Rennes runs courses on everything from cooking for kids to the art of French patisseries.

MANOIR DE LA RIVIÈRE (www.manoirdelariviere.net) Residential courses held in St-Louet-sur-Seulles. You'll also go shopping for your own ingredients.

ON RUE TATIN (www.onrue tatin.com) Scribe-chef Susan Hermann Loomis runs courses at her famous cookery school in Louviers, south of Rouen.

OUI CHEF (www.ouichef .com) Lively countryside-inspired cooking lessons in Neuvilles-sur-Touques.

REGIONAL CUISINE

Food's not just a fact of life in this corner of France, it's a *way* of life. Traditional Norman cooking is rich, indulgent and heavy, dominated by prodigious portions of meat and game smothered in butter, cheese and cream-based sauces. True to its roots, Brittany takes a more down-to-earth approach, making plentiful use of locally grown produce, especially onions, cauliflowers, potatoes and other root vegies. Seafood is the one constant between the two: with over 2000km of coastline, fish unsurprisingly plays a central role in both regions' cuisines. But it's the simple things that make this region so rewarding: browsing the bustling stalls of a village food market, stocking up on fresh-caught fish straight from the boats, or setting off for a countryside picnic of cheese, cider and fresh crusty bread. *Yehed mad,* as they say around these parts…

GREG ELMS

TOP LEFT A seafood platter featuring prawns **BOTTOM LEFT** Cups of sweet cider **RIGHT** A pâtisserie selection including *kouign amann* (butter cake) **FAR RIGHT** Norman cheese for sale

TOP CHEFS

FONTAINE AUX PERLES (www.fontaineauxperles.com) Rachel Gesbert is one of Brittany's up-and-coming names (p54).

GILL (www.gill.fr) Gilles Tournadre's Rouen restaurant has received the Michelin seal of approval – twice (p242).

JEAN-LUC TARTARIN (www.jeanluc-tartarin.com) You're in for an experience (p224).

LA COQUILLAGE (www.maisons-de-bricourt.com) Brittany's celebrity chef, Olivier Roellinger, has chucked in three Michelin stars to open new premises (p45).

DON'T MISS EXPERIENCES

* Place des Lices market – Rennes' weekly food fair is the second-biggest in France (p52)

* Oysters in Cancale – shuck your own from the quayside stalls (p44)

* Livarot – take a cheesy tour in the home of Livarot (p204)

* Fish markets – watch the fishermen sell their catch in Roscoff (p86), Concarneau (p108) and Le Guilvinec (p108)

* Honey-making at Ferme Apicole de Térénez – and taste 100% organic honey (p96)

* Honfleur – sip something cold and savour seafood at a harbourside restaurant (p215)

* Foire aux Dindes – turkeys fill Sées' streets in December

STAPLES

* Crêpes and galettes

* Seafood, especially oysters and scallops

* Cheese (of course)

* *Cotriade* (fish stew)

* *Kig ha farz* (Breton meat and veg stew)

* *Kouign amann* (a buttery Breton cake)

* *Far breton* (Breton flan with prunes)

* Calvados, Normandy's apple-scented spirit

* Cider and Breton beer

* *Beurre salé* (salted butter)

FOOD & DRINK

MARTIN MOOS

FOOD BOOKS

AT MY FRENCH TABLE (Jane Webster) Foodie reminiscences from an Aussie expat.

COOKING AT HOME ON RUE TATIN (Susan Hermann Loomis) Recipes from the Louviers-based cooking school.

FRENCH CHEESES (Eyewitness) Handy pictorial guide to all the top French cheeses.

OLIVIER ROELLINGER'S CONTEMPORARY FRENCH CUISINE Learn the culinary secrets of Cancale's famous chef.

TOP TREATS

CAMEMBERT AND LIVAROT Cheese straight from the source (p204).

CONSERVERIE LA BELLE-ILOISE Visit the Quiberon's last fish cannery (p126).

DISTILLERIE CHRISTIAN DROUIN Try Normandy's two top tipples – Calvados and cider (p180)

GALETTES DE PONT AVEN Shop for buttery biscuits in Pont-Aven (p112).

KOUIGN AMANN Our favourite version of this Breton cake comes from Hotel Lulu-Larnicol (p112).

MACAROONS Sample handmade macaroons from a master-maker in Quimper's old town (p104).

NORMAN CHEESES

If there's one thing this part of France is famous for, it's cheese. Some of the most enduring names of French *fromage* come from Normandy, including Pont L'Évêque, Livarot and, most famous of all, Camembert. Norman monks first experimented with cheesemaking during the 11th century, and it's now a multimillion-euro industry – Camembert's factories churn out 15,000 tonnes of the stuff every year, and the industry is still a massive local employer. All the big cheeses are protected by their own AOC (*appélation d'origine controlée*), a culinary copyright that prevents other manufacturers from cashing in on the hallowed name.

TOP LEFT Making crêpes at the Festival de Cornouaille (p105) in Quimper **RIGHT** A sizzling plate of oysters, Cancale's specialty (p44)

FRUITS OF THE SEA

Seafood features on practically every menu. The signature dish to look out for is the *plateau de fruits de mer* (seafood platter), which varies according to the daily catch, but generally includes langoustines, spider crab, oysters, prawns, shrimps, clams, scallops and mussels. Fish is often served fairly simply to bring out the flavours: popular sauces are *à la normande* (in a creamy sauce) or *au beurre blanc* (in a butter sauce). Other dishes to look out for are *homard à l'armoricaine* (lobster in a herb and tomato sauce), *bar de ligne au sel de Guérande* (line-caught sea bass crusted in Guérande salt), *cotriade* (a hearty fish and shellfish soup), and of course the ubiquitous bistro staple of *moules-frites* (mussels and chips).

FOOD FESTIVALS

★ Foire au Boudin – if black pudding's your passion, head for Mortagne-au-Perche in March

---

★ Fête de la Coquille St-Jacques – savour scallops in Erquy, St-Quay-Portrieux and Loguivy in April

---

★ Fête du Fromage – Pont L'Évêque champions its cheese in mid-May

---

★ Fête de la Morue – this May cod festival in Binic commemorates the town's fishing heritage

---

★ Fête de la Crevette – Honfleur's shrimps are honoured in late September

OLIVIER CIRENDINI

OUTDOORS

CAROLE MARTIN

TOP NATURE PARKS

There are several glorious *parcs naturels régionals* (PNR).

PNR ARMORIQUE (www.parc -naturel-armorique.fr) Wild hilltops, granite moors and rugged cliffs stretching across central Brittany (p94).

PNR BOUCLES DE LA SEINE NORMANDE (www .pnr-seine-normande.com) Has 4500 hectares of bird-friendly wetlands (p221).

PNR BRIÈRE (www.parc-naturel -briere.fr) Canals, salt marsh and reedland support rare migratory birds in Loire-Atlantique (p151).

PNR MARAIS DU COTENTIN ET DU BESSIN (www.parc-cotentin-bessin.fr) Lowland nature park straddling Manche and Calvados (p161).

PNR PERCHE (www.le-perche.org) Some 2035 sq km of fields, forests and farms in southern Normandy, and not an autoroute in sight (p203).

THE WILD SIDE

With a pastoral patchwork of green fields, ancient woodland, humpbacked hills and over 2000km of rugged coastline, outdoorsy types will be spoilt for choice in Brittany and Normandy. Hard-core hikers, iron-legged bikers and dedicated sailors will find a wealth of opportunities to indulge their passions, and local tourist offices are well setup for providing advice on loads of outdoor activities. While you certainly won't be able to escape the summer crowds along the most popular stretches of coastline, a quiet beach, remote cliff-top or unspoilt patch of countryside is never more than a quick drive or ride away; and if you're looking to get back to nature, the area's many *parc naturels régionals* (regional nature parks) and *réserves naturelles* (nature reserves) are ideal, protecting huge tracts of natural landscape that collectively support all sorts of rare flora and fauna.

BETHUNE CARMICHAEL

TOP LEFT A forest walk in the Morbihan countryside BOTTOM LEFT A sweeping view of Étretat (p224) CENTRE RIGHT A puffin poses on rocks near Le Conquet (p89) FAR RIGHT Plage de Toul Drez (p74)

TOP HIKES

BAIE DE MONT ST-MICHEL (p163) Take a guided walk across one of the world's largest tidal bays.

BELLE-ÎLE-EN-MER (p127) Strike out along the island's coastal path.

FORÊT D'HUELGOAT & MONTS D'ARRÉE (p95) Volcanic boulders, Celtic camps and legends, and a mysterious forest, as well as marshes and tors.

PARC NATURAL RÉGIONAL DU PERCHE (p203) There's hiking and horse riding galore in this huge Normandy nature park.

DON'T MISS EXPERIENCES

★ Birdwatching – the Réserve de Cap Sizun (p100) and the Sept Îles (p74) offer some of France's finest twitching

---

★ Canal Cruising – steer your own houseboat along the Nantes–Brest and Ille-et-Rance canals (p136)

★ Golfe du Morbihan – explore the miniature islands of this huge coastal bay (p133)

★ Île d'Ouessant – take a boat trip to this wild, wind-lashed Atlantic island (p89)

★ Wild Woods – trek the forest trails of Paimpont (p37) and the Forêt de Lyons (p256).

★ D-Day Beaches (p185) – pay homage to the heroism of the D-Day veterans

LIFE'S A BEACH

Top tips for beach-bums:

★ Côte d'Albâtre (p217) Sunbathe beside chalk-white cliffs

★ Crozon Peninsula (p96) Spotted with secluded coves

★ Quiberon (p126) Packed and proud of it

★ Pointe de la Torche (p108) Brave the Atlantic swells

★ D-Day Beaches (p185) Grand and golden

★ Côte de Granit Rose (p73) A family fave

★ Côte de Penthièvre (p66) Home of the *station balneaire*

MARTIN MOOS

OUTDOORS

TOP WEBSITES

All but the first option are in French only.

WWW.BRETAGNE-RANDO.COM Hikes within Brittany.

WWW.LESROCH.ORG Tips on mountain-bike trips in the Monts d'Arrée.

WWW.NAUTISMEBRETAGNE.FR Online guide to water activities.

WWW.RANDOBREIZH.ORG Great resource for Breton hiking and cycling itineraries.

WWW.RANDONNEE-NORMANDIE.COM Hikes with a Norman focus.

RESOURCES

All but the last option are in French only.

COMITÉ RÉGIONAL NORMANDIE CANOË-KAYAK (www.crck-normandie.fr) Information on kayaking and canoeing throughout Normandy.

FÉDÉRATION FRANÇAISE DE CYCLO-TOURISME (FFC; www.ffc.fr) Cycle-specific maps, booklets and trail guides.

FÉDÉRATION FRANÇAISE DE LA RANDONNÉE PÉDESTRE (www.ffrp.asso.fr) The main hiking contact in France, with *topoguides* covering trails including the GR34.

FÉDÉRATION FRANÇAISE DE LA VOILE (www.ffvoile.net) France's national sailing federation, with links to accredited sailing schools.

INSTITUT GÉOGRAPHIQUE NATIONAL (IGN; www.ign.fr) France's main map company.

THE GR34

This trail ranks is one of France's longest *Sentiers de Grande Randonnée* (GRs; long-distance trails). Hugging the Brittany coast, it runs for over 2000km all the way from Mont St-Michel to Port-Navalo on the Golfe du Morbihan. The trail is marked by red-and-white striped trail markers – wherever you see one, you can be sure you're on a maintained trail offering spectacular coastal walking. Many stretches, especially near coastal towns, are known as *Sentiers des Douaniers* (customs officers' trails), a reminder of the days when the paths were patrolled by armed officers on the lookout for smugglers.

TOP LEFT Brittany's countryside and superb roads are perfect for cycling **RIGHT** Sand-yachting on a Brittany beach

VOIES VERTES

Brittany has some of the nation's most extensive *voies vertes* ('greenways'). These trails stretch for over 1000km along old canal towpaths, disused logging roads and decommissioned railways, and can be used by hikers, cyclists and horse riders. Many sections are paved to enable access for wheelchair users. There are currently three main sections in Brittany: St-Malo to Rennes along the Ille-et-Rance Canal (Voie 2, 105km); St-Malo to Rhuys via the Forêt de Paimpont (Voie 3, 150km) and St-Méen-le-Grand to Carhaix via the Monts d'Arrée and Lac Guerlédan (Voie 6, 111km). Extra sections are slowly taking shape along the coastline and between Roscoff and Rosporden; you'll also find a smaller network in Normandy. See www.voiesvertes.com for more info.

USEFUL CONTACTS

★ Cycling holidays – with Breton Bikes (www.bretonbikes.com), a British-owned but Breton-based company

★ Golf-breaks – with Golfing in Brittany (www.golfinginbrittany.co.uk)

★ Sand-yachting – at Penthièvre, run by Passageurs du Vent (www.aeroplage.com)

★ Diving – Paul Éluard (www.pauleluard-plongee.com) goes to wrecks off Normandy

★ Hiking – Explore the Monts d'Arrée, guided by ADDES (www.arree-randos.com)

★ Sailing lessons – with France's celebrated school, Îles de Glénan (www.glenans.asso.fr)

JEAN-BERNARD CARILLET

TOP WEBSITES

BIENVENUE À LA FERME
(www.bienvenue-a-la-ferme.com)
Check it out for farmstays and
farm activities all over France.

**WWW.FRANCE4FAMILIES
.COM** Advice on travelling
with kids in France, with
sections for Brittany and
Normandy.

**WWW.GITES-BRITTANY
.COM** Online directory of
family-friendly, self-catering
accommodation.

DON'T MISS EXPERIENCES

★ Meet deep-sea denizens at the aquariums in
St-Malo (p41) and Brest (p93)

★ Go wild at the Bourbansais Safari Park (p50),
Branféré animal park (p135) or Parc de Clères
(p243)

★ Play Gallic games at the Village Gaulois at
Cosmopolis (p75)

★ Visit a decommissioned nuclear sub at Cherbourg's Cité de la Mer (p172)

★ Visit the fairy-tale castles of Fougères (p56),
Josselin (p136) and Château du Champ de
Bataille (p247)

★ Explore the beaches and rock-pools of the
Côte de Granit Rose (p73)

★ Stay in a treehouse at Dihan (p295)

TRAVEL WITH CHILDREN

Brittany and Normandy are both well used to catering for travellers *en famille,* and
you'll find plenty of child-friendly attractions dotted around both regions, ranging
from animal parks to fairy-tale châteaux and world-class aquariums. For most activities and sights, kids generally pay around half price, and in many places under 5s get
in for free. Most restaurants will happily cater for kids, and you'll often find a *menu
enfant* that's been specially designed to appeal to younger palates (remember that
lunch is generally a much less formal affair than dinner). Family hotel rooms can be
expensive, so self-catering *gîtes* and campsites are popular options for family travellers. Many are specifically geared towards families, with facilities such as water parks,
playgrounds and organised activities.

TOP Children fishing for crabs on the coast near Brest (p92)

CONTENTS

THE AUTHORS

OLIVER BERRY

Introducing Brittany & Normandy, Itineraries, Brittany chapters, Background, Accommodation

Oliver's French love affair began at the tender age of two, and he's since travelled practically every inch of l'Hexagone while contributing to several editions of the best-selling Lonely Planet guide to France, among other projects. For this book he braved Atlantic swells en route to Brittany's islands, got stuck inside a prehistoric burial tomb and tried 23 different sorts of fish.

PETER DRAGICEVICH

Normandy chapters, Accommodation, Transport, Directory

After a dozen years stuck behind a desk at various newspapers and magazines, Peter has spent much of the last four years on the road – contributing to over a dozen Lonely Planet titles in the process. In the course of researching this book he added more than 3100km to his odometer and at least a couple of centimetres to his waistline – cheese being an occupational hazard for a Normandy travel writer.

LONELY PLANET AUTHORS

Why is our travel information the best in the world? It's simple: our authors are passionate, dedicated travellers. They don't take freebies in exchange for positive coverage so you can be sure the advice you're given is impartial. They travel widely to all the popular spots, and off the beaten track. They don't research using just the internet or phone. They discover new places not included in any other guidebook. They personally visit thousands of hotels, restaurants, palaces, trails, galleries, temples and more. They speak with dozens of locals every day to make sure you get the kind of insider knowledge only a local could tell you. They take pride in getting all the details right, and in telling it how it is. Think you can do it? Find out how at lonelyplanet.com.

ITINERARIES

BEST OF BRITTANY

TWO WEEKS // ST-MALO TO ROSCOFF // 650KM

Begin taking in Brittany's essential sights at the old town and ramparts of St-Malo (p33) followed by a day trip to elegant Dinard (p45) and then go upriver to medieval Dinan (p59). Indulge in shopping and sightseeing in Rennes (p50), visit wonderfully

preserved Vannes (p130) and admire the prehistoric Carnac megaliths (p122). Head west via maritime Concarneau (p108) to the lively city of Quimper (p102). Trace the coastline north, stopping to see the Pointe de Penmarc'h (p108) and Pointe du Raz (p101) headlands, stroll around the old-world village of Locronan (p102) and visit the boat museum in Douarnenez (p99). Explore the Parc Naturel Régional d'Armorique (p94) before heading to the old port of Roscoff (p84), after visting Morlaix (p82) and making a detour to the coastline of Côte de Granit Rose (p73).

NORMAN HIGHLIGHTS

TWO TO THREE WEEKS // ROUEN TO MONT ST-MICHEL // 900KM

Start in **Rouen** (p234) with its medieval centre. Take day trips to Monet's gardens at **Giverny** (p251), the châteaux of **Beaumesnil** (p248) and nearby **Champ de Bataille**

(p247). Then visit the port of **Dieppe** (p228) and explore the Impressionists' favourite coastline, the **Côte d'Albâtre** (p217). Compare concrete-central, **Le Havre** (p217), with futuristic **Pont de Normandie** (p215) and picture-book **Honfleur** (p211). Roll the dice at **Deauville** (p208) and visit the sombre **Mémorial de Caen** (p191), the **D-Day Beaches** (p185) and the **American Military Cemetery** (p187). Then it's on to beautiful **Bayeux** (p177) and its famous tapestry, followed by a few days exploring the **Haut-Cotentin** (p168) en route to laid-back **Barfleur** (p171) and the imposing abbey of **Mont St-Michel** (p157).

NATURAL SPLENDOUR

ONE WEEK // PNR BRIÈRE TO THE CROZON // 400KM

This trip starts with a barge trip around the marshes of the **Parc Naturel Régional (PNR) de Brière** (p151). Next, wander along the beaches of the **Presqu'île de Rhuys** (p134), spot seabirds at the **Réserve de Séné** (p134) and explore other parts of the gor-

geous **Golfe du Morbihan** (p133) before heading for the aptly named **Belle-Île-en-Mer** (p127) and its diminutive neighbours, **Houat** and **Hoëdic** (p129). Cycle the quiet towpaths of the **Nantes–Brest Canal** (p136) en route to the peaceful shores of **Lac de Guerlédan** (p138). The forest trails of **Paimpont** (p37) or **Huelgoat** (p95) warrant a visit. Explore the wild hilltops of the **Monts d'Arrée** (p95) on horseback or by mountain bike, and finish up at the bays and headlands of the **Crozon Peninsula** (p96).

ITINERARIES

MEDIEVAL MARVELS

10 DAYS // BAYEUX TO VANNES // 550KM

Kick off at the world's most ambitious comic strip, the **Bayeux Tapestry** (p177). Explore the area around William the Conqueror's **château** (p196), while the village of

St-Céneri-le-Gérei (p201) is one of the prettiest in France. Spin on to **Coutances Cathedral** (p166) and the sea-captains' city, **St-Malo** (p33). Head up along the River Rance to **Dinan** (p59), renowned for its helter-skelter half-timbered houses. Goggle at the great cathedral in **Dol-de-Bretagne** (p49), before visiting the fortified towns of **Fougères** and **Vitré** (p56), which once guarded Brittany's border. Delve into what's left of **Rennes' old city** (p52) after the fire of 1720, before viewing aristocratic architecture at **Josselin** (p136) and ending up at one of Brittany's best-preserved medieval towns, **Vannes** (p130).

A GASTRONOMIC TOUR

10 DAYS // RENNES TO DIEPPE // 600KM

From fresh fish to salted butter, fiery ciders and smelly cheeses, this corner of France is the perfect place to indulge your inner connoisseur. Begin with a visit to the Saturday food market in **Rennes** (p52), followed by trips to **Erquy** (p67) for scallops, **Cancale**

(p44) for oysters, and **Mont St-Michel** (p157) for salt-marsh lamb and an *omelette de Mère Poulard*. In **Caen** (p188), you'll need a strong stomach to handle **tripes à la mode de Caen** (p194). You'll need a strong liver to cope with **Calvados** (p180) and a strong nose to appreciate cheese at **Pont l'Évêque** (p207), **Livarot** (p204) and **Camembert** (p204). Along the coast try mussels in **Trouville** (p210), shrimp in **Honfleur** (p211), *sole normande* in **Fécamp** (p226) and fishermen's stew in **Dieppe** (p233).

THE ENDS OF THE EARTH

FIVE DAYS // ROSCOFF TO THE POINTE DU RAZ // 300KM

If it's spume and spindrift that set your pulse racing, the Finistère area is the place to head for. This wind-whipped coastline has a history packed with shipwrecks and smugglers: the old port of Roscoff (p84) makes a perfect start combined with a cruise to the Île de Batz (p86). Head west via the dunes of Keremma (p88) to the estuaries of the Pays des Abers (p88) and then climb the landmark lighthouses of Trézien and Pointe St-Mathieu (p89). The Crozon Peninsula (p96) has some stunning cliff scenery, especially around Pointe de Pen-Hir and Cap de la Chèvre (p97), while huge seabird colonies can be seen at Cap Sizun (p100) and awesome sunsets are guaranteed from the famous Pointe du Raz (p101).

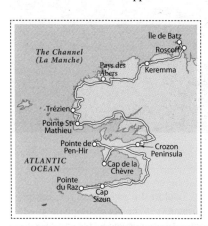

ARCHITECTURAL TREASURES

TWO WEEKS // DIEPPE TO CARNAC // 800KM TO 1000KM

Begin near Dieppe at the landscaped estate of Bois des Moutiers (p228) before visiting Rouen's old city (p236), renowned for its medieval buildings, landmark cathedral (p238) and Gothic architecture (p239). Extravagant abbeys litter the Seine Valley (p245), while the Haute-Normandie countryside is chock-a-block with spectacular chateaux – Martainville (p244), Vascœuil (p256) and Champ de Bataille (p247). The nearby abbey of Le Bec-Hellouin (p246), and Fécamp's stunning Palais Bénédictine (p226) are impressive, but for sheer architectural ambition, the postwar re-imagining of Le Havre (p217) and the space-age Pont de Normandie (p215) take some topping. Factor in stops for Coutances Cathedral (p166), Mont St-Michel (p157) and Josselin (p136) before finishing at the Carnac alignements (p122).

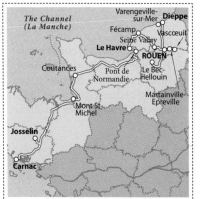

ILLE-ET-VILAINE

3 PERFECT DAYS

☙ DAY 1 // THE CORSAIRE CITY
Kick off in the walled city of St-Malo (opposite). Explore the backstreets, visit the re-built cathedral (opposite) and the château's museum (p38) before climbing the tower for 360-degree views. Treat yourself to a sea cruise (p39) followed by tea and cake at Timothy (p43), or a stellar supper at Le Chalut or Bouche En Folie (p42).

☙ DAY 2 // STYLE BY THE SEA
Catch the ferry over to delightful Dinard (p45), still one of France's most sophisticated seaside getaways. Bag a beach tent on the Plage de l'Écluse (p47), or stroll the Pointe du Moulinet (p47) and the Promenade du Claire de Lune (p47). Check into the old-fashioned Hôtel Printania (p290) or the stylish Hôtel de la Reine-Hortense (p290), and indulge in a twilight supper at L'Escale à Corto (p49) or Didier Méril (p48).

☙ DAY 3 // INLAND ILLE-ET-VILAINE
Day three is devoted to exploring the region's inner charms. Arrange your itinerary around visits to the châteaux of Combourg (p49), Fougères or Vitré (p56), factoring in an expedition to the safari park of Bourbansais (p50) if you've got the kids in tow. Alternatively, you could devote the whole day to Brittany's historic capital city, Rennes (p50). If you do, round things off with a meal at Rachel Gesbert's fantastic restaurant, Fontaine aux Perles (p54).

ST-MALO

· · · · · ·

pop 52,700

Jutting from the Channel waters like a honey-stoned super-tanker, the walled city of St-Malo cuts one of northern France's most unforgettable silhouettes. Often referred to as the 'City of Corsaires' – a nod to its pirate heritage – St-Malo was first settled by a Welsh monk by the name of MacLow in the 6th century, and served for centuries as a fishing harbour before establishing itself as one of the country's most important ports during the 17th and 18th centuries.

St-Malo became a key base for merchant ships and government-sanctioned pirates (known as privateers), and the city's independent spirit survives to this day in its motto, *'ni français, ni breton, malouin suis'* ('Neither Frenchman, nor Breton, but of St-Malo am I'). To protect the city from reprisals (especially from the hated English), the great military architect Vauban oversaw the construction of the city's defensive walls in the 17th century, one of the few areas of the city to survive WWII almost unscathed. Since its postwar reconstruction, St-Malo has reinvented itself as a Channel port and seaside getaway; visit in high summer and you won't have the streets to yourself.

ESSENTIAL INFORMATION

EMERGENCIES // Centre Hospitalier Broussais (Map p38; ☎ 02 99 21 21 21; 1 rue de la Marne); Police Station (Map p38; ☎ 02 99 40 02 06; 6 av Franklin Roosevelt)

TOURIST OFFICES // St-Malo Tourist Office (Map p40; ☎ 02 99 56 64 48; www.saint-malo -tourisme.com; Esplanade St-Vincent; ⏰ 9am-7.30pm Mon-Sat, 10am-6pm Sun Jul & Aug, 9am-12.30pm & 1.30-6.30pm Mon-Sat, 10am-12.30pm & 2.30-6pm Sun Apr-Jun & Sep, 9am-12.30pm & 1.30-6pm Mon-Sat Oct-Mar) Has maps, walking leaflets and a St-Malo audioguide (€12), plus makes bookings for boat trips, activities and hotels. It provides useful info on windsurfing, sailing, scuba-diving and fishing options.

ORIENTATION

St-Malo consists of the harbour towns of St-Malo and St-Servan and the modern suburbs of Paramé and Rothéneuf to the east. The walled city of St-Malo is known as Intra-Muros ('within the walls'). From the train station, it's a 20-minute walk west along av Louis Martin.

EXPLORING ST-MALO

❧ **INTRA-MUROS (WALLED CITY) // STROLL THE RAMPARTS AND STREETS OF ST-MALO'S OLD TOWN** St-Malo's tangle of streets (Map p40) are a highlight of a visit to Brittany. Grand merchants' mansions and sea captains' houses line the alleys; one of the smartest residences houses the **Maison de Corsaire** (☎ 02 99 56 09 40; www.demeure-de-corsaire.com; 5 rue d'Asfeld; tours in French adult/child €5.50/4; ⏰ 10-11.30am & 2.30-5.30pm summer & school holidays, 3pm Tue-Sun at other times Feb-Nov), built in 1725 by François-Auguste Magon de la Lande, an influential shipowner and director of the East India Trading Company.

It may be hard to believe but St-Malo's old town was almost entirely rebuilt following the ferocious fighting of August 1944, when the battle to unseat the German forces left 80% of the town's buildings in ruins. The **Cathédrale St-Vincent** (place J de Châtillon; ⏰ 9.30am-6pm) was particularly badly hit; much of the original structure (including its spire) was reduced

(Continued on page 38)

ILLE-ET-VILAINE

ILLE-ET-VILAINE

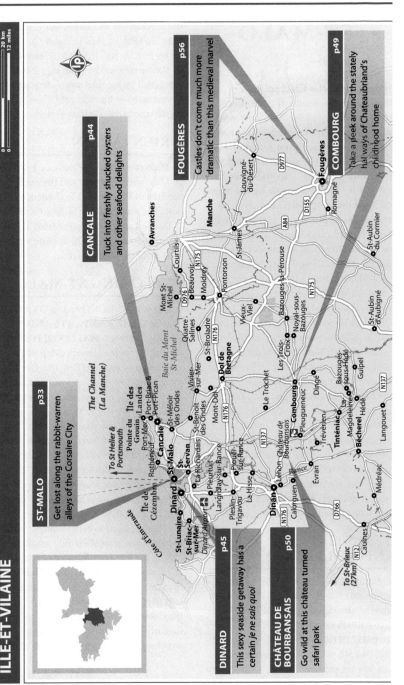

0   20 km
0   12 miles

ST-MALO   p33
Get lost along the rabbit-warren alleys of the Corsaire City

CANCALE   p44
Tuck into freshly shucked oysters and other seafood delights

FOUGÈRES   p56
Castles don't come much more dramatic than this medieval marvel

COMBOURG   p49
Take a peek around the stately halls of Chateaubriand's childhood home

DINARD   p45
This sexy seaside getaway has a certain *je ne sais quoi*

CHÂTEAU DE BOURBANSAIS   p50
Go wild at this château turned safari park

The Channel (La Manche)

Baie du Mont St-Michel

Côte d'Emeraude

To St Heller & Portsmouth

To St-Brieuc (27km)

Avranches
Manche
Courtils
St-James
Louvigné-du-Désert
Fougères
Romagné
St-Aubin du Cormier
St-Aubin d'Aubigné
Pontorson
Beauvoir
Moidrey
Bazouges-la-Pérouse
Mont St-Michel
Quatre Salines
St-Broladre
Noyal-sous-Bazouges
Vieux-Viel
Les Trois-Croix
Dol de Bretagne
Mont-Dol
Vivier-sur-Mer
St-Benoît-des-Ondes
Le Trochet
Dingé
Bazouges-sous-Hédé
Guipel
Pleugueneuc
Combourg
La Magdeleine
Tréverien
Hédé
Langouet
Bécherel
Tinténiac
Médréac
Évran
Rance
Lénon
Château de Bourbansais
Calorguen
Cauhes
Dinan
La Hisse
Plouër-sur-Rance
Langrolay-sur-Rance
Pleslin-Trigavou
Pleurtuit
Dinard Airport
La Richardais
St-Servan
St-Malo
St-Méloir des Ondes
Port-Brillet & Port-Pican
Île des Ondes
Port-Mer
Pointe du Grouin
Île des Landes
Cancale
Rothéneuf
St-Lunaire
St-Briac-sur-Mer
Dinard
Île de Cézembre

D977
D155
A84
N175
D976
N175
N176
N137
N176
N137
D766
N12

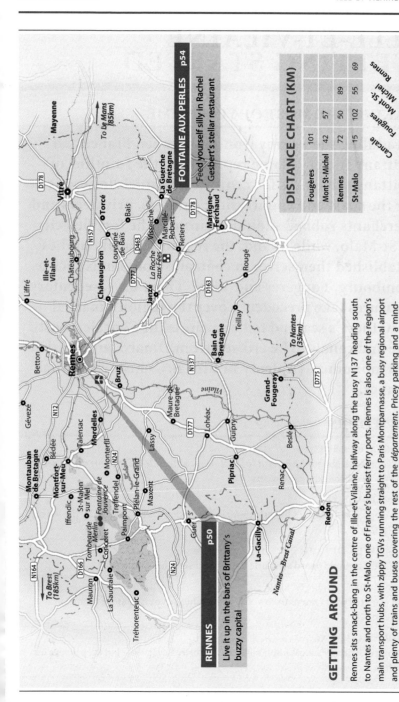

FONTAINE AUX PERLES p54

Feed yourself silly in Rachel Gesbert's stellar restaurant

RENNES p50

Live it up in the bars of Brittany's buzzy capital

DISTANCE CHART (KM)

	Cancale	Fougères	Mont St-Michel	Rennes
Fougères	101			
Mont St-Michel	42	57		
Rennes	72	50	89	
St-Malo	15	102	55	69

Note: Distances between destinations are approximate

GETTING AROUND

Rennes sits smack-bang in the centre of Ille-et-Vilaine, halfway along the busy N137 heading south to Nantes and north to St-Malo, one of France's busiest ferry ports. Rennes is also one of the region's main transport hubs, with zippy TGVs running straight to Paris Montparnasse, a busy regional airport and plenty of trains and buses covering the rest of the *département*. Pricey parking and a mind-bending one-way system make driving in the big city a serious headache.

ILLE-ET-VILAINE GETTING STARTED

MAKING THE MOST OF YOUR TIME

Straddling the stormy frontier between France and Brittany Ille-et-Vilaine represented the frontline of Brittany's defences for centuries. Historic locations litter the coast and countryside: painters, privateers and merchants rubbed shoulders around the fortified city of St-Malo, while inland, the region's feudal families established themselves in château strongholds such as Combourg, Fougères and Vitré. These days, sedentary pleasures take precedence over the region's martial past: there's seafood to be savoured in Cancale, coastline and canals to be cruised from Dinard, and markets and monuments aplenty in Brittany's historic capital, Rennes.

TOP TOURS

♣ CORSAIRE CRUISE
Book your berth aboard *Le Renard* (p39), a restored *corsaire* of the type once used by St-Malo's swashbuckling privateers

---

♣ RENNES' OLD CITY
Get to grips with Brittany's historic capital on a guided tour organised by the tourist office (p52)

♣ DISCOVER DINARD
Take a tour around Dinard's historic houses and seaside sights (p46)

♣ CANCALE OYSTER FARMS
If you can't tell your *creuses* from your *belons,* educate yourself at the Ferme de la Marine (p44)

♣ FORT NATIONAL
Visit one of Brittany's most impressive coastal fortresses (p39) – but keep an eye on the tide…

GETTING AWAY FROM IT ALL

This scenic corner of Brittany transforms into a tourist hell in high season, but that doesn't mean you can't escape the crowds.

* **Cycle or hike the voies vertes** Greenways criss-cross the Ille-et-Vilaine countryside (p23), perfect for exploring on two wheels, two feet or four legs.

* **Forêt de Paimpont** (www.paimpont.fr) This lush forest spanning the border between Ille-et-Vilaine and Morbihan is supposedly the last remains of the mythic Brocéliande Forest, where King Arthur received Excalibur and the wizard Merlin met his ill-fated lover Viviane. Whatever the truth of the legends, it's a fine spot for some walking and cycling. Paimpont town is the base for exploring the forest; there's a tourist office here. Buses go to Paimpont from Rennes.

ADVANCE PLANNING

* **Accommodation** Hotel rooms in St-Malo and Dinard can be rarer than hen's teeth in the high season, so it pays to book ahead.

* **Le Chalut** Get organised if you want to bag a table at this stellar St-Malo seafood restaurant.

* **Rennes** Ditch the car to avoid navigating Rennes' one-way nightmare.

* **Check it's open** The opening hours for many of Ille-et-Vilaine's châteaux, museums and houses can be very erratic, especially out of season.

TOP VIEWS

❦ CHÂTEAU DE ST-MALO
The view from the top of St-Malo's historic castle (p38) is only rivalled by the one from the Tour Solidor (p41)

❦ POINTE DU GROUIN
Follow the coastal path north from Cancale to reach this stunning headland (p45)

❦ FOUGÈRES
For a flavour of Brittany's medieval past, the battlements of Fougères (p56) are hard to beat

❦ DINARD
Admire Dinard's sparkling sands from Pointe de la Malouine (p47) or see St-Malo's smartest side viewed from the Promenade du Claire de Lune (p47)

❦ VITRÉ
Vitré's medieval ramparts (p56) afford wonderful views of the atmospheric old city

RESOURCES

* **Haute Bretagne** (www.bretagne35.com) Regionwide information from the Ille-et-Vilaine tourism authorities.

* **Saint Malo Tourist Office** (www.saint-malo-tourisme.com) Specific advice on accommodation and activities for the *Cité des Corsaires*.

* **Rennes** (www.rennes.fr) Essential info for visiting the Breton capital.

ILLE-ET-VILAINE

(Continued from page 33)

to rubble. The cathedral was subsequently rebuilt and reconsecrated in 1971; the gloomy medieval part contrasts strikingly with the light, airy feel of the eastern end, complete with its new rose window, modernist altar and reconstructed spire. A mosaic **plaque** marks the spot where the explorer Jacques Cartier received the blessing of the bishop of St-Malo before his voyage of discovery to Canada in 1535.

St-Malo's massive **ramparts** make an (almost) complete circuit of the old city, interspersed by gardens overlooked by the city's famous seafarers: the **statue of Jacques Cartier** looks out over on the Bastion de la Hollande, while the *corsaire* captain **Réné Surcouf** stands guard over the Place du Québec. The ramparts can be accessed at several points including all the main city gates.

❧ CHÂTEAU DE ST-MALO // A FAIRY-TALE TOWER WITH EYE-POPPING VIEWS

Opposite Porte St-Vincent stands **Château de St-Malo** (Map p40), built by the

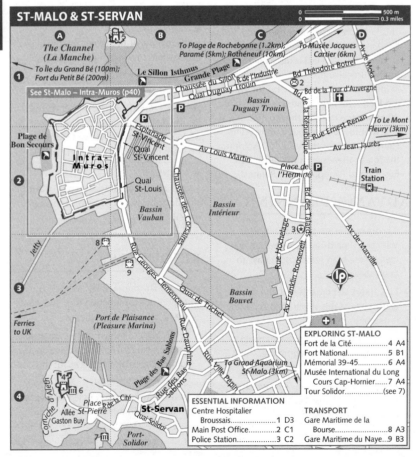

ST-MALO & ST-SERVAN

EXPLORING ST-MALO
Fort de la Cité................4 A4
Fort National..................5 B1
Mémorial 39-45..............6 A4
Musée International du Long
  Cours Cap-Hornier......7 A4
Tour Solidor.................(see 7)

ESSENTIAL INFORMATION
Centre Hospitalier
  Broussais....................1 D3
Main Post Office............2 C1
Police Station................3 C2

TRANSPORT
Gare Maritime de la
  Bourse........................8 A3
Gare Maritime du Naye...9 B3

dukes of Brittany in the 15th and 16th centuries, and briefly occupied by Duchesse Anne (see p261). The castle now houses the **Musée du Château** (☎ 02 99 40 71 57; adult/child €5.40/2.70; ☑ 10am-12.30pm & 2-6pm Apr-Sep, 10am-noon & 2-6pm Tue-Sun Oct-Mar), which explores the town's history through nautical exhibits, model boats and maritime artefacts, as well as an exhibition covering the city's cod-fishing heritage (in the Tour Générale). There's also background info (mostly in French; ask for an English leaflet) on the city's sons, including Cartier, Surcouf and the writer Chateaubriand. If you can handle heights, the castle's lookout tower offers stupendous views of the old city – but be prepared for some narrow, twisty, steep, steep steps.

FORT NATIONAL // VISIT VAUBAN'S FORTRESS AT LOW TIDE

From the northern ramparts of the Walled City, you can look out across the sands to this **fort** (Map p38; ☎ 02 99 85 34 33; www.fortnational.com; ☑ Jun-Sep), another stronghold designed by Vauban in 1689. Standing atop a rocky outcrop accessible only at low tide, the castle can be visited on a guided **tour** (adult/child €5/3) – ask at the tourist office for times and details.

♥ ÎLE DU GRAND BÉ // PAY YOUR DUES TO CHATEAUBRIAND

At low tide, you can walk out via the Porte des Bés to the rocky islet of **Île du Grand Bé**, where the great St-Malo–born writer Chateaubriand is buried. Once the tide rushes in, the causeway remains impassable for about six hours – check tide times before you set out. About 100m further west is the **Fort du Petit Bé** (☎ 06 08 27 51 20; www.petit-be.com, in French; admission free), another strongpoint built by Vauban (who else?).

♥ BOAT TRIPS // CRUISE THE BRINY BLUE AND EXPLORE THE COASTLINE

St-Malo's history is inextricably bound up with the sea, so a scenic boat trip is de rigueur. **Compagnie Corsaire** (☎ 08 25 13 81 00; www.compagniecorsaire.com, in French; ☑ Apr–mid-Nov) is the main operator, offering cruises around St-Malo Bay (one hour trip adult/2-18yr €13.50/8, 1½-hour trip adult/2-18yr €18.50/11), as well as trips to Cap Fréhel (€27/16), the Îles Chausey (€29/17.50), the Baie de Cancale (€23/14), Île de Cézembre (€13.50/8) and Dinan via the pretty Rance River (€29/17.50). It also runs the **Bus de Mer** (Sea Bus; adult/2-12yr return €6.20/4, 10 minutes, hourly) shuttle service between St-Malo and Dinard. **Vedettes de Saint-Malo** (☎ 02 23 18 41 08; www.vedettes-saint-malo .com, in French; ☑ Apr-Nov) offers similar trips. Both companies depart from the Cale de Dinan (Map p40).

For a real flavour of St-Malo seafaring, **Le Renard** (The Fox; Map p40; ☎ 06 73 86 12 85; www.cotre-corsaire-renard.com, in French; adult/8-12yr €66/35) offers trips aboard a restored *corsaire,* complete with rigging, spinnakers and billowing sails; the crew will even blast off a round from the cannon if you ask. Trips run several times a week between April and September; book well ahead. The boat's usually moored up alongside quai St-Vincent opposite the Grande Porte.

ILLE-ET-VILAINE

ST-MALO MUSEUM PASS

A **combination ticket** (adult/child €12.70/6.30) covers St-Malo's three main museums – the Musée du Château de St-Malo, Musée International du Long Cours Cap-Hornier and Mémorial 39-45. It can be bought at any of the museum ticket offices or the St-Malo tourist office.

ILLE-ET-VILAINE

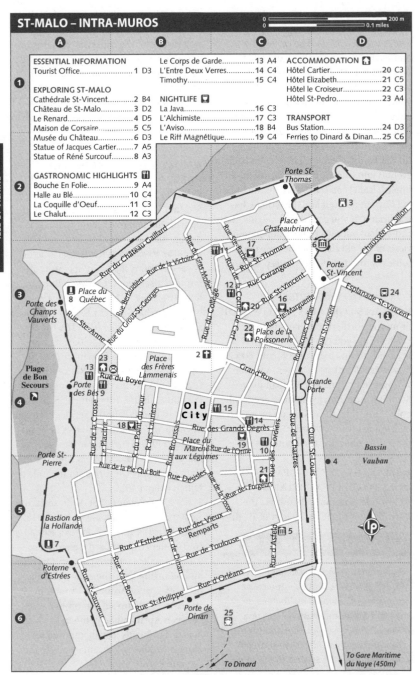

ST-MALO – INTRA-MUROS

0 — 200 m
0 — 0.1 miles

Ⓐ   Ⓑ   Ⓒ   Ⓓ

ESSENTIAL INFORMATION
Tourist Office.........................1 D3

EXPLORING ST-MALO
Cathédrale St-Vincent............2 B4
Château de St-Malo...............3 D2
Le Renard...............................4 D5
Maison de Corsaire.................5 C5
Musée du Château..................6 D3
Statue of Jacques Cartier........7 A5
Statue of Réné Surcouf...........8 A3

GASTRONOMIC HIGHLIGHTS 🍴
Bouche En Folie......................9 A4
Halle au Blé...........................10 C4
La Coquille d'Oeuf................11 C3
Le Chalut..............................12 C3

Le Corps de Garde...............13 A4
L'Entre Deux Verres.............14 C4
Timothy................................15 C4

NIGHTLIFE 🍷
La Java..................................16 C3
L'Alchimiste.........................17 C3
L'Aviso..................................18 B4
Le Ritt Magnétique..............19 C4

ACCOMMODATION 🏠
Hôtel Cartier........................20 C3
Hôtel Elizabeth.....................21 C5
Hôtel le Croiseur...................22 C3
Hôtel St-Pedro......................23 A4

TRANSPORT
Bus Station...........................24 D3
Ferries to Dinard & Dinan....25 C6

❦ ST-SERVAN // BUNKERS, BOATS AND BEACHES

South of the old city, the coastline curves around the Port de Plaisance to the rocky peninsula of St-Servan (Map p38), the site of the old Roman settlement of Cité d'Alet. The peninsula is crowned by the 18th-century **Fort de la Cité**, used as a German marine base during WWII; one of the blockhouses is now the **Mémorial 39-45** (☎ 02 99 82 41 74; adult/child €5.20/2.60; ⊙ guided visits 6 times daily Jul & Aug, 2pm, 3.15pm & 4.30pm Tue-Sun Apr-Jun & Sep-Nov), which explores the savage battle for St-Malo through photographs, artefacts and a 45-minute film (in French).

Seadogs should set a course for the 14th-century **Tour Solidor**, which houses the **Musée International du Long Cours Cap-Hornier** (Museum of the Cape Horn Route; ☎ 02 99 40 71 58; adult/child €5.20/2.40; ⊙ 10am-12.30pm & 2-6pm daily Apr-Sep, Tue-Sun Oct-Mar) – look out for some fascinating nautical instruments and scale models of ships that once plied the Cape Horn trading route. The top of the tower offers panoramic views.

❦ GRAND AQUARIUM ST-MALO // DIVE THE DEEP WITHOUT GETTING WET

The city's **aquarium** (☎ 02 99 21 19 00; av Général Patton; adult/4-14yr €15.50/9.50; www .aquarium-st-malo.com; ⊙ 9.30am-10pm mid-Jul– mid-Aug, 9.30am-8pm early Jul & late Aug, 10am-7pm Apr-Jun & Sep, 10am-6pm Oct-Feb) – one of Europe's finest – is about 4km south of the city centre. The underwater displays include a buried galleon, a tropical reef and a mangrove forest, as well as a simulated descent aboard an underwater submarine. Budding Jacques Cousteaus will love the *bassin tactile* (touch pool), where you can fondle rays, turbot and even a baby shark.

❦ BEACHES // SOAK UP THE SUN ON ST-MALO'S SANDS

St-Malo's beaches might not be Brittany's prettiest, but that doesn't deter the summertime hordes. Just west of the old city walls is **Plage de Bon Secours** (Map p38), which has a protected tidal pool for bathing. St-Servan's **Plage des Bas Sablons** (Map p38) has a cement wall that keeps the sea from receding completely at low tide. The **Grande Plage** (Map p38), much larger, stretches northeast along the isthmus of Le Sillon. **Plage de Rochebonne**, 1km to the northeast, is usually a good deal quieter.

❦ MUSÉE JACQUES CARTIER // VISIT THE HOME OF THIS PIONEERING SEAFARER

St-Malo's globe-trotting explorer made his name on a historic expedition to Canada in 1541, but his first voyages were essentially failures: he set out twice between 1534 and 1536 in search of gold, spices and a passage to Asia, but drew a blank on all three and was forced to return home empty-handed. Not that this is remembered now: these days Cartier is lionised as the quintessential St-Malo seaman, and his former manor has been transformed into the **Musée Jacques Cartier** (☎ 02 99 40 97 73; rue David-MacDonald-Stewart, Rothéneuf; adult/12-18yr/5-12yr/under 5yr €4/3/1.50/free; ⊙ 10-11.30am & 2.30-6pm daily Jul & Aug, Mon-Sat Jun & Sep, guided visits 10am & 3pm Oct-May), which recounts the story of his voyages as well as everyday life at the manor house. It's in the suburb of Rothéneuf to the northeast of St-Malo; buses 3 and 8 stop nearby.

FESTIVALS & EVENTS

Route du Rock (www.laroutedurock.com) Big-name acts hit town for St-Malo's music fest, held twice yearly, in mid-February and mid-August.

ILLE-ET-VILAINE

Étonnants Voyageurs (www.etonnants-voya geurs.com) Literature fest with an adventurous edge, held in late May/early June.

Folklores du Monde Traditional dancers from across the globe strut their stuff in this lively dance-athon in early July.

Festival de Musique Sacrée Choral music rings out in the shadow of the cathedral from mid-July to mid-August.

GASTRONOMIC HIGHLIGHTS

The wall-to-wall restaurants along rue Jacques Cartier, Porte St-Vincent and the Grande Porte are cheap, cheesy and totally forgettable. Good spots for a quick coffee stop include the lively squares of place du Marché aux Légumes and place Chateaubriand.

Fresh fruit, vegetables, Breton biscuits and other local goodies are on offer at the **Halle au Blé** (Map p40; rue des Cordiers) every Tuesday and Friday from 8am to 1pm. There's another big market on Sundays on place de l'Herminé outside the old city.

☙ BOUCHE EN FOLIE €€

☎ 06 72 49 08 89; 14 rue du Boyer; ☺ lunch & dinner Wed-Sun
The Mouth Gone Mad (Map p40) oozes Gallic gorgeousness from every nook and cranny. Decked out in designer wallpaper, hanging baskets and tiny tables, it feels like dining out in a super-stylish friends' living room. The menu gives a modern spin to French staples – lamb is fricasséed with garlic and artichokes, while red tuna's served *á la tartare* and monkfish is partnered by peas, black olives and asparagus. Sumptuous.

☙ LA COQUILLE D'OEUF €€

☎ 02 99 40 92 62; 20 rue de la Corne de Cerf; menus €21-28

'Cuisine creative' is the order of the day at the Eggshell (Map p40), which blends playful French classics with an engaging sense of jumble-shop chic. The menu is split between *viandes* (meats) and *crustaces* (crustaceans) – lobsters and St-Jacques scallops often feature – and the dining room brims with boho charm (beer barrels, lampshades, flowerpots).

☙ LE CHALUT €€€

☎ 02 99 56 71 58; 8 rue de la Corne-du-Cerf; mains €22-30, menus €25-55; ☺ closed Sun & Mon out of season
For seafood in St-Malo, there's only one choice. Thanks to its renowned chef, Le Chalut has become one of the best addresses (Map p40) for fishy fare in northern France, so while the prices are steep and the feel is formal, the food more than lives up to the hype. The menu's chock-a-block with the best the Breton coastline has to offer – buttered turbot, line-caught sea bass, scallops in champagne sauce – and you can pick your lobster from the dining-room tank. One to savour.

☙ LE CORPS DE GARDE €

☎ 02 99 40 91 46; www.le-corps-de-garde.com; 3 Montée Notre-Dame; mains €6-14
You couldn't ask for a posher position (Map p40), hidden away beside the ramparts above the Porte du Bés (bag an outside table if you're a sucker for sunset views). Crêpes and galettes form the menu's backbone, with a couple of experimentals thrown in among the standards. The communal benches and rustic tables provide a down-home feel.

☙ L'ENTRE DEUX VERRES €€

☎ 02 99 40 18 91; www.restaurant-lentredeux verres.com; 7 rue des Grands Degrès; mains €13-17; ☺ dinner Tue-Sun

Another gem tucked away down St-Malo's back streets (Map p40). Slate, low ceilings and a hearth conjure the classy setting, while the supper-only menu showcases fresh, modern French cuisine. Market ingredients are used to maximum effect – cod is served with a zingy blast of chilli and red pepper, while scallops shine in orange *beurre blanc* and duck steak simmers in cider.

☘ TIMOTHY €
☎ 02 99 40 35 36; 7 rue de la Vielle Boucherie; cakes €5-7.50, teas €3-5; ☯ 9am-5.30pm
Raspberry tarts, tutti-frutti fancies, Breton flans and extravagant gateaux fill the window of this super-smart *salon du thé* (Map p40), the town's top spot for afternoon tea. The house special is the *Rocher St-Malo*, a chocolate extravaganza of truly Wonkaesque proportions.

NIGHTLIFE

Bars, cafés and drinking dens are scattered along St-Malo's alleyways. In summer, classical concerts are hosted here for the Musique Sacrée festival (opposite).

☘ LA JAVA
☎ 02 99 56 41 90; 3 rue St-Barbe
Vintage puppets and theatrical knick-knacks cover every inch of the walls at this eccentric corner bar (Map p40), favoured by St-Malo's artsy crowd. Squeeze into one of the old-fashioned booths and sink a Breton beer or two, and look out for the rickety lift when you retire to the powder room.

☘ L'ALCHIMISTE
☎ 02 23 18 10 06; 7 rue St-Thomas; ☯ 5pm-1am Tue-Sun Oct-Apr, to 2am daily May-Sep
Ben Harper–style music creates a mellow backdrop at this magical place (Map p40) filled with old books and a toy flying fox. Take a seat either at the bar draped with a red, tasselled theatre curtain, or on the carved timber mezzanine, or at the wood-heated basement.

☘ L'AVISO
☎ 02 99 40 99 08; 12 rue du Point du Jour; ☯ 5pm-2am
Beers, beers, beers – about 300 of them in fact – are the tipple of choice at the Aviso (Map p40). For getting into the flavour of your visit, go for one of the local brews – Blanche Hermine and Telenn Du are both on tap.

☘ LE RIFF MAGNÉTIQUE
☎ 02 99 40 85 70; www.leriffmagnetique.com; 20 rue de la Herse; ☯ 5pm-1am Tue-Sun
Hipsters, musos and bright young things make a beeline for this lively café-club (Map p40), one of the town's *bonnes addresses* for visiting bands and weekend DJs. For decor, think stone and chrome; for drinking, think coffee and designer cocktails.

TRANSPORT

AIRPORT // The nearest airport to St-Malo is the Aéroport de Dinard-Pleurtuit-St-Malo, 5km southwest of Dinard (see p49).

BOAT // **Brittany Ferries** (☎ in France 08 25 82 88 28, in UK 0870 556 1600; www.brittany-ferries.com) runs regular ferries between St-Malo and Portsmouth, and **Condor Ferries** (☎ in France 08 25 13 51 35, in UK 0870 243 5140; www.condorferries.co.uk) runs boats to/from Poole and Weymouth via Jersey or Guernsey (known in French as the Îles Anglo-Normandes); car ferries leave from the Gare Maritime du Naye (Map p38). **Compagnie Corsaire** (☎ 08 25 13 81 00; www.compagniecorsaire.com) provides ferries (adult/child return €6.20/4) every hour between St-Malo (Map p40) and Dinard. For full details on ferries to Brittany, see p320.

ILLE-ET-VILAINE

BUS // Kéolis (☎ 02 99 56 06 06; www.ksma.fr) runs buses to Cancale (€1.05) and the surrounding area. Tibus (☎ 08 10 22 22 22; www.tibus.fr) has services to Dinan and Cap Fréhel (summer only). For Mont St-Michel, Dinard, Fougères and Rennes, contact Illenoo (☎ 08 10 35 10 35; www.illenoo.fr). All bus companies stop outside the train station (Map p38).

TRAIN // Regular trains run between St-Malo and Rennes (€12.40 to €14.30, 50 to 60 minutes, frequent). Three direct TGVs run daily to Paris' Gare Montparnasse (€61.30 to €75.50, 3½ hours). For travel to Dinan, St-Brieuc and Caen, change at Dol-et-Bretagne. The Ligne Baie (www.lignebaie.fr, in French) project connects St-Malo with Mont St-Michel, Dol-de-Bretagne, Pontorson, Avranches and Granville via a combination of trains and buses; a day-pass costs adult/child €10/5.

CÔTE D'ÉMERAUDE

· · · · · ·

The beautiful Côte d'Émeraude (Emerald Coast) stretches west from the oyster beds of Cancale to the broad beaches of Pléneuf-Val-André. It's a tempting coastline of rocky reefs and islets fringed with golden sand, emerald-green shallows and aquamarine depths.

CANCALE

pop 5200

Tucked into the curve of a shimmering shell-shaped bay, Cancale is the capital of the region's great delicacy, the oyster. Orderly oyster beds stretch for kilometres along the surrounding coastline, and the quayside is filled with seafood restaurants and fishermen's stalls serving up every crustacean you could care to imagine. There's even a museum dedicated to the art of oyster farming.

ESSENTIAL INFORMATION

TOURIST OFFICES // Cancale tourist office (☎ 02 99 89 63 72; www.cancale-tourisme. fr; 44 rue du Port; ☺ 9am-7pm Mon-Sat, 9.30am-1pm Sun Jul & Aug, 9am-1pm & 2.30-6pm Mon-Sat Sep-Jun); Information kiosk (port de la Houle; 10am-noon & 4-7pm Mon-Sat, 4-7pm Sun Jul & Aug only) In the Halle à Ma'rée by the quayside.

ORIENTATION

From the upper town, clustered around the church on Place de l'Église, rue du Port leads steeply downhill to the harbour at Port de la Houle, where buses stop. Quai Gambetta is to the right, quai Thomas to the left.

EXPLORING CANCALE

❦ **OYSTER STALLS //** SHUCK YOUR OWN STRAIGHT FROM THE SEA
Nowhere in France will you taste a fresher oyster than on Cancale's quayside. Local fishermen sell their catch directly from stalls at the northern end of the town's harbour, near the little Pointe des Crolles lighthouse. Point to the ones you want, and they'll be shucked, dashed with lemon and served before your eyes. Oysters are numbered according to size and quality; the smallest *huîtres creuses* (No 5) go for around €4 per dozen, while you could pay over €20 for a saucer-sized *Cancalaise*.

❦ **LA FERME MARINE //** GET AU FAIT WITH OSTRÉICULTURE
For the low-down on Cancale's oyster industry, head a couple of kilometres southwest of the port to the Ferme Marine (Marine Farm; ☎ 02 99 89 69 99; corniche de l'Aurore; adult/child €6.80/3.60; ☺ tours in English 2pm daily Jul–mid-Sep, in French at 11am, 3pm & 5pm daily Jul–mid-Sep, at 3pm Mon-Fri mid-Feb–Jun

ILLE-ET-VILAINE

& mid-Sep–Oct), which takes its visitors on a whistle-stop tour through the art of *l'ostréiculture* (oyster farming). Mother-of-pearl and shell-themed souvenirs are available at the museum shop, but you'll have to head back into town for a tasting session.

☙ LA POINTE DU GROUIN //
BRETON COASTLINE AT ITS BEST
North of the lighthouse at Port de la Houle, a coast path leads 7km north to the stunning headland of Pointe du Grouin, a glorious coastal nature reserve renowned for its wildflowers, rare seabirds, butterflies and craggy cliff-top views. Just offshore is the **Île des Landes**, a wild island that shelters a colony of giant black cormorants. If you're feeling energetic, the GR34 hiking and cycling trail continues for another 18km to St-Malo.

GASTRONOMIC HIGHLIGHTS

☙ AU PIED DE CHEVAL €
☎ 02 99 89 76 95; 10 quai Gambetta; seafood €7-20
This rustic restaurant can trace its oyster-catching ancestry back four generations, and it's still one of the port's choicest places for fruits of the sea. It's much cheaper than many places in Cancale – mussels from around €7, langoustines from around €13 – and you can choose your crustaceans from baskets beside the pretty patio.

☙ LE COQUILLAGE €€€
☎ 02 99 89 64 76; www.maisons-de-bricourt.com; 1 rue Duguesclin; menus €29-110; ⊙ Mar-Dec
Cancale's celeb chef Olivier Roellinger is one of the few Frenchmen to attain three Michelin stars. The great man's Cancale empire includes a *salon du thé,* a spice shop and a cooking school, but his original three-starred restaurant shut in 2008

to make way for a new project, the swish Château Richieux and its equally swish restaurant, Le Coquillage. Roellinger's trademark *Saint Pierre 'retour des Indes'* (John Dory 'Return to the Indies') appears, but that's just the start of the culinary fireworks. The château is about 4km south of town along the D76.

☙ LE SURCOUF €€
☎ 02 99 89 61 75; 7 quai Gambetta; menus €15.50-44; ⊙ closed Tue & Wed except Jul & Aug
For something smarter, Le Surcouf has long been a fave among the foodie guides. Nautically themed and run by a talented husband-and-wife team, its seafood is a cut above most of the harbour bistros. Crusty turbot, roast scallop kebabs and buttered lobster all feature, and the seafood platters are a real sight to behold.

☙ MAISON DE LA MARINE €€
☎ 02 99 89 88 53; 23 rue de la Marine; mains €17-40, menu €22; ⊙ lunch Tue-Sun, dinner Tue-Sat
Burnished wood, squeaky brown leather and red-velour chairs create an opulent atmosphere at this tempting restaurant-with-rooms just off the harbour drag. It's housed in the old harbour office, so the menu's unsurprisingly marine-themed – look out for a few fusion surprises and Thai spices among the French-orientated fare.

TRANSPORT

BUS // Kéolis (☎ 02 99 40 19 22; www.ksma.fr) runs regularly from Port de la Houle to St-Malo.

DINARD

pop 11,000
Seaside towns are ten-a-penny along the Breton coast, but Dinard has a sexy, sophisticated swagger all of its own. In the late 19th century well-to-do British

ILLE-ET-VILAINE

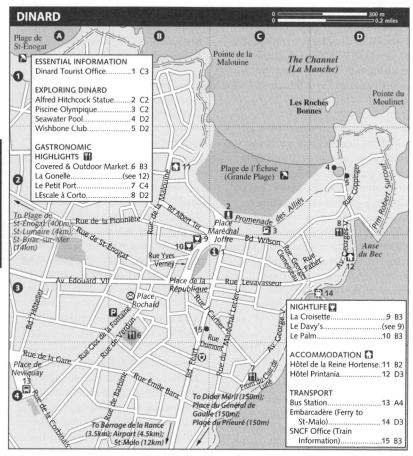

ILLE-ET-VILAINE

DINARD

0 ————————— 300 m
0 ————————— 0.2 miles

Plage de
St-Énogat

A   **B**   **C**   **D**

Pointe de la
Malouine

*The Channel
(La Manche)*

Les Rochés
Bonnes

Pointe du
Moulinet

ESSENTIAL INFORMATION
Dinard Tourist Office............1 C3

EXPLORING DINARD
Alfred Hitchcock Statue........2 C2
Piscine Olympique...............3 C2
Seawater Pool.....................4 D2
Wishbone Club....................5 D2

**GASTRONOMIC
HIGHLIGHTS**
Covered & Outdoor Market..6 B3
La Gonelle.......................(see 12)
Le Petit Port......................7 C4
L'Escale à Corto..................8 D2

Plage de l'Écluse
(Grande Plage)

Prm Robert Surcouf

Anse
du Bec

To Plage de
St-Énogat (400m);
St-Lumaire (4km);
St-Briac-sur-Mer
(14km)

Rue de la Pionnière
Rue de St-Énogat

Rue de la Malouine
Bd Albert Ter

Place
Maréchal
Joffre

Promenade des Alliés

Bd Wilson

Rue Georges
Clemenceau

Rue
Faber

Av Georges V

Rue Coppinger

Rue Yves
Verney

Av Édouard VII

Place
Rochaid

Place de la
République

Rue Levavasseur

Rue J Cartier

Rue du Maréchal Leclerc

Bd Féart

Rue Clos de la Fontaine

Rue de Verdun

Rue
Dumont

Prom du Garde

Av George V

NIGHTLIFE
La Croisette........................9 B3
Le Davy's.........................(see 9)
Le Palm.............................10 B3

ACCOMMODATION
Hôtel de la Reine Hortense..11 B2
Hôtel Printania..................12 D3

TRANSPORT
Bus Station.......................13 A4
Embarcadère (Ferry to
St-Malo)........................14 D3
SNCF Office (Train
Information)..................15 B3

Av Hôtelier

Rue de la Gare

Place de
Newquay

Rue des Corbinais

Rue de Barbine

Rue Émile Bara

To Didier Méril (150m);
Place du Général de
Gaulle (150m);
Plage du Prieuré (150m)

To Barrage de la Rance
(3.5km); Airport (4.5km);
St-Malo (12km)

aristocrats transformed the town into
one of France's first (and finest) *stations
balnéaires* (seaside resorts), and built *belle
époque* mansions along the lofty cliff-tops
around town. The aristocrats have moved
on, but the 'Nice of the North' still has an
air of old-fashioned exclusivity, with its
stripy beach-tents, smart restaurants and
elegant seafront promenades.

ESSENTIAL INFORMATION

TOURIST OFFICES // Dinard (☎ 02 99 46 94
12; www.ot-dinard.fr; 2 bd Féart; 9.30am-1pm & 2-7pm

Mon-Sat, 10am-12.15pm & 2.15-6.30pm Sun Jul & Aug,
9am-12.30pm & 2-6pm Mon-Sat Sep-Jun) It runs tours
of the town.

EXPLORING DINARD

Dinard is made for strolling; its orderly
grid of streets make navigation easy. The
tourist office runs several guided **tours**
(adult/child €5/2; ⏱ 3pm) between April and
October, exploring the town's history,
culture and architecture; most are in
French, but there are usually at least a
few in English. Ask for details.

❦ BEACHES // BAG YOUR BEACH TENT AND SUNBATHE IN STYLE
Dinard's sweeping **Plage de l'Écluse** has been the centre of attention in town ever since the first *belle époque* bathers turned up in the late 19th century. Its blue-and-white bathing tents, which carpet the beach in summer, have become a town trademark. Despite the best efforts of postwar planners, who plonked a string of concrete eyesores (including a huge casino) behind the beach, Dinard's *grande plage* is still a beauty.

You can bathe under cover in the **Piscine Olympique** (☎ 02 99 46 22 77; promenade des Alliés; adult/student €4/2.55; ☺ 10am-12.30pm & 3-7.30pm Mon-Sat, 10am-6.30pm Sun), filled with heated sea water; otherwise a large open-air swimming pool is tucked away at the beach's eastern end. Water activities such as windsurfing, kayaking and sailing a catamaran are on offer at the **Wishbone Club** (☎ 02 99 88 15 20; ☺ 9am-9pm Jun-Sep, 10am-noon & 2-6pm Oct-May) nearby.

When the Grande Plage gets too crowded, savvy Dinardais take refuge at the town's smaller beaches, including **Plage du Prieuré**, 1km to the south, and **Plage de St-Énogat** on the far side of Pointe de la Malouine.

You'll find plenty more beaches in the neighbouring resorts of **St-Briac-sur-Mer** and **St-Lunaire**, both reached by bus from Dinard.

❦ VILLAS & VIEWS // ADMIRE DINARD'S BELLE ÉPOQUE ARCHITECTURE
Walking trails wind out along the coast from the Plage de l'Écluse, leading west to **Pointe de la Malouine**, and east around **Pointe du Moulinet** onto the Promenade du Clair de Lune. The coastal paths provide a grandstand view of Dinard's magnificent villas, showcasing every architectural style in the French textbook; the most famous of all is the **Villa des Roches Brunes**, a lavish Louis XIII–pile built right on the tip of the Pointe de la Malouine. Most of the houses are privately owned, although a few sometimes open their doors to visitors in summer.

❦ PROMENADE DU CLAIR DE LUNE // TAKE A TWILIGHT STROLL ALONG THIS ROMANTIC PROMENADE
Spotted with palm trees, mimosas and exotic flowers, the turn-of-the-century **Promenade du Clair de Lune** (Moonlight Walk) rolls out from the old harbour at the Anse du Bec and goes all the way south to the Plage du Prieuré, offering a wonderful panorama across the Rance Estuary to St-Malo. As its name suggests, the promenade is at its finest at dusk or after dark, when it becomes the centrepiece for a spectacular summertime *son-et-lumière* (sound-and-light show).

HITCHCOCK CONNECTION

If the Plage de l'Écluse looks vaguely and eerily familiar, don't be surprised; the great cinematic shockmeister Alfred Hitchcock was a long-time Dinard fan, and filmed some of the beach sequences of his classic avian thriller *The Birds* here in the early 1960s. Some eagle-eyed film-buffs also think Hitchcock based the gloomy Gothic house featured in *Psycho* on one of Dinard's imposing cliff-top mansions. A statue of the great man (flanked, fittingly, by a brace of seagulls) stands just behind the beach.

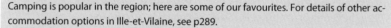

TOP CAMPING

Camping is popular in the region; here are some of our favourites. For details of other accommodation options in Ille-et-Vilaine, see p289.

★ **Domaine des Ormes** (☎ 02 99 73 53 00; www.lesormes.com; Épiniac, near Dol-de-Bretagne; sites €19.20-32.50; ⊗ mid-May–mid-Sep) All-star campsite with a horse-riding centre, tree-top cabins and aqua-park.

★ **Domaine de Tremelin** (☎ 02 99 09 73 79; www.domaine-de-tremelin.fr; Iffendic; sites for tent & 2 adults €11; ⊗ Apr–mid-Oct) Backwoods camping on the shores of a lake, west of Rennes.

★ **Le Pont Laurin** (☎ 02 99 88 34 64; www.location-camping-bretagne.fr; St-Briac; adult/site with car €4.40/7.20; ⊗ Easter-Nov) Quiet country campsite near the St-Briac beaches.

★ **Camping Paimpont-Brocéliande** (☎ 02 99 07 89 16; www.camping-paimpont-broceliande.com; Paimpont; adult/site €3/2.50; ⊗ Apr-Sep) Gorgeous spot in the middle of the Brocéliande forest.

★ **Camping La Touesse** (☎ 02 99 46 61 13; www.campinglatouesse.com; St-Lunaire; adult €4.20-5.20, site €5.20-7.50; ⊗ Apr-Sep) Busy but family-friendly site near Dinard and the St-Lunaire beaches.

♥ BOAT TRIPS // CATCH THE BOAT TO ST-MALO

Compagnie Corsaire (www.compagnie corsaire.com) runs the St-Malo ferry and other coastal cruises from its base at the Embarcadère along the Promenade du Clair de Lune. For prices see p39.

FESTIVALS & EVENTS

Festival du Film Britannique (www.festival dufilm-dinard.com) Dinard celebrates its cross-channel connections with a yearly film festival dedicated to the best new British flicks.

GASTRONOMIC HIGHLIGHTS

There are plenty of bistros and cafés on rue Yves-Verney. Dinard's **covered market** (⊗ 7am-1.30pm) is on place Rochaid.

♥ DIDIER MÉRIL €€€

☎ 02 99 46 95 74; www.restaurant-didier-meril.com; 1 place du Général de Gaulle; menus €22-65
Dinard's best-known chef has recently upped sticks to a new 'restaurant with rooms' on place Général de Gaulle. The food's as genre-bending as ever – think truffled monkfish, lobster gazpacho, or foie gras *crème brulée* – and the new setting is lovely, all starchy tablecloths, modern minimalism and garden views.

♥ LA GONELLE €€

☎ 02 99 16 40 47; Promenade du Clair de Lune; mains from €8; ⊗ Thu-Mon mid-Apr–Sep, daily Jul & Aug
Perched beside the granite quays of the Anse du Bec, Dinard's sophisticated answer to a seafood takeaway serves fabulously fresh crab, lobster, langoustines and mussels from the open-fronted counter, or you can grab one of the portside patio tables; whichever you choose, you won't find finer seafood anywhere in town.

♥ LE PETIT PORT €€

☎ 02 99 46 16 41; Le Port; mains €16-20
A fine portside position set back from the downtown din makes this friendly restaurant a favourite getaway for Dinardais diners. A big picture window gives lovely views of the marina and St-

ILLE-ET-VILAINE

Malo's skyline, while inside, terracotta tiles, *banquette* seats and a colourful maritime mural conjure a cosy feel. The menu's mainly meat and seafood, often with an Oriental fizz – most dishes are *à la carte*, but it's still excellent value.

♥ L'ESCALE À CORTO €€

☎ 02 99 46 78 57; 12 av George V; mains €12.60-22; ⏰ dinner Tue-Sun

Hidden away on a quiet street near the Anse du Bec, this fab (and very French) bistro specialises in all things seafood. The focus is firmly on food rather than decorative frips – so while the decor might be scruffy, its signature dishes (langoustines in a champagne sauce, monkfish in ginger cream) could happily grace a much posher *menu*.

NIGHTLIFE

The town's nightlife is concentrated on the bars along rue Yves-Verney. Hip young things favour **Le Palm** (☎ 02 99 46 84 34; 6 rue Yves-Verney), while a slightly older crowd congregates on **La Croisette** (☎ 02 99 46 43 32; 2 rue Yves-Verney) or the ever-popular **Le Davy's** (☎ 02 99 46 10 35; 2 rue Yves-Verney) with its neon signs, movie memorabilia and diner style. Most places open till around midnight, with longer hours on weekends and in summer.

TRANSPORT

AIR // Dinard's **airport** (☎ 08 25 08 35 09) is 5km south along the D168. **Ryanair** (☎ 02 99 16 00 66; www.ryanair.com) flies regularly to London Stansted and the Channel Islands.

BOAT // See p39 for details of the St-Malo–Dinard ferry.

BUS // Dinard's bus station is on place de Newquay. **Illenoo** (www.illenoo-services.fr) travels to St-Malo (Line 16, €1.65, 20 minutes) and Rennes (Line 7a, €3.75, two hours, hourly Monday to Saturday).

CAR // Parking in Dinard is expensive (€0.50 for 30 minutes), and limited to two hours in the town centre, but you can park all day at the Parking des Halles.

TRAIN // The nearest trains run to St-Malo.

ST-MALO TO RENNES

· · · · · ·

The rolling fields and gentle hills surrounding Rennes, Breton's capital, once marked the fiery frontline between Brittany and the rest of France, and the countryside is littered with defensive castles – one of which, the Château de Bourbansais, has transformed itself into a world-class zoo.

♥ DOL-DE-BRETAGNE // GOGGLE AT BRITTANY'S GRANDEST GOTHIC CATHEDRAL

Dominating the centre of this sleepy village is the monumental **Cathédrale St-Samson**, arguably Brittany's greatest example of Gothic architecture. Its most famous feature is the grand 14th-century doorway, decorated with complex medieval stonemasonry, but it's almost as famous for its sheer size – the nave stretches for an incredible 93m, topped by a 20m-high central dome. About 2km south of the village on the D795 is an even more ancient monument: the **Menhir du Champ-Dolent**, which at 9.5m high is the tallest menhir in Brittany.

♥ COMBOURG // WANDER THE HALLWAYS OF CHATEAUBRIAND'S MANOR HOUSE

Combourg's turret-topped 15th-century **château** (☎ 02 99 73 22 95; www.combourg .net; ⏰ castle 10-11.15am & 2-5.30pm daily Jul & Aug, 2-5.30pm Apr-Jun, Sep & Oct) is best known for its associations with the French writer Réné de Chateaubriand, who lived here and commemorated the castle in his book *Mémoires d'Outre-Tombe*. You can see Chateaubriand's favourite furniture, including his bed and writing desk, not to mention plenty of lavishly furnished rooms; outside, the castle's 19th-century landscaped **park** (☽ 9.30am-12.30pm & 2-6pm Apr-Sep) was designed by the great French landscapers, Denis and Eugène Buhler.

♥ L'ECRIVAIN // **PREPARE TO HAVE YOUR PALATE PAMPERED**
Combourg's **The Writer** (☎ 02 99 73 01 61; 1 pl St-Guildin, Combourg; menus €16-37) has long been rated as one of Ille-et-Vilaine's best rural restaurants, and with good reason. The menu is French through and through, but the dishes change according to the whims of the chef, so sit back and enjoy the châteauesque atmosphere.

♥ CHÂTEAU DE BOURBANSAIS // **TAKE A CHÂTEAU SAFARI**
Tamarind monkeys, giraffes, zebras and cockatoos are some of the exotic inhabitants of **Bourbansais** (☎ 02 99 69 40 07; www .labourbansais.com; adult/child €16.50/12; ☽ 10am-7pm Apr-Sep, 2-6pm Oct-Mar), which has established itself as one of France's finest safari parks. Between April and September there are twice-daily displays by the resident birds of prey, as well as a simulated hunt (complete with 50 baying hounds) in the castle grounds. If you'd like to see the castle's interior, you'll have to join a **guided tour** (€5/3; ☽ 5 daily Apr-Sep, 1 Sun Oct-Mar). It is located west of Combourg.

♥ HÉDÉ & AROUND // **EXPLORE VILLAGES DE CARACTÈRES**
Perched beside the peaceful Ille-et-Rance Canal, the village of **Hédé** marks the start of a famous flight of 11 locks known as

the **Onze Écluses**, and the towpath now makes a beautiful spot for an afternoon picnic and a promenade.

Bookworms will want to head to the streets of **Bécherel**, west of Hédé, which is famous for its second-hand bookshops and Easter book festival, while industrial aficionados should head over to Tinténiac's **Musée de l'Outil et des Métiers** (☎ 02 99 23 09 30; 5 quai de la Donac; admission €2; ☽ 10am-noon & 3-6pm Tue-Sat & Sun Jul-Sep), which houses 2000 artefacts relating to traditional handicrafts such as black-smithing, rope-making and coopering.

TRANSPORT

Dol-et-Bretagne is served by both train and bus from Rennes and St-Malo. Trains also run west from Dol to St-Brieuc and east to Manche *département*. Buses run by **Illenoo** (www.illenoo-services .fr) might help but getting to the sights is problematic without your own wheels.

RENNES

· · · · · ·

pop 212,500
Ask any French person for a list of must-see cities, and chances are Rennes won't figure near the top. But ask a Breton and it'll be a different story; locals know their capital is one of northern France's best-kept secrets, and they're happy for it to stay that way. Admittedly, the process of post-war reconstruction hasn't always been kind to Rennes – the outer suburbs are a mess of concrete tower blocks, high-rise flats and faceless industrial parks – but those who dig a little deeper will discover a lively student city crammed with Breton character, a beautifully restored medieval centre

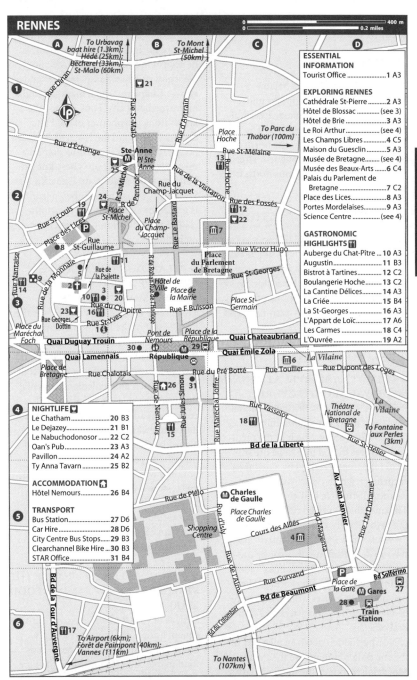

RENNES

0   400 m
0   0.2 miles

ILLE-ET-VILAINE

and one of the liveliest food markets in all of France.

ORIENTATION

The city is bisected by La Vilaine, a canalised river that disappears underground just before the massive central square, place de la République. The pedestrianised old city lies to the north of the river, while modern suburbs stretch to the south. The metro runs north from the train station.

ESSENTIAL INFORMATION

Tourist Office (☎ 02 99 67 11 11; www.tourisme -rennes.com; 11 rue St-Yves; ⊙ 1-6pm Mon, 9am-7pm Tue-Sat, 11am-1pm & 2-6pm Sun Jul & Aug, 1-6pm Mon, 10am-6pm Tue-Sat, 11am-1pm & 2-6pm Sun Sep-Jun) In a converted church near the old quarter, with a small museum exploring the city's history. Runs guided tours of the old city.

EXPLORING RENNES

❦ OLD CITY // MARVEL AT RENNES' MEDIEVAL ARCHITECTURE

Rennes has served as Brittany's capital ever since its incorporation into France in the 16th century. Much of the medieval city was gutted by a huge fire in 1720 (apparently started by a drunken carpenter), which destroyed many of Rennes' distinctive half-timbered houses. The ones that survived centre around the 17th-century Cathédrale St-Pierre (⊙ 9.30am-noon & 3-6pm), particularly along the rue de la Psalette; the wonky timbered house at No 12 is Rennes' oldest, dating back to the 16th century. The neighbouring houses would once have been occupied by choristers and cathedral officials.

Nearby, hidden down an alleyway off the rue de la Monnaie, are the Portes Mordelaises, one of the medieval city's original gatehouses, complete with chain-strung drawbridge and defensive towers.

More intriguing architecture can be seen along rue St-Michel, rue St-Georges, rue du Champ-Jacquet and rue du Chapitre, which mark the limits of the medieval city. Look out for the lavish stone townhouses of the Hôtel de Brie (1624) and the Hôtel de Blossac (1728), both built for well-to-do parliamentarians. The old city's best-known building is the Maison du Guesclin (3 rue St-Guillaume), whose half-timbered frontage is graced by a knight and a loincloth-clad peasant. It's now occupied by a nightclub.

❦ PALAIS DU PARLEMENT DE BRETAGNE // VISIT BRITTANY'S FORMER SEAT OF POWER

This grand 17th-century palace was the former seat of the Breton parliament. Built by the architect Salomon de la Brosse (the man behind Paris' Palais du Luxembourg), the building blends Italianate, French and Palladian elements; its rooms include the chandelier-lit courtroom and the Grande' Chambre, decorated with allegorical murals designed by Charles Errard, who helped furnish the palace of Versailles. The building was badly damaged by fire in 1994, started during a protest by angry fishermen; it was reopened after a major restoration in 2004 and now houses the city's appeal courts. The tourist office organises guided tours.

❦ PLACE DES LICES // BROWSE THE STALLS OF RENNES' FAMOUS FOOD MARKET

In days of yore Rennes' massive central square hosted jousting tournaments, but it's now famous for the enormous food market that explodes into life here every Saturday morning. It's the second-biggest in France (topped only by the Rungis market in Paris); local suppliers travel from all around the region to tout their freshest produce. From seafood to spices and from chocolate to cauliflowers, chances are it's for sale somewhere on the place des Lices. Crowded, chaotic, and very, very French.

☙ MUSEUMS // FROM MODERN ART TO KING ARTHUR

The city's cultural complex, **Les Champs Libres** (☎ 02 23 40 66 00; www .champslibres.fr; cours de Alliés; adult/child per exhibit €4/3, €7/5 for day pass; ☽ noon-7pm Tue-Fri, 2-7pm weekends Jul & Aug, noon-9pm Tue, noon-7pm Wed-Fri, 2-7pm weekends Sep-Jun) houses several exhibitions under one space-age roof. Breton history takes centre stage at the **Musée de Bretagne**, while you can explore Breton legends in **Le Roi Arthur**, and gaze across the galaxies at the planatarium or ponder the laws of physics, at the **Science Centre**.

The highlights at the modest **Musée des Beaux-Arts** (☎ 02 23 62 17 45; 20 quai Émile Zola; adult/student/under 18yr €4.20/2.15/free; ☽ 10am-noon & 2-6pm Tue-Sun) include works by Rubens, Picasso and Tanguy, as well as local artist Ernest Guérin and the Pont-Aven painters (p111).

Housed in a converted market on place Honoré Commeurec, **La Criée** (☎ 02 99 79 59 86; www.criee.org; admission free; ☽ noon-7pm Tue-Fri, 2-7pm weekends) is the city's main venue for contemporary art exhibitions.

☙ CANAL CRUISES // EXPLORE ONE OF RENNES' CANALS

You can cruise Canal St-Martin aboard an electric boat with **Urbavag** (☎ 02 99 33 16 88). It's located about 2km north of the city centre.

FESTIVALS & EVENTS

Les Mercredis du Thabor Traditional Breton dancing takes place on Wednesday afternoons throughout June and July in the city's lovely Parc du Thabor, 100m east of place Hoche along rue St-Mélaine.

Tombées de la Nuit (www.lestombeesdelanuit .com, in French) The streets of the old city burst into life for this street festival in the first week of July.

Les Transmusicales (www.lestrans.com, in French) In early December, Rennes hosts one of France's biggest music festivals at venues all across the city.

GASTRONOMIC HIGHLIGHTS

Rennes' **La Criée** (fish market; ☽ 7am-7pm Mon-Sat, 9.30am-12.30pm Sun) is on place Honoré Commeurec. The city's top bakeries include **Boulangerie Hoche** (☎ 02 99 63 61 01; 17 rue Hoche) and **Augustin** (☎ 02 99 79 46 92; 11 rue de la Monnaie). Good places for a quick coffee and a croissant include the busy cafés around place Ste-Anne, place St-Michel and rue Hoche.

☙ AUBERGE DU CHAT-PÎTRE €€

☎ 02 99 30 36 36; 18 rue du Chapitre; menus €20-25; ☽ dinner Tue-Sat

Eat your heart out, Monty Python – the Middle Ages come alive at this *auberge d'autrefois,* where the waitresses are dressed in medieval costume and some minstrels provide the inter-course entertainment. The menu's a royal banquet – knight's hotpot, boar stew, roast duck – but take it slow, since there are five gut-busting courses to get through. Tacky? Maybe, but top fun.

☙ BISTROT À TARTINES €

☎ 02 99 38 76 70; 2 rue des Fosses; tartines €4-9; ☽ noon-midnight

Another period piece, dressed to resemble a prewar Parisian café. Vintage food packets are stacked on the shelves, battered signs adorn the walls, and the food is served on mismatched bits of old china. Salads and gourmet *tartines* (toasted sandwiches) are the mainstays, but it's just as good for a morning coffee or a late-night beer.

❦ FONTAINE AUX PERLES €€€

☎ 02 99 53 90 90; www.fontaineauxperles.com; 96 rue de la Poterne; menus €36-78; ⓧ lunch Tue-Sun, dinner Tue-Sat, closed Sun & Mon Aug
This stellar restaurant is overseen by one of the city's most talented names, Rachel Gesbert, whose cooking has been championed by most of the major culinary critics, including Michelin, Pudlo, Champérard and Bottin Gourmand. Rightly so: the food's fresh and innovative and the menu's a seasonally tinged treat of stuffed pigeons, roast lobsters and line-caught bass. Pricey, but seriously good.

❦ LA CANTINE DÉLICES €€

☎ 02 99 31 36 36; 16 rue Nantaise; 3-course menu €28; ⓧ closed dinner Sun & Mon
One of our favourite finds in Rennes: it's a relaxed neighbourhood bistro where the food is served with a minimum of fuss or frills. Ingredients fresh from the Lices market are whipped into shape by the talented chef, Laurence Rissel, and served in simple, unpretentious surroundings.

❦ L'APPART DE LOÏC €€

☎ 02 99 67 03 04; 67 Ter, bd la Tour d'Auvergne; menus €23-29.50; ⓧ lunch Mon-Fri, dinner Tue-Sat
It's a townhouse bistro, with an air of big-city style. It's flooded with light through a half-moon window and decked out in chic greys, reds and glossy whites. The food's modern French, underpinned by local ingredients – rabbit, Erquy scallops and Breton fish often feature.

❦ LA ST-GEORGES €

☎ 02 99 38 87 04; 11 rue du Chapitre; crêpes €7-14
For crêpes look no further than the St-Georges, where the gourmet galettes are named after notable Georges (George Pompidou, George Sand, George Harrison). The cappuccino-and-blue decor gives it a fresh, modern feel, and the crêpes are first class. It's open on Sunday as well.

❦ LES CARMES €€€

☎ 02 99 79 28 95; 2 rue des Carmes; menus €28-50; ⓧ lunch Tue-Sun, dinner Tue-Sat
This is a smart restaurant with a fast-growing reputation, run by a Parisian-trained chef with a razor-sharp eye for culinary trends. Contemporary decor is matched by food with an experimental edge, so if you're looking for something traditional you'll probably be better off elsewhere. Definitely one to watch.

❦ L'OUVRÉE €€

☎ 02 99 30 16 38; 18 place des Lices; menus €14.80-33.20; ⓧ lunch Sat & Sun, dinner Tue-Fri
This upmarket restaurant overlooking place des Lices has long been one of the city's *bonnes addresses,* although it might feel too stuffy for some. The food is quintessential French *haute cuisine* – foie gras, smoked salmon, crusty *carré d'agneau* (lamb) – and the setting is formal.

NIGHTLIFE

With 60,000-odd students, Rennes is one of Brittany's liveliest towns come the weekend. Most of the after-dark action centres on the wall-to-wall bars along rue St-Malo and rue St-Michel (locally nicknamed rue de la Soif, or 'Street of Thirst') – things can get very rowdy on weekends. Kicking-out time is generally around 1am.

♥ LE CHATHAM

☎ 02 99 79 55 48; 5 rue de Montfort

This legendary spot has been slaking the city's thirst for decades, and it's still a beauty – part Irish pub, part French bar, furnished in rich burnished wood, nautical bits-and-bobs and even a reclaimed ship's wheel.

♥ LE DEJAZEY

☎ 02 99 38 70 72; 54 rue St-Malo

It's a Parisian-style club that hosts twice-weekly concerts – jazz is generally the main theme, but folk and French *chansons* occasionally make an appearance as well.

♥ LE NABUCHODONOSOR

☎ 02 99 27 07 58; 12 rue Hoche

The choice of the city's arty set, this place lays claim to being the city's oldest wine-bar. Suggested vintages and bar snacks are chalked up on the blackboards, and you'll find yourself mixing with an intelligent crowd.

♥ OAN'S PUB

☎ 02 99 31 07 51; 1 rue Georges Dottin

This cavernous pub is one of the best spots in town for hearing live Breton music. There are plenty of beers on tap, and impromptu jam sessions often kick into life courtesy of the clientele; gigs are usually more organised on Friday and Saturday.

♥ PAVILLON

☎ 02 99 78 22 22; 7 place St-Michel

With its black-and-chrome decor and prime place des Lices position, this 'café-resto' has established itself as one of the city's more stylish venues, but if you're after something grungier, the down-and-dirty drinking dens of rue St-Michel are steps away.

♥ TY ANNA TAVERN

☎ 02 99 79 05 64; 19 place Ste-Anne

Another favourite for the city's Breizh music crowd, with a rough-and-ready decor and tables spilling onto pretty place Ste-Anne.

TRANSPORT

AIR // **Rennes airport** (RNS; ☎ 02 99 29 60 00; www.rennes.aeroport.fr) is about 6km southwest of town, with Air France flights to French cities, plus Manchester, Newcastle, Exeter, Southampton and Edinburgh with **Flybe** (www.flybe.com) and Cork and Dublin with **Aerlingus** (www.aerlingus.com). Bus 57 leaves from place de la République and drops you about 800m from the airport. Buses run hourly from 6.50am to 7.45pm; there's a reduced weekend service.

BICYCLE // Free bikes can be borrowed for seven hours from **Clearchannel** (🕐 9am-7pm) in the Vilaine car park; you'll need a €76 deposit.

BUS // Rennes' **bus station** (☎ 02 99 30 60 00; www.gareroutiererennes.fr) is just east of the train station. *Départemental* buses are provided by **Illenoo** (www.illenoo-services.fr) to destinations including St-Malo (1¾ hours, 10 to 12 Monday to Friday, three on Saturday, one on Sunday), Fougères (one hour, hourly Monday to Friday, six on Saturday, two on Sunday), Dinard (Line 7a, two hours, four daily) and Pontorson (80 minutes, four to six daily Monday to Saturday).

CAR & MOTORCYCLE // All the major car-hire firms have offices at the train station.

TRAIN // Rennes is a major train hub. Fast TGVs travel east to Paris' Gare Montparnasse (€54, two hours, hourly) via Vitré (from €6.80, 35 minutes), and north-west to Brest (€34.50, 2¼ hours) via St-Brieuc (€14.90 to €17.90, 50 minutes). Regular services also travel north to St-Malo (€12.40, one hour); west to Vannes (€18.30, 1½ hours) and Quimper (€30.60 to €36, 2½ hours); and south to Nantes.

METRO & LOCAL BUSES // Rennes' city buses and futuristic metro are run by **STAR** (☎ 08 20 03 20 02; www.star.fr). Single tickets cost €1.20, a day pass is €3.20. The metro line cuts from northwest to southeast via place de la République and the train station.

ILLE-ET-VILAINE

EAST OF RENNES

······

FOUGÈRES, VITRÉ & AROUND

❤ FOUGÈRES // MARCH ALONG MEDIEVAL BATTLEMENTS

The region's most impressive fortress is **Fougères** (☎ 02 99 99 79 59; place Pierre-Symon; adult/10-16yr €3.65/2.15, guided visit €4.80; ⏰ 10am-noon & 2-5pm Feb-Dec, guided visits every hr), which towers over the banks of the River Nançon. It's the quintessential medieval fortress, ringed by a defensive moat and crenellated ramparts, and studded by 11 massive pepperpot towers. Although the interior has largely disappeared, the layout has remained practically unchanged since the 15th century, with three defensive 'zones', the medieval cannon decks, and a panoramic view from the ramparts.

The town's **tourist office** (☎ 02 99 94 12 20; www.ot-fougeres.fr; 2 rue Nationale) overlooks place du Théatre, a 500m uphill walk from the castle.

❤ VITRÉ // EXPLORE A CASTLE WITH WITCHES-HATS TURRETS

Fougères' defensive duties were shared with a sister fortress 48km to the south. The **Château de Vitré** (☎ 02 99 75 50 13; ⏰ 10am-12.45pm & 2-6pm Wed-Sun May-Sep) was built by a Breton baron in the 11th century and later embellished with a 15th-century gatehouse and witch's-hat turrets. The castle's lordly lodgings are now occupied by the local council; entry to the central courtyard is free, but you'll have to pay extra if you want to visit the castle's historical museum.

ILLE-ET-VILAINE

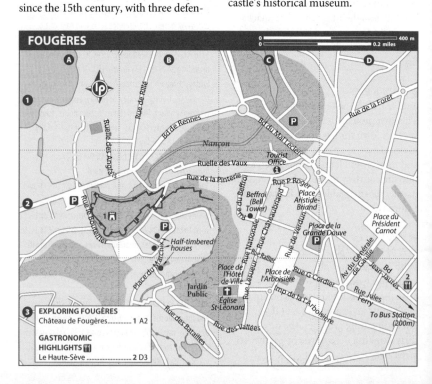

FOUGÈRES

0 ········ 400 m
0 ········ 0.2 miles

Rue de Rillé · Bd de Rennes · Ruelle des Anglais · Bd du Mail Le Déic · Rue de la Forêt · Nançon · Tourist Office · Ruelle des Vaux · Rue de la Pinterie · Rue P Roger · Rue du Beffroi · Beffroi (Bell Tower) · Place Aristide-Briand · Place de la Grande Douve · Place du Président Carnot · Rue de Bouteiller · Rue Nationale · Rue de Verdun · Rue Châteaubriand · Rue Lavoisier · Rue Raillet · Half-timbered houses · Place du Martchix · Place de l'Hôtel de Ville · Place de l'Arboisière · Rue G Cordier · Av du Général de Gaulle · Bd Jean-Jaurès · Jardin Public · Église St-Léonard · Imp de la l'Arboisière · Rue Jules Ferry · To Bus Station (200m) · Rue des Batailles · Rue des Vallées

Vitré's compact old town is easy to get around, with the tourist office, train station and a parking area right next to one another on the town's southern edge.

☙ LA ROCHE AUX FÉES // UNCOVER AN ANCIENT BURIAL CHAMBER

One of the region's most atmospheric ancient monuments is hidden away in the countryside about 30km southwest of Vitré. The Fairies' Rock is a roofed burial chamber, 11m long and 2m wide, constructed from huge slabs of schist around 4500 years ago. It's a few kilometres west of Marcillé-Robert, but the local signposts aren't terribly helpful, so a good-quality map will come in very handy.

GASTRONOMIC HIGHLIGHTS

☙ AR MILIN // CHATEAUBOURG €€€

☎ 02 99 00 30 91; 30 rue de Paris; mains €18-39

This ravishing hotel-restaurant on the banks of La Vilaine occupies a converted mill, which once supplied nearby Vitré with electricity. There's a brace of restaurants to choose from, both offering sophisticated French fare, and the lovely landscaped grounds (not to mention the upstairs rooms) are an utter delight.

☙ AUBERGE DU PONT D'ACIGŃE // NOYAL-SUR-VILAINE €€

☎ 02 99 62 52 55; lunch menu €27, dinner menus €38-75; ☽ lunch Tue-Fri & Sun, dinner Tue-Sat

This banquet beauty nestles on the banks of the River Vilaine, with views over the quiet village of Noyal-sur-Vilaine, about 12km east of Rennes. It's run by a Breton-born chef, Sylvain Guillemot, who's known for his use of regional produce and love of local veg and seafood – everything from artichoke hearts to curried mullet finds its way onto the menu,

but our tip is the salted butter caramel crisp. You'll need your own wheels to get here.

☙ AUBERGE DE ST-LOUIS // VITRÉ €€

☎ 02 99 75 28 28; 31 rue Notre Dame; menus €15.90-27.90

There's period character to spare at this old-world restaurant, tucked away on Vitré's backstreets, just steps from the château. Dark-wood panelling and vintage hearths create the atmosphere of a 18th-century gentleman's drawing room, and the food is rich and classic – duck pie, garlic snails and beef with *girolles* mushrooms.

☙ LE HAUTE-SÈVE // FOUGÈRES €€€

☎ 02 99 94 23 39; 37 bd Jean-Jaurès; menus €25.50-44; ☽ lunch Tue-Sun, dinner Mon-Sat

This sexy number comes as a shock in old Fougères; its groovy crimson-and-cappuccino colours, cherry-red chairs and wild-lighting feel wouldn't look out of place in downtown Paris. Thierry and Isabelle Robert's restaurant is a treat, showcasing bold flavours and even bolder ingredients – quail-and-truffle kebabs, anyone?

TRANSPORT

BUS // Buses to Fougères are mostly handled by Illenoo (www.illenoo-services.fr), which has at least a couple of buses to Rennes (Line 9a, 70 minutes), St-Malo (Line 17, 2¼ hours) and Vitré (Line 14, 40 minutes) from Monday to Saturday.

TRAIN // SNCF trains run to Vitré, which has connections to Rennes and many other local towns.

CÔTES D'ARMOR

3 PERFECT DAYS

❦ DAY 1 // A MEDIEVAL MARVEL

Begin with a morning exploring Dinan's old town (opposite), followed by lunch at Les Trois Lunes (p66) or L'Atelier Gourmand (p66) and a leisurely afternoon cruise along the Ille-et-Rance (p64). Practically everywhere is within easy driving distance, so base yourself either in a self-catering chalet at Malik (p291) or up the luxury ante at the Hôtel-Manoir de Rigourdaine (p291) or La Demeure in Guingamp (p291).

❦ DAY 2 // COASTAL EXPLORATIONS

On day two, head west along the coast, making detours to the beaches of St-Cast-le-Guildo (p66), the wild and windy promontory of Cap Fréhel (p67) and the coastal castle at Fort la Latte (p67). Have a long lazy lunch of scallops and seafood in Erquy (p67), and work off some of the calories with a stroll around Pléneuf-Val-André (p68) before piling them on again at the fantastic Voile d'Or (p67) in Sables d'Or les Pins.

❦ DAY 3 // AND AGAIN!

On day three, you could either opt for a day-trip over to the Île de Bréhat (p71), or continue your coastal explorations with a visit to Paimpol's street market and sea museum (p70), Tréguier's cathedral (p73) and the seaside resorts of the Côte de Granit Rose (p73) and the Côte des Ajoncs (p73).

DINAN

· · · · · ·

pop 11,000

When it comes to medieval mood, there aren't many Breton towns that can measure up to Dinan. Picturesquely perched above the River Rance, it boasts one of the loveliest old towns in northern France, a muddle of cobbled squares, half-timbered cottages and snaking ramparts tumbling down to the old port, where barges and river boats still putter along beside the old town quays.

ESSENTIAL INFORMATION

TOURIST OFFICES // Dinan (☎ 02 96 87 69 76; www.dinan-tourisme.com; 9 rue du Château; ☽ 9am-7pm Mon-Sat, 10am-12.30pm & 2.30-6pm Sun Jul & Aug, 9am-12.30pm & 2-6pm Mon-Sat Sep-Jun) Hour-long guided tours of the old town cost €5.50/3.50 for adults/5-18yr child.

EXPLORING DINAN

♣ CHÂTEAU & MUSÉE DE DINAN // DISCOVER DINAN'S MARTIAL PAST
Dinan's part-ruined castle (☎ 02 96 39 45 20; rue du Château; adult/12-18yr €4.40/1.75; ☽ 10am-6.30pm Jun-Sep, 1.30-5.30pm Oct-May) was begun in 1380 by Jean IV, Duke of Brittany, and later refortified with two towers and a drawbridge between 1585 and 1598. First a ducal residence, and later a prison, it's now home to the town museum, with artefacts detailing the town's history as a textile-industry and religious centre.

♣ THE OLD TOWN // STEP BACK TO THE MIDDLE AGES
Dinan's medieval centre radiates around **place des Cordeliers** and **place des Merciers**, where colourful multistoreyed houses teeter precariously above the cobbles and covered colonnades. Nearby on rue de l'Horloge is the town's 15th-century clock tower, the **Tour de l'Horloge** (adult/under 18yr €2.95/1.90; ☽ 10am-6.30pm Jun-Sep, 2-6pm Apr-May), whose tinny chimes ping every quarter of an hour. Winding stairs lead to a bird's-eye view over Dinan's jumbled rooftops.

The Gothic cloisters are all that remain of Dinan's 15th-century **Couvent des Cordeliers**, off rue de la Lainerie, but the town's striking **Basilique St-Sauveur** (place St-Sauveur; ☽ 9am-6pm) is still very much in situ; its buttressed basilica looms over place St-Sauveur, blending elements of Romanesque and Byzantine architecture – look out for the fabulous carved arch above the main doorway. Just east of the church is little **Jardin Anglais** (English Garden) and the 13th-century **Tour Ste-Cathérine**, which provides a postcard panorama over the river – just try to zone out the traffic buzzing over the town's 19th-century **viaduct**.

Though Dinan's ramparts have taken a battering down the centuries – most famously in 1357, when the heroic knight Bertrand du Guesclin saw off a determined English siege – many of the old watchtowers have been carefully restored. You can walk along one section between the old city gates of **Porte St-Malo** and the **Porte de Jerzual**, leading past the 15th-century artillery tower of the **Tour de Gouverneur**. The access gates on rue Haute-Voie and rue de l'Ecole are open from 8am to 9pm.

Be sure to head downhill along the steep cobbles of **rue Jerzual** and **rue du Petit Fort**, two of the best-preserved medieval streets in Brittany. The oldest house is the **Maison du Gouverneur**

(Continued on page 64)

CÔTES D'ARMOR

CÔTES D'ARMOR

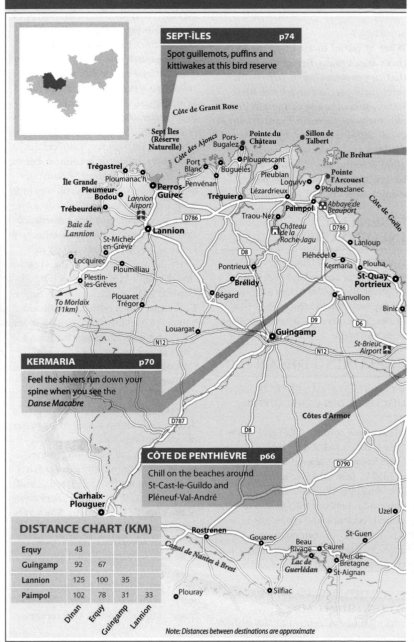

SEPT-ÎLES p74

Spot guillemots, puffins and kittiwakes at this bird reserve

Côte de Granit Rose

Sept Îles (Réserve Naturelle)

Côte des Ajoncs

Pors-Bugalez

Pointe du Château

Sillon de Talbert

Île Bréhat

Port Blanc

Buguélés

Plougrescant

Trégastrel

Ploumanac'h

Penvénan

Pleubian

Loguivy

Pointe l'Arcouest

Ploubazlanec

Île Grande
Pleumeur-Bodou

Perros-Guirec

Tréguier

Lézardrieux

Côte de Goëllo

Trébeurden

Lannion Airport

Paimpol

Abbaye de Beauport

Baie de Lannion

Traou-Nez

D786

Château de la Roche-Jagu

D786

Lannion

St-Michel-en-Grève

D8

Pléhédel

Lanloup

Locquirec

Ploumilliau

Pontrieux

Kermaria

Plouha

Plestin-les-Grèves

Brélidy

St-Quay-Portrieux

To Morlaix (11km)

Plouaret Trégor

Bégard

Lanvollon

Binic

Louargat

N12

Guingamp

D9

D6

St-Brieuc Airport

N12

KERMARIA p70

Feel the shivers run down your spine when you see the *Danse Macabre*

D787

D8

Côtes d'Armor

CÔTE DE PENTHIÈVRE p66

Chill on the beaches around St-Cast-le-Guildo and Pléneuf-Val-André

D790

Carhaix-Plouguer

Uzel

DISTANCE CHART (KM)

Rostrenen

Gouarec

St-Guen

Canal de Nantes à Brest

Beau Rivage

Caurel

Mur-de-Bretagne

Lac de Guerlédan

St-Aignan

Plouray

Silfiac

	Dinan	Erquy	Guingamp	Lannion
Erquy	43			
Guingamp	92	67		
Lannion	125	100	35	
Paimpol	102	78	31	33

Note: Distances between destinations are approximate

GETTING AROUND

The fastest route through the region is the busy N12, which passes nearby the major towns of Dinan, St-Brieuc and Guingamp, but for sightseeing the D786 is a much better option, providing some super views as it runs between the main coastal towns. Unfortunately, it gets clogged with traffic between June and August, when parking is also at a premium. The *département* is well served by trains and buses.

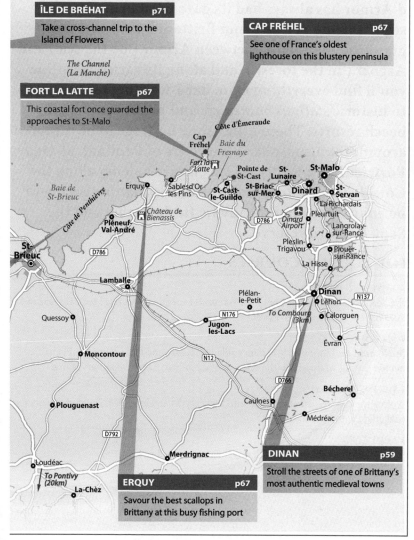

ÎLE DE BRÉHAT   p71
Take a cross-channel trip to the Island of Flowers

CAP FRÉHEL   p67
See one of France's oldest lighthouse on this blustery peninsula

The Channel
(La Manche)

FORT LA LATTE   p67
This coastal fort once guarded the approaches to St-Malo

Côte d'Émeraude

Cap Fréhel

Baie du Fresnaye

Fort la Latte

Pointe de St-Cast

St-Lunaire

St-Malo

Baie de St-Brieuc

Erquy

Sables d'Or les Pins

St-Cast-le-Guildo

St-Briac-sur-Mer

Dinard

St-Servan

La Richardais

Côte de Penthièvre

Château de Bienassis

Pléneuf-Val-André

Pleurtuit

Dinard Airport

Langrolay-sur-Rance

St-Brieuc

D786

Pleslin-Trigavou

Plouër-sur-Rance

La Hisse

Lamballe

Plélan-le-Petit

Dinan

Léhon

N137

Quessoy

N176

To Combourg (3km)

Calorguen

Jugon-les-Lacs

Évran

Moncontour

N12

D766

Bécherel

Plouguenast

Caulnes

Médréac

D792

Merdrignac

Loudéac

To Pontivy (20km)

La-Chèz

DINAN   p59
Stroll the streets of one of Brittany's most authentic medieval towns

ERQUY   p67
Savour the best scallops in Brittany at this busy fishing port

0 ——— 30 km
0 ——— 20 miles

CÔTES D'ARMOR GETTING STARTED

MAKING THE MOST OF YOUR TIME

Like much of Brittany, the *département* of Côtes d'Armor has always had its gaze fixed firmly on the sea. Its name derives from Brittany's traditional geographical distinction between Armor ('by the sea') and Argoat ('in the forest'), and along its varied coastline you'll find everything from hard-working fishing ports to historic *stations balnéaires* and bucket-and-spade beach resorts. There's maritime heritage to be explored around the atmospheric harbours of Paimpol, St-Quay-Portrieux and Erquy, beach culture aplenty along the Côte de Granit Rose and world-class nature-gazing to be enjoyed around the idyllic Île de Bréhat and the Sept-Îles bird reserve.

TOP TOURS & COURSES

❦ THIERRY TEFFAINE
The head chef at Les Trois Lunes (p66) reveals his culinary secrets (☎ 02 96 85 10 32; www.les3lunes.fr; €80; 1st Tue & Wed every month).

- -

❦ SILLON DE TALBERT
The Maison du Littoral (p70) offers guided walks around this unique peninsula that include getting an insight to the centuries-old industry of *goémon* harvesting.

- -

❦ ÎLE DE BRÉHAT
Explore the car-free isles and delve into their myths and legends through the eyes of a local guide with Kerano (p72).

- -

❦ SEPT-ÎLES
Take an unforgettable boat trip to this twitcher's paradise (p74).

- -

GETTING AWAY FROM IT ALL

Several gardens make gorgeous getaways from the coastal buzz.

* **Jardins Kestellic** Exotic trees, oaks and pines overlooking Tréguier's port. (☎ 06 73 84 00 15; www.kestellic.fr, in French; admission €5; ☺ 2-6pm Mon-Fri mid-July–mid-Aug, 2-6pm Mon, Wed & Fri early-Jul & mid-Aug–mid-Sep, 2-5pm Mon & Wed mid-Apr–Jun)

* **Jardin Naturel de l'Atelier** Wander around the orchards and arboretums of a professional *arboriste* (tree-grower). (www.claudelemaut.com, in French; Kervasclet, near Perros-Guirec; admission €4; ☺ 2-6pm Fri-Sun May-Sep)

* **Jardin Vivaces** A joint ticket to the Jardin Naturel de l'Atelier also buys entry to this show garden and botanical centre. (☎ 02 96 47 27 64; www.lepage-vivaces .com, in French; Pleumeur-Bodou).

ADVANCE PLANNING

* **Dinan** Crushing summer crowds can seriously take the shine off visiting this delightful medieval town, so try to time your visit for the quieter months between September to May.

* **Boat trips** Advance reservations for boats to the Île de Bréhat and the Sept-Îles are always a good idea.

* **Restaurant reservations** The *département* is one of Brittany's busiest areas, and tables at its top restaurants are like gold dust in peak season – book well ahead for La Clarté (p75), La Voile d'Or (p67), Aux Pesked (p69) and La Ville Blanche (p75).

TOP RESTAURANTS

♥ L'ESCURIAL
The place to savour Erquy's stellar scallops (p67)

♥ AUX PESKED
Michelin-starred dining in St-Brieuc (p69)

♥ LA VOILE D'OR
Sumptuous food with a coastal setting (p67)

♥ LA CLARTÉ
Masterchef Daniel Jaguin's latest culinary project (p75)

♥ LES TROIS LUNES
New, inventive dining in old Dinan (p66)

♥ LA COTRIADE
Try our new find along Paimpol's sweet quayside (p71)

RESOURCES

* **www.cotesdarmor.com** This website provides lots of general information on the entire coast, with suggestions for accommodation, upcoming events, leisure activities and recommended restaurants.

CÔTES D'ARMOR

(Continued from page 59)

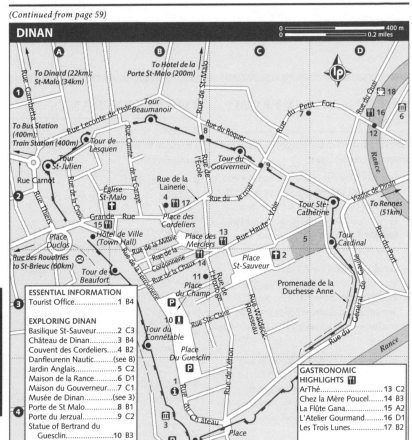

DINAN

0 ——————— 400 m
0 ——————— 0.2 miles

To Dinard (22km);
St-Malo (34km)

Rue Gambetta

To Bus Station
(400m);
Train Station (400m)

To Hôtel de la
Porte St-Malo (200m)

Rue Leconte de l'Isle

Tour
Beaumanoir

Rue du Petit Fort

Rue du Quai

18

16

6

12

Rance

Tour de
Lesquen

Tour
St-Julien

Rue Carnot

Rue Thiers

Rue de la Croix

Rue du Comte de la Garaye

Rue du Roquet

Rue de l'École

Tour du
Gouverneur

Rue de la
Lainerie

Rue du Jerzual

4   17

Tour Ste-
Catherine

Viaduc de Dinan

To Rennes
(51km)

Église
St-Malo

Grande   Rue

15

Place Duclos

Hôtel de Ville
(Town Hall)

Rue des Rouairies
to St-Brieuc (60km)

Tour de
Beaufort

Place des
Cordeliers

Place des
Merciers

Rue de la Mittrie

Rue de la
Cordonnerie

Rue de la Chaux

Rue de la Ferronnerie

13

14

Rue Haute-Voie

Place
St-Sauveur

2

5

Tour
Cardinal

Rue du Port

Place
du Champ

Rue de l'Horloge

11

Promenade de la
Duchesse Anne

Rance

Rue du Général de

Rue Waldeck-Rousseau

10

Tour du
Connétable

Rue Ste-Claire

Place
Du Guesclin

Rue de la Station

1

Rue du Château

3

Tour du Coëtquen

Place
St-Louis

ESSENTIAL INFORMATION
Tourist Office...................1 B4

EXPLORING DINAN
Basilique St-Sauveur.........2 C3
Château de Dinan............3 B4
Couvent des Cordeliers.....4 B2
Danfleurenn Nautic.........(see 8)
Jardin Anglais....................5 C2
Maison de la Rance...........6 D1
Maison du Gouverneur....7 C1
Musée de Dinan.............(see 3)
Porte de St Malo..............8 B1
Porte du Jerzual................9 C2
Statue of Bertrand du
     Guesclin.....................10 B3
Tour de l'Horloge............11 B3
Vieux Pont.....................12 D1

**GASTRONOMIC
HIGHLIGHTS**
ArThé..........................13 C2
Chez la Mère Poucel.......14 B3
La Flûte Gana.................15 A2
L'Atelier Gourmand.........16 D1
Les Trois Lunes...............17 B2

TRANSPORT
Boat Terminal.................18 D1

(Governor's House) at number 24, which dates from the late 1500s and was occupied by the city governor; you can peek inside on certain afternoons between July and September. The street meanders onwards to Dinan's old **port**, where the quayside cafés make an ideal place for some R&R before braving the leg-sappingly steep slog back into town.

❦ **BOAT TRIPS // CRUISE THE ILLE-ET-RANCE TO ST-MALO**
The Ille-et-Rance canal is popular with pleasure boaters; if you fancy hiring your

own vessel, head for the quayside kiosk of **Danfleurenn Nautic** (☎ 06 07 45 89 97; www.danfleurenn-nautic.com; per hr €29-35, half-day €69-79, full day €129-146; 🕙 10am-7pm Easter-Nov), which hires self-drive motorboats. If you prefer to have someone else at the helm, **Jaman IV** (☎ 02 96 39 28 41; www.vedettejamaniv .com; adult/2-12yr €11/7), offers commentated river cruises passing under three local bridges and through the pretty Léhon lock, while **Compagnie Corsaire** (☎ 08 25 13 81 00; www.compagniecorsaire.com; adult/2-18yr €29/17.50) runs on all the way to Dinard and St-Malo.

❤ MAISON DE LA RANCE //
BRUSH UP ON YOUR BRUSHWORK
On the opposite bank of the Rance
River, the **Maison de la Rance** (☎ 02 96
87 40 00; quai Talard; adult/child €4.60/3; ☺ 10-7pm
Jul & Aug, 2-6pm Tue-Sun Apr-Jun & Sep-Nov) is
an interactive centre that explores the
natural history and industrial heritage
of the river. In addition to this, it runs
guided **nature walks** (adult/child 6-12yr
€6.50/2.60) and photography and painting
expeditions (€20) along the canal's quiet
towpaths.

FESTIVALS & EVENTS

Fête des Remparts (☎ 02 96 87 94 94; www
.fete-remparts-dinan.com) This two-yearly festival
held in July sees Dinannais and 40,000 visitors dress up
in medieval garb for markets, military re-enactments,
parades and jousting contests. The next ones are to take
place in 2010 and 2012.

GASTRONOMIC HIGHLIGHTS

There are cafés around the old port area.

❤ ARTHÉ €
☎ 02 96 87 48 45; 19 rue de l'Apport; teas €3-6;
☺ around 10am-5pm Tue-Sun
Hundreds of tea-themed trinkets fill
every inch of space at this endearingly
chaotic tearoom-cum-antique-shop. You
can buy rare estate teas to take away, or
settle down for a brew served from antique china – if you can find any room,
that is.

❤ CHEZ LA MÈRE POURCEL €€
☎ 02 96 39 03 80; 3 place des Merciers; mains €22-28;
☺ Tue-Sat, lunch Sun
Delightfully set in a pale-blue timbered
house, this place is all about home-style

CÔTES D'ARMOR

TOP CAMPING

Here are a few of our favourite alfresco accommodation options in Côtes d'Armor. For
other accommodation options, see p290:

★ **Camping Bellevue** (☎ 02 96 70 41 84; www.campingbellevue.net; St-Quay-Portrieux; site €6-8, adult
€4.10-5.10, child €3-3.20; ☺ May-Sep) Sweeping views of the Goëlo coast, although it can
get crowded in high season.

★ **Camping de Kerdual** (☎ 02 96 23 54 86; jphostiou@voila.fr; Trébeurden; site €18.50-23; mid-
May–mid-Sep) Absolutely tiny site (26 pitches at the last count) hidden away by little
Pors-Mabo beach near Trébeurden. Simple but secluded.

★ **Camping Domaine de Keravel** (☎ 02 96 22 49 13; www.keravel.com; near Plouha; site €19-28
depending on season; ☺ Jun-Sep; ☒) Superior camping (heated swimming pool, woods,
tennis court) in the grounds of an old manor. Worth every one of its four stars.

★ **Camping Le Chatelet** (☎ 02 96 41 96 33; www.lechatelet.com; St-Cast-le-Guildo; site €12-21.50,
adult €4-7; ☺ late-Apr–mid-Sep; ☐ ☒) St-Cast has plenty of campgrounds, but this
posh family-friendly site is our current pick. Pitches have a choice of sea or lake
view.

★ **Camping Le Vieux Moulin** (☎ 02 96 72 34 23; www.camping-vieux-moulin.com; Erquy; site
€10-19.90, adult €4.90-6.10, child €3.80-4.80; ☺ mid-Apr–Sep; ☒) Another great option for
families, with a lovely swimming pool, several playgrounds and a rather spiffing
water park.

French cooking, with menus taking in everything from salt-marsh lamb to country *cocottes* (casseroles). *Menus* are named after Poucel family members (Eugènie, Virginie, Père Alfred) for that extra-intimate touch.

🌱 LA FLÛTE GANA €
☎ 02 96 85 29 76; 23 Grande Rue / 26 Rue Du Marchix (double entrance)

You'll feel the heat belting out from the baker's oven as you step into this artisan bakery, which turns out the town's finest *pains de campagne* and hand-baked cakes.

🌱 L'ATELIER GOURMAND €
☎ 02 96 85 14 18; 4 rue du Quai; mains €8-15; ☽ lunch Tue-Sun, dinner daily in summer, lunch Tue-Sun, dinner Wed-Sat rest of year

The food almost plays second at this handsome waterside brasserie: bookings are essential for the top tables, squeezed onto a sun-trap patio hovering above the Rance River. The menu's plain and unpretentious – think salads, creamy haddock stews and fish kebabs – and you couldn't ask for a better spot when the sun's shining.

🌱 LES TROIS LUNES €€
☎ 02 96 85 10 32; 22 rue de la Lainerie; menus €23-49; ☽ lunch Mon-Sat, dinner Tue-Sat

Thierry Teffaine is Dinan's hottest young chef, and his bistro, the Three Moons, is *the* place to eat in Dinan. In contrast to its old town setting, the interior is über-contemporary – fuschia pinks, smoke greys, chrome lamps – and the menu gives an inventive twist to classics such as rabbit, duck, pigeon and scallops.

TRANSPORT

BUS // Tibus (☎ 0 810 22 22 22; www.tibus.fr) has at least a couple of daily buses to Dinard, St-Malo and St-Cast-le-Guildo, while the No 7 run by Illenoo (☎ 08 10 35 10 35; www.illenoo-services.fr) stops at Dinan en route between Rennes and Dinard.

TRAIN // There are regular local trains to Dinan from Dol-de-Bretagne (€5.40, 25 minutes), on the TGV route between Pairs and St-Malo. These local trains continue to St-Brieuc.

CÔTE DE PENTHIÈVRE & AROUND
· · · · · ·

Stretching between the blustery promontory of Cap Fréhel and the busy commercial centre of St-Brieuc, this pretty stretch of coastline is pocked by pink granite cliffs, sandy beaches and seaside resorts.

The area's name commemorates one of the ancient fiefdoms of Brittany, Penthièvre, and was once ruled by its own feudal counts before being subsumed into the Duchy of Brittany and, much later, the Côtes d'Armor *département*.

ST-CAST-LE-GUILDO & CAP FRÉHEL

🌱 ST-CAST-LE-GUILDO // TIME TO HIT THE BEACH

If beaches are what you're after, you can't beat St-Cast. Thousands of visitors descend on this seaside resort to cook themselves to a crisp on one of its seven sandy beaches: the big boys are the **Grande Plage** and **Plage de Pen-Guen**, but you'll find several quieter patches further west.

If beach-bronzing's not your thing, St-Cast makes a good starting point for exploring the GR34 coastal path: you can follow the trail south to the blustery headland of **Pointe de Garde**, and north to **Pointe St-Cast**, from where there's a fantastic view across the Baie de Fresnaye all the way to the Cap Fréhel lighthouse.

♥ CAP FRÉHEL // EXPLORE BEACONS AND BASTIONS

Swathed in gorse, heather and colourful wildflowers, this wind-battered peninsula boasts not one, but two cliff-top lighthouses. The most recent one dates from the mid-1950s, but there's a much older example further out along the coast, the **Phare Vauban**, built in 1685. On a clear blue day, views stretch all along the northern Breton coastline, and if it's really fine you might even glimpse the hazy outline of Jersey on the faraway horizon.

The cape is mainly frequented by walkers and bird-spotters these days, but in days gone by this headland was an important strategic strongpoint for protecting the approaches to St-Malo. Several abandoned gun emplacements left over from WWII are dotted around the headland, but they're completely dwarfed by the **Fort La Latte** (☎ 02 96 41 30 31; www.castlelalatte.com; adult/4-12yr €4.90/2.80; ⊙ 10am-7pm Jul & Aug, 10am-12.30pm & 2-6pm Apr-Jun & Sep, 2-6pm weekends Oct-Mar), a hulking 14th-century fort that was expanded during the reign of Louis XIV. If it looks familiar, don't be surprised – back in 1958, Tony Curtis and Kirk Douglas swashbuckled their way round the battlements in the classic sword-and-sandals epic *The Vikings*.

GASTRONOMIC HIGHLIGHTS

♥ LA VOILE D'OR
SABLES D'OR LES PINS €€€

☎ 02 96 41 42 49; allée des Acacias; lunch menu €28, dinner €38-99; ⊙ lunch Thu-Sun, dinner Tue-Sun
Feel like splashing out? Then there's only one choice – the Golden Sail, west of Cap Fréhel, has rapidly acquired a reputation as one of Brittany's most renowned restaurants thanks to the culinary talents of Maximin Hellio. Big windows and big views provide the backdrop for Hellio's superb brand of *terre-mer* cuisine – adventurous, but with just a soupçon of tradition to keep the purists happy.

ERQUY & PLÉNEUF-VAL-ANDRÉ

♥ ERQUY // SAVOUR FRANCE'S FINEST SCALLOPS

This bustling fishing port is the number-one spot in Brittany to try the local delicacy of **coquilles St-Jacques**. Erquy accounts for over half of France's annual scallop catch – some 2500 tonnes each year – and you'll find 'em served every which way around the town's quayside cafés: garlic-buttered, pan-fried, oven-roasted, stewed in Breton cider or served in their shell accompanied by crusty bread and a glass of chilled white.

The top place to try them is upmarket **L'Escurial** (☎ 02 96 72 31 56; menus €26-41; ⊙ lunch & dinner Tue-Sun in summer), but for something more laid-back try **La Cassolette** (☎ 02 96 72 13 08; 6 rue de la Saline; dishes €19-34; ⊙ daily in season, closed Wed & Thu in winter).

Alternatively, you could arrange a cooking lesson or a visit to the local fish market with the **Syndicat des Caps** (☎ 02 96 41 50 83; www.syndicat-des-caps.bzh.fr); better still, pitch up for the April **Coquilles St-Jacques festival**, held in alternate years in Erquy, St-Quay-Portrieux and Loguivy.

A coastal path leads northwest from the harbour for 2km to **Cap d'Erquy**, a nature reserve bounded by cliffs of pink sandstone and several fine beaches, including the magnificent 2km sweep of **Plage de Caroual**.

CÔTES D'ARMOR

❦ **CHÂTEAU DE BIENASSIS //**
FEUDAL FINERY NEAR THE COAST
About 6km west of Erquy, this 16th-century château (☎ 02 96 72 22 03; www
.chateau-bienassis.com; adult/child €5/3; 🕙 10am-12.30pm & 2-6.30pm Sun mid-Jun–mid-Sep, 2-6.30pm Sun mid-May–mid-Jun) has been owned by the same family since 1880. It still boasts its original moat and machicolated walls, and inside the castle you can wander around the inner courtyard and tranquil chapel, as well as a medieval *jardin potager* (kitchen garden).

❦ **PLÉNEUF-VAL-ANDRÉ //** **RELAX IN THIS QUINTESSENTIAL STATION BALNÉAIRE**
Wind the clock back to the 1870s and you'd find little more than a few fishermen's shacks and cod boats in **Pléneuf-Val-André**, but spin forward a couple of decades and you'd find yourself smack-bang in the middle of one of France's most fashionable *stations balnéaires* (seaside resorts). Canny developers cashed in on the seaside craze in the late 19 century and constructed a casino, promenade and a host of elegant art deco villas in Pléneuf, and it's still one of the area's top seaside resorts – the huge beaches of **Plage Val-André**, **Plage des Vallées** and **Plage de la Ville Berneuf** attract massive summer crowds of sunbathers and water-sport enthusiasts.

GASTRONOMIC HIGHLIGHTS

Apart from the *coquilles* (scallops) places listed, p67, consider the following.

❦ **ART ET SAVEUR //**
PLÉNEUF-VAL-ANDRÉ €
☎ 02 96 63 19 17; 28 quai des Terres-Neuves; mains €8-14; 🕙 Apr-Oct

The name says it all – art and flavour. This boho haven started life as a gallery for local artists, but it's now branched out into bistro food, including crispy *tartines* (toasted sandwiches) and great platters of smoked tuna, sardines and fish pâté. The port views are rather lovely, too.

❦ **RELAIS ST-AUBIN //** **ERQUY €€**
☎ 02 96 72 13 22; www.relais-saint-aubin.fr; St-Aubin; menus €18-38; 🕙 dinner Tue-Sun Jul & Aug, closed Wed in low season
This ivy-clad priory just outside Erquy is packed to the rafters with Breton character. The food's hale and hearty – spicy marinated sardines, big slabs of cidery pork, chimney-cooked sea-bass – and you can eat either *auberge*-style in the beamed dining room, or alfresco on the patio terrace.

TRANSPORT

BUS // Tibus (www.tibus.fr) operates most of the coastal buses; line 2 is the most useful, with four daily buses (two on Sunday) running between St-Brieuc and St-Cast, stopping at Pléneuf, Erquy, Sables d'Or and Cap Fréhel en route.
TRAIN // St-Brieuc's the area's main train hub, with zippy TGVs east to Paris Montparnasse (€54 to €63, 3½ hours), south to Rennes (€15.30 to €18.40, 50 minutes) and west to Brest (€21.30 to €24.70, 1½ hours).

CÔTE DU GOËLO

· · · · · ·

Zigzagging along the western side of the Baie de St-Brieuc, the Goëlo Coast shares the attractions of its sister shore across the bay – salty fishing harbours, busy *stations balnéaires* and long, photo-friendly stretches of cherry-pink cliffs.

ST-BRIEUC

Let's be honest – the Côtes d'Armor's concrete capital is never going to top any must-visit lists, but it's worth a detour to see the elegant 16th-century **Cathédrale St-Étienne** and some attractive medieval houses – the most venerable of which, the **Maison Ribault** (32 rue Fardel), dates back to 1480, making it one of Brittany's oldest residences.

The train and bus stations are located south of the town centre. To get to the tourist office and the main sights, head up rue de la Gare then go left along rue de Rohan.

☙ AUX PESKED // STUFF YOURSELF SILLY AT ST-BRIEUC'S TOP RESTAURANT

☎ 02 96 33 34 65; 59 rue du Legué; lunch €19-23, dinner €38-68; ☺ lunch Sun-Fri, dinner Mon-Sat
Gird your gastronomic loins – Aux Pesked's Brest-born chef Mathieu Aumont is known for his zingy flavours and offbeat culinary approach. The decor blends modern materials with bold splashes of colour and quirky furniture, and the food is deliberately eclectic; seafood predominates, but everything's laced with a creative twist.

TRANSPORT

BUS // Tibus (☎ 08 10 22 22 22; www.tibus.fr) has several lines connecting St-Brieuc with Lannion, Lamballe and towns all along the Côte du Goëlo and beyond.

TRAIN // St-Brieuc's a busy transport hub. It's on the main TGV route to Paris Montparnasse as well as Brest to the west and Rennes to the east. There are also regional connections to Guingamp (€6, 17 minutes) where you can catch onward trains to Paimpol (€11, 1½ to 2½ hours), and also trains east to Dinan and Dol-et-Bretagne (for a connection to St-Malo).

BINIC TO PAIMPOL

☙ BINIC & ST-QUAY-PORTRIEUX // CLIFFS AND COD-FISHING

Between the 16th and 19th centuries, these side-by-side harbours were at the centre of **La Grande Pêche à la Morue** (cod-fishing industry). Braving the stormy waters off the coasts of Newfoundland and Iceland, the *morutiers* (cod boats) left home for up to six months at a time and endured unimaginable hardship and danger – the Paimpol region alone lost 100 ships and over 2000 men in just 80 years.

Although the cod-fishing industry began to decline from the 1930s onwards, small fishing fleets still operate out of St-Quay thanks to its deep-water port (the only one between Cherbourg and Brest). In honour of its piscatorial traditions, Binic hosts a **cod festival** in May, and every third year St-Quay takes its turn in the April **scallop festival** along with nearby Erquy and Loguivy.

These days, though, it's tourists that are the towns' main catch – visitors throng the towns' beaches and cafés during the summer, or strike out along the coastal path to peep over the edge of Brittany's highest cliffs at **Pointe de Plouha**, which plunge 100m straight-down into the foaming waters of the Channel.

The chef at the **Hôtel Saint-Quay** (☎ 02 96 70 40 99; 72 bd du Maréchal-Foch, St-Quay-Portrieux; menus €25-59; ☺ lunch & dinner) spent several years working at a top Singapore hotel, and his globe-trotting travels have left their mark on his country restaurant. The menu's mostly French with a Provençal bias, but you'll often see a spicy Asian accent thrown into the mix.

See Transport, left, for details on getting to these towns.

❦ KERMARIA // ASHES TO ASHES, DUST TO DUST...

This tiny village hosts a famous *pardon* on the third Sunday in September, but it's better known for the 13th-century **Chapelle de Kermaria-an-Iskuit** and its chilling medieval fresco, the *Danse Macabre* (Dance of Death). The spooky skeletal figure of Ankou leads a procession of monks, ploughmen, knights, kings and cardinals – a macabre reminder of our shared mortality. There is no public transport to Kermaria.

PAIMPOL & AROUND

Paimpol is still a busy commercial harbour, and hosts one of the area's largest **fish and produce markets** every Tuesday morning. The **Festival du Chant Marin** is a music festival with a maritime flavour held in Paimpol every August. It's also a good town to find out about the local fishing traditions and stories about boats that never returned to port.

EXPLORING PAIMPOL & AROUND

❦ MUSÉE DE LA MER // VISIT A FASCINATING FISHING MUSEUM

This **museum** (☎ 02 96 22 02 19; rue Labenne; adult/7-18yr €4.70/2; ⊗ 10.30am-12.30pm & 2.30-6pm mid-Jun–Aug, 2-6pm mid-April–mid-Jun & early Sep), housed in one of the town's old cod-drying factories, is a treasure-trove of nautical artefacts, from seine nets and canvas sails to vintage posters and fishing outfits. Sepia photos depict a lost age of bewhiskered Breton fishermen and elegant fishing schooners, locally known as *goélettes*. A joint ticket includes entry to the **Musée du Costume Breton** (☎ 02 96 22 02 19; ⊗ same hrs as Musée de la Mer).

❦ VAPEUR DE TRIEUX // ALL ABOARD FOR THIS VINTAGE STEAM ENGINE

Steam-buffs and lovers of fine scenery will be in seventh heaven aboard the chuffing carriages of the **Vapeur du Trieux** (Trieux Steam; ☎ 08 92 39 14 27; www.vapeurdutrieux.com; Gare de Paimpol; adult/4-16yr return €22/11; ⊗ May-Sep), a 1920s steam engine that plies the old railway line between Paimpol and Pontrieux to the southwest, through the scenic Trieux Valley. The outward leg includes a stop for crêpes, ice creams and Breton music at the manor of Traou-Nez.

❦ ABBAYE DE BEAUPORT // EXPLORE THE RUINS OF A TUMBLEDOWN ABBEY

About 2.5km southeast of Paimpol's town centre lie the graceful ruins of the **Abbaye de Beauport** (☎ 02 96 55 18 55; www.abbaye-beauport; Kérity; adult/11-18yr €5/2; ⊗ 10am-7pm mid-Jun–mid-Sep, 10am-noon & 2-5pm mid-Sep–mid-Jun). Founded in 1202, the abbey flourished for several centuries as a port and overnight stop for English pilgrims heading for Santiago de Compostela in Spain. The guided tour takes in the Gothic abbey and its sheltered harbour, apple orchards and rose gardens.

❦ SILLON DE TALBERT // WALK TO THE TIP OF BRITTANY

Jutting out from the coastline 10km northwest of Paimpol, this strange shingly spit is a natural phenomenon formed by the opposing currents of two nearby rivers, the Trieux and Jaudy. It's now a protected nature reserve, where terns and ringed plovers nest in spring and *goémon* (seaweed) is harvested by hand from the surrounding tidal flats. The **Maison du Littoral** (☎ 02 96 16 54 67;

CÔTES D'ARMOR

maison-littoral-pleubian@orange.fr; 1 impasse de la Tossen, Pleubian; ⏰ 10am-noon & 2-4.30 Wed, 2-4.30pm Fri) organises regular coastal walks exploring the area's unusual geology and the centuries-old industry of *goémon* harvesting.

GASTRONOMIC HIGHLIGHTS

♥ LA VIELLE TOUR // PAIMPOL €€

☎ 02 96 20 83 18; 13 rue de l'Église; menus €39-50; ⏰ lunch & dinner Tue-Sun

There's only a handful of tables at this Paimpol grandee, so reservations are essential. Burnished wood and antique furnishings make for a sober ambience, and as you might expect in Paimpol, seafood predominates: for example, scallops with girolles mushrooms, poached turbot, cod steak in a herring juice.

♥ LA COTRIADE // PAIMPOL €€

☎ 02 96 20 81 08; 16 quai Armand Dayot; mains €21-30; ⏰ lunch Tue, Thu, Fri & Sun, dinner daily in peak season

Things are altogether lighter and brighter at this portside establishment, where laid-back brasserie food is dished up at café-style tables. There are five different starters, four mains and three desserts to choose from each day, but exactly what's on offer depends on what the chef's picked up during his daily expedition to the market.

TRANSPORT

BUS // Tibus (☎ 08 10 22 22 22; www.tibus.fr) has several lines connecting Paimpol with St-Brieuc and Lannion and towns all along the Côte du Goëlo and beyond.

TRAIN // A local train connects Paimpol with Guingamp (€11, 1½ to 2½ hours), which is on the main TGV route between Paris Montparnasse and Brest via St-Brieuc.

ÎLE DE BRÉHAT

· · · · · ·

pop 425

Just 3.5km long and 1.5km wide, the Île de Bréhat is known for its beautiful coastline and an unusually balmy climate. It's actually more an archipelago than an island – the two largest landmasses (Île Nord and Île Sud) are connected by the Pont ar Prat, a teeny 17th-century footbridge built by Vauban, while the coast is littered with rugged atolls and reefs frequented by seals and seabirds.

The island is only 1.5km north of the Breton coastline, but its unique microclimate supports an abundance of exotic trees, shrubs and flowers such as palms, figs, eucalyptus, mimosas and huge hydrangeas, some of which grow to gargantuan proportions. Apart from the beaches and coastal paths, there's not a great deal to see, but that doesn't deter the 4000-odd visitors who pitch up daily in summer – so if it's a quiet island escape you're looking for, you'd be wise to avoid the summer months. There are no cafés, no coffee shops, nothing, here on the island.

ESSENTIAL INFORMATION

TOURIST OFFICES // Le Bourg (☎ 02 96 20 04 15; www.brehat.infos.fr; ⏰ 10am-6pm Mon-Sat in summer) In the island's only village.

EXPLORING ÎLE DE BRÉHAT

♥ HIKING & CYCLING // PACK YOUR WALKING SHOES

Bréhat is completely car-free, so the only way of getting around is by bike or on foot. Depending on the tide, ferries land at one of three points near Port-Clos,

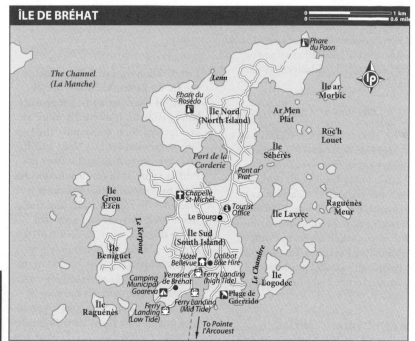

ÎLE DE BRÉHAT

The Channel (La Manche)

Phare du Paon

Île ar-Morbic

Lenn

Phare du Rosédo

Île Nord (North Island)

Ar Men Plat

Roc'h Louet

Île Séhérès

Port de la Corderie

Pont ar Prat

Chapelle St-Michel

Île Grou Ezen

Le Kerpont

Tourist Office

Le Bourg

Île Lavrec

Raguénès Meur

Île Sud (South Island)

Île Beniguet

Hôtel Bellevue

Dalibot Bike Hire

Le Chambre

Camping Municipal Goareva

Verreries de Bréhat

Ferry Landing (high Tide)

Île Logodec

Île Raguénès

Ferry Landing (Low Tide)

Ferry Landing (Mid Tide)

Plage de Guerzido

To Pointe l'Arcouest

at the southern end of the island. From here it's about a two-hour, 4km walk to the tip of the north island and the **Phare du Paon**, a 1950s carbon-copy of the original lighthouse which was blown up by the occupying Germans during WWII. You can circle back via the island's second lighthouse, the **Phare du Rosédo**, and the miniscule **Chapelle St-Michel**, built in 1852 at the island's highest point; though barely 30m above sea level, it provides a superb outlook over the whole island.

The only real settlement is **Le Bourg**, home to the tourist office and a tiny 12th-century chapel. About 500m further south is the **Plage du Guerzido**, Bréhat's most popular beach, but you'll find lots more secluded coves hidden away on the Île Nord, especially along the northern coast of the Port de la Corderie.

Kerano (☎ 02 94 20 06 75; www.kerano .com; adult €12-25) runs four tailored walks around the island, taking in local myths and legends, local beauty spots and the *littoral* (coastline).

There are a couple of very basic campsites on the island – check ahead with the tourist office to see if there's space.

❦ **VERRERIES DE BRÉHAT // TAKE HOME A HANDMADE SOUVENIR**
Twenty years ago this 17th-century fort was a crumbling ruin, but a pair of passionate glass-blowers have since transformed it into the **Verreries de Bréhat** (Bréhat Glassworks; ☎ 02 96 20 09 09; La Citadelle; admission mid-Jun–mid-Sep €2), a combined glass workshop, gallery and boutique where you can watch the artists at work and buy some of their fragile ornaments, modelled on everything from colour-

ful elephants, cats and paper weights to plates and banister finials.

TRANSPORT

BIKE // For bikes, contact **Dalibot** (☎ 02 96 20 03 51; www.locationvelosbrehat.com; per half-/full day €10/13) near the ferry landings.

BOAT // **Vedettes de Bréhat** (☎ 02 96 55 79 50; www.vedettesdebrehat.com) makes the 10-minute hop from Pointe de l'Arcoest (adult/4–11yr €8.50/7) 16 times daily April to September, eight times daily in winter. Buses from Paimpol go to l'Arcoest. Extra summer ferries run from Pléneuf-Val-André, Erquy, Binic and St-Quay-Portrieux in season.

CARS // There aren't any.

CÔTE DE GRANIT ROSE

· · · · · ·

Christened after its distinctive rosy-pink rocks, the Côte de Granit Rose (Pink Granite Coast) is one of Brittany's most popular tourist spots, a jumble of tree-fringed coves and offshore islands backed by busy seaside resorts.

It's geared mainly towards family travellers and bucket-and-spade holidays – ideal if you've got the kids in tow, but perhaps not so perfect if you prefer your coastline wild and rugged. Despite the coastal clutter, there are still a few pockets of wilderness – most notably around the Côte des Ajoncs and the Sept-Îles, a tiny island archipelago turned ornithological reserve.

TRÉGUIER & CÔTE DES AJONCS

❦ TRÉGUIER // AWESOME ECCLESIASTICAL SPLENDOUR

Tréguier's magnificent Gothic **Cathédrale St-Tugdual** (place du Martray) complete-

ly dominates the centre of this old market town. It was built on the foundations of a 12th-century chapel, but all that remain of the original church are two Romanesque arches at the base of the **Tour Hastings**, just inside the south porch as you enter from place du Martray.

The rest of the building is textbook 15th-century Flamboyant Gothic, an exuberant architectural fantasy of flying buttresses, belfries and portals, as well as a charming enclosed cloister. The soaring nave contains the tomb of **St-Yves**, patron saint of lawyers; it's a 19th-century copy of the original, which was destroyed during the Revolution. Tréguier honours the saint with its annual **pardon**, one of the region's largest, held on the third Sunday in May.

Give yourself time to visit the **Jardins Kestellic**, overlooking the town's port.

❦ PLOUGRESCANT // BRITTANY'S ANSWER TO THE LEANING TOWER OF PISA

At the other end of the architectural spectrum is Plougrescant's oddball church, the **Chapelle St-Gonéry**, whose punch-drunk steeple lurches alarmingly to one side. Inside are a series of startling frescoes, painted over the course of a couple of centuries from the early 1500s. Naively drawn on a tawny-coloured background, the paintings depict various Old Testament scenes – see if you can spot Adam and Eve and other episodes from the Book of Genesis.

❦ CÔTE DES AJONCS // VENTURE ALONG THE GORSE COAST

Yellow gorse, grassy heath and weatherworn granite characterise the dramatic coastline between Tréguier and Perros-Guirec – pack a picnic and take your time exploring. The most northerly point is **Pointe du Château**, with views of the Sept-Îles offshore. About 1km to the west at Castel Meur is **Le Gouffre**, a spectacular cleft in the cliffs, and **La Maison Entre Les Deux Rochers**, a diminutive house built between two huge great granite outcrops – the subject of countless Breton postcards.

TRANSPORT

BUS // Tibus (☎ 08 10 22 22 22; www.tibus.fr) has services that link the coastal areas.

PERROS-GUIREC & AROUND

♥ PERROS-GUIREC, TRÉGASTEL & TRÉBEURDEN // BREAK OUT THE BEACH TOWELS

Stripy beach tents and colourful windbreaks cover every inch of sand of the hectic beaches around **Perros-Guirec**, the Côtes d'Armor's busiest seaside resort. Sprawling across a rocky peninsula, the town is split into two main areas: cafés, hotels and a concrete casino cluster around the main beach, **Plage de Trestraou**, while the town's modern marina is tucked away along the headland's eastern side. If beaches aren't your thing, there's not much to detain you in Perros-Guirec: life in this corner of Brittany revolves almost exclusively around baking on the beach, messing about in the water and chilling out in the many waterfront cafés.

Neighbouring **Trestrignel** is a smaller and prettier town, while the family-friendly **Plage de St-Guirec** is 3km to the east in the coastal town of Ploumanac'h.

After your umpteenth ice cream, you might feel like stretching your legs along the **Sentier des Douaniers** between Perros-Guirec and Ploumanac'h. It's one of the best bits of the GR34 coastal path,

passing via the dramatic promontory known as the **Pointe de Squewel**, where the rock stacks and rosy boulders have been eroded into fantastic shapes by centuries of erosion by the wind, weather and sea.

There's more good walking around **Trégastel**, another popular family resort 5km west of Perros-Guirec. Day-trippers cram onto the **Plage de Toul Drez**, but there are little inlets and rock pools to explore around the shoreline of the **Presqu'île Renote**, a pine-topped island joined to the mainland by a car-park-cum-causeway.

Tucked in among the granite rocks, the ingenious **Aquarium Marin** (☎ 02 96 23 48 58; www.aquarium-tregastel.com; bd Coz Pors; adult/4-16yr €7/5; ☉ 10am-7pm Jul & Aug, 10am-6pm Tue-Fri, 2-6pm Sat-Mon Apr-Jun & Sep, 2-5pm Tue-Sun Oct-Mar) has 28 tanks filled with underwater inhabitants plucked from along the Breton coastline.

Trébeurden, 10km southwest of Trégastel, is the last of the beach resorts along the Côte de Granit Rose, but usually feels less hectic than its brash, busy sisters.

♥ SEPT-ÎLES // PACK THE BINOCULARS FOR THIS ISLAND BIRD RESERVE

In spring and summer, 20,000 pairs of nesting seabirds congregate on the rocky specks of the Sept-Îles (Seven Islands), a nature reserve that has been managed since 1912 by the Ligue pour la Protection des Oiseaux (LPO). One of the islands, the **Île aux Moines** (Monks' Island) can be visited on foot: gannets, puffins, guillemots, razorbills, shags, kittiwakes, fulmars and herring gulls are just a few of the species to spot. The views of the surrounding islands and distant islands are superb.

The **Gare-Maritime** (☎ 02 96 91 10 00; www.armor-decouverte.fr; adult trips €14-19, 3-12yr €9-13) in Perros-Guirec runs expeditions to the islands lasting between 1¼ hours and 2½ hours. There are also special **bird-watching trips** organised by the **Station Ornithologique** (☎ 02 96 91 91 40; adult/child €2.50/1.50; ☺ 10am-1pm & 2.30-7pm Jul & Aug, 2-6pm weekends Sep-Jun) in Trébeurden, which also provides background info and guidebooks on the region's birdlife, as well as live video-feeds from several bird-cams hidden away within the island undergrowth.

GASTRONOMIC HIGHLIGHTS

❦ **LE SUROÎT** **PERROS-GUIREC** €€
☎ 02 96 23 23 83; 81 rue Ernest Renan; menus €17.90-38.90; ☺ lunch Tue-Sun, dinner Tue-Sat
Not far from Perros-Guirec's marina, this quietly stylish seafooderie makes a lovely haven from the hustle. Abstract art, wood floors and big windows create a contemporary vibe, and the menu is a tempting mix of fish dishes and stonking seafood platters.

❦ **LA CLARTÉ** **PERROS-GUIREC** €€€
☎ 02 96 49 05 96; www.la-clarte.com; 24 rue Gabriel Vicaire; menus €25-74
Top recommendation on the Pink Granite Coast goes to this Perros-Guirec address, run by Michelin-starred *maître-cuisinier* Daniel Jaguin (previously of Lannion's Ville Blanc). Jaguin's still showcasing his trademark *terre-mer cuisine* and championing the very best Breton ingredients, but running his own place seems to have brought a new freshness and creativity to his cooking. Highly recommended.

TRANSPORT

BUS // Tibus (☎ 08 10 22 22 22; www.tibus.fr) has services linking coastal towns.

LANNION & AROUND

❦ **LANNION //** **SAUNTER THE STREETS OF THIS MARKET TOWN**
These days **Lannion** is a centre for the electronics and communications industries, but during the Middle Ages it was one of the region's main market centres, and it's not too hard to picture a medieval bazaar in full swing on the town's atmospheric main square, hemmed in by higgledy-piggledy half-timbered houses.

Lannion's pleasant riverside setting and twisty streets make for a pleasant morning stroll, and there's a great view from the **Église de Brélévenez**, a 13th-century church that was supposedly founded by Templar knights, reached by 140 steep steps.

Later on, lunch on crispy *tartines* and gourmet platters of meat and cheese at **Le Lannionais** (☎ 02 96 46 74 79; 31 place du Général Leclerc), which also does a nice line in Breton-brewed beers and provides a perfect vantage point for some people-watching on the market square.

La Ville Blanche (The White Town; ☎ 02 96 37 04 28; www.la-ville-blanche.com; ☺ lunch & dinner Tue-Sun Jul-Aug, closed Mon, Wed and pm Sun Sep-Jun) might only have one Jaguin brother these days but it's still a fave of the foodie guides. Started by the brothers' grandma, the restaurant's focus has always been firmly on fine French cuisine such as oven-roasted lobster, langoustines with asparagus, and pigeon with Paimpol coconut. You'll need to book in peak season.

❦ **COSMOPOLIS //** **FROM ANCIENT HISTORY TO ASTRONOMY**
Northwest of Lannion, in Pleumeur-Bodou, is **Cosmopolis**, a complex of three kitsch, kid-friendly attractions that are ideal when the weather takes a turn

CÔTES D'ARMOR

for the worse. First up is **La Cité des Télécoms** (☎ 02 96 46 63 80; www.cite-telecoms .com; adult/child €7/5.60; ⊙ 10am-7pm Jul & Aug, 10am-6pm Mon-Fri Apr, May & Sep), a communications museum housed in a former ground station for the Telstar satellite. Next comes the **Village Gaulois** (☎ 02 96 91 83 95; www.levillagegaulois.org; adult/child Apr-Jun & Sep €4/3, €0.50 extra Jul & Aug; ⊙ 10.30am-7pm Jul & Aug, 2-6pm Sun-Fri Apr-Jun & Sep), a mock-up of a Gaulish village where the kids can amuse themselves by erecting menhirs or piloting a wooden barge. Last comes a trip through the stars at the **Planétarium de Bretagne** (☎ 02 96 15 80 32; www.planetarium -bretagne.fr; adult/child €7.50/5.60); it's only open for scheduled visits, so ring ahead to make sure.

TRANSPORT

BUS // Tibus (☎ 08 10 22 22 22; www.tibus.fr) has several lines connecting Lannion with other towns in the area.

TRAIN // Lannion has a regional train service to Plouaret-Trégor, which is on the main line between Paris, Rennes, St-Brieuc and Brest.

FINISTÈRE

3 PERFECT DAYS

☙ DAY 1 // THE SOUTH COAST
The former mill town of Pont-Aven (p111) was a favourite country getaway for lots of 19th-century artists including Paul Gauguin, and its water mills and woodlands still have bags of old-world charm. Indulge in a stellar lunch at Le Moulin de Rosmadec (p113) before heading on to Concarneau (p108), famous for its fortified *ville close* and authentic fishing-town feel.

☙ DAY 2 // CAPITAL IDEAS
Next up is Finistère's historic capital, Quimper (p102). Factor in visits to the twin-spired cathedral (p103) and the historic HB Henriot faïencerie factory (p105), before brushing up on Celtic culture at the Musée Départemental Breton (p104). A gastro-nomic cruise down the Odet River (p104) is a fine way to end the day, followed by a stay at the exclusive Villa Tri-Men (p294).

☙ DAY 3 // THE EDGE OF FINISTÈRE
Quit the city and head southwest to the pretty fishing ports and portside restaurants of the Pays Bigouden (p106). Picnic on the beaches around Pointe de la Torche (p108), spot seabirds at the Réserve du Cap Sizun (p100) or drink in the scenery from Pointe du Raz (p101). Douarnenez (p99) has some great places to stay – two of our favourites are the L'Auberge de Kervéoc'h (p293) and Ty Mad (p294).

FINISTÈRE

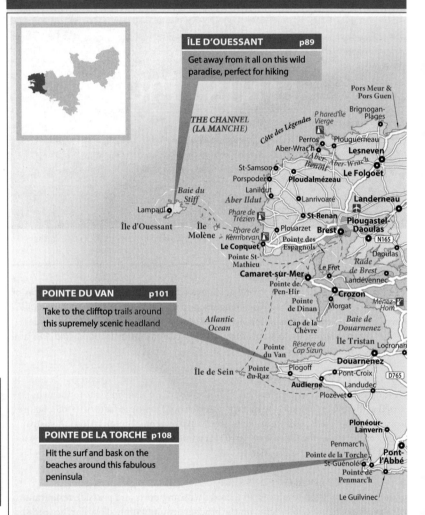

ÎLE D'OUESSANT p89

Get away from it all on this wild paradise, perfect for hiking

POINTE DU VAN p101

Take to the clifftop trails around this supremely scenic headland

POINTE DE LA TORCHE p108

Hit the surf and bask on the beaches around this fabulous peninsula

GETTING AROUND

Two main roads cut across Finistère: the north–south N165 between Quimper and Brest, and the west–east D12 from Brest towards Guingamp and the Côtes d'Armor, but the smaller regional roads, especially around the coasts and abers, can be slow-going. The main TGV route from Paris Montparnasse runs to Morlaix and Brest, with good regional train connections and bus links around the rest of the *département*. Roscoff's a busy ferry port, with regular boats to Plymouth and Rosslare.

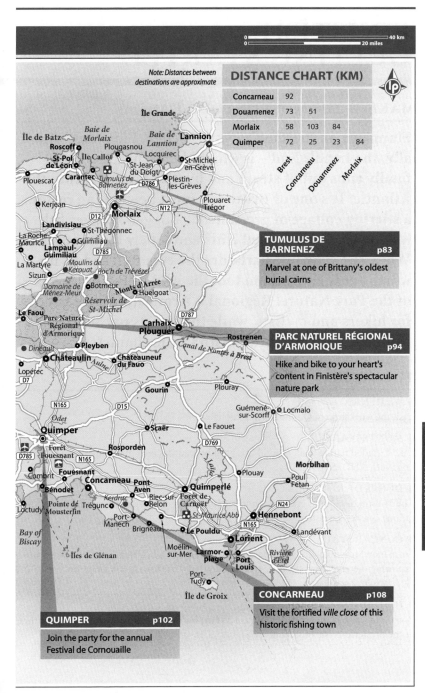

DISTANCE CHART (KM)

Note: Distances between destinations are approximate

	Brest	Concarneau	Douarnenez	Morlaix
Concarneau	92			
Douarnenez	73	51		
Morlaix	58	103	84	
Quimper	72	25	23	84

TUMULUS DE BARNENEZ   p83

Marvel at one of Brittany's oldest burial cairns

PARC NATUREL RÉGIONAL D'ARMORIQUE   p94

Hike and bike to your heart's content in Finistère's spectacular nature park

CONCARNEAU   p108

Visit the fortified *ville close* of this historic fishing town

QUIMPER   p102

Join the party for the annual Festival de Cornouaille

FINISTÈRE

FINISTÈRE GETTING STARTED

MAKING THE MOST OF YOUR TIME

Flung out on Brittany's westerly edge, Finistère – literally, the Land's End – is where the French mainland finally runs out of steam and hurtles headlong into the Atlantic. It's one of Brittany's most bewitching regions, a stirring collage of green fields, hugger-mugger fishing towns, sea-pounded cliffs and lonely lighthouses. While the coastline harbours the essential sights, it's worth venturing inland too: the wild hills and forests of the Parc Naturel Régional d'Armorique are a haven for hikers and cyclists, while the streets of the region's capital, Quimper, thrum with Celtic character.

TOP TOURS

♣ HB HENRIOT
Visit the workshop of Quimper's flagship faïencerie (p105).

♣ MONTS D'ARRÉE
Take a guided nature walk around this bleakly beautiful area of granite peaks and peat bogs with ADDES (p95).

♣ DUNES DE KEREMMA
The Maison des Dunes et de la Randonée (p88) arranges fascinating walks around this unique coastal ecosystem.

♣ CONCARNEAU
Local man Simon Allain is a mine of information on Concarneau, and he offers trips exploring the *ville close*, the *criée* (fish auction) and the town's fish canneries. (☎ 02 98 50 55 18; www.alassautdesremparts.com)

♣ ÎLE D'OUESSANT
Born-and-bred islanders run minibus trips exploring the history, culture and coastline of the mysterious isle of Ushant (p91).

ADVANCE PLANNING

★ **Tickets** If you're visiting some of the area's big draws including Océanopolis, the Château de Taureau, Ouessant and the Île de Batz, booking online or through local tourist offices can help dodge the queues.

★ **Ferry tickets** Trips to Ouessant, the Île de Sein and the Île de Batz get booked up lightning-fast in summer, so it pays to bag your seat early.

★ **Crowds** Finistère is packed during July and August, especially around Concarneau, Pont-Aven, the Crozon Peninsula and Pointe du Raz. Save these for the shoulder seasons to see them at their best.

★ **Festival de Cornouaille** Quimper's Celtic shindig in July makes accommodation scarce.

GETTING AWAY FROM IT ALL

★ **Monts d'Arrée** (p95) Seclusion can be scarce along the Finistère coastline in summer: head for the hills when you wish to give the crowds the slip.

★ **Cap Sizun** (p100) This blustery headland is a haven for birdwatchers, but it's just as suited to people looking for coastal quiet.

★ **Cruising the Abers** (p88) Boats putter around these picture-perfect inlets from Aber Wrac'h and Perros.

TOP HIKES

🌿 **POINTE DE VAN**
Stunning clifftop walks near Pointe du Raz (p101)

🌿 **POINTE ST-MATHIEU**
An old customs-officers' path from a lighthouse-topped headland (p89)

🌿 **THE MORLAIX–CARHAIX VOIE VERTE**
Follow the disused railway line between Morlaix and Carhaix (p95)

🌿 **SOUTHEAST OF PONT-AVEN**
Coastal paths surround Kerfany, Brigneau and Port-Merrien (p113)

🌿 **HUELGOAT**
An ancient woodland criss-crossed by sun-dappled trails (p95)

ONLINE RESOURCES

Most of these websites are in French only.

★ **www.cornouaille.com** Background info on the region's southwestern corner.

★ **www.finisteretourisme.com** Region-specific advice, with links to sister sites covering walking, family holidays and more.

★ **www.parc-naturel-armorique.fr** All you need to know about Brittany's largest natural reserve.

★ **www.viaoo29.fr** Schedules and timetables for Finistère's bus routes.

FINISTÈRE

NORTH COAST

· · · · · ·

MORLAIX & AROUND

pop 17,000

Set at the base of a deep valley straddled by a soaring 19th-century viaduct and a pleasure port, the bustling commercial centre of Morlaix is the principal city of northeastern Finistère. Apart from the narrow *venelles* (alleyways) and half-timbered houses of the old town, it's a bit short on sights, but it makes a handy base for exploring the Pays de Léon and northern Finistère.

ESSENTIAL INFORMATION

TOURIST OFFICES // Morlaix (☎ 02 98 62 14 94; officetourisme.morlaix@wanadoo.fr; place des Otages; ⏰ 9am-12.30pm & 1.30-7.30pm Mon-Sat,

10am-12.30pm Sun Jul & Aug, 9am-12.30pm & 2-6pm Mon-Sat Sep-Jun)

EXPLORING MORLAIX & AROUND

♥ **THE OLD TOWN // VENTURE ALONG THE VENELLES OF OLD MORLAIX**

The heart of modern Morlaix is the place des Otages, which sprawls between the old town and the Port du Plaisance; passing underneath Morlaix's great 58m-high viaduct, built in 1861 to carry the Brest–Paris railway. East of the tourist office is the Flamboyant Gothic **Église St-Melaine** (⏰ 9am-noon & 2-6pm), notable for its star-studded barrel-vault roof and saintly statues.

To the southeast, the city's oldest street is **Grand' Rue**, lined with restored medieval buildings including **La Maison**

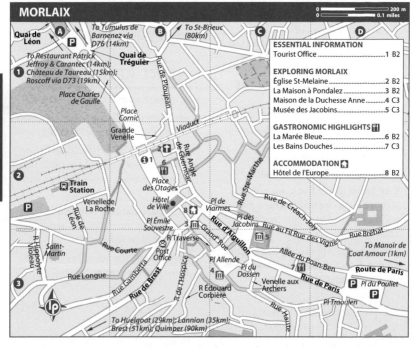

MORLAIX

| | 0 | 200 m |
| 0 | | 0.1 miles |

ESSENTIAL INFORMATION
Tourist Office 1 B2

EXPLORING MORLAIX
Église St-Melaine 2 B2
La Maison à Pondalez 3 B2
Maison de la Duchesse Anne 4 C3
Musée des Jacobins............................5 C3

GASTRONOMIC HIGHLIGHTS 🍴
La Marée Bleue 6 B2
Les Bains Douches 7 C3

ACCOMMODATION 🛏
Hôtel de l'Europe 8 B2

à Pondalez (☎ 02 98 62 14 94; 9 Grand' Rue; ☻ 10am-12.30pm & 2-6.30pm Jul & Aug, 10am-noon & 2-6pm Mon & Wed-Sat, 2-6pm Sun Apr-May & Sep, 10am-noon & 2-5pm Mon & Wed-Sat Oct-Mar & Jun), a typical example of a Morlaix *maison à lanterne* (house with an inner gallery). Nearby on place Allende is another example, the **Maison de la Duchesse Anne** (Queen Anne's House; ☎ 02 98 88 23 26; www .mda-morlaix.com; 33 rue du Mur; adult/child €1.50/ free; ☻ 11am-6.30pm Mon-Sat Jul & Aug, 11am-6pm Mon-Sat May, Jun & Sep). Despite the name, the link to Queen Anne is tenuous. It was probably built for a rich medieval merchant, and boasts medieval carving, an original oak staircase and huge hearth.

The **Musée des Jacobins** (☎ 02 98 88 68 88; joint ticket with La Maison à Pondalez adult/child €4/2.50; ☻ same hours & prices as Maison de la Duchesse Anne), displays period furniture, costumes and paintings in Morlaix's former convent.

♥ CHÂTEAU DE TAUREAU // CROSS THE ESTUARY TO THIS FORBIDDING FORTRESS

While most people steam out of Morlaix on the main D19, there's a more memorable road-trip along the D73, which tracks the twisty, tree-clad shoreline of the Rade de Morlaix to the seaside village of **Carantec**. Historically, this was a crucial waterway, and in 1544 the **Château de Taureau** (☎ 02 98 62 29 73; www.chateaudu taureau.com; adult/4-12yr €12/6) was constructed on a rocky island to protect the estuary from assault. Boats buzz across to the island from the **plage de Kelenn** in Carantec, and include a guided tour of the towers, battlements and casemates, while sound effects and explanatory panels help bring the place to life.

There are up to four boats daily from Carantec in season, plus extra vessels from Plougasnou. You can book online or at the tourist offices in Morlaix and Carantec, or buy tickets direct from the kiosk on plage de Kelenn.

♥ TUMULUS DE BARNENEZ // MARVEL AT FRANCE'S LARGEST ANCIENT BURIAL CAIRN

On the eastern side of the estuary, the winding D76 meanders through gorse-covered coastline to the hilltop **Tumulus de Barnenez** (Plouezoc'h; adult/18-25yr/under 18yr €5/3.50/free; ☻ 10am-6.30pm May-Aug, 10am-12.30pm & 2-5.30pm Tue-Sun Sep-Apr), a monumental ancient tomb built in stages over the last 6000 years. It currently stands around 6m tall, but would originally have been a couple of metres higher. Beneath the mass of carefully laid stones are 11 burial chambers, perfectly aligned with the sun's axis at the solstices; some have been excavated to reveal their inner construction. Astonishingly, the site was nearly demolished in the mid-'50s as road-building material, but was made an historic monument in 1955.

There are some lovely walks and quiet beaches along the peaceful shoreline between Barnenez, Plougasnou and Loquirec: the beach at **St-Samson** and the headland of **Pointe de Primel**, both north of Barnenez, are prime spots for a picnic.

GASTRONOMIC HIGHLIGHTS

♥ LA MARÉE BLEUE // MORLAIX €€

☎ 02 98 63 24 21; rampe St-Melaine; menus €15-26.50; ☻ Tue-Sat & lunch Sun

Morlaix's best restaurant by a country mile, the Blue Tide is tucked away along a backstreet opposite the Église St-Melaine. Seafood is partnered by hearty fare such as antelope steak, veal's liver and casseroles, and the setting combines country charm with modern accents: exposed stone and heavy drapes meet groovy uplighters and splashes of modern art.

FINISTÈRE

❤ LES BAINS DOUCHES //
MORLAIX €€

☎ 02 98 63 83 83; 45 allée du Poan-Ben; mains €12-20; ☻ lunch Mon-Fri, dinner Tue-Sat

The city's old municipal showers provide the offbeat setting for this reliable bistro (some original glass and porcelain tiles are still in situ). Solid brasserie food is the order of the day – think big bowls of mussels, generous salads and hearty steaks, or be adventurous with a kangaroo cutlet or maybe some garlic-buttered snails.

❤ PATRICK JEFFROY //
CARANTEC €€€

☎ 02 98 67 00 47; 20 rue du Kelenn; menus €62-119; ☻ lunch & dinner

You'll need deep pockets, but for a gastronomic adventure Patrick Jeffroy's renowned restaurant is the place. A divine glass-walled dining room looks out over the Baie de Morlaix, and the chef's known for his wildly playful approach to ingredients – prepare for sardine, cheese and chorizo cake, crayfish with onions and artichokes, or whelks fried with pork brawn, pancake and porridge.

TRANSPORT

BUS // The 52/53 bus runs north to St-Pol de Léon and Roscoff, while the LR8020 travels east along the coast via Plougasnou. There are also buses south to Huelgoat.

TRAIN // Morlaix is a useful TGV hub between Paris Montparnasse (€65.60 to €83, four to 4½ hours) and Brest (€9.80 to €11.80, 30 minutes) and stations in between; local connections go north to Roscoff (€5.40, 30 minutes) via St-Pol de Léon, and south to Quimper (€18.10, 1½ to 3½ hours depending on connections) via Landerneau.

ROSCOFF

pop 3600

Sheltered from the restless waters of the English Channel by the peaceful Île de Batz, Roscoff (Rosko in Breton) is by far the most charming of the cross-channel ferry ports. Set around an arcing harbour cluttered with granite cottages and seafront villas, it's a town that's inextricably tied to the sea; seaweed farming, fishing and smuggling have all played their part in shaping this seaport, and no matter where you stroll, you'll never quite shake the salty ocean tang or the seagulls' plaintive cries.

THE ENCLOS PAROISSIAUX

Between Morlaix and Brest lies the Élorn Valley, a traditional area that's renowned for its elaborate **enclos paroissiaux** (parish enclosures). These extravagant ecclesiastical *closes* were mostly constructed between the 15th and 17th centuries, and usually feature a triumphal entrance, a *calvaire* (calvary), an *ossuaire* (chapel for storing bones), and a central chapel decorated with fancy stonemasonery, brightly coloured rood screens and medieval woodwork. Look out for important members of medieval society in the carvings; monks, lawyers and bakers rub shoulders with archangels, bishops and apostles, and over all of these watches the ominous figure of Ankou, a spectral figure said to portend death in Breton legend.

Brittany has over 70 *enclos paroissiaux* in all, including notable examples in La Roche-Maurice, La Martyre, Sizun (with its triple-arched gateway, sculpture-covered ossuary and charming chapel), Guimiliau and Plougastel-Daoulas. A signposted road route connects the major parish enclosures; generally they're open from around 8am to 6pm, but it's always worth checking ahead with a local tourist office to make sure.

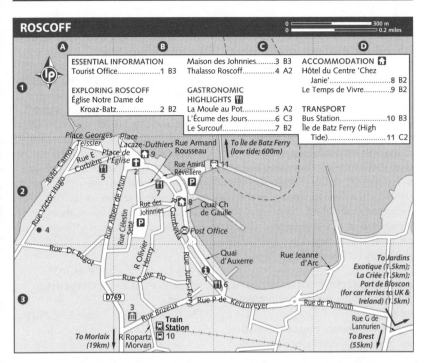

ROSCOFF

ESSENTIAL INFORMATION	
Tourist Office.................1 B3	
EXPLORING ROSCOFF	
Église Notre Dame de	
Kroaz-Batz...................2 B2	

Maison des Johnnies.........3 B3
Thalasso Roscoff..............4 A2

**GASTRONOMIC
HIGHLIGHTS**
La Moule au Pot..............5 A2
L'Écume des Jours............6 C3
Le Surcouf.....................7 B2

ACCOMMODATION
Hôtel du Centre 'Chez
Janie'.........................8 B2
Le Temps de Vivre...........9 B2

TRANSPORT
Bus Station....................10 B3
Île de Batz Ferry (High
Tide)...........................11 C2

Roscoff celebrates its illustrious pink onions in mid-August during the **Fête de l'Oignon Rose**. Expect music, dancing and onions by the bucketload.

ESSENTIAL INFORMATION

TOURIST OFFICES // **Roscoff** (☎ 02 98 61 12 13; www.roscoff-tourisme.com; quai d'Auxerre; ⏲ 9am-12.30pm & 1.30-7pm Jul & Aug, 9.15am-noon & 2-6pm Mon-Sat Sep-Jun) On the harbour.

EXPLORING ROSCOFF

♥ OLD ROSCOFF // AMBLE AROUND THIS CLASSIC BRETON SEAPORT

Former shipowners' houses line Roscoff's meandering streets, many decorated with carvings of ships, anchors and other nautical motifs. The best streets for strolling are **rue Amiral Réveillère, rue Albert de**

Mun and **rue Armand Rousseau,** supposedly the town's oldest street. Nearby on place de l'Église is the 16th-century **Église Notre Dame de Kroaz-Batz,** a Gothic church crowned with elaborate carvings and an over-the-top belfry tacked on during the Renaissance.

♥ MAISON DES JOHNNIES // DISCOVER THE HISTORY OF THE OIGNON ROSE

Ask anyone for their image of a Frenchman, and chances are berets, bicycles, stripy tops, elaborate moustaches and – most importantly – strings of onions will find their way into the mix. If you've ever wondered how this national caricature got started, quell your curiosity at the **Maison des Johnnies** (☎ 02 98 61 25 48; 48 rue Brizeux; adult/10-18yr €4/2.50; ⏲ guided tours 11am, 3pm & 5pm Mon-Fri mid-Jun–mid-Sep,

FINISTÈRE

3pm Mon, Tue, Thu & Fri during school holidays, 10.30am & 3pm outside school holidays, closed Jan), a folk museum dedicated to the itinerant 'Onion Johnnies' who, in the days before passenger ferries, regularly crossed the Channel to sell Roscoff's famous *oignons roses* (pink onions) to British housewives. They were still a common sight until well into the 1930s, and Roscoff's *oignon rose* remains an important export. Recent attempts have been made to secure AOC status, which would give the onion the same cachet as Champagne and Camembert. On Tuesday evenings from June and September, you can meet onion farmers and a bona fide ex-Johnny between 6pm and 7pm.

♥ THALASSO ROSCOFF // SOOTHE THOSE BONES WITH A SEAWEED CURE

Roscoff's temperate climate and bracing sea air turned it into France's first resort for *thalassotherapie*, a curative treatment regime involving hot sea-water baths and various other curious concoctions. The tradition is continued by **Thalasso Roscoff** (☎ 08 25 00 20 99; www.thalasso-roscoff .com; rue Victor Hugo), whose cure-alls include a heated sea-water pool, a Turkish *hammam* and all-over applications of *crème d'algues* (seaweed cream – very good for the skin, apparently).

♥ JARDIN EXOTIQUE // PICNIC AMONG PALMS AND PASSION FLOWERS

Perched on a granite hummock east of the harbour, Roscoff's paradisical **exotic garden** (☎ 02 98 61 29 19; adult/12-18yr €5/2; ⏰ 10am-7pm Jul & Aug, 10.30am-noon & 2-6pm Apr-Jun & Sep-Oct, 2-5pm Nov & Mar) has an enormous population of over 3500 plants drawn from all corners of the globe. Desert cacti, Mexican palms, eucalyptus,

dates, amaryllis and tea trees are just some of the unusual species nurtured by Roscoff's balmy climate.

♥ LA CRIÉE // CATCH ROSCOFF'S FISHERMEN IN ACTION

Roscoff's chaotic **fish auction** (☎ 02 98 62 39 26; adult/8-16yr €4/2.50; ⏰ visits 11am, 3pm & 5pm Mon-Thu Jul & Aug, 3.30pm Wed May-Jun & Sep-Nov, 3.30pm Tue-Thu Easter holidays) is a must-see. Over 4500 tonnes of fresh seafood pass through the port every year, and the newly built market on the Port de Bloscon has a special observation gallery from where you can watch the day's haul being auctioned off.

♥ ÎLE DE BATZ // SKIP ACROSS TO THIS PEACEFUL OFFSHORE ISLAND

The Île de Batz (pronounced *ba*; Enez Vaz in Breton) is known for its fine beaches, shoreline walks and prodigious vegetable crops (the farmland's fertility apparently stems from the use of seaweed-based fertilisers). A half-day is all you'll need to circumnavigate the island; factor in a day and you'll have time to visit the **Jardins Georges Delaselle** (☎ 02 98 61 75 65; adult/child €3.50/1.75; ⏰ 1-6pm daily Jul & Aug, 2-6pm Wed-Mon Apr-Jun & Sep, 2-6pm Sat & Sun Oct) and the **Île de Batz lighthouse** (⏰ 1-5.30pm Jul & Aug, 2-5pm Thu-Tue late-Jun & early-Sep).

Ferries run from Roscoff every half-hour between 8am and 8pm from June to mid-September; there are about eight daily sailings during the other months. Contact **Compagnie Maritime Armein** (☎ 02 98 61 75 47), **Armor Excursion** (☎ 02 98 61 79 66) or **Vedettes de l'Île de Batz** (☎ 02 98 61 78 87). Bikes can be hired on the island at **Le Saout** (☎ 02 98 61 77 65; ⏰ Feb-Nov) and **Prigent** (☎ 02 98 61 76 91; ⏰ year-round).

FINISTÈRE

GASTRONOMIC HIGHLIGHTS

♥ LA MOULE AU POT €€

☎ 02 98 19 33 60; 13 rue Édouard Corbière; mains €12-20; ⏱ Easter-Oct, closed Thu

You won't find a cosier place in Finistère than this much-loved hideaway, tucked away just off Roscoff's seafront. Rough-hewn stone, simple wooden tables and hefty beams create the snug, fisherman's-shack vibe, and the blackboard menus exude seafood goodness, from monkfish in a creamy seaweed sauce to a divine *parmentier aux poissons* (fish pie).

♥ L'ÉCUME DES JOURS €€€

☎ 02 98 61 22 83; quai d'Auxerre; menus €31-51; ⏱ usually closed Wed Jul & Aug, plus Tue other times

Push the boat out at Roscoff's top table. In a shipowner's house (complete with stone hearth), this elegant address serves some of the classiest *terre-mer* (sea and countryside) cuisine in the Léon: perfumed sea bream and roast pollock sit alongside classic cuts of pork, beef and game. It's formal, but these dishes are worth dressing up for.

♥ LE SURCOUF €€

☎ 02 98 69 71 89; 14 rue Amiral Réveillère; menus €16-27; ⏱ closed Wed

More top-class dining bang in the heart of Roscoff, smart without being remotely snooty. The menu's predominately (but not exclusively) seafood; you can choose your own lobsters, crabs and langoustines from the window tank, tuck into a classic bowl of fish soup or plump for the guaranteed-to-be-good *poisson du jour*. Plate-glass windows keep things light and bright, but it's a shame there's no terrace.

TRANSPORT

The bus and train station is on rue Ropartz Morvan.

BOAT // For details of cross-channel ferries, see from p321.

BUS // Roscoff is well-supplied by buses; the most useful line is the 52/53 to Morlaix via St-Pol and Carantec.

TRAIN // For trains, see Morlaix p84.

ST-POL DE LÉON

Founded as the seat of Brittany's first bishop, Pol Aurélien, the trim little town

---

TOP CAMPING

Finistère offers some fine camping options; here are our favourites. For details of some other accommodation options in the *département*, see p292.

★ **Camping de la Pommeraie** (☎ 02 98 50 02 73; www.campingdelapommeraie.com; St-Philibert; site €18.80-30; ⏱ May-Sep; 🛝 ⚲) Seven hectares of family-friendly camping between Pont-Aven and Concarneau.

★ **Camping Penn Ar Ster** (☎ 02 98 56 97 75; www.camping-pennarster.com; La Forêt Fouesnant; site €17-23; ⏱ mid-Feb–mid-Nov) In the grounds of a manor house.

★ **Camping Ty Provost** (☎ 02 98 86 29 23; www.typrovost.com; Dinéault; adult/site €3.80/7.90; ⏱ May–mid-Sep) Quiet country camping in the Parc Naturel Régional d'Armorique.

★ **La Pointe Superbe** (☎ 02 98 86 51 53; www.lapointesuperbecamping.com; Chateaulin; site €12-16; ⏱ mid-Mar–Oct; ⚲) Intimate campsite set in a wooded valley.

★ **L'Orangerie de Lanniron** (☎ 02 98 90 62 02; www.lanniron.com; adult €4.25-7.20, site €10.25-18.60; ⏱ mid-May–mid-Sep; 🛝 ⚲) Four-star château camping on Quimper's outskirts.

of **St-Pol de Léon** is now a bustling agricultural centre. No matter which direction you approach from, it's impossible to miss the town's twin landmarks, which rocket skywards among fields full of cauliflowers, broccoli and artichokes. The two 55m towers of the **Cathédrale St-Pol de Léon** (⊙ 9am-noon & 2-6.30pm) are impressive, but St-Pol's finest building is the **Chapelle Notre Dame du Kreisker** (⊙ 10am-noon & 2-6pm Jul & Aug, 10am-6pm Oct & Feb-Jun). Its sky-high spire is the tallest in Brittany at 78m, built to replace a bell tower that was felled by lightning. In July and August, you can climb the spire's steps for views over St-Pol's old town and the Roscoff coast.

The 52/53 bus between Morlaix and Roscoff stops outside St-Pol's tourist office five times daily. The Morlaix–Roscoff train also stops in town.

DRIVING TOUR: PAYS DES ABERS

Distance: 110km to 140km depending on route
Duration: 2 days

The ragged ribbon of coastline between Keremma and Le Conquet is interspersed by three lush estuaries known as *abers* (from a Celtic word meaning river mouth) created by retreating glaciers at the end of the last ice age. This driving tour takes in the three main *abers* and explores the surrounding coastline. The route is also suitable for cycling.

You'll find welcome space on the 5km of glorious dunes of **Keremma** or at the beaches of **Pors Meur** and **Pors Guen**. Guided nature walks of the dunes offered by the nearby **Maison des Dunes et de la Randonée** (☎ 02 98 61 69 69; www.maisondes

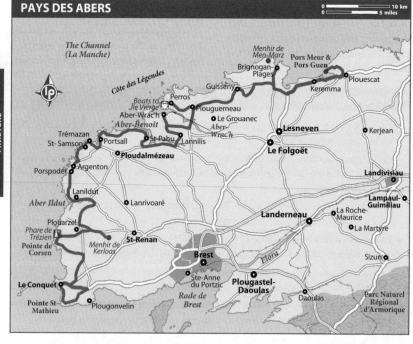

PAYS DES ABERS

dunes.org; rte de Goulven) explain Keremma's unique natural ecosystem. The beaches get crowded at touristy **Brignogan-Plages** but just west of town is the 8m-high **Menhir Men-Marz** (crowned by a small cross to make it more acceptable to Christians). Heading west, stop for a super country lunch at **L'Auberge de Keralloret** (☎ 02 98 25 60 37; www.keralloret .com; €19.50-37; ☽ lunch & dinner) in Guissény.

Explore the area's love affair with *les algues* (seaweed) at the **Musée des Goémoniers** (☎ 02 98 37 13 35) in Plouguerneau, before taking a boat trip along the Aber Wrac'h estuary to the **Phare de l'Île Vierge**, which at 82.5m is the tallest lighthouse in Europe. Trips are run by **Vedettes des Abers** (☎ 02 98 04 74 94; www.vedettes-des-abers.com; adult/4-12yr/under 4yr €16/11/4) from Perros; there's a second boat route that runs along the coastline en route to Aber Benoît and St-Pabu (adult/4-12yr/under 4yr €18/12/4).

Cross over Aber Wrac'h and round the day off in style with top-class oysters at **Huitres Prat-Ar-Coum** (☎ 02 98 04 00 12) or serious seafood at **L'Auberge des Abers** (☎ 02 98 04 00 29; menu €45-85; ☽ lunch & dinner Tue-Sat), both near **Lannilis**, followed by a night at the luxurious **Baie des Anges** (see p293) in Aber Wrac'h.

On day two, the coastline between **St-Pabu** and **Portsall** is dotted with fantastic beaches and coastal walks, several of which run on along the mudbanks of the **Aber Benoît**. Portsall is infamous as the site of one of the region's worst oil spills when the tanker *Amoco Cadiz* ran aground in 1978. A huge clean-up operation has since restored the area's splendour. Continue on the twisty D127 to **Argenton**.

Travel south along the D27 to **Lanildut**, the largest seaweed-farming port in Europe. Look out for *goémoniers* (seaweed boats) trawling the estuary and the old shoreline ovens in which seaweed was once roasted to produce soda and iodine. The road then circles around the last of the three *abers*, the **Aber Ildut**.

The D28 then takes you inland to Plouarzel and the **Menhir de Kerloas**, the largest standing menhir in France at an astonishing 9.5m. In July and August, you can visit the lighthouse at **Trézien**, 12km to the west, which has stood watch over the jagged **Pointe de Corsen**, the most westerly point of mainland Brittany, since 1894; you can often glimpse the faint spectres of distant ships negotiating the Ouessant strait on the horizon.

Make your way to the coastal village of **Le Conquet**. About 5km to the south of here is **Pointe St-Mathieu**, marked by the ruins of a 16th-century abbey and a red-topped 1865 **lighthouse** (adult/child €3/1); you can climb the 163 steps to the top for spectacular views of the Anse des Blancs Sablons and the distant Ouessant Islands.

ÎLE D'OUESSANT

pop 950

There's a real end-of-the-world feel to the wild, wind-lashed Ouessant archipelago, 32km off the Breton mainland. Only two islands are inhabited, Molène (Bald Island) and Ouessant (Enez Eusa, meaning 'Island of Terror', in Breton; Ushant in English), supporting a community of about 950 souls.

In days gone by fishing, farming and seaweed cultivation were the main industries, but life here has always been a precarious business – a fact that's commemorated in a famous Breton proverb: *qui voit Molène, voit sa peine, qui voit Ouessant, voit son sang* (those who see Molène see their sorrow, those who see

FINISTÈRE

Ouessant see their blood). Despite their fearsome reputation, the islands are blessed with a surprisingly balmy climate thanks to the Gulf Stream; unusual lichens, heathers and wildflowers flourish here in abundance, and the islands have become a sanctuary for all kinds of marine life and migratory seabirds, not to mention one of the world's tiniest (and hardiest) breeds of sheep, the chocolate-coloured *mouton d'Ouessant*. There are a few simple B&Bs and a couple of campsites dotted around the island. Reservations are essential in summer; contact the tourist office.

The islands' unique environmental credentials were underlined by Unesco's decision to designate the archipelago a World Biosphere Reserve in 1989, and the creation of France's very first marine park, the **Parc Naturel Marin d'Iroise** (www.parc-marin-iroise.gouv.fr, in French) in 2007.

ESSENTIAL INFORMATION

TOURIST OFFICES // Ouessant (☎ 02 98 48 85 83; www.ot-ouessant.fr; ⏲ 10am-noon & 1.30-5pm Mon-Sat, 10am-noon Sun) On place de l'Église in Lampaul, Ouessant's main 'village'.

EXPLORING THE ISLANDS

♣ ISLAND ROVING // STRIKE OUT ALONG THE COAST PATH

The archipelago's largest island is **Ouessant**, about 7km long and 4km wide, where you'll find the ferry landing and the only village, Lampaul. A 45km footpath encircles the island, passing through a paradise of isolated coves, patchwork fields, tumbledown sheep shelters and rocky clifftops – perfect country for exploring on foot.

A good day-target from Lampaul is the **Pointe de Pern,** a headland overlook-

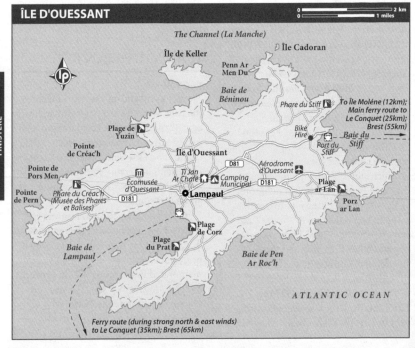

ing the offshore lighthouse of Nividic; the return route takes you past one of the world's most powerful lighthouses, the **Phare du Créac'h**, whose light (two white flashes every 10 seconds) can be seen 50km away. The round-trip covers about 8km.

A longer option is to follow the coast path east between the **plage de Yusin** and the **Phare du Stiff** on the island's east coast. Look out for seabirds and seals around the Baie de Béninou and the Île Cadoran, and head south for beach-lounging at **Porz ar Lan**. Count on around 15km there and back from Lampaul.

Bikes are another great way to see the island: outlets include **La Bicyclette** (☎ 02 98 48 81 34; www.labicyclette-ouessant.fr; place de l'Église, Lampaul; per day €10-14). For the cultural perspective you could take a minibus trip with a born-and-bred islander (see right) or see the island from the saddle with **Ty Crenn** (☎ 02 98 48 83 58; Stang-ar-Glenn).

If you're looking for sustenance, **Le Ty Korn** (☎ 02 98 48 87 33; Lampaul; menus from €15; ⊗ closed Sun evening & Mon) is a cosy locals' bar that serves up cold beer, big seafood platters and crustaceans straight off the boats.

❦ MUSEUMS // PONDER OUESSANT'S STORMY PAST

Shipwrecks have long been a fact of life in Ouessant, and a string of lighthouses guard the island's shores, helping 100,000 vessels each year navigate the treacherous shipping lane of the Ouessant Strait. The history of these life-saving navigational aids is explored at the **Musée des Phares et Balises** (Lighthouse & Beacon Museum; ☎ 02 98 48 80 70; adult €4.30, joint ticket with Écomusée €7; ⊗ 10.30am-6.30pm Apr-Sep, 1.30-5pm Oct-Mar), housed in the generator room of the Créac'h lighthouse.

The small **Écomusée d'Ouessant** (☎ 02 98 48 86 37; Maison du Niou; ⊗ as above) offers an intriguing insight into island life. Two traditional houses are crammed with driftwood furniture, rustic tools, shipwrecked booty, Ouessant costume and *proëlla* (little wax candles lit to commemorate the souls of sailors lost at sea).

❦ ÎLE MOLÈNE // INVESTIGATE AN INFAMOUS SHIPWRECK

Scarcely 1km across, Île Molène (Mol Enez in Breton) feels even more remote than its neighbour; carless, practically treeless, and home to a population of just 270 people.

You can tick off the sights in a couple of hours. The only village is **Le Bourg**, a huddle of whitewashed fishermen's cottages clustered around a granite quay, which is still the focus for the island's principal industries, lobster fishing and seaweed farming. Behind the town hall is the little **Musée du Drummond Castle** (☎ 02 98 07 38 41; Le Bourg; adult €2; ⊗ 2-6pm Jul & Aug, 3-5pm May, Jun, Sep & Oct), which commemorates the heroic role islanders played in the rescue of a shipwrecked British passenger liner in 1896. Sadly, only three of the 248 passengers survived, but Queen Victoria was so grateful she stumped up for the island's new clock tower.

The island only has one hotel, the friendly **Kastell An Daol** (☎ 02 98 07 38 64; www.kastell-an-daol.com; r €62-65), plus a handful of *chambres d'hôtes*.

TRANSPORT

BOAT // Regular ferries to Ouessant and Molène are provided by **Penn Ar Bed** (☎ 02 98 80 80 80; www.pennarbed.fr; €30.20 Jun-Sep, €18.40/20.40 weekdays/weekends Oct-Mar), which sails from Brest, Le Conquet and Camaret up to five times daily during summer, dropping to just a single crossing in winter. Most boats stop at Île Molène.

FINISTÈRE

MINIBUS // Several islanders – including Domi-
nique Etienne (☎ 06 07 90 07 43), Robert
Quantin (☎ 06 07 90 07 36) and Jean-Michel
Thomas (☎ 06 12 22 92 73) – run minibus shuttles
from the Ouessant ferry port, and also offer guided tours
of the island from around €15. Reserve well ahead in
season.

AIR // Finist'air (☎ 02 98 84 64 87; www.finistair
.fr) makes the 15-minute hop to the Île d'Ouessant twice
daily from Brest airport (adult/child €65/38).

BREST

· · · · · ·

pop 149,600

**Situated alongside a magnificent nat-
ural harbour, Brest has been one of
northern France's busiest naval ports
since the mid-17th century. Unfortunately, like many Breton cities, it was
all but flattened by air attacks during
WWII, and while the postwar blend
of steel, concrete and ruler-straight
streets isn't going to win any urban
beauty contests, Brest is worth more
than a cursory glance.**

Peek beyond the Brutalist surface and
you'll discover a Vauban-built château,
a nationally renowned aquarium and
some excellent restaurants, not to mention one of the only naval bases in the
western hemisphere that you can visit on
a guided tour.

ORIENTATION

The modern city extends along the River
Penfeld and the northern coast of the
Rade de Brest. The city centre, château,
bus and train stations, and port spread
eastwards from the river; the city's main
thoroughfare is rue de Siam, which runs
northeast from the château to the monumental place de la Liberté. The Pont de
Recouvrance suspension bridge leads

across the river to the western suburbs
and L'Arsenal (naval base).

ESSENTIAL INFORMATION

TOURIST OFFICES // Brest (☎ 02 98 44 24 96;
www.brest-metropole-tourisme.fr; place de la Liberté;
☷ 9.30am-7pm Mon-Sat, 10am-noon Sun Jul & Aug,
9.30am-6pm Mon-Sat Sep-Jun)

EXPLORING BREST

❦ **CHÂTEAU DE BREST // TOUR
THE COLOSSAL CITADEL**
Dominating the River Penfeld, Brest's
castle was built on the site of a Roman
fort and medieval keep, and was heavily
refortified by Vauban in the mid-17th
century with his trademark combination
of ramparts, battlements and defensive
towers. It now houses the administrative
quarters for the French Admiralty and
the Musée de la Marine (Naval Museum; ☎ 02
98 22 12 39; adult/child €4.60/free; ☷ 10am-6.30pm
daily Apr–mid-Sep, 10am-noon & 2-6pm Wed-Mon
mid-Sep–Mar), which documents Brest's
naval history. Needless to say, there's a
great view of the harbour, bridge and
river from the castle battlements.

Across the river is the rocket-shaped
Tour Tanguy (☎ 02 98 00 88 60; place Pierre Péron;
admission free; ☷ 10am-noon & 2-7pm daily Jun-Sep,
2-5pm Wed-Thu, 2-6pm Sat & Sun Oct-May), a slate-
topped watchtower dating from the 14th
century. Inside, dioramas depict the city
prior to its postwar remodelling; look out
for one documenting the visit of three
Siamese ambassadors to the court of Louis
XIV in 1686, an event commemorated in
the name of the city's main street.

❦ **L'ARSENAL MARITIME // SNEAK
A PEEK AROUND THE NAVAL BASE**
If your home nation belongs to the EU
or NATO you can take a behind-the-

scenes tour around Brest's **naval base** (☎ 02 98 22 11 78; www.defense.gouv.fr/marine; ☽ 2 afternoon guided tours mid–end Jun, Jul, Aug & early Sep). The 1½-hour tours take in the arsenal of helicopters, frigates, minesweepers and patrol boats, and conclude with an on-board visit – although the nuclear subs moored off Île Longue are off limits.

Entry to the Arsenal is via the Porte de la Grande Rivière beneath the suspension bridge – you'll need to book in advance, and remember to bring some photo ID.

♥ OCÉANOPOLIS // GO JACQUES COUSTEAU AT BREST'S FLAGSHIP AQUARIUM

Three underwater zones – temperate, tropical and polar – make up Brest's aquarium complex, **Océanopolis** (☎ 02 98 34 40 40; www.oceanopolis.com; Port de Plaisance; 1 zone adult/4–17yr €7.50/5.20, all zones €16.20/11; ☽ 9am-7pm Jul & Aug, 9am-6pm May–Jun & Sep, 10am-5pm Oct-Apr). Rather sneakily, you have to buy a combination ticket if you want to see all three. The Tropical Zone is by far the best, with a superb tank containing sawfish, nurse sharks and reef sharks,

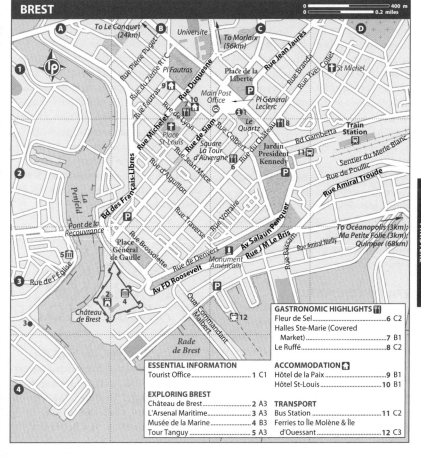

BREST

0 — 400 m
0 — 0.2 miles

FINISTÈRE

and smaller tanks stocked with coral reefs and technicoloured tropical fish. It's about 3km east of the city centre – catch bus 15 from place de la Liberté.

GASTRONOMIC HIGHLIGHTS

Self-caterers can stock up at **Halles Ste-Marie** (rue de Lyon).

❦ FLEUR DE SEL €€

☎ 02 98 44 38 65; 15 bis rue de Lyon; mains €22-42; ⌚ lunch Tue-Fri, dinner Mon-Sat

Clipped box hedges and plate-glass windows provide a chic intro to this renowned (if fussy) fine-diner, known across the city for its upmarket take on classic French cuisine. It's not a place to turn up to in jeans and flip-flops; dress smartly and indulge in artfully arranged plates of *cochon Breton* (piglet) or roast turbot infused with lemon and herbs.

❦ LE RUFFÉ €€

☎ 02 98 46 07 70; 1 bis rue Yves Collet; menus €18.50-33

Sunny yellows, sea blues and sailcloths suspended overhead create a nautical vibe at Jean-Michel Faijean's restaurant, much recommended by Brestois. Top dishes include a 'lobster cauldron' and abalone-and-scallops fried in snail-butter.

❦ MA PETITE FOLIE €€

☎ 02 98 42 44 42; Port de Plaisance, Moulin Blanc; menus €18-28; ⌚ lunch Tue-Sun, dinner Tue-Sat

Let's be honest – it's not every day you eat on a decommissioned lobster boat. The quirky setting alone would be enough to recommend it, but throw in sea views and a fine *fruits-de-mer* menu and you've got a real rarity. Get your act together – it's often booked out in summer. Head for the Port de Plaisance at Moulin Blanc, 3km east of the centre. Bus 15 from place de la Liberté goes this way.

TRANSPORT

AIR // Brest airport (☎ 02 98 32 86 00; www.brest.aeroport.fr/en/) hosts flights to Birmingham, Exeter, Manchester and Southampton with **Flybe** (www.flybe.com), plus London Luton with **Ryanair** (www.ryanair.com) and domestic flights with **Air France** (www.airfrance.com). A shuttle bus (adult/child return €8.40/4.20, eight to 10 daily, from 8.40am to 10.50pm from airport, from 5.30am to 7.30pm from city) runs to/from the city centre via the tourist office, place Albert 1er and the bus station.

BOAT // Ferries to Île Molène and Île d'Ouessant (see p91) leave from the Port de Commerce.

BUS // Brest has good bus links to Roscoff (Line 40, two hours, five Monday to Saturday, two on Sunday), Quimper (Line 1, 1¼ hours, eight Monday to Friday, two on weekends), Le Conquet (Line 31, one hour, eight Monday to Saturday, three on Sunday) and the northern Finistère coast. Local buses are handled by **Bibus** (☎ 02 98 80 30 30; www.bibus.fr; one way/day pass €1/3).

TRAIN // Brest is on the TGV route to Paris Montparnasse (€67.90 to €83.90, 4½ hours) via Morlaix, St-Brieuc and Rennes. Local trains run south to Quimper (€15, 80 minutes) and on to the south coast.

PARC NATUREL RÉGIONAL D'ARMORIQUE

· · · · · ·

Established in 1969, the huge Parc Naturel Régional d'Armorique covers around 172,000 hectares, taking in much of central Finistère, the Crozon Peninsula and a substantial slice of the Iroise coastline. It's Brittany's biggest regional park, and encompasses a broad range of habitats, from the dense woodland of Huelgoat to the barren granite hills of the Monts d'Arrée and the rocky cliffs of the Crozon.

This is a fantastic place to appreciate the region's wilder side, and makes ideal country for hiking, cycling and horse riding. For general info, contact the **Maison du Parc** (☎ 02 98 81 90 08; www.parc -naturel-armorique.fr, in French; 15 place aux Foires, Le Faou), which supplies maps, topoguides and trail leaflets, and provides details of bike-hire outlets, campsites and local activity companies.

HUELGOAT

At the park's eastern edge, countless legends swirl around the ancient trees and mossy boulders of Huelgoat (from the Breton for 'high forest'), the last remnants of a vast woodland that once covered most of inland Brittany. The forest is famous for its rocky landmarks including the **Ménage de La Vièrge** (Virgin Mary's Kitchen), the **Grotte du Diable** (Devil's Grotto), the mushroom-shaped **Le Champignon** and the **Roche Tremblante**, a 100-tonne monster that rocks back and forth if you push in the right place. You'll also find the remains of a Gaulish hill fort known as the **Camp d'Artus**; legend has it that King Arthur once kipped in the rock shelter known as the **Grotte d'Artus**.

Walking trails wind their way through the trees, ranging from short strolls to longer half-day hikes; ffrest maps and trail leaflets are available from the tourist office in **Huelgoat** (☎ 02 98 99 72 32; www .tourismehuelgoat.fr, in French; 18 place Aristide Briand; 🕙 10am-noon & 2-5.30pm Mon-Sat, 10am-noon Sun Jul & Aug, open weekends & bank holidays Sep-Jun).

Nearby Carhaix hosts one of Brittany's largest rock festivals, the **Festival des Vielles Charrues,** every July.

Buses from Huelgoat go to Morlaix and Carhaix.

LES MONTS D'ARRÉE

Often described as Brittany's spine, the whaleback hills, peat bogs and heather-cloaked uplands of the Monts d'Arrée cover 60,000 hectares between the Pays de Léon and Cornouaille areas. Formed by a band of granite bedrock that's more erosion-proof than the surrounding schist, the *monts* run in a southwest–northeast line for over 20km.

This wild country is hugely popular with hikers and cyclists, with options including six VTT (mountain-bike) trails and a wonderful **voie verte** (greenway) along the disused railway line between Carhaix and Morlaix. The Maison du Parc offices in Le Faou (left) and Huelgoat have plenty of trail maps and topoguides.

The area's highest point is the **Roc'h de Trévézel** (383m), which overlooks the Réservoir de St-Michel to its south and the barren, marshy area of the Yeun Elez. Natural-history tours and guided hikes are offered by **ADDES** (☎ 02 98 99 66 58; www.arree-randos.com), based in Botmeur, or you could trot the hills on your own trusty steed with **Rand'Arrée** (☎ 06 70 62 84 69; http://randarree.free.fr; day trips €60-72), located in Lopérec.

Ten kilometres west of the Roc'h de Trévézel, on the road to Sizun, are the **Moulins de Kerouat** (☎ 02 98 68 87 76; Commana; adult/child €4.50/2.10; 🕙 11am-7pm Jul & Aug, 10am-6pm Mon-Fri, 2-6pm Sat & Sun Jun, 10am-6pm Mon-Fri, 2-6pm Sun mid-Mar–May & Sep-Oct), a fascinating project that recreates a traditional Breton community of a century

FINISTÈRE

ago. Around the site's 19 restored buildings, you can watch grain being ground in the water mill, visit the working kitchen garden or even bake your own *kouign amann* (butter cake) in the wood-fired bakehouse.

Public transport is very limited; you're better off with your own (preferably two) wheels.

PRESQU'ÎLE DE CROZON

Stretching westwards into the Atlantic from the eastern border of the Parc Naturel Régional d'Armorique, the Crozon Peninsula is another must-see for coast lovers. In previous centuries this multifingered spit of land was a key strategic outpost, with dual aspects overlooking the Rade de Brest and the Baie de Douarnenez. Crumbling forts and ruined gun batteries can still be seen on the many headlands, but these days it's the Crozon's tucked-away coves and clifftop trails that attract the summertime invaders.

ESSENTIAL INFORMATION

TOURIST OFFICES // Crozon (☎ 02 98 27 07 92; officedetourisme@crozon.fr; bd Pralognan la Vanoise; ◷ 9.15am-7.30pm Mon-Sat, 10am-1pm Sun Jul & Aug, 9.15am-noon & 2-5.30pm Mon-Sat Sep-Jun); **Morgat** (☎ 02 98 27 29 49; ◷ 10am-1pm & 3-7pm Jul & Aug only)

LANDÉVENNEC & AROUND

🌱 LANDÉVENNEC // ABBEYS OLD AND NEW
The little coastal village of Landévennec conceals the ruins of Brittany's oldest Christian site. The **Abbaye St-Guenolé** was founded in the 5th century by its eponymous saint, and the building was successively sacked by the Normans and

the English before eventually being dissolved during the Revolution. Only the walls of this great ecclesiastical centre are now standing, although you can still make out the abbey's footprint, along with carved columns and a tomb rumoured to belong to Brittany's legendary warrior-king, Gradlon. Other artefacts are displayed at the abbey **museum** (☎ 02 98 27 35 90; admission €4; ◷ 10am-7pm Jul & Aug, 10am-6pm Sun-Fri Apr-Jun & Sep, 10am-5pm Sun or by reservation Oct-Mar).

In 1958 a new **abbey** (☎ 02 98 27 73 34; http://abbaye-landevennec.cef.fr) was established and now supports around 20 full-time monks. The abbey church is usually open for visits, and you mustn't miss the monks' homemade **pâtés de fruits** (fruit jellies), made using fruit from the abbey orchard. Divine – in more ways than one.

Bus 43 connects Landévennec with Crozon, Camaret, Le Faou and Brest twice daily Monday to Saturday and once on Sunday.

🌱 FERME APICOLE DE TÉRÉNEZ // STAY ON A WORKING BEE FARM
A short drive north of the D791 between Pont de Térénez and Le Faou, the **Ferme Apicole de Térénez** (☎ 02 98 81 06 90; www .ferme-apicole-de-terenez.com, in French; day visitors free; s €30-33, d €37-43, both incl breakfast) is a working bee farm, ecomuseum and *maison d'hôtes* rolled into one. Run by a family of passionate *apiculteurs* (beekeepers), the farm produces its own all-natural honey from 500 environmentally friendly hives, laced with a distinctive sweet, perfumed flavour stemming from the area's flower-filled *bocages* (hedgerows). Sweets, cakes, royal jelly and *hydromel* (a sweet mead, known as *chouchen* in Breton) are sold in the shop, and there's an intriguing bee museum

PONT DE TÉRÉNEZ

A few kilometres south of Landévennec, the **Térénez Bridge** is the only crossing over the deep Aulne River. Its construction in 1925 shaved 25km off the journey between Le Faou and the isolated Crozon Peninsula, but the first bridge was blown to smithereens by occupying Germans during 1944. A replacement was hastily rebuilt in 1952, but its poor design and shoddy construction have caused constant headaches ever since; over the last 15 years, an astonishing €1.5m has been spent patching up the cracks and keeping the bridge in service.

At long last, in 2007, work began on a brand-new crossing. Measuring 515m end-to-end, flanked by twin 90m towers, the new cable-stayed bridge is taking shape alongside its ageing sister – work is scheduled to be completed in 2010.

and 40 hectares of private forest to explore. If you just can't tear yourself away, there are six simple, timber-lined *chambres d'hôtes,* and the breakfast brims with honey-based goodness.

❦ MÉNEZ-HOM // 360-DEGREE VIEWS FROM A PANORAMIC HILLTOP

The 330m-high, heather-clad hump of Ménez-Hom guards the eastern end of the peninsula. It's one of the region's loftiest lookouts, with views of all three Breton coastlines on a clear day. A tarmacked road leads to the top – look out for the signpost off the D887 between Crozon and Chateaulin. Buses between Crozon and Quimper pass near the rock.

THE CROZON COASTLINE

❦ CROZON HEADLANDS // CLIFFS, CAPES AND STANDING STONES

The peninsula's two main towns, Crozon and Morgat, aren't worth a detour; you're better off heading straight for the spectacular coastline. The peninsula's most southerly point, **Cap de la Chèvre**, is 8km south of Morgat, and offers sweeping panoramas of the Baie de Douarnenez and the Pointe du Raz. Along the headland's west side there's sunbathing aplenty on the 2km-long **Plage de la Palue**. If you're feeling inclined, the northern end, **Plage de Lostmarc'h**, is reserved for nude bathing.

Further north, the cliffs of **Pointe de Dinan** provide a dramatic lookout over the sands of the Anse de Dinan and the jumble of rock known as the Château de Dinan, linked to the mainland by a natural archway. Around the bay is **Pointe de Pen-Hir**, famous for a series of offshore rock stacks known as **Tas de Pois** (known rather less poetically in English as the Pile of Peas). Just inland are the 40-odd standing stones of the **Alignements de Lagatjar**.

Last stop on the coastal tour is the **Pointe des Espagnols**, to the north, a steep bluff overlooking Le Goulet (the Bottleneck), the narrow entrance to the Rade de Brest. As befits such a strategic position, the headland is riddled with fortifications and gun emplacements, some dating back to Napoleonic times.

❦ CAMARET-SUR-MER // THE CROZON'S POSTCARD-PERFECT PORT

Like many Breton towns, Camaret-sur-Mer was founded on the fruits of the sea: first as a centre for sardine-fishing, and later as France's premier crayfish

FINISTÈRE

port; crays are caught in traditional boats known as *dundées*. Today, the decaying hulks of abandoned vessels line the granite breakwater, a testimony to the industry's 20th-century decline.

Despite its economic troubles, Camaret is still well worth a visit. Cheek-by-jowl cafés and clanking yacht masts populate the attractive harbour, overlooked by a 17th-century red brick watchtower known as the **Tour Vauban** (☎ 02 98 27 65 00; adult/child €4/2; ☯ 2-6pm mid-Jun–mid-Sep), which houses a small display of military memorabilia. The town's other notable building is the 17th-century **Chapelle Notre Dame de Rocamadour**, a pocket-sized chapel dedicated to Camaret's sailors, who have left their own votive offerings of battered oars, life buoys and model ships.

♥ SEA FISHING // CATCH YOUR SUPPER WITH A CAMARET FISHERMAN

In July and August, **Pesketour** (☎ 02 98 27 98 44) runs fishing trips with Gérard Le Brenn, a local fisherman who knows the Crozon coastline like the back of his hand. Trips run to the Tas de Pois at dawn and dusk, and you'll be treated to some of Gérard's tall tales and natural-history lessons along the way. If you're after something less active, opt for a scenic cruise with **Vedettes Azénor** (☎ 02 98 41 46 23; www.azenor.com, in French; adult/4-16yr/ under 4yr €15.50/11.50/4; ☯ Jul &Aug).

GASTRONOMIC HIGHLIGHTS

♥ LES FRÈRES DE LA CÔTE // CAMARET-SUR-MER €€

☎ 02 98 27 95 42; 11 quai Toudouze
On the Camaret quayside, this restaurant bills itself as a 'Taverne de l'Ocean'. Model boats, old telescopes and Camaret artwork create a seaside feel, and the

blackboards are crammed with fishy delicacies laced with a tropical kick – the two brothers in charge previously ran a restaurant in the Caribbean and brew their own rum.

♥ SAVEURS ET MARÉES // MORGAT €€

☎ 02 98 26 23 18; 52 bd de la Plage; menus €16-45
There's plenty of choice along the Morgat waterfront, but our fave is 'Tastes and Tides'. It's a simple place, decked out in pastel colours and a maritime ceiling mural, but the beach views and friendly atmosphere make it perfect for a plate of *fruits de mer* and a glass of chilled Chablis. Shame about the passing traffic, though.

TRANSPORT

BOAT // Vedettes Azénor (☎ 02 98 41 46 23; www.azenor.com) runs a summer ferry service between Camaret and Brest (adult/4-16yr/under 4yr return €17/13/6; ☯ three daily Jul-Aug). Boats also run from the nearby port of Le Fret between April and September. For boats to Ouessant, see p91.

BUS // Bus 43 connects Camaret with Crozon, Landévennec, Le Faou and Brest twice daily Monday to Saturday and once on Sunday.

CORNOUAILLE

· · · · ·

The name of Cornouaille, Finistère's most southerly region, commemorates the early Celts who sailed across the Channel from Cornwall to settle here. The Breton language and culture still have a strong foothold here, especially around the area known as the Pays Bigouden; the area's capital city, Quimper, stages an annual summer festival celebrating the Celtic culture.

This region is also where you'll find some of Brittany's most striking coastal scenery, particularly around the Crozon Peninsula and the famous viewpoints of the Pointe du Raz and the Pointe du Van.

DOUARNENEZ

pop 17,000

A century ago, there was only one thing that mattered in Douarnenez, and that was the slippery, silvery commodity called the sardine. During the height of the boom in the late 19th century, a thousand boats called this rough-and-ready port home, and 30 canneries worked round the clock to package up the daily catch for export around the globe. Douarnenez's residents even earned the local nickname of *'penn sardin'* (sardine-head), but by the turn of the 20th century fish stocks were in freefall, and within a couple of decades most of the boats and canneries had shut up shop for good. For a flavour of Douarnenez' fishy heyday, head for the fantastic Port Musée, lodged in a converted sardine cannery.

The **Carnaval des Gras** is a lively Easter carnival held in the week before Mardi Gras.

ORIENTATION

The town is split into three main sections. The town centre focuses on place Stalingrad and place Édouard Vaillant, where you'll find the tourist office and bus stops. Downhill to the east, the narrow streets of the old town lead to the harbour at Port du Rosmeur. To the west is the narrow, river-mouth harbour of Port Rhu. A road bridge leads across the river to the modern suburb and beaches of Tréboul.

ESSENTIAL INFORMATION

Tourist Office (☎ 02 98 92 13 35; www
.douarnenez-tourisme.com; 2 rue Docteur-Mével;
☺ 10am-7pm Mon-Sat, 10.30am-1pm & 4-6.30pm Sun
Jul & Aug, 10am-12.30pm & 2-5.30pm Mon-Sat Sep-Jun)
Leaflets detailing walks, accommodation info and guided tours (adult/child €4.80/3.30) around the old quarters and the fishing port.

EXPLORING DOUARNENEZ

❧ LE PORT MUSÉE // SAIL THROUGH THE HISTORY OF BOAT BUILDING

Fresh from a multimillion-euro refit, the **Port Musée** (☎ 02 98 92 65 20; www.port-musee
.org; adult/6-16yr €6.20/3.80; ☺ 10am-7pm Jul-Aug,
10am-12.30pm & 2-6pm Tue-Sun Apr-Jun & Sep-Nov)
is the perfect place to get au fait with the town's sea-going heritage. Situated by the now quiet quais of Port Rhu, the museum owns France's leading collection of working sea-vessels, many of which are moored along the quay: you can climb aboard an old *langoustier* (crayfish boat) and a flat-bottomed cargo barge, or wander the decks of a British-built steamboat dating from 1929. Inside, the museum displays everything from Inuit kayaks and African canoes to steamboats and rigged sailboats. As you'd expect, there's plenty of background on Douarnenez' sardine industry, too.

❧ SARDINETOWN // AMBLE AROUND THE TOWN'S CHARMING OLD QUARTERS

Douarnenez' sardine business centred on the ramshackle port of **Rosmeur**, whose narrow streets were once crammed with fishing families hoping to cash in on the sardine explosion – the population increased tenfold in the late 1800s, and many people had to live in slumlike conditions on paltry rates of pay. It's no

FINISTERE

coincidence that France's first commu-
nist mayor was elected in Douarnenez
in 1924. The modern fishing port is on
the tip of the headland to the north of
Rosmeur.

A kilometre west of downtown
Douarnenez is the neighbouring port of
Tréboul, now the centre of the town's
busy beach industry thanks to the **Plage
des Sables Blancs** and smaller **plage St-
Jean.** There's another wonderful stretch
of sand 2km to the east of town at **Plage
du Ris.** The tourist office runs guided
walks to the **Île Tristan,** accessible at low
tide.

If you fancy trying some local produce, seafood is sold daily at **Les Halles**
(place des Halles), and there's a big fish and
produce market every Wednesday and
Saturday on the Tréboul port. Better still,
head across the square from the covered
market to **Penn Sardin** (☎ 02 98 92 70 83;
7 rue Le-Breton), where the shelves are loaded
with enough collectible sardine cans to
sink a trawler.

GASTRONOMIC HIGHLIGHTS

❦ LA VÉRANDA €€
☎ 02 98 45 53 84; 15 bis rue des Professeurs Curie;
menus €17-29; ☯ lunch & dinner Tue-Sun Oct–mid-
Jun, daily mid-Jun–Aug
A fashionable find near the Tréboul harbour, blending lounge-bar stylings with
fresh fusion cooking. The menu veers
from straightforward *moules-frites* (mussels and chips) to hearty slabs of local
steak or fish fresh from the Douarnenez
market. It has stone, wood and groovy
lighting inside; and outside, a sun-trap
terrace for when the weather's good.

❦ L'INSOLITE €€
☎ 02 98 92 00 02; 4 rue Jean Jaurès; lunch menus
€13-17, dinner menus from €25; ☯ lunch & dinner

This elegant restaurant occupies the
ground floor of the Hôtel de France,
Douarnenez' main city-centre hotel. Re-
finement is the watchword – crisp white
tablecloths and modern art provide a
zen setting for the food, which mixes
top-notch *terroir* ingredients with a fine
showing of Douarnenez-caught fish. *À
noter* – the killer chocolate pudding laced
with popping candy.

❦ TY MAD €€
☎ 02 98 74 00 53; Tréboul; mains €10-20; ☯ dinner
Light floods in through tall French windows into the ground-floor restaurant
of the Ty Mad hotel (p294), and the
fare concentrates on a revolving menu
of just-so seafood – apart from Sunday,
which is designated as 'curry day'.

TRANSPORT

BUS // Daily buses run between Douarnenez and
Quimper from Monday to Saturday. At least four travel
via the Pointe du Raz and Audierne.

AROUND DOUARNENEZ

❦ RÉSERVE DU CAP SIZUN //
**BREAK OUT THE BINOCULARS AT
THIS BIRD RESERVE**
This rocky headland, 8km northwest
of Audierne, has become a birdwatch-
er's paradise thanks to the work of the
French ornithologist Michel Hervé
Julien, who established one of Europe's
most important bird reserves here in
1958. The **reserve** (☎ 02 98 70 13 53; admission €2; ☯ 10am-6pm Jul & Aug, 10am-noon &
2-6pm Apr-Jun) is a haven for cormorants,
fulmars, kittiwakes and several sorts of
seagull; it's also one of only three places
in France that supports breeding guillemots. If your French is up to it, guided
tours (€6.50) are run by the reserve's
ornithologists.

♥ POINTE DU RAZ & POINTE DU VAN // LAST STOP, FINISTÈRE – NEXT STOP, AMERICA

If you're seeking an unforgettable sunset, there's only one place in Finistère that fits the bill, and that's the Pointe du Raz. Known in Breton as the Beg Ar Raz, there are few places in France which can match it for coastal splendour. On every side, gorse-cloaked cliffs plummet into the waves 70m below, gulls trace lazy arcs overhead and a statue of **Notre Dame des Naufragés** (Our Lady of the Shipwrecked) gazes out to sea toward the Île du Sein and the winking light of the Ar Men lighthouse.

Incredibly, the point was earmarked in the late 1970s as a potential site for a new nuclear power station. Thankfully, the powers-that-be came to their senses – cancelling the project was one of President Mitterand's manifesto pledges during the '81 election – and the area is now a nationally protected reserve. A car park and **visitor centre** (admission €3; ☽ Apr-Sep) was built behind the point proper; shuttle buses ferry visitors the last 800m, or you can just walk the scenic coast path.

Five million trippers visit the Pointe du Raz every year, but only a fraction make the trek over to the equally stunning **Pointe du Van**, a short spin along the coast road. Between the two headlands is the **Baie des Trépassés** (Bay of the Dead), where legend has it deceased druids were ferried over to the Île de Sein for burial. The panoramic bar of **Hôtel de la Baie des Trépassés** (☎ 02 98 70 61 34; www.hotelfinistere.com; mains €12-25) makes a glorious place for a sunset tipple and a slap-up supper, with views across the shoreline; the hotel has a varied menu.

There are at least four daily buses to the Pointe du Raz from Quimper (1½ hours) via Douarnenez (30 minutes) and Audierne.

♥ ÎLE DE SEIN // BRAVE THE SWELLS AROUND BRITTANY'S LOWEST ISLAND

The tiny Île de Sein – 3km long and just a few hundred metres across – is more an offshore reef than an island. Barely 6m above the tideline, it's notoriously flood-prone; when severe Atlantic storms combine with unusually high tides – as happened in 1839, 1866 and 1919 – the island can be completely swamped. Despite a steady population drain over the last century, around 200 hardy islanders still opt to eke out an existence here, to the considerable consternation of the French government.

Some 12km west of the island stands the lonely **Phare d'Ar Men**, built to protect ships from the tidal races of the Raz de Sein, one of Brittany's most perilous shipwreck spots. Perched atop a rocky reef and exposed to the full force of the Atlantic waves, the lighthouse was one of the greatest engineering accomplishments of the late-19th century; it took 14 years to build, and was completed in 1881. Like most of Brittany's lighthouses, it has been automated since 1990.

The only way to get to the island is by boat. **Penn Ar Bed** (☎ 02 98 70 70 70; www.pennarbed.fr; adult weekdays/weekends €18.40/20.40 Oct-May, €30.20 Jul & Aug, €30.20 Jun-Sep) runs ferries year-round from Audierne, Brest and Camaret; there are up to four daily boats in July and August, dropping to one over winter. **Vedette Biniou II** (☎ 02 98 70 21 15; www.vedettebiniou.freesurf.fr) runs three daily boats from Audierne (adult/3-15yr €25/13) during July and August.

♥ AUDIERNE // STROLL THE PORT AND RELAX ON THE SANDS

Audierne is one of the busiest fishing towns along this stretch of the Finistère coastline. Smart sea-captains' houses stack up across the hillside above the old port, while brightly coloured boats set out in search of langoustines, monkfish, plaice and sea bass from the bustling quays.

The town's main attraction is its epic beach, the kilometre-long **Plage de Trescadec**, a popular spot for swimming and water sports. You can also take half-day trips aboard the langoustine vessel **Cap Sizun** (☎ 06 99 28 15 08) or view the skeletal hulls of scrapped vessels in the **ships' graveyard** along the **Anse de Loquéran**.

Nearby, the seven zones at **Aquashow** (☎ 02 98 70 03 03; rue du Goyen; adult/4-11yr €13.80/10.80; ⏰ 10.30am-7pm Apr-Sep, 2-6pm Oct & school holidays) include a 3D cinema, *bassin tactile,* coastal tank and a section exploring the flora and fauna of Brittany's rivers. There is also a live bird display where you can compare the hunting practices of cormorants, bald eagles and barn owls.

♥ LOCRONAN // EXPERIENCE A TRADITIONAL PARDON

Locronan has barely changed in appearance since the mid-18th century, and its old-world ambience and photogenic granite houses – not to mention its lack of phone cables or electricity wires – have made it hugely popular with film crews. Locronan's most famous silver-screen role was doubling as a Dorset village in Roman Polanski's 1979 version of *Tess;* following his notorious under-age sex scandal in 1977, Polanski couldn't film in Britain for fear of being extradited back to the USA for trial.

Locronan was once famous for its sailcloth, but it's now better known for hosting one of Brittany's oldest *par-dons* (religious processions), the **Petite Troménie,** held on the second Sunday in July. Barefooted pilgrims bearing saintly banners and singing traditional songs follow a 6km route from the Église St-Ronan, at the centre of the village, to a sacred grove nearby known as Le Néméton, originally used as a site of pagan worship. The event attracts huge crowds of onlookers, and every six years the festival goes supersized for the **Grande Troménie,** which follows an even longer 12km route: the next one is in 2013.

TRANSPORT

BUS // Daily buses run between Douarnenez and Quimper from Monday to Saturday. At least four travel via the Pointe du Raz and Audierne. Less-frequent buses also link Douarnenez with Locronan.

QUIMPER

pop 59,400

Dominated by the double spires of its towering cathedral, riverside Quimper (pronounced *kam-pair*) is the capital of Finistère, but its influence stretches far beyond *départemental* boundaries. Supposedly founded in the 5th century by the Breton hero, King Gradlon, Quimper has become a touchstone for local Celtic culture; it's the home of Brittany's flagship museum and hosts one of the region's liveliest cultural celebrations, the Festival de Cornouaille, every July. Historically, it was also the centre for one of the region's great exports – the brightly coloured, pastorally patterned china known as *faïence* – and if you want to pick up some pottery, this is definitely the place to do it. Factor in some excellent museums, one of Brittany's loveliest old quarters and a delightful setting along the Odet River, and you've got a city that deserves serious exploration.

ORIENTATION

The pedestrianised old quarter clusters around the cathedral on the north bank of the Odet. The city's main thoroughfares run either side of the river before joining up and leading to the train and bus stations about 600m east of the city centre.

ESSENTIAL INFORMATION

TOURIST OFFICES // Quimper (☎ 02 98 53 04 05; www.quimper-tourisme.com; place de la Résistance; ◷ 9am-7pm Mon-Sat, 10am-12.45pm & 3-5.45pm Sun Jul & Aug, 9am-12.30pm & 1.30-6.30pm Mon-Sat, 10am-12.45pm Sun Jun & early Sep, 9.30am-12.30pm & 1.30-6pm Mon-Sat mid-Sep–Mar) Sells the Pass Quimper (€10), which includes entry to four museums, a guided tour of the city and other discounts.

EXPLORING QUIMPER

♥ CATHÉDRALE ST-CORENTIN // GOGGLE AT THE SPIRES OF QUIMPER'S CATHEDRAL

The twin spires of Quimper's cathedral have become a much-loved Breton landmark, but they actually weren't part of

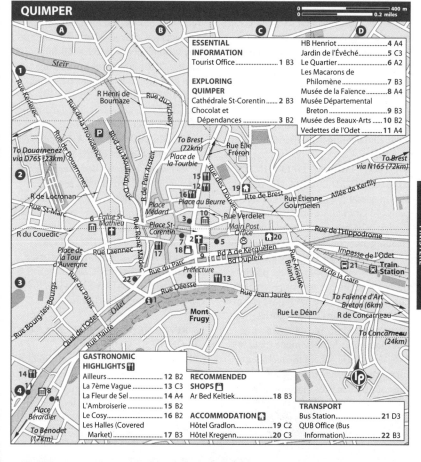

QUIMPER

ESSENTIAL INFORMATION	
Tourist Office	1 B3

EXPLORING QUIMPER	
Cathédrale St-Corentin	2 B3
Chocolat et Dépendances	3 B2

HB Henriot	4 A4
Jardin de l'Évêché	5 C3
Le Quartier	6 A2
Les Macarons de Philomène	7 B3
Musée de la Faïence	8 A4
Musée Départemental Breton	9 B3
Musée des Beaux-Arts	10 B2
Vedettes de l'Odet	11 A4

GASTRONOMIC HIGHLIGHTS	
Ailleurs	12 B2
La 7ème Vague	13 C3
La Fleur de Sel	14 A4
L'Ambroiserie	15 B2
Le Cosy	16 B2
Les Halles (Covered Market)	17 B3

RECOMMENDED SHOPS	
Ar Bed Keltiek	18 B3

ACCOMMODATION	
Hôtel Gradlon	19 C2
Hôtel Kregenn	20 C3

TRANSPORT	
Bus Station	21 D3
QUB Office (Bus Information)	22 B3

FINISTÈRE

the original design; they were added as an afterthought in the 1850s, modelled on similar spires at a church in Pont-Croix. The cathedral was supposedly founded on the orders of King Gradlon, but construction didn't get started until 1239. You can see a statue of Gradlon himself, seated on his trusty charger high up on the west facade between the cathedral's spires.

Apart from the spires and the magnificent west portal, the cathedral's most notable feature is its nave, set at a distinctive 5-degree kink to the choir, and said by some to represent the inclination of Christ's head as he was dying on the cross. The real reason for the kink is rather less poetic; it was designed to incorporate the inconveniently located tomb of Alain Canhiard, the Breton hero who vanquished Norman invaders in 913. There's some fine medieval carpentry on the choir stalls and pulpit, and several blazing stained-glass windows around the nave, some dating from the 15th century.

♥ OLD QUIMPER // DELVE INTO THE CITY'S MEDIEVAL HEART

The higgledy-piggledy streets of Quimper's **old city** radiate out around the cathedral. The best spots for architectural strolling are around rue Kéréon, rue du Guéodet and place Terre-au-Duc, where half-timbered buildings teeter precariously above the cobbled lanes, creating a convincing air of medieval days gone by.

There are some fantastic pâtisseries dotted around the old city, including **Les Macarons de Philomène** (☎ 02 98 95 21 40; 13 rue Kéréon), where the technicoloured confections are made by one of the country's master macaroon-makers. **Chocolat et Dépendances** (☎ 02 98 95 56 06; 32 place St-Corentin) produces the city's best *kouign amann* – the lunch *menu* includes

something savoury, something sweet and something hot to drink for just €5.

The city's best address for browsing is **Ar Bed Keltiek** (☎ 02 98 95 42 82; 2 rue au Roi Gradlon), which stocks a huge array of Breton and Celtic books.

♥ MUSEUMS // BROWSE BRETON CULTURE OLD AND NEW

Lodged inside the former Bishop's Palace, in the shadow of the cathedral, the **Musée Départemental Breton** (☎ 02 98 95 21 60; 1 rue du Roi Gradlon; adult/child €3.80/2.50; ⓨ 9am-6pm daily Jun-Sep, 9am-noon & 2-5pm Tue-Sat, 2-5pm Sun Oct-May) houses the nation's greatest collection of Breton artefacts, ranging from ancient archaeological artefacts to Celtic jewellery, Roman mosaics and plenty of priceless Quimperois *faïence*. The highlight is a huge collection of traditional costume, including several skyscraping examples of Breton *koef* (laced headdresses). The **Jardin de l'Évêché** adjoins the museum.

The **Musée des Beaux-Arts** (☎ 02 98 95 45 20; 40 place St-Corentin; adult/12-18yr €4.50/2.50; ⓨ 10am-noon & 2-6pm Wed-Mon) is especially strong on local artists, with sections devoted to the Pont-Aven school and the works of Quimperois poet-painter Max Jacob. For something more contemporary, head for **Le Quartier** (☎ 02 98 55 55 77; www.le-quartier.net, in French; 10 esplanade F Mitterrand; adult/under 26yr €1.50/free, free Sun; ⓨ 10am-noon & 1-6pm Tue-Sat, 2-6pm Sun), the city's main modern-art venue.

♥ RIVER CRUISES // CATCH A BOAT ALONG THE ODET

The rushing River Odet cuts through the centre of Quimper and once served as the city's commercial thoroughfare. The riverboats and barges have long since been replaced by traffic jams, but you can still enjoy a downriver cruise to Bénodet with **Vedettes de l'Odet** (☎ 02 98 57 00 58; www.vedettes-odet.com; adult €15-25, 4-12yr €10-15, under 4yr €5 depending on cruise). If you're feeling flash, you could even indulge in lobster and langoustine washed down with a chilled glass of bubbly on the *croisière gastronomique* (€59 to €93).

FESTIVALS AND EVENTS

Grand Pardon de Ty Mamm Doué The city's largest religious procession is held on the first Sunday in July.

Festival de Cornouaille (www.festival-corn ouaille.com) This major Breton celebration in late July has been entertaining the city every year since 1928 with folk groups, *festou-noz* (night musical concerts) and Quimperois *en costume*.

Les Jeudis de l'Évêché Outdoor concerts are held in the bishops' gardens on Thursdays from July to September.

GASTRONOMIC HIGHLIGHTS

On quai du Steir, fresh fish, fruit and picnic goodies are on offer at **Les Halles** (covered market; ☺ 9am-noon & 2-5pm Mon-Sat). Stalls spill out onto the surrounding streets for the food market on Wednesday and Saturday mornings. There are

QUIMPER FAÏENCE

For three centuries, Quimper has been synonymous with the art of **faïence,** a pottery process in which pieces of earthenware or porcelain are painstakingly painted by hand before being coated in a special tin-based glaze and fired at temperatures in excess of 1000°C. The process can trace its roots back to ancient Persia, but the kilns needed to reach the necessary temperatures weren't developed until the mid-16th century.

The Italian city of Faenza was the first place to produce *faïence* on a serious scale (hence the name). Moustiers, Nevers and Rouen later became important *faïence* centres, but their success was eclipsed by Quimper, which attracted many famous artists and developed its own distinctive style, characterised by vibrant colours and designs inspired by pastoral scenes and Breton legends.

Quimper's crockery boom peaked during the late 18th and early 19th centuries, but the industry has since enjoyed a 20th-century revival. The most sought-after pieces are produced by **HB Henriot** (☎ 02 98 90 09 36; www.hb-henriot.com; rue Haute; ☺ guided tours Mon-Sat Jul & Aug, Mon-Fri Sep-Jun), in business for over 300 years and one of the only French faïenceries that paints entirely by hand (all Henriot pieces are individually signed by the artist, making them highly prized among crockery collectors). You can watch Henriot artists at work on a **guided tour** (€5) around the workshop, before picking up souvenirs in the shop or browsing 2000 classic pieces in the **Musée de la Faïence** (☎ 02 98 90 12 72; www.quimper-faiences.com; 14 rue Jean-Baptiste Bousquet; adult/child €4/2.30; ☺ 10am-6pm Mon-Sat Apr-Oct) behind the factory.

The town's other major producer is **Fäincerie d'Art Breton** (☎ 02 98 52 85 28; www .faience-quimper.com), founded in 1994 by a cooperative of Quimperois artists. Although its pieces aren't quite as collectible as Henriot's, they're usually considerably cheaper and still 100% Quimper-made. Be careful if you're buying outside the factories, as there are plenty of knock-off companies looking to cash in on the Quimper name. Authentic pieces always come with a Certificate of Authenticity, which should be stamped by the shop at the time of purchase.

FINISTÈRE

lots of little coffee shops dotted around the cathedral square.

♨ AILLEURS €€

☎ 02 98 95 56 32; 43 rue Élie Fréron; mains €19-23; ☺ dinner Mon-Sat

As its name suggests, 'Elsewhere' takes a globetrotting approach to its cuisine – the menu takes in everything from chicken curry to authentic sushi and the house special, beef served à la 'cowboy' with its own spitfork and flaming grill. The service can be hit-and-miss, but the food's usually more reliable.

♨ LA 7ÈME VAGUE €€

☎ 02 98 53 33 10; 72 rue Jean Jaurès; mains €10-18; ☺ closed dinner Wed, lunch Sat & all day Sun

The Seventh Wave is the locals' tip, where hungry Quimperois squeeze onto wooden tables for straightforward French grub served *sans fuss*. Fresh oysters, *andouillette* (tripe sausage) and top-notch foie gras are always on offer, while daily specials are chalked up on the blackboard; the *menu du terroir* ('menu of the land') is fab value at €19.90.

♨ LA FLEUR DE SEL €€

☎ 02 98 55 04 71; 1 quai Neuf; menus €27-38; ☺ lunch Mon-Fri, dinner daily

There's nothing remotely pretentious about this cute bistro along the old quay, but the food has charmed many culinary critics. Tiny tables and a crimson-and-cream theme make for a cosy setting, and the menu mixes up top-notch fish, meat and game with some superb puddings; look out for the house special *tarte tatin*.

♨ L'AMBROISERIE €€€

☎ 02 98 95 00 02; www.ambroiserie-quimper.com; 49 rue Élie Fréron; menus €32-59; ☺ closed Mon

Abstract art, blindingly white tablecloths and a gleaming chequerboard floor set the just-so tone at the Ambroiserie, Quimper's long-standing address for fine French cuisine, and a reliable favourite among the foodie guides. Expect upmarket Michelin-type food – roast pigeon *en cocotte*, langoustine tart with ginger – presented in sophisticated style, although it might be a bit too clever-clever for some.

♨ LE COSY €

☎ 02 98 95 23 65; 2 rue du Sallé; mains €10.50-14; ☺ lunch daily, dinner Fri & Sat

It's a gourmet emporium with a split personality: downstairs, a treasure trove of oils, wines, biscuits, mustards and handmade choccies; upstairs, a boho café stocked with mix-and-match furniture and a menu that ditches crêpes and *frites* in favour of hearty *tartines* (toasted sandwiches) and a set daily lunch. Lovely.

TRANSPORT

BUS // Useful bus links include Brest (Line 1, 1½ hours, four Monday to Friday, two on Saturday), Concarneau (Line 14B, 2½ hours, four Monday to Saturday via La Forêt Fouesnant) and Pont l'Abbé (Line 3, 25 minutes, six Monday to Saturday, four on Sunday).

TRAIN // Quimper has TGV services to Paris Montparnasse (€73.40 to €80.30, 4½ to 5½ hours) as well as services to Nantes (€47.10 to €53.70, 2½ to 3½ hours), Rennes (€30.60 to €36, 2½ hours), Vannes (€17.40 to €22.90, 1½ hours) and local trains north to Brest (€15, 1¼ hours) or Morlaix (€18.10, 1½ to 3½ hours).

PARKING // Quimper's city-centre traffic is hectic, and on-street parking is pricey. If you have to drive, station yourself in the big car park on rue de la Providence.

DRIVING TOUR: LE PAYS BIGOUDEN

Distance: 50km to 60km
Duration 1 day

Tucked into the southwestern corner of Cornouaille, bounded to the north by

Plozévet and to the east by the Ste-Marine peninsula, the Bigouden is one of the traditional bastions of Breton culture – *koef*, *kabig* (waterproof coats) and other local garments were still a common sight here at the turn of the 20th century. It's a lovely corner of Brittany, spotted with tiny fishing harbours, quiet villages and some of the region's finest beaches around the Pointe de la Torche. You could cycle it but you'd best give yourself more than a day.

From **Quimper**, head southwest along the D785 to the Bigouden's unofficial capital, **Pont-l'Abbé**. Here, the **Musée Bigouden** (☎ 02 98 66 09 03; adult/12-18yr €3.50/2; ⏰ 10am-12.30pm & 2-7pm Jul & Aug, 10am-12.30pm & 2-6.30pm Jun & Sep, 2-6pm Tue-Sun Apr-May) is housed in the town's former château and boasts a fine collection of local costumes and lace *koefs*. The château dates to the 14th century.

Detour southeast along the D2 to the **Manoir de Kerazan** (☎ 02 98 87 40 40; www.kerazan.fr; adult/7-15yr €6/4; ⏰ 10.30am-7pm mid-Jun–mid-Sep, 2-6pm Tue-Sun Apr–mid-Jun & late Sep), a lavish 16th-century manor house left to the Institut de France in 1928 by

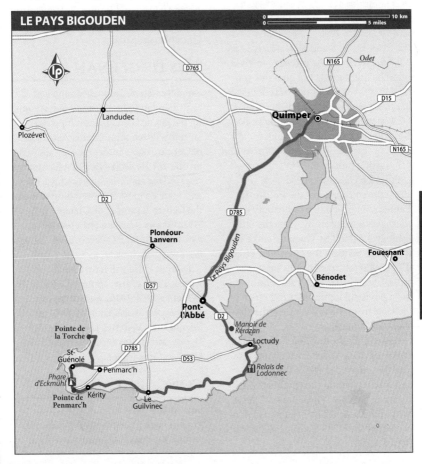

the local notable Joseph Georges Astor. Inside the manor you can visit the stately billiard room, chapel and the *salon des dames* (ladies' parlour); outside there are 5 hectares of picturesque parkland. Head 2km past the harbour at Loctudy for a seaside lunch at the **Relais de Lodonnec** (☎ 02 98 87 55 34; plage du Lodonnec; menus €15-33; ☺ closed Mon Jul & Aug, closed Tue & Wed other times).

The Bigouden is still a heartland for the Breton fishing industry, and in nearby **Le Guilvinec** there's a fun interactive museum called **Haliotika** (☎ 02 98 58 28 38; adult/child €5.50/3.50, guided visit & fish auction €2 extra; ☺ 9.30am-7pm Mon-Fri, 3-6.30pm Sat & Sun Jul & Aug, 10am-12.30pm & 2.30-6.30pm Mon-Fri Apr-Jun, Sep & some school holidays, 3-6pm Oct), which brings the industry to vivid life. The highlight is the quayside terrace that provides a grandstand view for *la criée*, the daily **fish auction** (☺ 6am & 4-5.30pm Mon-Fri). If you're feeling peckish, you can join the fishermen for an evening session of *soupe de poissons* and fish-sorting (adult/child €9/7.50).

From Le Guilvinec, head west along the coast road to the **Pointe de Penmarc'h**, which marks Brittany's southwestern extremity. Here the little fishing villages of **St-Guénolé** and **Kérity** huddle beneath the 65m-high **Phare d'Eckmühl** (admission €2; ☺ 10.30am-6pm Apr-Sep), built in 1897 and still one of the most powerful lighthouses in France – the view from the top is worth the 300-step slog (honest).

Round things off with a sunset picnic at **Pointe de la Torche**, which juts out into the Atlantic north of Penmarc'h and is renowned for its epic surf and stunning beaches. There are surf shops behind the beach. The headland is signposted off the D785 leading back towards Pont-l'Abbé.

SOUTH COAST

· · · · · ·

BÉNODET

Once a favourite retreat of both Marcel Proust and Winston Churchill, Bénodet is an upmarket holiday resort and yachting harbour at the mouth of the River Odet. There are some good beaches nearby, including the **Plage du Trez** and **Plage du Coq**, but neither can match the stunning white-sand dunes stretching for 4km between Le Letty and **Pointe de Mousterlin**.

For river cruises from Bénodet to Quimper, see p104.

ÎLES DE GLÉNAN

Sapphire waters, untouched sand and nary a soul in sight – that just about sums up the Îles de Glénan, an archipelago of around a dozen mini-islands 20km south of Concarneau. Visitors are only allowed on one, the **Île de St-Nicolas** – the rest are reserved for seabirds, super-rich yachties and France's most famous sailing school, the **Centre Nautique de Glénan** (☎ 01 53 92 86 00; www.glenans.asso.fr; quai Louis Blériot), which usually offers a few courses in English every year.

Everyone else will have to make do with a scenic cruise: contact **Vedettes de l'Odet** (☎ 02 98 57 00 58; www.vedettes-odet .com; return ticket adult/4-12yr/under 4yr €39/20/5) in Bénodet and **Vedettes Glenn** (☎ 02 98 97 10 31; www.vedettes-glenn.fr; return ticket adult/5-13yr €25/13) in Concarneau.

CONCARNEAU

pop 18,600
Trawlers and tourist boats rub bulwarks around the quays of Concarneau (Konk-

Kerne in Breton), one of southern Brittany's largest working fishing ports and the home of the country's third-largest fish market. Like Douarnenez, Concarneau's fortunes were founded on the sardine boom of the 19th century, but with the subsequent collapse of sardine stocks, local fishermen were forced ever further afield in search of their catch; Concarneau's 200-odd boats can now be found everywhere from Iceland to the Indian Ocean. The town is still often referred to as the *ville bleue* because of the bright blue seine nets used by local fishermen.

ESSENTIAL INFORMATION

TOURIST OFFICES // Concarneau (☎ 02 98 97 01 44; www.tourismeconcarneau.fr; quai d'Aiguillon; ⊙ 9am-7pm Jul & Aug, 9am-12.30pm & 1.45-6.30pm Mon-Sat, 10am-1pm Sun Apr-Jun & early Sep, 9am-noon & 2-6pm Mon-Sat mid-Sep–Mar)

EXPLORING CONCARNEAU

♥ VILLE CLOSE // BRAVE THE CROWDS IN CONCARNEAU'S CITADEL

Protruding from the east side of the port, Concarneau's distinctive bastion, known as the **ville close**, was built between the

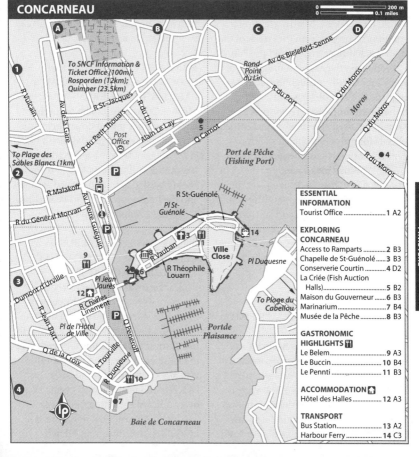

CONCARNEAU

0 ————— 200 m
0 ————— 0.1 miles

To SNCF Information &
Ticket Office (100m);
Rosporden (12km);
Quimper (23.5km)

To Plage des
Sables Blancs (1km)

Rond-
Point
du Lin

Av de Bielefeld-Senne

Port de Pêche
(Fishing Port)

R St-Guénolé

Pl St-
Guénolé

Ville
Close

Pl Duquesne

To Plage du
Cabellou

Port de
Plaisance

Pl de l'Hôtel
de Ville

Baie de Concarneau

FINISTÈRE

**ESSENTIAL
INFORMATION**
Tourist Office 1 A2

**EXPLORING
CONCARNEAU**
Access to Ramparts 2 B3
Chapelle de St-Guénolé 3 B3
Conserverie Courtin 4 D2
La Criée (Fish Auction
Halls)..5 B2
Maison du Gouverneur 6 B3
Marinarium 7 B4
Musée de la Pêche 8 B3

**GASTRONOMIC
HIGHLIGHTS**
Le Belem.................................9 A3
Le Buccin 10 B4
Le Pennti 11 B3

ACCOMMODATION
Hôtel des Halles 12 A3

TRANSPORT
Bus Station..........................13 A2
Harbour Ferry 14 C3

14th and 17th centuries to protect the town's harbour. While the threat of an English invasion is long gone, the *ville close* is subjected to a different assault these days; in peak summer this is one of Brittany's popular spots, and its streets feel about as tranquil as a cattle auction. July and August are months to avoid if you can.

The *ville close* is ringed by ramparts and linked to the mainland by a stone footbridge and barbican. Just past the citadel's clock tower and western courtyard, look out for the 18th-century **Maison du Gouverneur** above the main gate, where the citadel's military captain would have lodged. Nearby are several cannons recovered from the wreck of the *Venus,* a 300-man frigate built in 1780.

From here, the main thoroughfare of rue Vauban leads through the citadel to **place St-Guénolé**, passing a string of postcard shops, ice-cream stalls and *crêperies,* as well as a small chapel, which once belonged to the citadel's 15th-century hospital (spot the statue of St Guénolé nestled into a handy niche). On the east side of the citadel is a pleasant garden and a little outdoor auditorium that hosts summer plays and concerts. Just outside the ramparts, a regular **ferry** transports passengers across the harbour to the rive Gauche (left bank), the city's historic fishing quarter.

♥ MUSEÉ DE LA PÊCHE // DISCOVER CONCARNEAU'S FISHY CONNECTIONS

Concarneau's marvellous **fisheries museum** (☎ 02 98 97 10 20; 3 rue Vauban; adult/5-15yr €6/4; ⏰ 9.30am-8pm Jul & Aug, 10am-6pm Apr-Jun & Sep, 10am-noon & 2-6pm Feb-Mar & Oct-Nov) is just inside the west gate, and delves into the history of the local fishing industry using everything from archive film to scale models, nautical paintings and vintage boats. You can even clamber aboard the museum's very own fishing vessel, the retired 34m trawler *L'Hémérica,* permanently docked just outside the city walls.

♥ MARINARIUM // STUDY THE COASTLINE AT THIS HISTORIC RESEARCH STATION

On the southern side of the harbour, the **Marinarium** (☎ 02 98 50 81 64; place de la Croix; adult/6-14yr €5/3; ⏰ 10am-7pm Jul & Aug, 10am-noon & 2-6pm Apr-Jun & Sep, 2-6pm Oct-Dec & Feb) is the world's oldest institute of marine biology, founded in 1859. The institute's 10 aquariums and seawater tanks are brimming with local marine life; several species can be inspected in microscopic detail.

♥ CONSERVERIE COURTIN // STOCK UP AT CONCARNEAU'S LAST FISH CANNERY

Most of Concarneau's fish canneries have long since pulled down their shutters, but the **Conserverie Courtin** (☎ 02 98 97 01 80; 3 quai du Moros) has stayed in business and is still the top place in town for freshly bottled fish soup, tinned sardines and the house special, *confit de noix de St-Jacques* (tinned scallops).

♥ FÊTE DES FILETS BLEUS // CELEBRATE WITH LOCALS AT THIS SHIPSHAPE FESTIVAL

Concarneau's annual piscatorial party can trace its roots back to the collapse of sardine stocks at the turn of the 20th century, when local people organised the first festival to raise funds for needy fishing families. It's been a town tradition ever since; costumed parades, dances, concerts and fishy-themed events take over Concarneau's streets on the last Sunday in August. Find out more at http://filetsbleus.free.fr, in French.

GASTRONOMIC HIGHLIGHTS

♥ LE BELEM €€

☎ 02 98 97 02 78; 2 rue Hélène Hascoet; menus €19.90-38.90, seafood platters €34-74; ☺ closed Wed, dinner Thu & Sun

Nautical prints, fishing floats, ships' lanterns and reclaimed lifebuoys decorate the walls of this small but popular seafooderie (one room is panelled in dark wood to resemble a ship's interior). The market's right across the way, so the ingredients are as fresh as it gets – opt for a simple sea-snack (mussels served five ways, or a combo plate of crab, oyster and langoustines) or splash out on a supersized seafood platter for two.

♥ LE BUCCIN €€

☎ 02 98 50 54 22; 1 rue Dougay Trouin; menus €16-34; ☺ lunch Sun-Wed & Fri, dinner Sat-Wed & Fri

With its creamy tablecloths, tasteful tones and impeccably folded napkins, 'The Whelk' might feel a smidgen conservative, but it's been the town's foremost fishy address for nearly two decades. Roast lemon sole, steaming pots of *cotriade du pêcheur* (fishermen's stew) and stuffed clams from the Îles de Glénan keep the devotees happy, while organised gourmets plump for the lobster 'degustation' menu, which needs to be ordered a day ahead.

♥ LE PENNTI €

☎ 02 98 97 46 02; 6 place St-Guénolé; crêpes €3-7.50; ☺ lunch & dinner

The restaurants of the *ville close* leave a lot to be desired, but this outrageously floral *crêperie* is the place if you're feeling peckish. Climbing ivy and potted plants cover the stone-clad facade, and in the homely dining room you can tuck into generous galettes and crêpes. Unsurprisingly in Concarneau, fishy flavours feature heavily.

TRANSPORT

BOAT // For boats to the Îles de Glénan, see p108.

BUS // Concarneau's most useful bus line is the 14A/B, which runs northwest to Quimper (35 minutes) and southeast to Pont-Aven (20 minutes) and Quimperlé (1¼ hours). There are four to six services daily Monday to Saturday, and one or two on Sunday.

TRAIN // The nearest train station is at Rosporden, 12km northeast between the Quimper–Lorient line and linked to Concarneau by SNCF bus.

PONT-AVEN & AROUND

Breton villages don't come much prettier than Pont-Aven, a former port and mill town huddled at the end of a wooded creek about 20km east of Concarneau. Its old water mills, river quays and smart terraced houses are a reminder of the town's heyday as an industrial centre, but Pont-Aven is better-known these days for its artistic connections – during the 19th century it became a favourite getaway for Parisian-based artists seeking fresh air, country inspiration and (most importantly) cheap rent.

ESSENTIAL INFORMATION

TOURIST OFFICES // Pont-Aven (☎ 02 98 06 04 70; www.pontaven.com; 5 place de l'Hôtel de Ville; ☺ 9.30am-7pm Mon-Sat, 10am-1pm & 3-6.30pm Sun Jul & Aug, 10am-12.30pm & 2-5pm Mon-Sat Sep-Jun)

EXPLORING PONT-AVEN

♥ ARTISTIC CONNECTIONS // FOLLOW IN THE FOOTSTEPS OF GAUGIN AND CO

Pont-Aven's most famous visitor was the stockbroker-turned-artist Paul Gauguin, who first arrived here in the mid-1880s. It was while working in Pont-Aven that Gauguin, along with like-minded artists such as Emile Bernard and Paul Sérusier, laid the foundations for his new

FINISTÈRE

anti-Impressionist artistic movement known as synthetism, which emphasised the importance of symbolic subjects and bright, saturated colours.

Paintings by major artists of the 'Pont-Aven School' are displayed at the **Musée de Pont-Aven** (☎ 02 98 06 14 43; place de l'Hôtel de Ville; adult/child €4/2.50; ⏱ 10am-7pm Jul & Aug, 10am-12.30pm & 2-6/6.30pm Sep-Dec & Feb-Jun), although there are only a couple of works by the master himself. More recent work by Pont-Aven artists is the focus at **Le Centre International d'Art Contemporain** (☎ 02 98 09 10 45; 10 rue de la Belle Angèle).

Sadly, the legendary boarding house where Gauguin and his chums lodged, **La Pension Gloanec**, is now a newsagency. Keep your eyes peeled for the plaque on place Paul Gauguin.

☙ EXPLORING ON FOOT // MOSEY AMONG WATERMILLS AND WOODLAND

Pont-Aven's eponymous bridge sits right in the centre of the village and marks the start of some lovely walks. Upstream from the bridge is **Promenade Xavier Grall**, a leafy walkway that leads to the **Bois d'Amour** (Wood of Love), scene of a famous meeting between Gauguin and Sérusier. Another walking trail takes in 14 mills and 15 notable houses around Pont-Aven – ask for the leaflet at the tourist office.

Downstream from the bridge, the road forks along the riverbank, leading past a pretty jumble of old houses and millponds to Pont-Aven's harbour. The road ends here, but a walking trail leads on another 9km to the heart-meltingly pretty *station balnéaire* (seaside resort) of **Port-Manech**. If you fancy continuing the walk, there's more fantastic coast and white sandy beaches between **Raguénez** and the **Pointe de Trévignon**.

From mid-April to September, the **Vedettes Aven Belon** (☎ 02 98 71 14 59; www .vedettes-aven-belon.com; adult €9.50-14.50, child €6.50-9.50) runs boat trips to Port-Manech, taking in the side-by-side estuaries of the Aven and Bélon.

☙ SWEET TREATS // SAMPLE PONT-AVEN'S BUTTERY BICKIES

Along with its artistic connections, the town is also famous for producing the rich, crumbly biscuits known as *galettes de Pont-Aven*. There are endless places to buy them around town; try **Le Boutique de Pont-Aven** (☎ 02 98 06 07 65; place Paul Gauguin) or the cake-cum-fashion shop, **Hotel Lulu-Larnicol** (☎ 02 98 06 18 51; Le Pont). You can even pay a visit to one of the major biscuit factories, **Galettes Penven** (☎ 02 98 06 02 75; Zone Artisanale de Kergazuel, 1 quai Théodore Botrel; €3) by arrangement from July to August.

GASTRONOMIC HIGHLIGHTS

☙ ESTABLISSEMENT OSTRÉICOLES LAURENT PUBLIER // KERDRUC €€

☎ 02 98 06 62 60; Kerdruc; mains €10-25, seafood platters on demand; ⏱ lunch & dinner Jul & Aug, dinner Fri & Sat, lunch Sat & Sun Apr-Jun
This wonderful oyster farm has been a local secret for years. Huge platters of crab, langoustines and top-quality *creuses* and *belons* (oysters) are served on wooden tables overlooking the river estuary in Kerdruc. You'll need to book in season, and credit cards are a no-no.

☙ LE CLOS DU MINAOUET // TRÉGUNC €€€

☎ 02 98 50 29 30; Trégunc; menus €15-40; ⏱ closed Mon
Overseen by up-and-coming chef Jean-Luc Golliot, this relaxed country restaurant in nearby Trégunc is worth seeking out for its exciting *terre-mer* dishes, par-

ticularly a fabulous salt-crust *bar de ligne* (line-caught sea bass) and a huge *coté de boeuf* (side of beef) for two.

♥ LE MOULIN DE ROSMADEC // PONT-AVEN €€€

☎ 02 98 06 00 22; Venelle de Rosmadec; menus €35-76; 🕑 closed dinner Thu & Sun

Owned by the same team of brothers behind Sur Le Pont (see following), this place is an utter spoil from start to finish. You couldn't wish for a more perfect setting, lodged in a 15-century water mill beside the Aven. Tables tumble out along the riverbank or shelter among shrubs in the back garden, and the food is seriously posh: think twice-buttered lobster, turbot with Indian spices or home-made rye bread served with the best *belon* oysters.

♥ LES GRANDES ROCHES // TRÉGUNC €€€

☎ 02 98 97 62 97; Trégunc; menus €25-47; 🕑 lunch & dinner Thu-Mon

This much-lauded address occupies a perfect pastoral setting outside Trégunc, surrounded by 5 hectares of idyllic farmland (it even has its own menhir). The restaurant is inside the old farmhouse:

seasonality and local produce underpin the menu, and the rooms are rather lovely if you fancy sleeping over.

♥ SUR LE PONT // PONT-AVEN €€

☎ 02 98 06 16 16; 11 place Paul Gauguin; menus lunch €22-28, dinner €28-32; 🕑 closed lunch Wed & Sun

This place offers stylish and contemporary dining by the Pont-Aven bridge. A just-so palette of cool greys, blacks and whites creates the feel of a big-city bistro, and the menu oozes culinary confidence – the main ingredients are listed in big, bold type, with sauces and ingredients added almost as an afterthought. Expect modern French blended with fusion flavours.

TRANSPORT

BUS // The 14A bus (two to four daily Monday to Saturday) travels between Concarneau (20 minutes) and Quimperlé (55 minutes).

QUIMPERLÉ

About 12km inland at the head of the Laïta estuary is stately **Quimperlé**, which marks the meeting-point of two rivers, the Isole and Ellé. The town's major

FINISTÈRE

∼ WORTH A TRIP ∼

From Pont-Aven the southern coastline zigzags all the way to the Morbihan border, passing through a string of pocket-sized ports that are well off the tourist track.

About 5km east of Pont-Aven, the pretty port of **Riec-sur-Bélon** lends its name to one of Brittany's most celebrated oysters, the flat, nutty *belon;* you'll find them chalked up on menus all around the old port, but our top tip is **Chez Jacky** (☎ 02 98 06 90 32; www.chez-jacky.com; mains from €15, seafood platter for 2 €83; 🕑 lunch Tue-Sun, dinner Tue-Sat).

To the south, seaside villas cluster around **Kerfany**, while fishermen's cottages huddle along the twisting lanes of **Brigneau**. Prettiest of all is tiny **Port-Merrien**, hidden away along a wooded inlet that was once a favourite hideout for Breton smugglers. **Hiking trails** first tramped by the region's *douaniers,* or customs officers, make this stretch of coastline fantastic for hikes.

landmark is the 11th-century **Church of Ste-Croix** (⊙ 9am-6pm), one of Brittany's finest examples of Romanesque architecture: inside the crypt, the 15th-century tomb of St Gurloës is said to have the power to cure migraines; a hole allows sufferers to pop their heads inside.

For a gourmet detour, don't miss Quimperlé's renowned **Bistro de la Tour** (☎ 02 98 39 29 58; 2 rue Dom Morice; menus €22-61; ⊙ lunch & dinner), where the jumble-shop decor of brass, burnished wood, vintage posters and reclaimed gramophones provides the perfect setting for superior French food, not to mention one of the finest wine lists for miles around.

Quimperlé is connected to Paris by the train line that runs to Quimper. There are also train services to Nantes and Rennes. Bus 14A (two to four daily Monday to Saturday) travels between Quimperlé and Quimper via Concarneau and Pont-Aven.

FINISTÈRE

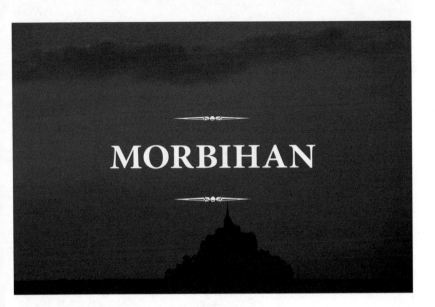

MORBIHAN

3 PERFECT DAYS

❦ DAY 1 // ANCIENT HISTORY

The Carnac *alignements* (series of standing stones; p122) are Morbihan's most un-missable sight. You'll need at least half a day to explore them, but count on a full day if you want to factor in a guided tour or a visit to other nearby sites at Locmariaquer (p127). The Carnac area is awash with great places to stay: try nearby La Villa Mane Lann (p295) for a homely welcome, or Le Lodge Kerisper (p295) for designer lines.

❦ DAY 2 // COASTLINE CRUISING

Day two is reserved for the *littoral* (coastline). Take a cobblestone wander around Vannes (p130) and a leisurely lunch at Le Roscanvec (p132), before spending the after-noon cruising around the islands of the Golfe du Morbihan (p133). See the sunset next to the Port-Navalo lighthouse, at the tip of the Presqu'île de Rhuys peninsula (p134). Overnight in luxury at the Villa Kerasy (p296).

❦ DAY 3 // CASTLE COUNTRY

Day three is for exploring Morbihan's inland charms. Top of the list are the atmos-pheric châteaux of Pontivy (p137) and Josselin (p136); if you're bringing the kids you might want to factor in a visit to the animals at Branféré (p135) or Pont-Scorff (p121), or take your time with a leisurely stroll and a country picnic on the towpaths of the Nantes–Brest Canal (p136). Spend a night in the trees at Dihan (p295), west of Auray.

MORBIHAN

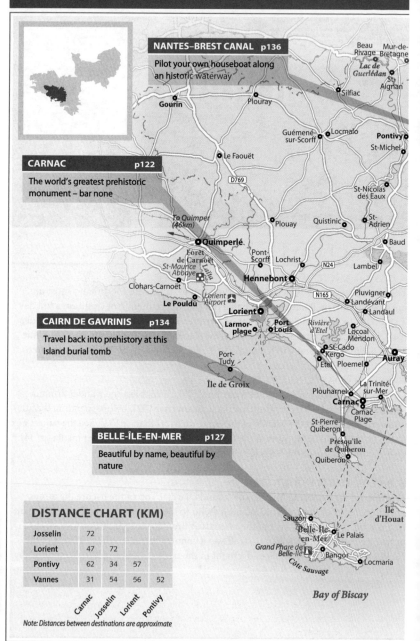

NANTES–BREST CANAL p136

Pilot your own houseboat along an historic waterway

CARNAC p122

The world's greatest prehistoric monument – bar none

CAIRN DE GAVRINIS p134

Travel back into prehistory at this island burial tomb

BELLE-ÎLE-EN-MER p127

Beautiful by name, beautiful by nature

Beau Rivage
Mur-de-Bretagne
Lac de Guerlédan
St-Aignan
Silfiac
Plouray
Gourin
Guémené-sur-Scorff
Locmalo
Pontivy
St-Michel
Le Faouët
St-Nicolas des Eaux
D769
Plouay
Quistinic
St-Adrien
Baud
To Quimper (46km)
Quimperlé
Pont-Scorff
Lochrist
N24
Lambel
Forêt de Carnoët
St-Maurice Abbaye
Hennebont
Clohars-Carnoët
Pluvigner
Le Pouldu
Lorient Airport
Landévant
Landaul
Lorient
Rivière d'Etel
Locoal Mendon
Larmor-plage
Port-Louis
St-Cado
Kergo
Auray
Port-Tudy
Etel
Ploemel
Île de Groix
La Trinité-sur-Mer
Plouharnel
Carnac
Carnac-Plage
St-Pierre-Quiberon
Presqu'île de Quiberon
Quiberon
Île d'Houat
Sauzon
Belle-Île-en-Mer
Le Palais
Grand Phare de Belle-Île
Bangor
Locmaria
Côte Sauvage

Bay of Biscay

DISTANCE CHART (KM)

	Carnac	Josselin	Lorient	Pontivy
Josselin	72			
Lorient	47	72		
Pontivy	62	34	57	
Vannes	31	54	56	52

Note: Distances between destinations are approximate

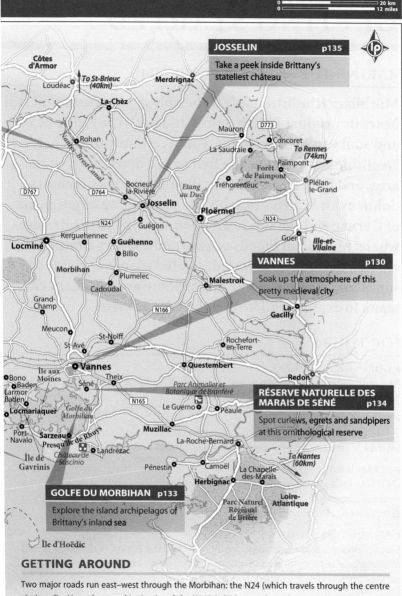

JOSSELIN p135
Take a peek inside Brittany's stateliest château

VANNES p130
Soak up the atmosphere of this pretty medieval city

RÉSERVE NATURELLE DES MARAIS DE SÉNÉ p134
Spot curlews, egrets and sandpipers at this ornithological reserve

GOLFE DU MORBIHAN p133
Explore the island archipelagos of Brittany's inland sea

GETTING AROUND

Two major roads run east–west through the Morbihan: the N24 (which travels through the centre via Josselin, Hennebont and Lorient) and the N165 (which runs along the coast via Vannes, Auray and Lorient, and roughly parallels the main TGV route). Local trains and buses connect all the coastal cities and the larger inland towns. Be prepared for traffic jams along the coast in summer, especially around Quiberon and Carnac.

MORBIHAN

MORBIHAN
GETTING STARTED

MAKING THE MOST OF YOUR TIME

Morbihan (the 'little sea') is the only *département* that still bears its original Breizh name, and if it's the Celtic heart and soul you're looking for, you'll certainly find it here. Neolithic settlers were the first to put down roots in the area, and littered around are their mysterious menhirs, dolmens and cairns, notably the upstanding *alignements* of Carnac and the mystical island tomb of Gavrinis. Elsewhere, Morbihan blends coastal and country charm: beach resorts, nature reserves and isolated islands sprinkle the southern coastline, while inland there are landmark châteaux to explore and historic canals to cruise.

TOP TOURS

❦ GOLFE DU MORBIHAN
Take an unforgettable boat trip around the atolls of the Golfe du Morbihan (p133), stopping off at the idyllic Île aux Moines en route.

❦ GAVRINIS
Guided tours are the only way to visit this atmospheric island tomb (p133) in the Golfe du Morbihan. A cross-bay boat-ride is included in the price.

❦ BELLE-ÎLE-EN-MER
Arzic Tours is a knowledgeable tour company that offers thematic trips around this beautiful island (p127), taking in Claude Monet, Sarah Bernhardt and the coastline. (☎ 06 16 25 79 46; www.arzictours.com; ☷ year-round)

❦ PRESQU'ÎLE DE RHUYS
A local, Gwen Mallajac, runs inspiring tours around the Presqu'île de Rhuys (p134) including bike trips, oyster farm visits and bird-spotting expeditions on the local marshes. (☎ 06 82 18 34 36; St-Gildas-de-Rhuys)

❦ ÎLE DE GROIX
Based in Port-Louis, Bro-Warok runs voyages to the Île de Groix (p120) aboard a langoustine boat built in Camaret in 1948. (☎ 06 09 96 26 84, 02 97 28 80 57; www.bageal.com; adult/under 12yr €45/20)

ADVANCE PLANNING

* ★ **Quiberon** Don't even think about driving there in summer.

* ★ **Carnac** Reserve ahead for guided tours around the *alignements*.

* ★ **Belle-Île** Half of Brittany heads for the beautiful island in July and August; book your boat in advance.

* ★ **Binoculars** Bring some if you're exploring the coastline.

GETTING AWAY FROM IT ALL

* ★ **Île de Groix** (p120) This island receives smaller crowds than its better-known neighbour, Belle-Île-en-Mer.

* ★ **Canal cruising** Leave the outside world behind aboard your very own barge on the Nantes–Brest Canal (p136).

* ★ **Séné Nature Reserve** (p134) Spot rare birds in unspoilt natural surroundings on the Presqu'île de Rhuys.

* ★ **Lac de Guerlédan** If the coast gets too busy, hire a kayak or relax with a picnic on the shores of this tranquil man-made lake (p138), fringed by forest and sandy bays.

TOP ANCIENT SITES

♥ MUSÉE DE PRÉHISTOIRE
Take an informative prehistorical primer (p124)

♥ ALIGNEMENTS DE KERLESCAN
The most atmospheric of the Carnac *alignements* (p123)

♥ GÉANT DU MANIO
Obelix would envy this massive menhir (p123)

♥ GRAND MENHIR BRISÉ
Morbihan's largest stone – now in bits (p127)

♥ CAIRN DE GAVRINIS
Where the ancients buried their dead (p133)

ONLINE RESOURCES

* ★ **www.culture.gouv.fr/culture/arc nat/megalithes/en/index_en.html** Excellent online resource on Morbihan's megaliths.

* ★ **www.golfedumorbihan.fr** Go on a virtual visit to the islands of this impressive gulf.

* ★ **www.morbihan.com** In French, it's an online resource for the whole of the Morbihan.

MORBIHAN

THE MORBIHAN COAST

· · · · · ·

Compared to the wild, wind-battered clifftops of Finistère, the coastline of Morbihan is a much gentler affair: white sandy beaches sprawl along much of the south coast, interspersed by two slender peninsulas, the Presqu'île de Rhuys and the Presqu'île de Quiberon, and a breathtakingly beautiful inland sea, the Golfe du Morbihan.

The coast is also where you'll find most of the *département's* sights, including the picture-perfect medieval town of Vannes and the world-famous ancient monuments of Carnac.

LORIENT & AROUND

💀 **LORIENT // THE U-BOAT CITY**
Let's face it – postwar Lorient has about as much architectural charm as a car park, but it's still an important shipbuilding and sailing centre, as well as the venue for the **Festival InterCeltique** (see boxed text, opposite). The Port de l'Orient (later shortened to Lorient) was established in the 17th century by the French East India Company, and grew into an important 18th-century trading harbour. Unfortunately, the Germans also chose it as a station for their U-boats, which meant that the city was pulverised by Allied bombing during 1945.

You can still visit the old U-boat pens at the **Base de Sous-Marins de Keroman** (☎ 02 97 21 07 84; adult/12-18yr/under 18yr €6/4/free), although the submarines themselves are long gone. Lorient's maritime heritage also features aboard the converted marine research boat, **La Thalassa** (☎ 02 97 35 13 00; www.la-thalassa.fr; Port de Plaisance; adult/5-17yr/under 5yr €6.90/5.30/free; ⊙ 10am-7pm Jul-Aug, 9.30am-12.30pm & 2-6pm Tue-Fri, 2-6pm Sat-Mon Apr-Jun & Sep).

The bus and train stations are about 600m north of the city centre; the port area, which hosts a tourist office, is a short distance further south of the centre.

PORT-LOUIS // DISCOVER THE TREASURES OF THE ORIENT
About 5km south of Lorient, Port-Louis' 16th-century **citadel** (☎ 02 97 82 56 72; adult/under 18yr €5.50/free incl both museums; ⊙ 10am-6.30pm May-Aug, 1.30-6pm Wed-Mon Feb-Apr & Sep–mid-Dec) houses two excellent museums.

The **Musée de la Compagnie des Indes** traces the history of the French East India Company and its lucrative trade with the Far East and the New World: among its exotic exhibits you'll discover Chinese porcelain, African art, lavish Indian fabrics and some fascinatingly inaccurate historical maps.

Nearby, the **Musée National de la Marine** collects together a wealth of underwater treasures recovered by the French submariner Franck Goddio, including the cannons of a ship belonging to the East India Company, and plenty of gold, porcelain and other salvaged booty. A new section is devoted to the history of marine rescue.

💀 **ÎLE DE GROIX // AN ISLAND ESCAPE**
About 14km offshore from Lorient lies the Île de Groix, a teeny island that once sustained its inhabitants solely on the tuna trade, but now serves mainly as a stopover for passing pleasure yachts. Fringed by quiet beaches and cliff paths, as well as a protected bird reserve, it's a

FESTIVAL INTERCELTIQUE

Every August, 500,000 visitors pack into Lorient's concrete streets for the **Festival InterCeltique** (www.festival-interceltique.com), France's largest cultural festival. For 10 days the city swings to the sound of pipes, drums, horns and strings from all Europe's Celtic regions – Cornwall, Galicia, the Isle of Man, Ireland, Wales, Scotland and, of course, Brittany. The more unusual instruments on show include the *bodhrán* (Celtic drum) and the *bombarde* (an oboe-like instrument) and *biniou kozh* (a type of Breton bagpipe), but the festival isn't just about music – street theatre, circus troupes and comedy all have their place in the celebrations.

Events take place all over the city, and the highlight is a grand street parade on the opening weekend. You'll need tickets to the bigger events, but off-the-cuff gigs and free *festou-noz* (night concerts) are all part of the fun of this great cultural knees-up. Event guides, maps and festival information are available from the **Lorient Tourist Office** (☎ 02 97 84 78 00; accueil@lorient-tourisme.fr; Maison de la Mer, quai de Rohan; 9am-8pm during festival, 9.30am-1pm & 2-7pm Mon-Sat, 10am-1pm Sun Jul-Aug, 10am-noon & 2-6pm Mon-Fri, 10am-noon & 2-5pm Sat Apr-Jun & Sep, 10am-noon & 2-5pm Mon-Fri, 10am-noon Sat Oct-Feb).

paradise for nature lovers. If you're curious about how life was once lived on the island, you can drop by the **Écomusée de Groix** (9.30am-12.30pm & 3-7pm Jul-Aug, 10am-12.30pm & 2-5pm Tue-Sun Apr-Jun & Sep-Nov, 10am-12.30pm & 2-5pm Wed, Sat & Sun Dec-Mar), which collects archaeological finds, vintage fishing gear and Breton costumes in the island's old tuna cannery.

Companies including **SMN** (☎ 08 20 05 60 00; www.smn-navigation.fr) and the **Compagnie des Îles** (☎ 08 25 13 41 00; www.compagnie desiles.com) run trips between April and September from Clohars-Carnoët, about 20km west of Lorient, but our favourite operator is **Bro-Warok** (see p118).

❦ LE PARC ZOOLOGIQUE DE PONT-SCORFF // BEARS AND BABOONS IN THE MORBIHAN COUNTRYSIDE

Budding Doctor Doolittles are spoilt for choice in Morbihan, with a wealth of wild attractions to explore. Top of the popularity list is this **zoo** (☎ 02 97 32 60 86; www.zoo-pont-scorff.com, in French; adult/child

€16/10.50; 9am-7pm Jun-Aug, 9.30am-6pm Apr-May & Sep, 9.30am-5pm Oct-Mar), whose residents include tigers, lions, monkeys, elephants, rhinos and bears, as well as a colony of extrovert parrots who put on a daily aerial display.

❦ HARAS NATIONAL D'HENNEBONT // HORSEY HEAVEN

Napoleon founded his *haras* (stud farm) at Langonnet in 1806, but the stables later upped sticks to **Hennebont** (☎ 02 97 65 56 55; www.haras-hennebont.fr; adult/5-17yr/under 5yr €7.10/5.50/free; 10am-7pm Jul-Aug, 9.30am-12.30pm & 2-6pm Mon-Fri, 2-6pm Sat & Sun Apr-Jun & Sep-Nov), which currently houses around 60 pedigree stallions. Guided tours take in the stables, tack room and smithy, and there are regular equestrian displays throughout the year, including a nighttime spectacular in August (€16/12 per adult/child). The stables also own a collection of vintage *hippomobiles* (horse-drawn vehicles); you can take a trip in an antique *calèche* (carriage) from July to August for €3/2 per adult/child.

MORBIHAN

GASTRONOMIC HIGHLIGHTS

♥ LE JARDIN GOURMAND // LORIENT €€

☎ 02 97 64 17 24; 46 rue Jules Simon; menus €28-40; ☯ lunch Wed-Sun, dinner Wed-Sat

Lorient has some fancy establishments but our current fave is this laid-back bistro run by local culinary star Nathalie Beauvais (who's just published her first recipe book, *Trop Mad*). Her raison d'être is locally bought, market-fresh ingredients, cooked with a minimum of fuss to bring out their natural flavours.

♥ RESTAURANT AVEL VOR // PORT-LOUIS €€€

☎ 02 97 82 47 59; 25 rue de Locmalo; menus €28-69

This up-and-comer in Port-Louis has just picked up a shiny new Michelin star, so reservations have become a must. The chef's culinary inspiration comes from the 'whims of the winds and the tides' – in other words, expect top-quality seasonal produce with a fishy focus. Modern art and bold colours complete the classy package.

TRANSPORT

Lorient is a major train hub, with frequent links east to Auray, Vannes and beyond, and west to Quimper. Public transport to Hennebont and Port-Louis is patchy outside of school term times, so your own wheels will be useful.

CARNAC

pop 4600

Brittany isn't short on megalithic sites, but nowhere packs the same prehistoric punch as Carnac. Spreading out across the plains inland from the Baie de Quiberon is one of the great wonders of the ancient world – a huge complex of ancient stone *alignements* constructed by Neolithic people between 5000 BC and 3500 BC. Consisting of more than 3000 menhirs, it's the world's greatest prehistoric site, and inevitably draws huge crowds in summer. Ancient attractions aren't the only draw – beach bums and water babies make a beeline for Carnac's glittering white beaches, which fan along the coastline for 3km to the south of town.

ORIENTATION

Carnac is split into two sections: the beach resort of Carnac-Plage and the commercial centre of Carnac-Ville, 1.5km to the north. The nearest megalithic site, Ménec, is about 1km north of Carnac-Ville.

ESSENTIAL INFORMATION

TOURIST OFFICES // Carnac-Plage (☎ 02 97 52 13 52; www.ot-carnac.fr; 74 av des Druides, Carnac-Plage; ☯ 9am-7pm Mon-Sat, 3-7pm Sun Jul-Aug, 9.30am-noon & 2-6pm Mon-Sat Sep-Jun); Carnac-Ville (☎ 02 97 52 13 52; place de l'Église, Carnac-Ville; ☯ 9.30am-12.30pm & 2-6pm Mon-Sat Apr-Sep)

EXPLORING CARNAC

♥ ALIGNEMENTS DE CARNAC // WANDER THE WORLD'S GREATEST PREHISTORIC COMPLEX

It's difficult to appreciate the scale of Carnac's megaliths from the ground – it's only when you see them from an aerial perspective that you realise what a monumental project this must have been for the ancient architects. Carnac's 3000 stones are arranged in a series of side-by-side rows, covering 6km end to end and a total area of around 40 hectares, making it by far and away the largest ancient site ever discovered.

MORBIHAN

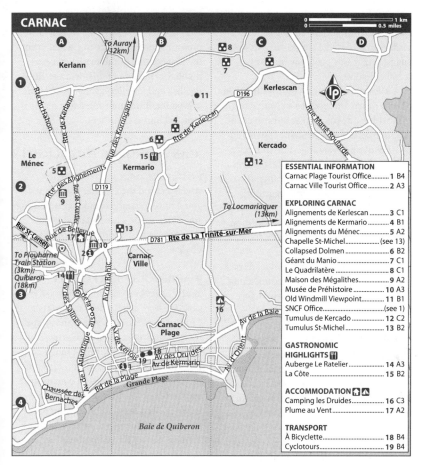

CARNAC

The menhirs are divided between three main fields. Most people start at the **Alignements du Ménec**, the largest field with a total of 1099 stones. Directly opposite is the **Maison des Mégalithes** (☎ 02 97 52 89 89; rte des Alignements; ☷ 9am-8pm Jul-Aug, 9am-7pm May-Jun, 10am-5pm Sep-Apr), which explores the history of the site and has a rooftop viewpoint overlooking the *alignements*.

In fact, the *alignements* are better followed in an east–west direction. Head along the D196 from Ménec for 3km, following signposts to the Kerlescan car park. From here it's a short stroll to the **Alignements de Kerlescan**, the smallest grouping, consisting of 555 menhirs arranged in 13 lines. A 15-minute woodland walk brings you to **Le Quadrilatère**, a rectangular arrangement of mini-menhirs, and the **Géant du Manio**, the tallest menhir in the complex at over 6m high.

About 500m west, a turn-off leads from the D196 to the **Tumulus de Kercado** (admission €1). Dating from around 3800 BC, it's one of the best-preserved tumuli in France, still covered by its

MORBIHAN

original grassy burial cairn and menhir. Inside the tomb, a carved double-axe is visible on one of the supporting stones, suggesting it was probably built for a tribal chieftain.

A kilometre further west on the D196, another turn-off leads to a stone windmill which affords a great view over the **Alignements de Kermario**, consisting of 1029 menhirs arranged in 10 lines, each over 1km long. The tallest stones (some over 2m high) are arranged towards the western end, suggesting the positioning of a particularly sacred area. A small, partly collapsed **dolmen** sits opposite the entrance to La Côte restaurant.

Further west, a walking trail leads past the Chez Céline *crêperie*, winding along the northern flank of Kermario before circling back to the Ménec stones.

On your way back into Carnac, 400m northeast of place de l'Église, a little chapel sits on top of the **Tumulus St-Michel**, a great 15m-high burial mound that dates back to at least 5000 BC. Sadly, it's off limits to everyone except visiting archaeologists.

The *alignements* are fenced off between Easter and September to allow vegetation to regrow, although sections of all three are accessible from October and Easter. The rest of the year, **guided visits** (adult/18-25yr €4.50/4; in English at least once daily Jul & Aug) are organised by the Maison des Mégalithes.

❦ MUSÉE DE PRÉHISTOIRE // PREHISTORY 101

In the centre of Carnac-Ville, the **Museum of Prehistory** (☎ 02 97 52 22 04; www .museedecarnac.com; 10 place de la Chapelle; adult/child €5/2.50; ☽ 10am-6pm daily Jul-Aug, 10am-12.30pm & 2-6pm Wed-Mon Apr-Jun & Sep, 10am-12.30pm & 2-5pm Wed-Mon Oct-Mar) is a must for ancient history buffs. Jointly founded in 1881 by a Scotsman, Robert Miln, and a Breton archaeologist, Zacahrie Le Rouzic, the museum chronicles life in Carnac from the Palaeolithic to the medieval era: highlights include prehistoric axe-heads, needles and jewellery, some fascinating carved menhirs and even a few reconstructed burial chambers.

GASTRONOMIC HIGHLIGHTS

Restaurants, cafés and bars line the streets behind the Grande Plage, but you'll have to head inland for something smarter. Carnac's food market is on Wednesday and Sunday, just off place de l'Église.

❦ AUBERGE LE RATELIER €€

☎ 02 97 52 05 04; 4 chemin du Douet, Carnac-Ville; menus €21-48; ☽ daily May-Sep, Thu-Mon Oct-Apr
This former stables, covered in ivy and built from Breton stone, is Carnac-Ville's best address for traditional French cooking. Nouvelle cuisine it ain't – dishes are rich, hearty and dominated by country staples (duck leg, ham hock, beef entrecôte) – but the raftered dining room is lovely, and the €48 'lobster adventure' *menu* is a must for seafoodies.

❦ LA CÔTE €€€

☎ 02 97 52 02 80; Kermario; menus €24-85; ☽ lunch Wed-Sun, dinner Tue-Sun in summer
Lodged inside a converted farmhouse opposite the Kermario megaliths, The Coast is rightly championed as one of the district's top tables. Overseen by its chef-patron, Pierre Michaud, it's made its name with subtle and adventurous *terre-mer* (sea and countryside) food served with a dash of designer style. There's a choice of dining rooms: one with rustic beams and Breton bricks, another with bucolic garden views.

BRITTANY'S MEGALITHS

Carnac might be Brittany's best-known (and biggest) prehistoric site, but there are many more to discover, including the Alignements de Lagatjar (p97), dolmens and menhirs near Locmariaquer (p127) and the burial cairns of Barnenez (p83) and Gavrinis (p133).

The majority were built between 4500 BC and 2500 BC at a time when Neolithic hunter-gatherers were abandoning their seminomadic life in favour of a more settled agricultural existence. Around this time, ancient people all across Europe developed burial practices involving massive stone blocks, ranging from simple **cairns** (stone heaps) and **menhirs** (from the Breton 'men hir', meaning standing stone) to complex **dolmens** (chambers supported by menhirs and capstones) and **cromlechs** (stone circles). Curiously, in Brittany the fashion seems to have been for erecting rows of menhirs (known as *alignements*), rather than the stone circles found in other parts of Europe, although no-one really knows why.

Regardless of the shapes they chose, the question that still has academics and ancient historians twiddling their bowties in frustration is exactly why these ancient builders expended so much effort in creating these great stone structures. Some of the largest blocks at Carnac weigh several tonnes, and were transported from faraway quarries in an age when the wheel wasn't even a twinkle in its inventor's eye. Just why were these sites so important to ancient people?

Unsurprisingly, theories abound. Some experts believe that they're the remnants of an ancient phallic fertility cult, while others maintain they're celestial timepieces, seasonal calendars, meeting places or even extraterrestrial landing-stations.

Despite the more outlandish suggestions, the consensus is that they probably served some sort of spiritual or religious function. Most of the sites are closely linked with the solar axis (especially during the summer and winter solstices), perhaps suggesting religious rites in which the perpetual process of life, death and rebirth was symbolically reflected by the course of the rising and setting sun. Many of the Carnac blocks also bear decorative carvings, including abstract geometric symbols as well as axes, animals, figures and faces. Is it possible the blocks represented individual people, families or even tribes? Are they a massive communal memorial or perhaps some kind of prehistoric census? The truth is, no-one really has the foggiest idea.

TRANSPORT

BUS // Carnac's main bus stops are in Carnac-Ville outside the police station on rue St-Cornély and outside the Carnac-Plage tourist office. Useful buses go to Auray, Vannes and Quiberon.

BIKE // Bikes are an excellent way of exploring Carnac. Contact **Cyclotours** (☎ 02 97 52 06 51; 88 av des Druides) or **À Bicyclette** (☎ 02 97 52 75 08; 92 av des Druides), which rent out bikes (€7 to €10 per day) and multi-seater 'rosalies' (pedal carts; €20 to €60 per day).

TRAIN // The nearest station is in Auray (p127), though Plouharnel station is operational when the Auray–Quiberon shuttle is running during summer.

AROUND CARNAC

The coastline around Carnac is one of the Morbihan's most popular summertime holiday spots, with plenty of beaches and coastal walks to explore, not to mention one of Brittany's most attractive offshore islands – the aptly

MORBIHAN

named Belle-Île-en-Mer – easily accessible via ferry from most of the major ports.

♥ QUIBERON PENINSULA // CATCH THE CORKSCREW TO QUIBERON'S BEACHES

Another popular spot for worshippers of the sun is the **Quiberon Peninsula**, a narrow 14km-finger of land poking out into the Atlantic, west of Carnac. Once an important sardine-canning centre, these days Quiberon is prime tourist real estate; day-trippers cram onto the busy beaches along the peninsula's eastern side, while the rocky western Côte Sauvage (wild coast) is favoured by cliff-walkers and nature-watchers. The **Plage de Penthièvre**, on the peninsula's northwest side, is a fave hang-out for windsurfing, kitebuggying and the latest craze, sand-yachting.

While the sardine industry is a shadow of its former self, you can take a guided tour around one of the last remaining canneries, the **Conserverie Belle-Iloise** (☎ 02 97 50 08 77; www.labelleiloise.fr, in French; ☑ tours 10am, 11am, 3pm, 4pm Mon-Fri , 11am & 3pm Sat) before replenishing your supplies of tinned tuna, mackerel, sardines and fish spreads.

Quiberon can be hellish in the high season; you're better off ditching the car and catching the Tire-Bouchon (corkscrew) train from Auray via Plouharnel instead (opposite). There are boats from Quiberon to Belle-Île-en-Mer (p127).

♥ LA TRINITÉ-SUR-MER // SAVOUR SEAFOOD AT ITS FRESHEST

On the road towards Locmariaquer from the pretty harbour of La Trinité-sur-Mer, stop off at **Aquaculture Jaouen** (☎ 02 97 30 00 24; http://jaouenaquaculture.objectis.net, in French; St-Philibert; mains €8-20; ☑ dinner & Sun lunch in season, otherwise dinner Fri-Sun) for one of the most authentic seafood experiences you'll ever have. The cream of the day's catch – oysters, scallops, mussels, winkles, clams – is served up in the cramped, cosy surroundings of a converted boat-shed, or if you're in a hurry, you can order your *fruits de mer* to go. *À faire*, as the French might say.

TOP CAMPING

Morbihan offers some fine camping options; here are our favourites. For details of some other accommodation options in the *département,* see p295.

* ★ **Camping l'Ocean** (☎ 02 97 31 83 86; www.camping-ocean-belle-ile.com; Belle-Île-en-Mer; adult €3.60-5.20, site €5.20-8.40; ☑ Mar–mid-Nov; ☒) Top-notch pine-shaded site on Belle-Île.

* ★ **Camping des Sables Rouges** (☎ 02 97 86 81 32; www.campingdessablesrouges.com; adult €4.70-5.10, site €5-5.60; ☑ May–mid-Sep) Simple camping on the Île de Groix.

* ★ **Domaine Le Bohat** (☎ 02 97 41 78 68; www.domainelebohat.com; Sarzeau; site €19.70-41.50; ☑ mid-Apr–mid-Sep; ☒) Spacious pitches near Sarzeau and the Presqu'île de Rhuys.

* ★ **Camping Les Druides** (☎ 02 97 52 08 18; www.camping-les-druides.com; Carnac; ☑ mid-Apr–mid-Sep; ☒) The pick of Carnac's many campsites: plenty of room, shady sites and fab facilities.

* ★ **Camping des Îles** (☎ 02 99 90 30 24; www.camping-des-iles.fr; Pénestin; site €16-36; ☑ Apr–mid-Oct; ☒) Four-star camping on the coast, with heated pool, hedge-edged pitches and a beach on your doorstep.

MORBIHAN

☙ LOCMARIAQUER // ANCIENT HISTORY BY THE SEA

There are more fascinating ancient sites around Locmariaquer, a small seaside town 13km east of Carnac-Ville. The major monuments are the **Grand Menhir Brisé**, a massive 20.6m-high menhir that now lies broken on its side, and the nearby **Table des Marchand**, an impressive 30m-long dolmen. Both sites are included in the one admission price (adult/under 18yr €5/free; ⏰ 10am-7pm Jul-Aug, 10am-6pm May-Jun, 10am-12.30pm & 2-5.15pm Sep-Apr).

Just to the south near the beach is the **Dolmen des Pierres Plates**, a 24m-long chamber decorated with ancient engravings.

☙ AURAY // STROLL THIS TYPICAL BRETON PORT

Auray is a bustling commercial town scattered among the banks of its eponymous river. Its old port of **St-Goustan** is well worth a stroll, with a cluster of 16th- and 17th-century half-timbered houses dotted along the old quays – one of which, quai Franklin, commemorates the spot where the politician and polymath Benjamin Franklin first set foot on French soil while trying to win support for American independence. Place St-Sauveur has cafés and seafood restaurants. The road to St-Goustan is lined with little galleries and antique shops.

TRANSPORT

BOAT // For boats from Quiberon to Belle-Île, see p130.
TRAIN // Trains from Auray go to Vannes (€5.50, 11 minutes), Lorient (€6.30, 20 to 30 minutes), Quimper (€14.90 to €17.90, one hour), Rennes (€20.50, 80 minutes), Nantes and Paris Montparnasse (€66.60 to €88.80, 3½ hours direct). From July to August only, the **Tire-Bouchon** train runs several times daily between Auray and Quiberon (€2.50, 40 minutes), replaced by buses from September to June.

BELLE-ÎLE-EN-MER

Rarely has an island suited its name as well as Belle-Île-en-Mer, Brittany's 'beautiful island in the sea', which juts out from the rolling Atlantic 15km south of Quiberon. At 20km by 9km, it's the largest of Brittany's offshore islands, and arguably the most dramatic: rugged cliffs and rock stacks line the island's west coast, while gorse and wildflowers carpet the interior and quiet coves, and sleepy seaside communes nestle along the eastern side. For centuries the island served as a key naval base, and later attracted a stream of 18th- and 19th-century artists including Van Gogh, Monet, Matisse and the famous French actress Sarah Bernhardt. These days 35,000 visitors make the hop across to Belle-Île every year, and if you've only got time to visit one Breton island, you'd be wise to follow in their footsteps.

ORIENTATION

Belle-Île has four main settlements: the main port of Le Palais is on the east side of the island, with smaller Sauzon in the northeast, Bangor in the south and little Locmaria in the southeast.

ESSENTIAL INFORMATION

TOURIST OFFICES // Le Palais (☎ 02 97 31 81 93; www.belle-ile.com, in French; quai Bonnelle; ⏰ 9am-7.30pm Mon-Sat, 8.45am-1pm Sun Jul-Aug, 9am-12.30pm & 2-6pm Mon-Sat Sep-Jun)

EXPLORING BELLE-ÎLE

☙ LE PALAIS // TOUR THE ISLAND CITADEL

Belle-Île is dominated by its forbidding citadel, fortified by Vauban in 1683 to protect the island from seaborne raids, and later used as a military prison and

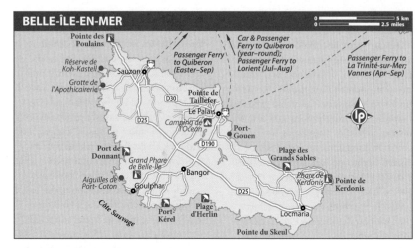

BELLE-ÎLE-EN-MER

a German stronghold during WWII (it was eventually liberated in May 1945, nearly a year after D-Day). The citadel's **ramparts** make for a fascinating walk, studded with fortified gates and bastions, and you can delve into local history at the **Musée Historique** (☎ 02 97 31 84 17; adult/child €6.10/3.05; ☯ 9.30am-7pm Jul & Aug, 9.30am-6pm Sep, Oct & Apr-Jun, 9.30am-noon & 2-5pm Nov-Mar) or wander around the town quays, lined with bobbing fishing boats and people downing an afternoon pastis.

♥ POINTE DES POULAINS //
COASTAL VIEWS AND SARAH
BERNHARDT CONNECTIONS

The island's northernmost point juts out at **Pointe des Poulains**, 3.5km to the northwest of the pastel port of **Sauzon**. Flanked by craggy cliffs, this windswept headland was the favourite summer getaway for Sarah Bernhardt, the celebrated French actress and doyenne of the 19th-century French stage. Bernhardt first visited the island in 1894 during an affair with the painter Georges Clairin, and despite losing a leg to gangrene in 1915 (the result of a freak stage accident), continued to visit the island

until her death in 1923. Although her original summer house was largely destroyed during the German occupation in WWII, an **exhibition** (adult/under 13yr €4/free; ☯ 10.30am-5pm Apr-Sep) now explores her life and work.

♥ EXPLORING THE COASTLINE //
SPOT SEAGULLS AND KITTIWAKES
ALONG THE CÔTE SAUVAGE

Belle-Île's sea-smacked coastline is pocked by rugged inlets and tucked-away coves. The most spectacular stretch is along the island's west side, known as the **Côte Sauvage**. Southwest of the Pointe des Poulains is the **Grotte de l'Apothicairerie**, a great sea cave where the waves thunder in from both sides. Sea caves and rock stacks pepper the shore, notably at the **Aiguilles de Port-Coton**, depicted in a series of canvases by Claude Monet.

The island also has some lovely beaches; the largest is **Plage des Grands Sables**, which cuts a stately curl for 2km between Le Palais and the island's eastern tip. **Port de Donnant**, on the island's opposite side, is more secluded, but swimming is dangerous due to rip-tides.

Port-Kérel and Plage d'Herlin, on the south side, are best for kids.

The best way to appreciate the island's coastal charms is from the 95km *sentier côtier* (coastal footpath), which rings the island and allows access to the more secluded spots. Ask at the tourist office for a leaflet detailing possible routes and overnight stays.

For tours of the island, see p118. From July to August, there are organised **bird-watching expeditions** (☎ 06 43 88 04 43, 02 97 31 63 67; sepnb.belle-ile@wanadoo.fr; ☉ 10am, 2pm & 4pm) to the island's bird reserve at Koh Kastell.

☙ ÎLE D'HOUAT & ÎLE D'HOËDIC // PLAY ROBINSON CRUSOE FOR A DAY

The tiny twin islands of Houat and Hoëdic (Breton for 'duck' and 'duckling') lie east of Belle-Île, topped by crumbling Vauban-built forts and fringed by patches of golden sand. Île de Houat is the larger, at around 5km long and barely 1km wide, but you can circumnavigate the coast path in a day, factoring in stops at the island's old fishing harbour of **Houat** and the **Éclosarium** (☎ 02 97 52 38 38; admission €4; ☉ 10am-6pm Jul-Aug, 10am-noon & 2-6pm Easter-Jun & Sep), a marine research station devoted to the study of plankton (it's more interesting than it sounds). The best beach is the **Plage de Tre'ach-er-Goured**, on the southeastern side of the island.

Île d'Hoëdic is even titchier – home to just 150 people and a handful of hardy fishing smacks. You can comfortably conquer the island in a couple of hours, although its fine sandy beaches will probably cause a few delays along the way.

Compagnie des Îles (☎ 08 25 13 41 00; www.compagniedesiles.com) runs boat trips to Houat and Hoëdic from Le Palais, as well as mainland ports including Loc-mariaquer, Port-Navalo, Le Croisic and Vannes. **Krog e Barz** (☎ 06 86 40 71 52; www .krog-e-barz.com; half-/full-day €30/50), in Port Navalo, offers expeditions to Houat, Hoëdic and along the River Auray in a lovingly restored *langoustier* (langoustine boat).

GASTRONOMIC HIGHLIGHTS

☙ LA TABLE DU GOUVERNEUR €€€
☎ 02 97 31 82 57; Le Palais; menus €25-68; ☉ lunch Mon-Sat, dinner daily

A regal location in the former governor's mansion sets the tone for this classy restaurant, where the formal French food is mirrored by a penchant for period elegance (antique tables, old-world wallpaper, 18th-century chimney). The setting is sober, so the Governor's table attracts a suitably well-heeled clientele.

☙ LE CONTRE QUAI €€€
☎ 02 97 31 60 60; rue St-Nicolas, Sauzon; menus €42-60; ☉ dinner

This Sauzon restaurant has a reputation that reaches far beyond its island setting thanks to an inventive chef who serves up some of the most creative seafood in southern Brittany. The menu is a real sea-sourced smorgasbord, and revolves around whatever happens to flop onto the quayside – if they're on offer, plump for the marinated sardines, stuffed crab or sea bass in spider crab *jus*.

☙ LE GOÉLAND €€
☎ 02 97 31 81 26; 3 quai Vauban, Le Palais; mains €22-30; ☉ closed lunch Tue & Wed in low season

For laid-back dining in Le Palais, you can't really top the Seagull's choice of settings: plump for the ground-floor brasserie or a more formal room upstairs. Menuwise, look out for island-raised lamb crusted with Guérande salt or turbot and monkfish caught off the Morbihan coastline.

MORBIHAN

TRANSPORT

BOAT // The quickest trip to Belle-Île is from Quiberon with SMN (☎ 08 20 05 60 00; www.smn-navigation .fr), which runs ferries (adult/four to 18 years/under four years €26/13/free) to Sauzon April & September. Navix (☎ 08 25 13 21 00; www.navix.fr) goes to Le Palais from Vannes (adult/four to 14 years/under four years €30/20/5, €2 supplement in July & Aug), and from La Trinité-sur-Mer in July and August.

BIKE // Scooters and pushbikes are the best way of getting around Belle-Île – take your pick from various outlets in Le Palais.

BUS // Les Cars Bleus (☎ 02 97 31 56 64; www .lescarsbleus.com, in French) and Les Cars Verts (☎ 02 97 31 81 88; www.cars-verts.com, in French) provide round-island bus tours (half-/full-day €12/14). Tickets are sold at the *gare maritime* (ferry terminal) in Quiberon or the Le Palais tourist office.

VANNES

pop 55,000

Overlooking the glittering Golfe du Morbihan, Vannes is one of the unmissable towns of southern Brittany. Encircled by sturdy walls and defensive gates, crisscrossed by meandering alleys and cobbled squares, Vannes still preserves much of its medieval atmosphere, but it's a long way from being a museum piece. Lively bistros, cafés and street markets keep the old town ticking, while around the redeveloped marina you'll find smart yachts, fishing boats and the base for one of France's top boat designers, Multiplast. Vannes is a great base for exploring the Morbihan region, and if it all gets too hectic, the scattered archipelagos of the Golfe du Morbihan (p133) are a boat ride away.

ORIENTATION

Vannes' Port de Plaisance sits at the end of a waterway, 1.5km north of the Golfe du Morbihan. The old city extends north from the port, enclosed by the modern thoroughfares of rue Thiers and rue Francis Decker. The train station is about 1.2km northeast of the old city.

ESSENTIAL INFORMATION

TOURIST OFFICES // Vannes (☎ 08 25 13 56 10; www.tourismevannes.com; 1 rue Thiers; ☺ 9am-7pm Mon-Sat, 10am-6pm Sun Jul-Aug, 9.30am-12.30pm & 1.30-6pm Mon-Sat Sep-Jun)

EXPLORING VANNES

❤ THE OLD CITY //
COBBLESTONES AND CARVINGS IN VANNES' HISTORIC CENTRE
Once the capital of the Veneti tribe, Vannes briefly established itself as one of the area's most important market towns during the early Middle Ages. It was here in Vannes that the historic Treaty of Union between the Duchy of Brittany and the Kingdom of France was signed in 1532.

The old city is a delightful jumble of timber-framed houses and wonky merchants' mansions, especially around the medieval squares of **place des Lices** and **place Henri IV** (once the site of the city's bird market). On the eastern side of the square looms the grand edifice of the **Cathédrale St-Pierre**, a picture-perfect example of Flamboyant Gothic architecture – note the apostle statues nestled around the elaborate doorway. To the south, on the corner of rue Noë and rue Pierre Rogue, is the famous **Maison de Vannes et Sa Femme**, which sports a timber carving of a portly 16th-century shop owner and his equally well-endowed wife.

Swing to the south to view the elegant **Château de l'Hermine**, built for the Dukes of Brittany, and the **Porte Poterne**, which leads past some 19th-

MORBIHAN

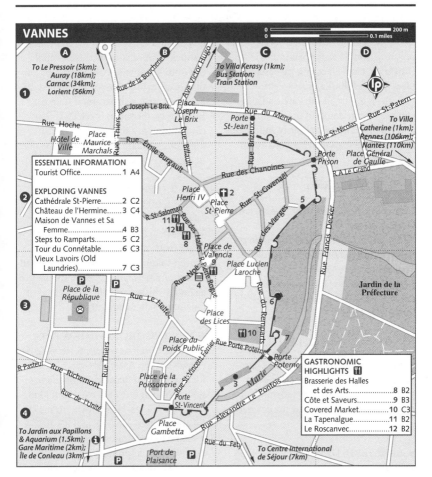

VANNES

0 _____ 200 m
0 _____ 0.1 miles

To Le Pressoir (5km);
Auray (18km);
Carnac (34km);
Lorient (56km)

To Villa Kerasy (1km);
Bus Station;
Train Station

To Villa
Catherine (1km);
Rennes (106km);
Nantes (110km)

Rue de la Boucherie
Ave Victor Hugo
Rue Joseph Le Brix
Place Joseph Le Brix
Rue du Mené
Rue St-Patern
Rue Hoche
Rue Thiers
Rue St-Nicolas
Hôtel de Ville
Place Maurice Marchais
Rue Émile Burgault
Porte St-Jean
Rue Brizeux
Porte Prison
Place Général de Gaulle
R A Le Grand
Rue Billault
Rue des Chanoines
Place Henri IV
Place St-Pierre
Rue St-Gwenaël
R St-Saloman
Place de Valencia
Rue des Vierges
Rue Noé
Rue des Halles
Place Lucien Laroche
Rue Porte Roque
Rue Francis Decker
Jardin de la Préfecture
Place de la République
Rue Le Helloco
Place des Lices
Rue du Rempart
Place du Poids Public
Rue Porte Poterne
Porte Poterne
R Pasteur
Rue Richemont
Rue Thiers
Rue de l'Unité
Place de la Poissonerie
Rue St-Vincent Ferrier
Rue Marie Le Franc
Porte St-Vincent
Rue Alexandre Le Pontois
Place Gambetta
Rue du Fety
To Jardin aux Papillons
& Aquarium (1.5km);
Gare Maritime (2km);
Île de Conleau (3km)
Port de Plaisance
To Centre International
de Séjour (7km)

MORBIHAN

century laundries into the city's lovely ornamental gardens. There's a great view from the old city **ramparts**, which can be accessed along rue des Vierges. Nearby is the **Porte Prison**, once the city's main gateway; as its name suggests, it was once used to incarcerate local miscreants and ne'er-do-wells.

♥ **BUTTERFLIES & BLACK-TIPS //
WATCH BUTTERFLIES FLUTTER BY
IN A GIANT GREENHOUSE**
Tropical plants, birds and butterflies co-habit at the **Jardin aux Papillons** (☎ 08 10

40 69 01; www.jardinauxpapillons.com; rue Daniel Gilard; adult/4-11yr/under 4yr €8.60/6/free, joint ticket with aquarium €15.10/10.60/free; ☺ 10am-7pm Jul & Aug, 10am-noon & 2-6pm Apr-Jun & Sep), a vast green-house devoted to nature's blingiest insect. Kept at a constant temperature of 27° and 80% humidity, the park houses many spe-cies including the world's largest moth, the Atlas, whose wingspan can reach 30cm across. Time your visit right and you might see butterflies emerging from their chrysalids in the hatching chamber.

Joint tickets are available with Vannes' nearby **aquarium** (☎ 08 10 40 69 01; adult/

6-11yr/under 6yr €9.50/6.50/free; ☉9am-7.30pm Apr-Sep, 10am-noon & 2-6pm Feb-Mar, 2-6pm Oct-Jan), boasting over 50 tanks brimming with clownfish, tropical corals, turtles and black-tip reef sharks.

Both sights are in the Parc du Golfe complex to the south of the port. In July and August, there's an hourly shuttle bus from Port de Plaisance between 10am and 7pm.

FESTIVALS & EVENTS

Festival de Jazz Festival Vannes swings to street-side jazz in late July.

Nuits Musicales du Golfe Classical concerts are hosted throughout August at the Cathédrale St-Pierre, and in surrounding towns.

Fêtes d'Arvor Bombardes (oboes), binious (bagpipes) and folk groups play it up at this fest-noz (night festival) in late August.

GASTRONOMIC HIGHLIGHTS

Cafés are scattered around place Gambetta, and there's a food market every Wednesday and Saturday morning on place du Poids Public, near the covered market.

☻ BRASSERIE DES HALLES ET DES ARTS €

☎ 02 97 54 08 34; 9 rue des Halles; menus €15-25; ☉lunch & dinner

Light, bright and buzzy, this modern brasserie is a fine bet for Mediterranean flavours. Tuck into a club sandwich or a steaming bowl of mussels for lunch, or plump for langoustines or buttered sea bass by night. The interior is a blend of chrome, stone and bold Breton artwork courtesy of a Concarneau-based painter.

☻ CÔTE ET SAVEURS €

☎ 02 97 47 21 94; 8 rue Pierre-Réné Rogue; menus €12-25; ☉lunch & dinner

Solid French cooking in an old merchant's house steps from the Maison de Vannes. Umbrella-topped tables spill out onto the outside cobbles, or you can duck inside into a cosy stone-walled dining room with a smart spiral staircase. Either way, the menu is eclectic – bay-caught oysters and mango monkfish meet unusual fare such as kangaroo fillet in a green pepper sauce.

☻ LA TAPENALGUE €

☎ 02 97 42 69 65; 23 rue des Halles; ☉9am-7pm daily

The place in town for Breton goodies: sweet treats including kouign amann (butter cake), Pont-Aven bickies and salt-butter caramels, plus savoury spoils such as Eddu whisky, and big canvas bags of Guérande salt. Mmmmm.

☻ LE PRESSOIR // SAINT-AVÉ €€€

☎ 02 97 60 87 63; 7 rue de l'Hôpital; menus €35-94; ☉lunch Wed-Sun, dinner Wed-Sat

Renowned chef Bernard Rambaud has set up shop in quiet St-Avé, about 8km north of Vannes. He's known for his artful approach to cooking, and it's almost a shame to tuck into some of his more extravagant sculptural creations. Expect meat, fish and game presented with serious panache.

☻ LE ROSCANVEC €€€

☎ 02 97 47 15 96; www.roscanvec.com; 17 rue des Halles; menus €30-60; ☉lunch & dinner Tue-Sat

Lost among the timbers of the old city, this fine-diner is the address to recommend in Vannes. Its chef, Thierry Seychelle, has trained with some of Brittany's top names, and it shows: his trademark six-course 'Hedonist Menu' combines seasonal French classics with global flavours. The 15th-century building is a treat as well: all ancient

MORBIHAN

wood, rough stone and an old-country atmosphere.

TRANSPORT

BOAT // See p130 for boats to Belle-Île and below for trips around the Golfe du Morbihan.

TRAIN // Vannes has regular TGVs west to Quimper (€17.40, 70 minutes), Lorient (€8.80, 30 minutes) and Auray (€3.70, 10 minutes). Eastbound trains serve Paris (€65 to €87.20, 3¼ hours), Rennes (€18.30 to €21.50, 70 minutes) and Nantes (€19.20 to €21.60, 1¼ hours).

BUS // Local buses travel to the Presqu'île de Rhuys and other local destinations, but services are limited outside summer. Ask at the tourist office.

GOLFE DU MORBIHAN

This sparkling island-studded bay was fashioned at the end of the last ice age, when rising sea levels flooded a lowland plain to the southwest of Vannes, creating dozens of tiny islands and a unique habitat for all kinds of marine life and migratory seabirds. A narrow 1km-wide channel is all that stops Brittany's 'little sea' from becoming an enclosed lagoon, and it's a glorious place to experience Breton nature at its most unspoilt – a fact that's clearly not lost on the nation's powers-that-be, who've recently made the Golfe de Morbihan Brittany's newest *parc naturel régional*. About time too.

♥ BAY CRUISING // EXPLORE ISLAND ARCHIPELAGOS

Around 40 islands peep out from the shallow waters of the Morbihan gulf: some are barely sandy specks of land, while others harbour communities of fishermen, farmers and artistic types seduced by the island lifestyle, not to mention the odd incognito celeb looking for the ultimate escape from the paparazzi's unwelcome attentions.

The bay's largest island is the 6km-long **Île aux Moines** (Monks' Island), so-called because it was once occupied by a community of Cistercian monks. They weren't the island's first inhabitants; ancient Bretons were here over 3000 years before, building the spectacular stone circle of **Kergonan** (Brittany's largest). The island's other notable features are its woodlands, whose romantic names (the Wood of Sighs, the Wood of Love, the Wood of Regrets) have unsurprisingly inspired a panoply of local legends.

Nearby **Île d'Arz** (Bear Island) is smaller – just 3km long and 1km wide – but it's worth a visit for its secluded sands and coastal walks, as well as several high-class sailing schools.

Lots of companies offer scenic cruises: the big boys include **Compagnie des Îles** (☎ 08 25 13 41 00; www.compagniedesiles.com) and **Navix** (☎ 08 25 13 21 00; www.navix.fr), both based in Vannes. Quick half-day trips start from €15/9 per adult/child; longer cruises taking in the major islands cost around €29/19.

If you want to cruise in style, the only way to go is aboard a traditional *sinagot,* a rigged sailboat that was once synonymous with this stretch of the Morbihan coastline. **Les Amis de Sinagot** (☎ 06 14 93 04 69; www.amis-du-sinagot.net) owns the only original *sinagot* still in existence, *Les Trois Frères* (since 1985 it's been classed as an historic monument). These days it's been joined by a modern sister vessel, *Le Joli Vent;* cruises start at €30/50 for a half-/full-day, but you'd be wise to book well ahead.

♥ GAVRINIS, AN ISLAND TOMB // VISIT A BURIAL CHAMBER IN THE HEART OF THE BAY

The tiny **Île de Gavrinis**, at the western end of the gulf, conceals one of

Morbihan's most evocative prehistoric monuments. The **Cairn de Gavrinis** (☎ 02 97 57 19 38; www.gavrinis.info; adult/8-17yr/under 8yr €12/5/free incl guided tour & ferry; ☺ 9.30am-7pm Jul-Aug, 9.30am-12.30pm & 1.30-6.30pm Apr-Jun & Sep) is the longest dolmen in France, 14m long, 50m across, 8m high and over 3500 years old. Many of the 29 supporting menhirs are scrawled with intricate carvings – spirals, shields, snakes, double-headed axes – but the real mystery is exactly how the ancient builders transported these great stone blocks across 4km of open water. Guided tours include the ferry trip and leave from the village of Larmor-Baden, 14km southwest of Vannes.

♥ BIRDWATCHING ON THE BAY // BRING OUT YOUR INNER TWITCHER

The bay's powerful tides, temperate climate and varied vistas of salt marsh, mudflat and isolated island make this one of the region's best places for birdwatching. Hundreds of rare species take a break here en route to warmer climes, from spoonbills, white egrets, curlews and sandpipers to a whole host of assorted waders, ducks and grebes.

The **Réserve Naturelle des Marais de Séné** (☎ 02 97 66 92 76; www.reservedesene.com, in French; adult/child €4/2.50; ☺ 10am-1pm & 2-7pm Jul-Aug, 2-7pm Apr-Jun, 2-6pm early-Feb–early-Mar), 6km southeast of Vannes, is the perfect place to start, with several observation hides overlooking the local tidal marshes, and a visitor centre stocked with maps, guidebooks and twitching supplies.

♥ PRESQU'ÎLE DE RHUYS // CHÂTEAUX, SPOONBILLS AND SANDY BEACHES

This slender peninsula curls around the gulf's southern edge, ending at the picturesque harbour of **Port-Navalo**,

crowned by a coastal lighthouse and separated by a scant kilometre of open water from the neighbouring headland. The area is littered with ancient tombs, including another impressive burial cairn at **Petit Mont** (☎ 06 03 95 90 78; adult/8-17yr/under 8yr €6/3/free; ☺ 11am-6.30pm Jul-Aug, 2.30-6.30pm Apr-Jun & Sep), whose menhirs bear similar symbols to Gavrinis.

Further east is the **Château de Suscinio** (☎ 02 97 41 91 91; adult/8-17yr/under 8yr €7/2/free; ☺ 10am-7pm Apr-Sep, 10am-noon & 2-6pm Oct & Feb-Mar, 10am-noon & 2-5pm Nov-Jan), constructed in stages between the 13th and 15th centuries as a residence for Brittany's dukes. Carefully restored over the last three decades, it's a textbook example of a medieval castle, ringed by a deep moat and protected by pointy turrets; but its most famous feature is a richly decorated floor consisting of over 30,000 hand-painted tiles, featuring a menagerie of dragons, serpents, hydra, harpies and other mystical beasties.

About 4km north of the château near Sarzeau, the **Réserve de Duer** offers fantastic walking and bird-spotting – keep your peepers peeled for spoonbills, winter teals, avocets, hen harriers, terns and shelducks – or if you're feeling lazy, plonk yourself down for a picnic on the sands of **Landrézac**, a 5km beach that unfurls along the southern coastline.

For tours of the area, see p118.

INLAND MORBIHAN

· · · · · ·

Morbihan is one of the few Breton *départements* where the countryside attractions rival those of the coast. Carpeted by broad green fields and quiet copses, spotted with market towns and stately chateaux, and bisected by one of the great French engineering projects of the 19th century, the Nantes–Brest Canal, it's an area that's tailor-made for touring – either by car or, better still, on two wheels.

ROCHEFORT-EN-TERRE & AROUND

♥ ROCHEFORT-EN-TERRE // TAKE AN ARCHITECTURAL TRIP INTO THE MIDDLE AGES

You won't spy any signposts or telephone wires on the cobbled streets of Rochefort-en-Terre – this lovely village perched on a rocky outcrop above the Gueuzon River has made a concerted effort to preserve its old-world appearance. It's a wonderful wander; place des Puits and Grande-Rue are lined with granite mansions, slate-roofed houses and flower-filled window boxes, and the town's château (☎ 02 97 43 31 56; adult €4; ☺ 10am-6.30pm Jul-Aug, 2-6.30pm Jun & Sep, 2-6.30pm Sat & Sun Apr-May) contains a regional museum, as well as various bits-and-bobs belonging to its former owner, the American painter Alfred Klots, who bought the castle in 1907 and spent the rest of his days restoring it to its former splendour.

♥ QUESTEMBERT // BE ASTONISHED BY THIS MEDIEVAL MARKET

This tiny village's landmark is its magnificent timber-beamed market, carved by skilled craftsmen in 1552 and restored in 1675. It's a shining example of medieval carpentry: 55m long, 10m high, with a roof surface in excess of 1100 sq metres. There are other fine examples in other Breton towns including Le Faouët, Plouescat and Clisson.

PARC ANIMALIER ET BOTANIQUE DE BRANFÉRÉ // SET OUT ON A BRETON SAFARI

North of Le Guerno, this animal park (☎ 02 97 42 94 66; www.branfere.com, in French; adult/13-17yr/4-12yr €13/11.50/8.50; ☺ 10am-6pm Jul-Aug, 10am-5pm Apr-Jun & Sep, 1.30-4pm Feb-Mar & Oct-Nov) follows the safari-park angle, with around 120 species including red pandas, flamingos, gibbons, zebras and giraffes sharing the grounds of a 40-hectare botanical park.

♥ L'AUBERGE BRETONNE // SHARE JACQUES THOREL'S PASSION FOR LOCAL PRODUCE

☎ 02 99 90 60 28; 2 place Duguesclin, La-Roche-Bernard; menus €35-135

This quietly stunning *ferme-auberge* (farm-hostel) in La-Roche-Bernard is a beauty, overseen by the Michelin-starred Jacques Thorel, a chef of Breton descent governed by an all-pervading passion for local produce. The inn is cosy, relaxed and not a smidgen snooty, and while the food is pricey, it's full of panache – giant scallops served in their shell, delicately spiced Breton lobster, pigeon pâté partnered with homemade bread.

PLOËRMEL & JOSSELIN

♥ PLOËRMEL // ADMIRE THE WORK OF MEDIEVAL CARPENTERS

Once occupied by the Dukes of Brittany, the market town of Ploërmel is worth a peep for its medieval architecture, including the Maison des Marmousets (1586), which features several intricate figures carved into its timbered facade. It's opposite the tourist office. The nearby Hôtel des Ducs de Bretagne dates back to 1150. Also check out the intricate carvings at the Église de St-Armel.

MORBIHAN

❦ **JOSSELIN // A FAIRY-TALE CASTLE ON THE OUST RIVER**
The **Château de Josselin** (☎ 02 97 22 36 45; www.chateaudejosselin.fr; adult/child €7.30/5 incl guided tour; ✆ 11am-6pm mid-Jul–Aug, 2-6pm, Apr–mid-Jul & Sep, 2pm Sat & Sun Oct) is the jewel in the crown of Brittany's castles. Founded in 1008 by Guéthenoc, Count of Porhoët, Rohan and Guéméné, the fortress was expanded in the 13th century with nine towers and a keep by Olivier de Clisson, another member of the Rohan clan (whose descendants still own the castle). Five of the towers were subsequently destroyed on the orders of Cardinal Richelieu, but Josselin received a lavish 19th-century remodelling and now boasts the finest interior of any of Brittany's castles.

Beyond the entrance gate, the castle fans out into tree-filled grounds and a central courtyard, which affords a great view of the castle's Flamboyant Gothic facade and the river below. Inside, the guided tour (in French) takes in the medieval-style dining room, a 3000-tome library, and a grand salon filled with Sèvres porcelain, Gobelins carpets and an astronomical clock donated by Louis XV. Look out for a bust of the castle's former owner, Alain de Rohan, completed by Auguste Rodin in 1910.

BRITTANY'S CANALS

Stretching between Nantes and Brest, Brittany's most historic waterway, the **Nantes–Brest Canal**, was begun in the early 19th century on the orders of Napoleon I, who wanted a secure transport route that could dodge the English frigates blockading the Breton coastline. It was one of the largest construction projects of its day, requiring 238 locks and the canalisation of several major Breton rivers. It was finally finished in 1836 at a cost of 160 million francs; after being inaugurated by Napoleon III, it was used to transport coal, timber and other raw materials, but within 50 years it had been almost completely superseded by its new-fangled rivals, the steam train and the motor car.

Brittany's canals have had a renaissance thanks to the explosion of interest in **river cruising**. Sadly the whole canal is no longer navigable thanks to the construction of the dam at Lac de Guerlédan (p138) in the 1920s, but it's still possible to sail from Nantes as far as Pontivy; in practice, many people choose to start their trip further west at **Redon**, the junction point with Brittany's other major waterway, the **Ille-et-Rance Canal**, which heads north to St-Malo via Méssac, Rennes and Dinan. If you want to extend your trip, there's another 70km of navigable water from Pontivy along the **Blavet River** to Hennebont. Even if you don't end up on the water, the canals are still well worth exploring, as the old towpaths now provide some of Brittany's loveliest hiking and cycling.

Live-on boats are available from several companies: **Cris'Boat** (☎ 02 99 71 08 05; www.crisboat.com, in French) and **Locaboat** (☎ 02 99 72 15 80; www.locaboat.com) are both based in Redon, perfectly positioned for cruising both the major canal routes. No licence is required to hire a boat, and there are various packages available depending how long you want to spend on the water – prices start from around €600 to €750 per week. For the full lowdown, contact the **Comité des Canaux Bretons** (☎ 02 97 25 38 24; www.canaux-bretons.net).

Most of the locks are manned and operated by lock-keepers, but it depends on your route – check with the boat-hire company before setting out.

MORBIHAN

On your way out, duck into the **Musée des Poupées** (Doll Museum; joint ticket with castle adult/7-14yr/under 7yr €12.20/8.40/free), a collection of over 3000 vintage dolls, toys and games amassed by Herminie de Rohan around the turn of the 20th century. The collection was lost for several decades and was eventually rediscovered hidden in the castle's granary store. Some of them are deeply, deeply spooky – don't say we didn't warn you…

☙ LA TABLE D'O // DINE WELL AND TAKE IN THE SCENERY

☎ 02 97 70 61 39; 2 rue Glatinier, Josselin; mains €15-35; ☙ sometimes closed dinner Sun & Wed out of season

The panoramic valley view from this much-recommended bistro, just a short walk from the château gates, is almost worth a review in itself. The château's turrets and the tiled rooftops of the St-Croix quarter make a lovely backdrop for Olivier Buffard's imaginative, French-orientated cooking, where you might find yourself tucking into salt-crusted cod served with *dauphinoises* potatoes, or perhaps a scallop and foie gras tart.

TRANSPORT

Public transport is very limited – SNCF coaches and several local bus companies run between Vannes, Pontivy and Josselin during school term, but timetables change on a regular basis.

NORTHWEST MORBIHAN

☙ PONTIVY // TOUR THE FORTRESS OF THE COUNTS OF ROHAN

Enormous tracts of central Brittany were once ruled by the all-powerful Rohan family, whose *seigneurial* stronghold was the **Château de Rohan** (☎ 02 97 25 12 93; adult/child €1.50/1.10; ☙ 10am-noon & 2-6pm) in Pontivy. The castle squats behind a massive encircling ditch, although only two of its original four corner turrets remain. Highlights include two decorative fireplaces (actually rescued from another manor), an incredible medieval oak-beamed roof at the top of one of the towers, and a great view across town from the enclosed ramparts. There's also a weird art installation in the base of one of the turrets by the Japanese artist Koki Watanabe.

Following the Revolution, Pontivy became Napoleon's main administrative base in Brittany. The great little general promptly ordered a swathe of new neoclassical buildings, a cutting-edge street grid system and the canalisation of the Blavet River. With customary modesty, he also decided to rename the town Napoléonville – although after the fall of the Napoleonic empire, many of the building projects remained unfinished and the locals went back to referring to themselves as Pontivyens.

☙ LA POMMERAIE // ONE OF MORBIHAN'S MOST RESPECTED TABLES €€

☎ 02 97 25 60 09; 17 quai Couvent, Pontivy; menus €20-45; ☙ lunch & dinner Mon-Sat

You could be forgiven for never stumbling across this place, hidden down by Pontivy's quays, but gastronomes will already be thoroughly au fait with The Apple Orchard. A very respected table in the *département,* it's solidly traditional in style: neat napkins, tasteful colours and formal service are the order of the day, and the menu is dominated by Breton fish and big country flavours.

❧ LAC DE GUERLÉDAN // HIKE, GO KAYAKING OR JUST HAVE A PICNIC

This beautiful, sinuous, man-made tree-fringed lake is popular with bathers, hikers and water-sports enthusiasts. There are bathing beaches and plenty of summer water-sports facilities at **Beau Rivage**, on the northern shore of the lake near the village of Caurel, and at the little bay of **Anse de Sordan** on the southern shore. A kilometre west of the lake is a picturesque old bridge, weir and lock on the Nantes–Brest Canal, near the ruined **Abbaye de Bon Repos**. The abbey was founded by Cistercian monks in 1184, but most of the grand ruins date from the 18th century.

The lakeshore can be reached by road at Beau Rivage or Anse de Sordan. Elsewhere, you'll have to walk or take a boat. The 40km **GR341 hiking trail** makes a complete circuit of the lake. There are many camping options and some other accommodation options around and near the lake. There's a **tourist office** (☎ 02 96 28 51 41; otsi.guerledan@wanadoo.fr; place de l'Église) in Mur-de-Bretagne.

❧ L'ABEILLE VIVANTE ET LA CITÉ DES FOURMIS // GET UP CLOSE TO A BEE HIVE

In Le Faouët is this **complex** (☎ 02 97 23 08 05; www.abeilles-et-fourmis.com, in French; adult/child €6/4; ◷ 10am-7pm Jul-Aug, 10am-noon & 2-6pm Apr-Jun, 2-6pm Sep-Nov), which offers a giant's-eye insight into a working bee hive and ant farm; home-made honey is for sale in the on-site shop.

LOIRE-ATLANTIQUE

3 PERFECT DAYS

❦ DAY 1 // THE URBAN ESSENTIALS

If there's one city that mustn't be missed in Brittany, it's Nantes (p144). Start at the restored château (p144), followed by visits to the fine-arts museum (p145), a picnic in the botanical gardens (p148) and an inspiring tour around the Musée Jules Verne (p145). Finish with supper at the city's quintessential brasserie, La Cigale (p149).

❦ DAY 2 // CITY EXTRAS

On day two, begin with an early morning wander around the city market (p149), followed by a tour around the mind-boggling mechanical creations of the Machines de l'Île (p148). Mosey around the Île de Nantes before heading back into town via the Île de Feydeau (p148). Have lunch at Le 1 (p149) and book an afternoon cruise with Bateaux Nantais (p148), arriving back in town for supper at Un Coin En Ville (p150) and after-hours culture at Le Lieu Unique (p150).

❦ DAY 3 // CALL OF THE WILD

Leave the city behind and head for the quiet canals and misty marshes of the Parc Naturel Régional de la Brière (p151). Factor in visits to St-Lyphard, Rozé and the chocolate-box village of Kerhinet, followed by an afternoon punt on a traditional *chaland* and a luxurious evening meal at La Mare aux Oiseaux (p153).

LOIRE-ATLANTIQUE

LOIRE-ATLANTIQUE

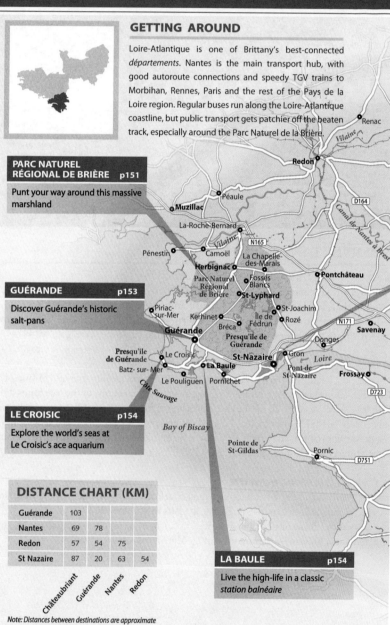

GETTING AROUND

Loire-Atlantique is one of Brittany's best-connected *départements*. Nantes is the main transport hub, with good autoroute connections and speedy TGV trains to Morbihan, Rennes, Paris and the rest of the Pays de la Loire region. Regular buses run along the Loire-Atlantique coastline, but public transport gets patchier off the beaten track, especially around the Parc Naturel de la Brière.

PARC NATUREL RÉGIONAL DE BRIÈRE   p151

Punt your way around this massive marshland

GUÉRANDE   p153

Discover Guérande's historic salt-pans

LE CROISIC   p154

Explore the world's seas at Le Croisic's ace aquarium

LA BAULE   p154

Live the high-life in a classic *station balnéaire*

DISTANCE CHART (KM)

	Châteaubriant	Guérande	Nantes	Redon
Guérande	103			
Nantes	69	78		
Redon	57	54	75	
St Nazaire	87	20	63	54

Note: Distances between destinations are approximate

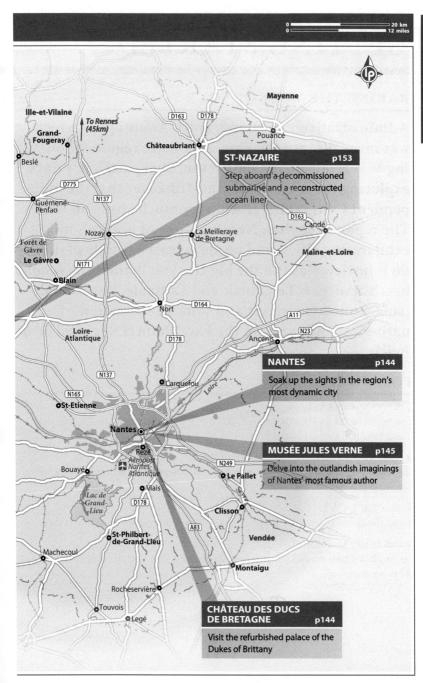

0 ━━━━ 20 km
0 ━━━━ 12 miles

Mayenne

Ille-et-Vilaine

To Rennes
(45km)

D163 D178

Pouancé

Grand-
Fougeray

Châteaubriant

Beslé

ST-NAZAIRE **p153**

Step aboard a decommissioned
submarine and a reconstructed
ocean liner

D775

N137

Guémené-
Penfao

D163

Candé

Nozay

La Meilleraye
de Bretagne

Forêt de
Gâvre

Maine-et-Loire

Le Gâvre

N171

Blain

Nort

D164

A11

Loire-
Atlantique

N23

D178

Ancenis

N137

NANTES **p144**

Carquefou

Soak up the sights in the region's
most dynamic city

N165

St-Etienne

Loire

Nantes

MUSÉE JULES VERNE **p145**

Rezé

Aéroport
Nantes-
Atlantique

N249

Delve into the outlandish imaginings
of Nantes' most famous author

Bouayé

Le Pallet

Viais

Lac de
Grand-
Lieu

D178

Clisson

St-Philbert-
de-Grand-Lieu

A83

Vendée

Machecoul

Montaigu

Rocheservière

**CHÂTEAU DES DUCS
DE BRETAGNE** **p144**

Touvois

Legé

Visit the refurbished palace of the
Dukes of Brittany

LOIRE-ATLANTIQUE GETTING STARTED

MAKING THE MOST OF YOUR TIME

Administratively speaking, Loire-Atlantique – which was hived off into the Pays de la Loire region following WWII – is no longer Breton, but spend a few days exploring the region and you'll discover that the independent Celtic spirit is still very much alive and well. The regional capital, Nantes, is one of France's most exhilarating cities, and needs at least a couple of days to do it justice. Beyond the big city you'll find *belle époque* beach resorts at Le Croisic and La Baule, historic salt-pans around Guérande and some of the nation's finest native wetlands around the Parc Naturel Régional de la Brière.

TOP TOURS

❦ NANTES CITY TOURS
The main Nantes tourist office runs tours covering the medieval city, the cathedral, Jules Verne and more (p144).

❦ BRIÈRE NATURE WALKS
Daniel Rambaud leads walking tours around the Brière (p151) focusing on the park's natural wonders. (☎ 06 62 85 29 68)

❦ AU GRE' DU VENT
Kayak the Loire-Atlantique coastline. (☎ 02 99 90 56 91; www.greduvent.fr, in French; La Baule)

❦ LES MARAIS SALANTS
Take a guided tour around the unique Guérande salt pans with Terre de Sel – Espace Sel et Nature (p153).

ADVANCE PLANNING

★ **Pass Nantes** (adult 24/48/72hr €18/28/36, 4-18yr 24/48/72hr €9/14/18) If you're spending a few days in the big city, Nantes' City Pass covers entry to the main museums, and also includes travel on public transport, shopping discounts and other freebies.

★ **Machines de l'Île** The opening hours and tour times for this Nantes art company's workshops change throughout the year and places are limited. Check and book ahead directly or via the tourist office.

GETTING AWAY FROM IT ALL

★ **Lac de Grand-Lieu** This huge lake about 14km south of Nantes is a must-see for twitchers – egrets, cormorants, herons are all residents, and with luck you might even spot a sacred ibis or two, transported here from the Branféré zoo.

★ **La Forêt du Gavre** About 45km north of Nantes, this huge forest – the region's largest – makes a soothing retreat from the coastal crowds. Guided walks are organised year-round – contact the **Maison de la Forêt** (☎ 02 40 51 25 14; http://maisondelaforet44.free.fr; 2 rte de Conquereuil, Le Gâvre).

TOP RESTAURANTS

❦ **LA MARE AUX OISEAUX**
A rural retreat par excellence with fabulous views (p153)

❦ **L'ATLANTIDE**
Fine dining that can be enjoyed with city views (p149)

❦ **LA CIGALE**
Historic brasserie in business for a century (p149)

❦ **LE 1**
Contemporary dining near the city courts (p149)

❦ **L'AUBERGE DE KERBOURG**
Country setting in Brière, cutting-edge food (p152)

ONLINE RESOURCES

★ **www.nantes-tourisme.com** Great starting point for your city explorations.

★ **www.ohlaloireatlantique.com** Information on the whole Loire-Atlantique region. In French.

★ **www.vinsdeloire.fr** Comprehensive site exploring the Loire Valley's classic wines.

NANTES

· · · · · ·

pop 534,200

Nantes' nickname, *La Reine de l'Erdre* (Queen of the Erdre), hints at the central role the city has played in Breton politics for the last thousand years – despite the fact it's no longer officially a part of Brittany (a decision that still rankles with many Nantais).

Founded by Celts around 70 BC, Nantes ('Naoned' in Breton) became the seat of power for the Duchy of Brittany and an important trading harbour and industrial centre (not to mention one of the nation's busiest slave ports). Despite the decline of many of its traditional industries, Nantes has continued the process of reinvention; with a balmy Atlantic climate, some fantastic museums, a freshly refurbished château, many cafés and restaurants and the most youthful population of any French city – 50% of Nantais are aged under 40 – it's hardly surprising that this dynamic metropolis topped a recent poll to find France's most liveable city. It's time to join the party.

ORIENTATION

Central Nantes sits snugly on the north bank of the Loire, 55km east of the Atlantic coast. The city's two main arteries are the north–south cours des 50 Otages (commemorating 50 hostages executed by the Nazis on 22 October 1941) and the long east–west boulevard connecting the station with quai de la Fosse. Both intersect at Commerce/Gare Centrale, the city-centre hub for buses and trams. The old city area stretches east to the château.

ESSENTIAL INFORMATION

EMERGENCIES // Hospital (CHR de Nantes; ☎ 02 40 08 38 95; quai Moncousu; ☾ 24hr); Police (☎ 02 40 37 21 21; 6 place Waldeck Rousseau; ☾ 24hr; ⌂ Motte Rouge) About 1km northeast of the Monument des 50 Otages.

TOURIST OFFICES // Feydeau (☎ 02 72 64 04 79; www.nantes-tourisme.com; cours Olivier de Clisson; ☾ 10am-6pm, from 10.30am Thu, closed Sun) Offers city tours (p142). St-Pierre (2 place St-Pierre; ☾ 10am-1pm & 2-6pm, from 10.30am Thu, closed Mon) Both offices sell the Pass Nantes (see p143) .

EXPLORING NANTES

♥ CHÂTEAU DES DUCS DE BRETAGNE // TOUR THIS PIMPED-UP DUCAL PALACE

Founded in the 13th century, and later used as a ducal palace, military fortress and soldiers' barracks, Nantes' ice-white castle (☎ 02 40 41 56 56; www.chateau-nantes.fr; 4 place Marc Elder; admission free; ☾ 9am-8pm Jul & Aug, 10am-7pm Sep-Jun) has had a somewhat chequered history, but after decades of neglect, a 15-year, multimillion-euro refit has restored it to its regal heyday. The refit has polished up the Renaissance facades of the Grand Logis (Dukes' Residence), Tour de la Couronne d'Or (Golden Crown Tower) and Grand Gouvernement (Governor's Palace), and even replaced missing architectural elements such as spires, gables, dormer windows and a couple of bell towers.

The castle's **museum** (adult/18-26yr €5/3; ☾ 9.30am-7pm Jul & Aug, 10am-6pm Wed-Mon Sep-May, 10am-6pm Tue-Sun Jun) has also had a thorough facelift: the old clutter has been stripped out in favour of cutting-edge multimedia exhibits documenting the city's history and evolving skyline. The weirdest exhibit is a gold-and-ivory case containing the heart of Anne de Bretagne, Duchess of Brittany, who was born at the castle in 1477.

Around the castle, a warren of medieval alleys make up the city's oldest quarter, the **Quartier Bouffay**. Many streets bear names hinting at their original inhabitants; look out for rue du Moulin (Mill St), rue des Petites Ecuries (Little Stables St) and rue des Echevins (Aldermen's St).

♥ MUSÉE JULES VERNE // TO INFINITY AND BEYOND...

Nantes' most famous son is the visionary writer Jules Verne (1828–1905), whose far-fetched tales of lunar pioneers, deep-sea explorers and globe-trotting adventurers laid the groundwork for a new literary genre known as science-fiction. Born in Nantes to seafaring parents, Jules embarked on short-lived stints as a runaway cabin boy and law student before settling into his writing career, which produced a string of classic novels including *Voyage au centre de la terre* (Journey to the Centre of the Earth, 1864), *De la terre à la lune* (From the Earth to the Moon, 1865), *Vingt mille lieues sous les mers* (Twenty Thousand Leagues under the Sea, 1869) and *Le Tour du Monde en 80 Jours* (Around the World in Eighty Days, 1872).

The family's former summer house, 2km southwest of the city centre, houses the **Musée Jules Verne** (☎ 02 40 69 72 52; 3 rue de l'Hermitage; adult/child €3/1.50; ☼ 10am-6pm Wed-Mon Jul & Aug, 10am-noon & 2-6pm Mon & Wed-Sat, 2-6pm Sun Sep-Jun; ☒ Gare-Maritime), crammed with first-edition books, annotated manuscripts and some delightful interactive displays exploring the writer's work. In the attached garden, look out for a pair of life-size **statues** depicting young Jules and his most famous creation, Captain Nemo, gazing wistfully out to sea. Tram 1 and buses 21 and 45 stop nearby.

♥ CATHÉDRALE ST-PIERRE ET ST-PAUL // ADMIRE THE CITY'S GOTHIC GLORY

Nantes' **cathedral** (place St-Pierre; ☼ 10am-6pm) may have taken over 400 years to finish, but the builders stuck to the Gothic script, and the building positively gleams after recent restoration. Its twin towers were built in 1508, but the interior was completely restored after a major fire in 1972. The soaring 37m-high nave is particularly noteworthy, as are the vibrant stained-glass windows, mostly replaced in the late '70s. Look out for the elaborate Renaissance tomb of François II, the last independent duke of Brittany (1458–88); it was commissioned by his daughter, Anne de Bretagne, and depicts François with his second wife, Margeurite de Foix, flanked by statues representing the four cardinal virtues: Prudence (with mirror), Temperance (reliquary and bridle), Fortitude (strangling a dragon) and Justice (sword and scales).

♥ OTHER MUSEUMS // FROM FINE ART TO FORMALDEHYDE

Nantes' **Musée des Beaux-Arts** (Fine Arts Museum; ☎ 02 51 17 45 00; 10 rue Georges Clemenceau; adult/child €3.50/2; ☼ 10am-6pm Wed-Mon, 6.30-8pm Thu) boast one of the most impressive fine-arts collections outside Paris, with works by Georges de La Tour, Chagall, Picasso and Kandinsky, plus a couple of Monet's *Nymphéas* (Water Lilies).

The **Musée Thomas Dobrée** (☎ 02 40 71 03 50; 18 rue Voltaire; adult/child €3.50/1.50; ☼ 1.30-5pm Tue-Fri, 2.30-5.30pm weekends) is the city's main archaeological museum, housed in a 15th-century palace restored by architect Viollet-le-Duc and funded by Thomas Dobrée, a wealthy ammunitions merchant. The building is more interesting than the artefacts, but check out the Revolutionary knick-knacks.

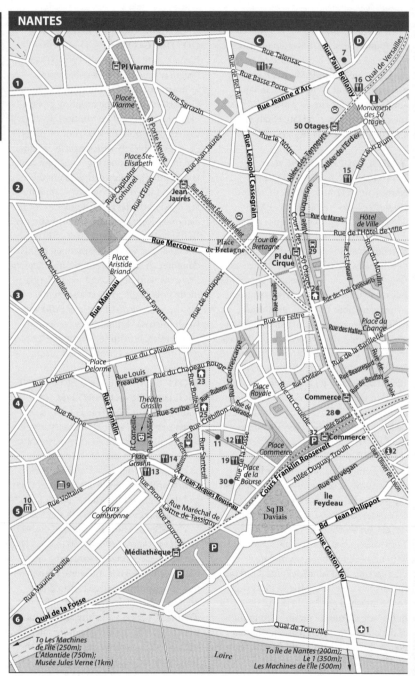

NANTES

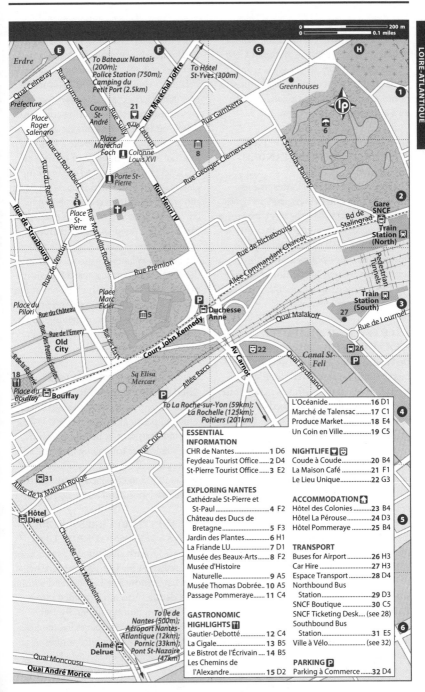

Also worth a peek is the fusty **Muséum d'Histoire Naturelle** (Natural History Museum; ☎ 02 40 99 26 20; 12 rue Voltaire; adult/child €3.50/2; ☉ 10am-6pm Wed-Mon), where glass-fronted cabinets display a cornucopia of dinosaur bones, stuffed pythons, transfixed birds and other quirky curiosities.

♥ JARDIN DES PLANTES // PACK A PICNIC FOR THE BOTANICAL GARDENS

On sunny days half of Nantes makes for the **Jardin des Plantes** (bd de Stalingrad; admission free; ☉ 8am-6pm), the city's exquisite botanic gardens. Founded in the early 19th century, it's a paradise of lawns, flower beds, duck ponds and tinkling fountains; amateur horticulturalists will spy rare palms, tropical orchids and even a few California redwoods.

♥ ÎLE FEYDEAU // EXPLORE THIS ISLAND-IN-THE-CITY

Île Feydeau (the quarter south of Commerce station) ceased to be an island after WWII when the channels of the Loire were filled in after the riverbeds dried up. You can still see where ships docked at the doors of the area's 18th-century mansions – some with stone carvings of the heads of African slaves. There's talk of reverting it to its original river status, but the huge cost has so far kept the project firmly on the drawing board.

Window-shoppers should swing by the lovely **Passage Pommeraye**, a three-storey shopping arcade filled by exclusive boutiques and designer shops.

♥ LES MACHINES DE L'ÎLE // TAKE A TRIP ASTRIDE A MECHANICAL ELEPHANT

After decades in the doldrums, the old industrial quarter on the **Île de Nantes** is slowly being reinvented as a civic and cultural hub. Since 2007, one of the old ships' hangars has housed the outlandish mechanical inventions of **Les Machines de l'Île** (☎ 08 10 12 12 25; www.lesmachines-nantes .fr; Machine Gallery adult/child €5.50/3, elephant ride adult/child €5.50/3; ☉ vary; ☑ Chantiers Navals), an innovative art/engineering company whose fantastical creations range from a giant crab and 'retropropelled' squid to a mechanised sea serpent and manta ray.

Tickets include entry to the machine gallery and the site workshop, where you can watch the latest creations being built; current projects include a triple-decker carousel decorated with sea creatures, and a 45m tree branch topped by two giant herons. Whatever you do, don't miss the chance take a ride aboard the company's showpiece, a 12m-high elephant that clanks along at 26cm per second and carries up to 50 passengers. Opening hours vary and places are limited in summer, so it's essential to book ahead.

♥ BOAT CRUISES // MESSING ABOUT ON THE RIVER

When the city bustle gets too much, take refuge with **Bateaux Nantais** (☎ 02 40 14 51 14; quai de la Motte Rouge; ☑ Motte Rouge), which offer scenic river trips along the Loire and Erdre, plus full-blown gastronomic voyages (adult €58 to €89) incorporating a twilight cruise, music and a slap-up supper.

♥ LES PETITS BEURRES // NIBBLE ON NANTES' FAMOUS BISCUITS

France's favourite biscuit, the *petit beurre,* was created in the late 19th century by local baker Monsieur Lefèvre, and within a few decades had mushroomed into a multimillion moneyspinner. By 1899, 1000 workers were employed at the LU biscuit factory, producing 3 tonnes of biscuits every day. The factory has long since been converted into an entertainment complex (see p150), although you can still see two biscuit-box-shaped towers and a giant *petit beurre* clinging to its facade; the best place for biscuit shopping these days is **La Friande LU** (☎ 02 40 20 14 68; 12 rue Paul Bellamy; ☯ 9.30am-7pm Tue-Sat, 9.30am-2.30pm Mon).

FESTIVALS & EVENTS

Carnaval de Nantes The city's annual street party explodes into life in April.

Fest Yves Celtic music hits bars and venues across the city in May.

Rendez-vous de l'Erdre (www.rendezvous erdre.com) Jazz on the river in August.

GASTRONOMIC HIGHLIGHTS

Under a gorgeous covered hall dating from 1934, Nantes' **Marché de Talensac** (rue Talensac) swings into gear every day except Monday. Place du Bouffay has a smaller produce market that goes organic every Wednesday, while rue Contrescarpe, northwest of Commerce station, is *the* street for food shops. You'll find cafés dotted around the city centre.

✤ GAUTIER DÉBOTTÉ €
☎ 02 40 48 23 19; 9 rue de la Fossé
If you're yearning for something sweet, Nantais know there's only one address that'll do, and that's Débotté's. This heritage-listed *maître-chocolatier* produces chocolicious treats including the house special *muscadet nantais*, a decadent concoction of dark chocolate, raisins and alcohol (€18.80 for 250g).

✤ L'ATLANTIDE €€€
☎ 02 40 73 23 23; 16 quai Ernest Renaud; menus €30-95; ☯ lunch Mon-Fri, dinner Mon-Sat
Sophisticated, if a smidgen stuffy, this fine-dining restaurant has long been one

of Nantes' *bonnes addresses*. Floor-to-ceiling windows overlook the Loire, and the menu is a textbook of rich, indulgent French cuisine – pigeon in coconut pastry, lemon turbot and sea-bass with Aquitaine caviar. Seriously good.

✤ LA CIGALE €€
☎ 02 51 84 94 94; 4 place Graslin; mains €12-25, dinner menu €18.90-28.90; ☯ 7.30am-midnight
If you only eat out once in Nantes, make sure it's at La Cigale – so good it's a classified national historic monument. This *belle-époque* beauty has been a Nantais institution since 1895, and it's still going strong. Art-deco tiles, gilded mirrors, sculpted wood and frescoed ceilings glimmer, while white-aproned waiters buzz about delivering coffee and aperitifs to a well-heeled clientele.

✤ LE 1 €€
☎ 02 40 08 28 00; 1 rue Olympe de Gouges; lunch menu €12-14, dinner menu €19-23; ☯ lunch & dinner
High-flying lawyers and cool creatives rub shoulders at this red-hot new tip (pronounced 'Le Un'), next to the city's futuristic law courts. Watch the chefs at work in the ultra-funky, open-plan kitchen while you tuck into tapas or select something more substantial from the modern, fusion-style menu.

✤ LE BISTROT DE L'ÉCRIVAIN €€
☎ 02 51 84 15 15; 15 rue Jean-Jacques Rousseau; mains €12-21; ☯ lunch & dinner Mon-Sat
Checked tablecloths, clattering pans and overworked waiters conjure a classically French vibe at the Writers' Bistro, an ideal place for sampling authentic *cuisine Nantaise* such as *sandre au beurre blanc* (pike in white sauce) and *escalope de saumon au beurre de muscadet* (salmon steak in muscadet butter).

❦ LES CHEMINS DE L'ALEXANDRE €€

☎ 02 40 48 62 27; 1 rue Léon Blum; menu €21-27; ☾ lunch Mon-Fri, dinner Tue-Sat

Hankering for home-cooking? Head for Alexander's, where the young chef takes his culinary inspiration from recipes handed down from his grandma. The dining room's country-cosy, with plenty of wood and stone for that down-home feel, and the menu takes the cream of traditional French and gives it a 21st-century spin. One to watch.

❦ L'OCÉANIDE €€€

☎ 02 40 20 32 28; 2 rue Paul Bellamy; mains €17-36; ☾ lunch & dinner Tue-Sat

Fish, fish and fish – that's all that matters at the little Oceanide, Nantes' premier address for *fruits de mer*. The starchy service and rather austere atmosphere might not be to everyone's taste, but you won't find better seafood anywhere in Loire-Atlantique.

❦ UN COIN EN VILLE €€

☎ 02 40 20 05 97; 2 place de la Bourse; lunch €12.90-16.90, dinner mains €15.50-18; ☾ lunch Tue-Fri, dinner Tue-Sat

This is a romantic bolthole blending rough stone with flickering tea-lights, baroque colours and a boho vibe. The feel's laid-back and relaxed, while the menu mixes up Asian and Italian flavours with Breton ingredients: think beef served *sashimi*-style or tuna served with a spicy crust. All-round lovely, really.

NIGHTLIFE

Nantes' students keep the city's nightlife ticking. You'll find countless drinking holes dotted around the old quarters – place du Bouffay, place Graslin and rue Jean-Jacques Rousseau are good places to start.

❦ COUDE À COUDE

☎ 02 40 69 75 82; 2 rue Gretry; ☾ 11am-2am Mon-Fri, 3pm-2am Sat

A much-loved locals' hangout decked out in vintage signs and *objets trouvées*, with a small decked terrace that gets crammed on weekends. Pick the *vin du mois* (wine of the month) from one of the mirrors, or wash down the chef's chorizo specials with a glass of something cold and fizzy.

❦ LA MAISON CAFÉ

☎ 02 40 37 04 12; www.lamaisonet.com; 4 rue Lebrun; ☾ 3pm-2am

Every room at this retro temple is decked out in bad '70s style, right down to the formica furniture and bucket seats – if the mood takes you, you could sip your drink by a stainless steel sink or plonk yourself down in a plastic bath-tub. Archly kitsch? Annoyingly camp? You decide...

❦ LE LIEU UNIQUE

☎ 02 40 12 14 34; www.lelieuunique.com; 2 rue de la Biscuiterie

Nantes' old biscuit factory has been converted into a buzzy cultural complex, complete with cinema, restaurant, theatre, club, sauna and, of course, a bar that's open until the wee small hours. Unique by name, unique by nature.

TRANSPORT

AIR // Nantes airport (☎ 02 40 84 80 00; www .nantes.aeroport.fr) is 12km southwest of the city. Air France serves major French cities, while Ryanair flies to the East Midlands, Liverpool, Dublin and Shannon. The TAN shuttle bus (☎ Espace Transport 08 10 44 44 44; www.tan.fr; 2 allée Brancas) coincides with flights and travels to the city centre and train station; tickets cost €7.
BIKE // Bikes can be hired from 79 places on the city-wide Bicloo network (☎ 08 10 44 44 44; www

.bicloo.nantesmetropole.fr), but you'll need to buy a membership card (€20) and put down a €150 deposit. Alternatively, **Ville à Vélo** (☎ 02 51 84 94 51; www.nge-nantes.fr/velo00.php; half-/full day €6/10; ⏰ 8am-8pm) is based at Parking du Commerce.

BUS // Buses throughout Loire-Atlantique are administered by **Lila** (☎ 08 25 08 71 56). Tickets cost a flat-rate €2, but most places can be reached quicker by train. Most buses (including the majority of Lila buses) depart the bus station on 13 allée de la Maison Rouge, although a few northbound buses leave from allée Duquesne.

LOCAL TRANSPORT // The city's public transport consists of trams, buses and a 'Busway' provided by **TAN** (☎ Espace Transport 08 10 44 44 44; www.tan.fr; 2 allée Brancas). Joint tickets (single/10-ticket carnet/24-hour pass €1.50/12/4) remain valid for an hour after time-stamping. The three tram lines (A, B and C) and major bus routes intersect at Commerce (Gare Centrale). Regular services run until around 9pm, followed by an hourly night service until around 2am, depending on the line.

TRAIN // The train station's two entrances, Accès Nord (27 bd de Stalingrad) and Accès Sud (rue de Lourmel) are linked by a foot tunnel. You can buy tickets at the city-centre **SNCF Boutique** (12 place de la Bourse) or TAN's Espace Transport office. TGVs run regularly to St-Nazaire, Vannes, Quimper, Rennes and Paris.

AROUND NANTES

♥ MUSCADET COUNTRY // TICKLE YOUR TASTEBUDS WITH THE LOCAL TIPPLE

The countryside to the east of Nantes produces one of France's favourite white wines, **muscadet**, made from the melon de Bourgogne grape and governed by its own AOC. The area is dotted with hundreds of *domaines* where you can try and buy the latest vintage, linked together by a signposted *route touristique*. Local tourist offices organise visits to major growers – there's a full list at www.vignoble-nantais.eu, in French.

Alternatively, you can browse vintage equipment and get wine-tasting tips at the **Musée du Vignoble Nantais** (☎ 02 40 80 90 13; 82 rue Pierre Abélard, Le Pallet; adult/12-17yr €4.50/2.50; ⏰ 10am-6pm mid-Jun–mid-Sep, 2-6pm mid-Apr-mid-Jun & mid-Sep–mid-Nov, by reservation mid-Nov–Mar) in Le Pallet.

♥ PORNIC // KICK BACK AT THIS PRETTY SEASIDE RESORT

During the 19th century, many famous French artists and writers – including Michelet, Flaubert and Rénoir – dipped their toes in the waters around **Pornic**, and it's still a popular thalassotherapy resort – the grand **Alliance Pornic** (☎ 08 00 03 03 76; www.thalassopornic.com; plage de la Source) offers luxurious treatments including hydrotherapy, kinestherapy and Ayurvedic massage.

PARC NATUREL RÉGIONAL DE BRIÈRE

· · · · · ·

While Nantes is the region's main draw, it's well worth taking some time to nose around the countryside to the northwest – especially the wonderful Brière nature park, a huge tract of protected wetland brimming with birdlife and traditional thatch-crowned houses.

EXPLORING PARC NATUREL RÉGIONAL DE BRIÈRE

Some 7000 hectares of reed beds, water meadows and peat bogs make up this **reserve** (☎ 02 40 66 85 01; www.parc-naturel-briere .fr; park office 38 rue de le Brière; La-Chapelle-des-Marais; ⏰ 10am-12.30pm & 2.30-6.30pm daily Jun-Sep,

LOIRE-ATLANTIQUE

10am-12.30pm & 2-6pm Mon-Sat Oct-May), the second-largest area of protected marshland in France after the Camargue. Brière is a natural sanctuary for all sorts of rare flora and fauna, from water voles, water ilies and otters to herons, kingfishers, egrets and cormorants, and it's crisscrossed by lovely walking trails and kilometres of canals, established centuries ago by local reed-cutters and peat-farmers.

The most atmospheric way of exploring is aboard a **chaland**, a traditional flat-bottomed barge that's been the traditional form of transport in the Brière for centuries. Trips leave from barge-ports dotted around the park: in Bréca, try **Yannick Thual** (☎ 02 40 91 32 02; http://calechesbrieronnes.free.fr, in French); from Île de Fédrun with local naturalist-historians **Philippe Garoux** (☎ 06 84 40 77 82) or **Valérie Aoustin-Huard** (☎ 02 40 40 91 28); from Fossés Blancs with **Les Chalands d'Or** (☎ 06 62 85 29 68); and from La Pierre Fendue (adjoining St-Lyphard) with **Brière Évasion** (☎ 02 40 91 41 96; www.briere-evasion.com). Count on around €10/45 per adult/child for a 45-minute *chaland*

trip. If you fancy having a go yourself, many operators have barges available for hire, but be warned – it's not as easy as it looks... For hiking tours, see p142.

The park's pretty villages are worth exploring in their own right, especially **St-Lyphard**, where you can climb the church bell tower for panoramic views (adult/child €3/1.50) and **Rozé**, where the history of the local canals are documented at **La Maison de l'Eclusier** (adult/child €5/2.50; ☷ 10.30am-1pm & 2.30-6.30pm Jul–mid-Sep, 2-6pm Apr-Jun), in an old lock-keeper's cottage.

Comeliest of all is **Kerhinet**, whose 18 thatch-topped cottages (locally known as *chaumièeres*) provide a fascinating glimpse of how life in the Brière was once lived. Guided tours are arranged by the park office between April and August.

GASTRONOMIC HIGHLIGHTS

♥ L'AUBERGE DE KERBOURG // ST-LYPHARD €€
☎ 02 40 61 95 15; 224 Village de Kerbourg; menus from €35; ☷ lunch Wed-Sun, dinner Tue-Sat

---

TOP CAMPING

Camping is popular in the region; here are some of our favourites. For details of other accommodation options in Loire-Atlantique, see p296.

★ **Camping de l'Ocean** (☎ 02 40 23 07 69; www.camping-ocean.com; rte de la Maison Rouge, Le Croisic; site €26-40; ☷ Apr-Sep; ☷) The full-blown French camping experience in sunny Le Croisic; water park, kids' clubs, tennis courts and all.

★ **Camping Le Port-Chéri** (☎ 02 40 82 34 57; www.camping-leportcheri.com; Pornic; site €12-20; ☷ year-round; ☷) Simple camping near the coast, with the added bonus that it's open year-round.

★ **Camping du Petit Port** (☎ 02 40 74 47 94; camping-petit-port@nge-nantes.fr; 21 bd du Petiti Port, Nantes; site €5.50-7.20 plus per car €1, adult €3.10-3.80, child €2-2.50; ☷ year-round) Who said sleeping in Nantes had to be expensive? It's small and simple but dead handy for the city.

★ **Camping Saint-Clair** (☎ 02 40 87 61 52; www.campingsaintclair.com; Guenrouet; site €5-7, adult €3.30-5.60, child €2-3.50; ☷ mid-Apr–Sep) Cute little site nestled beside the Nantes–Brest Canal.

Don't be tricked by the rustic country appearance of this Brière farmhouse – it's got a reputation for some of Brittany's most adventurous grub. If you've never tried shad *(alose)*, spider crab *(araignée)* or triggerfish *(baliste)*, this is the place to do it. Dress smartly and let Bernard Jeanson work his magic.

🌱 LA MARE AUX OISEAUX // ST-JOACHIM €€€

☎ 02 40 88 53 01; www.mareauxoiseaux.fr; 162 Île de Ferdrun; menus €39-85; ☽ closed lunch Mon

Let's not mess about – this is, quite simply, of our favourite places in Brittany. Eric Guérin's divine back-country retreat overlooks the Brière marshes, and his cooking makes full use of the ingredients on his doorstep, from grouse and frog to eel, pigeon and samphire. Despite its culinary credentials, it's relaxed and very child-friendly, with country views to die for. Don't miss.

TRANSPORT

Public transport to the Brière is very patchy, although there are a couple of seasonal buses to St-Lyphard via Kerhinet from St-Nazaire and Guérande.

PRESQU'ÎLE DE GUÉRANDE
. . . . . .

Over on the northwest coast of Loire-Atlantique, holidaymakers have been flocking to the flashy resorts of La Baule and Le Croisic for well over a century. A little inland, the region's celebrated saltpans have been supplying local chefs with one of their favourite ingredients, *sel de Guérande*, since time immemorial.

EXPLORING PRESQU'ÎLE DE GUÉRANDE

🌱 GUÉRANDE // WHERE EVERYTHING'S TAKEN WITH A PINCH OF SALT

This fortified town is famous for its fragrant **sea salt**, harvested from the local *marais salants* (saltpans) for the last 1000 years. It's collected by teams of *paludiers* (salt-panners), and remains a prominent ingredient in many Breton dishes – the delicate hand-collected crystals known as *fleurs de sel* (salt-flowers), command the highest price.

Sachets of Guérande salt are available from shops all around town, and the history of the industry takes centre stage at the **Musée du Pays de Guérande** (☎ 02 40 42 96 52; rue St Michel; adult/6-17yr €4/2; ☽ 10am-12.30pm & 2.30-7pm Tue-Sun, 2.30-7pm Mon Apr-Sep, closes 6pm Oct), located in the 15th-century gateway, the Porte St-Michel; a walk along the ramparts is included in the admission.

Nearby in Pradel, **Terre de Sel – Espace Sel et Nature** (☎ 02 40 62 08 80; www.seldeguerande.com; rte des Marais Salants; guided walks adult €7-11, child €4-8; ☽ 9.30am-7.30pm Jul & Aug, 10am-6pm spring & autumn, 10am-12.30pm & 2-5pm winter) offers fascinating guided walks in the company of a local *paludier*, exploring the unique natural environments of the saltpans and the working practices of this centuries-old industry.

🌱 ST-NAZAIRE // ALL ABOARD FOR OCEAN LINERS AND A DECOMMISSIONED SUBMARINE

Like Lorient and Brest, St-Nazaire paid heavily for WWII liberation – it was a major German U-Boat base, and 85% of the city was destroyed by Allied bombing before being rebuilt in uncompromising

LOIRE-ATLANTIQUE

concrete. St-Nazaire has since regained ihs status as a major aeronautical and shipbuilding centre: the largest passenger liner ever built, the *Queen Mary II*, was launched here in 2003.

Five separate museums around the harbour explore the city's industrial heritage: tickets can be bought from the central **ticket office** (☎ 08 10 88 84 44; bd de la Légion d'Honneur; www.saint-nazaire-tourisme .com) near the tourist office. The highlights are **Escal'Atlantic** (www.escal-atlantic .com; ◷ 10am-7pm Jul & Aug, 10am-12.30pm & 2-6pm Apr-Jun & Sep, 2-6pm Wed-Sun Feb & Mar & Oct-Dec, closed Jan), which traces the history of St-Nazaire's *paquebots* (passenger liners) in two converted U-Boat pens, and on the opposite side of the harbour, the decommissioned submarine **Espadon** (◷ 10am-12.30pm & 2-6pm Feb-Dec), launched in 1957 and in active service until 1986. Audioguides steer you around the cramped crew's quarters, control room and torpedo bays.

The train and bus stations are north of the town. Take av de la République 500m to the city centre; the ticket office and Escal' Atlantic are east of here.

❤ LA BAULE // LOUNGE ON THE BEACHES OF THIS BELLE ÉPOQUE RESORT

The 19th-century bathing craze transformed **La Baule** (www.labaule.com) from a quiet fishing port into one of the most glamorous resorts on the French Atlantic Coast. Art-nouveau villas and *belle-époque* mansions litter the streets of the older part of town, but a rash of modern high-rises, hotels and a huge casino have robbed the town of much of its charm. Still, its vast 8km curve of golden sand (the largest beach in Europe, according to the locals) is tailor-made for some serious sun-worshipping. If the crowds

get too much, you can usually find more breathing space in next-door **Pornichet**.

Kayaking and mountain-biking tours are available through **Au Gre' du Vent** (☎ 02 99 90 56 91; www.greduvent.fr, in French; La Baule).

❤ LE CROISIC // TRAVEL THE WORLD'S OCEANS WITHOUT GETTING WET

A dozen small beaches are dotted around the port-resort of Le Croisic, but the main draw is the **Océarium** (☎ 02 40 23 02 44; www.ocearium-croisic.fr, in French; av de St-Goustan; adult/3-12yr €12/9; ◷ 10am-7pm Jun-Aug, 10am-1pm & 2-7pm Feb-Dec), whose 45 tanks are stocked with species from ocean habitats including the Atlantic coast, Belle-Île-en-Mer, Cap Corse, Vancouver Island and a tropical lagoon; there's also a jellyfish tank, touch pool, shell display and a great underwater tunnel.

Le Croisic itself has some interesting buildings, such as the 19th-century Ancienne Criée (Old Fish Auction) on the waterfront and some charming half-timbered houses around the old town. If you've got time, the **Pointe du Croisic** makes a fine place for a sunset picnic, with views over the chaotic jumble of rocks known as **La Calebasse**.

GASTRONOMIC HIGHLIGHTS

❤ CASTEL MARIE-LOUISE // LA BAULE €€€

☎ 02 40 11 48 38; www.castel-marie-louise.com; 1 av Andrieu; menus from €65; ◷ dinner daily, lunch weekends Jul & Aug

It offers Lyonnaise cuisine in La Baule courtesy of Eric Mignard, the talented *patron* at this much-respected château-restaurant. Don your glad-rags and settle down in the spiffing dining room for

Michelin-approved buttered sole and cod flavoured with Guérande salt. Plenty of room for piggy dishes, too, as you'd expect from a Lyon-born chef.

☘ LA BOUILLABAISSE BRETONNE // LE CROISIC €€
☎ 02 40 23 06 74; 12 quai de la Petite Chambre; mains €20-35; ☺ lunch Wed-Sun, dinner Wed-Sat
You can enjoy seafood on the seafront in Le Croisic. Salt-crust cod, mussels, sole and langoustines feature, but as the name suggests, the house special is a rather fabulous Breton spin on Marseillaise *bouillabaisse*.

TRANSPORT

There are regular buses from St-Nazaire to Le Croisic, La Baule, Guérande and St-Lyphard, all adminstered by Lila (☎ 08 25 08 71 56; www.cg44.fr). Nantes also has frequent trains to St-Nazaire (€10.50, 35 minutes), La Baule (€13, 50 minutes) and Le Croisic (€14.30, 1¼ hours).

MANCHE

3 PERFECT DAYS

☙ DAY 1 // MOSEYING MONT ST-MICHEL

No French adventure would be complete without a visit to the celestial spires of Mont St-Michel (opposite). Avoid the crowds with a morning walk across the bay (p163), and aim for the abbey in late afternoon (opposite). If you're here in summer, stay for a night-time concert; otherwise, skip the local digs and base yourself in Pontorson (p298) or Granville (p298).

☙ DAY 2 // HIT THE CENTRE

Spend the morning in Granville (p163), enjoying the lower-town shops and the upper-town views. Head on to Villedieu-les-Poêles (p166), stopping for lunch at Manoir de l'Archerie (p166). Carry on to Coutances cathedral (p166) and continue north to Carteret (p168), where you can end the day with fine food and estuary views at La Marine (p168).

☙ DAY 3 // TACKLE THE TOP END

Head up to the Hague Peninsula (p175) and its blustery walking tracks, or admire wild and windy views at Nez de Jobourg and Goury. Bypass Cherbourg-Octeville and drive on to Barfleur (p171), Valognes (p168) and Ste-Mère-Église (p170), stopping wherever takes your fancy. If time allows, consider a boat trip to the Île Tatihou (p171) or a swampy trek in the Parc Naturel Régional des Marais du Cotentin et du Bessin (p161).

MONT ST-MICHEL

· · · · · ·

The slender towers and sky-scraping turrets of the abbey of Mont St-Michel are one of the quintessential images of northern France. Rising from a sea of white sands, the abbey sits atop a small island ringed by ramparts and battlements, connected to the mainland by a causeway and surrounded by one of Europe's largest tidal bays. Over three million visitors make the Mont St-Michel pilgrimage every year, and despite the coach tours and hordes of bellowing schoolkids, it's still a must-see for any first-time visitor – you will usually miss the worst of the crush by coming in late afternoon or, better still, by avoiding the summer season altogether.

According to local legend, the abbey was founded in the 8th century when Aubert, the bishop of Avranches, was visited by the Archangel Michael in a dream (a gilded statue of Michael slaying a dragon sits on the top of the abbey, symbolising the triumph of good over evil). Following his revelation, the bishop built a chapel in 708, and in 966 the site was gifted to the Benedictines by Richard I, Duke of Normandy. The island later served as an ecclesiastical fortress during the 11th century; during the Hundred Years' War it was the only place in northern France not to fall to the English. In 1966 the abbey was symbolically returned to the Benedictines as part of its millennial celebrations, and it became a Unesco World Heritage Site in 1979.

ORIENTATION

Mont St-Michel is linked to the mainland by a 2km causeway (soon to be a bridge – see the boxed text, p162). A gateway, the Porte de l'Avancée, leads to the Mont's main street, the Grande Rue, lined with restaurants, hotels and a string of tacky souvenir shops. There are car parks (€4 per day) at the foot of the Mont, two of which are covered by the rising tide – pay attention to the parking attendants unless you fancy your motor becoming a submarine. Nearby Beauvoir is a conglomeration of restaurants and hotels – the nearest proper town is Pontorson.

ESSENTIAL INFORMATION

TOURIST OFFICES // Mont St-Michel (☎ 02 33 60 14 30; www.ot-montsaintmichel.com; ☼ 9am-7pm Jul & Aug, 9am-12.30pm & 2-6pm or 6.30pm Mar-Jun, Sep & Oct, 10am-12.30pm & 2-5pm Nov-Feb) Just inside the Porte de l'Avancée. A tide-table *(horaire des marées)* is posted beside the door, and a detailed map costs €3.50. **Pontorson** (☎ 02 33 60 20 65; mont.st.michel.pontorson@wanadoo.fr; place de l'Église; ☼ 9am-12.30pm & 2-6.30pm Mon-Fri, 10am-12.30pm & 3-6.30pm Sat, 10am-noon Sun Jul & Aug, 9am-noon & 2-6pm Mon-Fri, 10am-noon & 3-6pm Sat Sep-Jun)

EXPLORING MONT ST-MICHEL

❦ THE ABBEY // MAKE YOUR OWN HEAVENLY ASCENT

Just glimpsing the Mont from the shore is reason enough to visit, but once you're here you can't miss visiting the stunning **abbey** (☎ 02 33 89 80 00; adult/18-25yr/under 18yr €8.50/5/free; ☼ 9am-7pm May-Aug, 9.30am-6pm Sep-Apr) itself, reached by the twisting cobbles of the Grand Rue and a 350-step

(Continued on page 162)

MANCHE

MANCHE

MANCHE

NEZ DE JOBOURG   **p175**

Gaze down from continental
Europe's highest sea cliffs

*The Channel
(La Manche)*

VALOGNES   **p168**

Strut down streets of stone in
Normandy's 'little Versailles'

GOURY   **p175**

Get wrapped up in the drama of
the rugged seascape

BARNEVILLE-CARTERET p168

Find a sandy spot to yourself in
this duo of low-key resorts

Barfleur

St-Pierre-
Église

St-Vaast-
la-Hougue

Île Tatihou

Quettehou

*Aéroport
Cherbourg
Maupertus*

**Cherbourg-
Octeville**

D902

Valognes

Ste-Mère-
Église

N13

Utah
Beach

*Baie des
Veys*

Grandcamp-
Maisy

La Cambe

Isigny-
sur-Mer

*To Bayeux
(25km)*

N174

Litteau

Balleroy

Calvados

D972

Carentan

Parc Naturel Régional
des Marais du
Cotentin et du Bessin

Le Hommet-
d'Arthenay

D900

*To Portsmouth
(UK)*

Gréville-
Hague

D901

N13

Bricquebec

D900

Picauville

St-Sauveur-
le-Vicomte

Périers

D900

D2

Lessay

La Haye-
du-Puits

D650

Pirou

**Cap de
la Hague**

Goury

La
Rouche

Auderville

AREVA

Nez de-
Jobourg

Bénoîtville

Diélette

Flamanville

D904

Barneville

Portbail

Carteret

To Guernsey

To Guernsey

*Baie
d'Ecalgrain*

Jersey (UK)

Gorey

St Helier

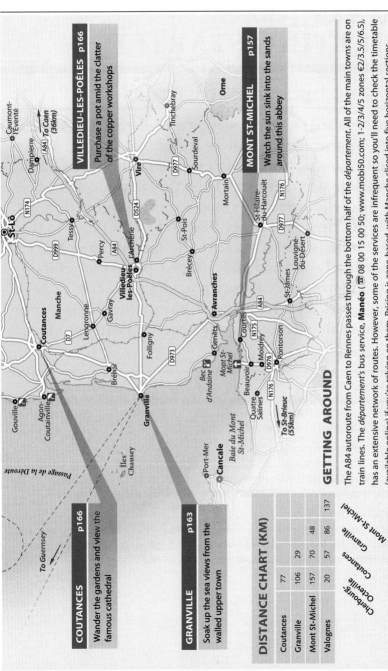

MANCHE

VILLEDIEU-LES-POÊLES p166

Purchase a pot amid the clatter of the copper workshops

MONT ST-MICHEL p157

Watch the sun sink into the sands around this abbey

COUTANCES p166

Wander the gardens and view the famous cathedral

GRANVILLE p163

Soak up the sea views from the walled upper town

GETTING AROUND

The A84 autoroute from Caen to Rennes passes through the bottom half of the *département*. All of the main towns are on train lines. The *département's* bus service, **Manéo** (☎ 08 00 15 00 50; www.mobi50.com; 1-2/3/4/5 zones €2/3.5/5/6.5), has an extensive network of routes. However, some of the services are infrequent so you'll need to check the timetable (available online) if you're relying on them. Pricing is zone-based, with Manche sliced into five horizontal sections.

DISTANCE CHART (KM)

	Cherbourg-Octeville	Coutances	Granville	Mont St-Michel
Coutances	77			
Granville	106	29		
Mont St-Michel	157	70	48	
Valognes	20	57	86	137

Note: Distances between destinations are approximate

MANCHE
GETTING STARTED

MAKING THE MOST OF YOUR TIME

Surrounded on three sides by the Channel (La Manche), the *département* of Manche is dominated by the Cotentin Peninsula, Normandy's western bulwark. Its 320km coastline stretches north from the fairy tale–like Mont St-Michel, Normandy's most iconic visage, to the port city of Cherbourg-Octeville and then southeast to the westernmost beach of the D-Day landing sites. Much of the coast is wild and undeveloped, perfect for solitary wind-blown walks above a pounding sea. The fertile inland areas, criss-crossed with bocage (hedgerows), produce an abundance of apples, beef and dairy products.

TOP TOURS & COURSES

❦ ÎLES CHAUSEY

This archipelago of dozens of rocky islands and outcrops can be visited as part of a 70-minute cruise from Granville's Gare Maritime. (☎ 02 33 50 31 31; www.vedettejoliefrance .com; adult/child €9/6; ⊙ daily Jul-Sep)

- -

❦ WILDE KITCHEN

Master the local cuisine in Irish-born but long-time Normandy resident Sinéad's 18th-century kitchen. Three-day courses include on-site accommodation and visits to local markets and producers. (☎ 06 03 17 83 73; www.wildekitchen.net; Benoîtville; 1/3 days €85/875)

- -

❦ FRANCE STATION NAUTIQUE

Learn to sail with an introductory course for €99 to €114, or try your hand at a range of other watery activities such as kayaking, rowing and paragliding. (☎ 02 33 78 19 29; www.cherbourg-hague-nautisme.com; Port Chantereyne, Cherbourg-Octeville)

- -

MANCHE

GETTING AWAY FROM IT ALL

★ **Parc Naturel Régional des Marais du Cotentin et du Bessin** Spanning both Manche and Calvados, this park comprises 250 sq km of lowlands. Criss-crossed with rivers, canals and hedgerows, the area teems with flora and fauna, but the highlight is undoubtedly the Baie des Veys in the east. Seagulls, woodcocks, cormorants and grebes make the bay one of France's most important habitats for migratory birds (see www.parc-cotentin-bessin.fr).

★ **Hague Peninsula** Manche's wild northwest hides many secluded bays (p175).

★ **The Bocage** Explore the back roads through this picturesque patchwork of hedgerows and farmland (p165).

TOP RESTAURANTS

❦ LA CITADELLE
Creative cuisine on Granville's waterfront (p165)

- -

❦ MANOIR DE L'ARCHERIE
Simple country goodness in rural surroundings (p166)

- -

❦ LA MARINE
Exquisite food and exceptional service make this Manche's best (p168)

- -

❦ CAFÉ DE PARIS
Bustling brasserie serving food with flair (p174)

- -

❦ LE VAUBAN
Placing seafood centre stage (p174)

- -

❦ AUBERGE DE GOURY
Simple barbecue perhaps, but thoroughly entertaining and delicious (p175)

- -

ADVANCE PLANNING

★ **Jazz Sous les Pommiers** (☎ 02 33 76 78 65; www.jazzsouslespommiers.com) The most important annual music event in Normandy, this jazz festival is held in Coutances during Ascension week in May. In cafés, in churches and on the streets, local and international musicians strut their stuff to an appreciative public.

★ **Grand Pardon** At the end of July, Granville's port is filled with decorated boats for this religious parade and Blessing of the Sea. There's lots of seafood to sample.

★ **Regatta** Barfleur's strong sailing tradition is celebrated on the second Sunday in August with a century-old regatta.

★ **Les Traversées de Tatihou** (www.tatihou.com) Head to the World Heritage–listed island for the annual folk-music festival in mid-August.

★ **Mont St-Michel** Dodge the queues and buy your tickets in advance from the Pontorson tourist office or online at http://monuments.fnacspectacles.com.

ONLINE RESOURCES

★ **Manche Conseil Général** (www.manche .fr) Information about the whole *département,* in French only

★ **Granville Tourisme** (www.granville -tourisme.fr)

★ **Ville de Valognes** (www.mairie-valognes.fr)

★ **Cherbourg & Haut-Cotentin Tourisme** (www.otcherbourgcotentin.fr) Covering both the city of Cherbourg-Octeville and the upper part of the Cotentin Peninsula

MANCHE

(Continued from page 157)

staircase known, appropriately, as the Grand Degré. Take it slow – it's a long, agonising slog to the top.

A guided tour is included in the admission price (English tours run hourly in summer, a couple a day in winter). If you prefer exploring on your own, pick up an audioguide (€4) or a guide brochure, both available in several languages.

The three-tiered construction of the abbey reflects both the ecclesiastical hierarchy and the monk's own lifelong plod towards heaven, with each level slightly more sacred than the last. At the very top sits the glorious **Église Abbatiale** (Abbey Church), famous for its harmonious blend of architectural styles, including a Romanesque nave and transept built between the 11th and 12th centuries, and a glorious Flamboyant Gothic choir supported by flying buttresses, seamlessly added three centuries later. Astonishingly, most of the masonry was shipped in by boat and pulled up the hillside by hand using ropes and pulleys.

The buildings on the northern side of the Mont are known as **La Merveille** (The Marvel); highlights include the wonderfully peaceful **cloister** and a 13th-century **guest hall** reserved for important pilgrims and royal visitors. Sacred texts would have been copied out in the **scriptorium** (sometimes called the Salle des Chevaliers), while in the luminous **refectory**, the monks would have eaten their meals in silence while listening to an educational sermon. One of the oldest parts of the complex is the **Crypte St-Martin**, renowned for its impressive barrel-vaulted roof, although the **Chapelle St-Martin** is usually off-limits to visitors.

One of the most atmospheric times to visit – if you can cope with the crowds – is on summer nights between July and September, when you can wander around the floodlit abbey and listen to special concerts of plainsong and church music from 9pm to midnight.

SAVING MONT ST-MICHEL

Despite its peaceful setting, Mont St-Michel has witnessed a surprising amount of controversy over recent years. In addition to the problems of spiralling visitor numbers and ever-longer traffic jams, the Mont has faced a more ominous threat: for decades the bay has been silting up at a rate of a million cubic metres each year, threatening to turn Normandy's world-famous island abbey into a peninsula. Years of research suggested several causes for the sedimentary build-up, including the local practice of agricultural *polders* (reclaimed pastures), the canalisation of the Coüesnon River and the construction of the Mont's causeway. What wasn't so clear is whether the problem could be stopped.

After years of deliberation, procrastination and consultation, the powers that be finally authorised a massive engineering project in 2006, costing an eye-watering €200 million, to help save the Mont from itself. There are three main stages: the construction of a new dam at the mouth of the Coüesnon River; the building of a new footbridge to replace the troublesome causeway; and the construction of a visitors centre and car park 2.5km inland, connected to the Mont by shuttle buses. The Coüesnon dam is currently under construction, and the rest of the project is scheduled for completion by 2012; by 2020, it's hoped that over 80% of the sediment will have been washed out to sea. The latest news is at www.projetmontstmichel.fr.

None of the **museums** (adult/child for 1 museum €8/4.50, all 4 €16/9) along the Grande Rue are much, although a couple might intrigue the kids. The **Archéoscope** (☎ 02 33 89 01 85) takes a 20-minute multimedia spin through the history of the Mont, while the **Musée de la Mer et de l'Écologie** explains the bay's complex tidal patterns.

❦ BALADE ON THE BAY //
CROSS MONT ST-MICHEL'S
SHIFTING SANDS

The Baie du Mont St-Michel is famed for its extraordinary tides. Depending on the lunar pull, the difference between low and high tides can reach 15m, although the Mont is only completely surrounded by the sea during the equinoxes. Regardless of the season, the waters sweep in across the bay at an astonishing rate, said to exceed the speed of a galloping horse. The Mont St-Michel sands are also notoriously treacherous – one panel in the Bayeux tapestry shows Norman soldiers being plucked from the quicksand by their resourceful comrades.

Walking across the bay on your own is an extremely bad idea; you'll need the expertise of an experienced local guide. The tourist office in Pontorson keeps details of scheduled walks, or you can book directly with **Découverte de la Baie** (☎ 02 33 70 83 49; www.decouvertebaie.com) or **Chemins de la Baie** (☎ 02 33 89 80 88; www.cheminsdelabaie.com).

GASTRONOMIC HIGHLIGHTS

❦ LA MÈRE POULARD €€€

☎ 02 33 89 68 68; lunch menu €39, dinner menus €65-85; ◷ 11.45am-4.30pm & 6.45-9.30pm, all day in summer

Mont St-Michel's restaurants are generally overbusy, overbooked and overpriced, but if you're desperate to eat out, you'd better make it Mother Poulard's, which has been churning out the old girl's trademark wood-fired omelettes since 1888. Are they worth the fuss (or the astronomical prices)? We'll leave that up to you…

TRANSPORT

BUS // **Kéolis** (☎ 02 99 19 70 70; www.keolis-emeraude.com) provides two or three daily buses to Pontorson and St-Malo.

TRAIN // The **Ligne Baie** (www.lignebaie.fr) project connects the Mont with St-Malo, Dol-de-Bretagne, Pontorson, Avranches and Granville via a combination of trains and buses; an adult/child day pass costs €10/5.

GRANVILLE
· · · · · ·

pop 13,500

Granville likes to call itself the 'Monaco of the north'. Like the tiny principality, it has an old town crowded onto a rocky promontory overlooking the sea and a lower town built on reclaimed land. The straight rows of granite houses and white shutters in the walled upper town, however, have a uniquely Norman austerity. Despite the no-nonsense buildings, Granville is a popular destination for pleasure seekers. In summer, the narrow beach and chic boutiques are crowded with visitors.

Much of the upper town is 18th century, when shipbuilders and privateers built residences. The 19th-century vogue for sea bathing brought the first beach lovers, speeded by a new train line. Liberated on 31 July 1944, Granville was surprised to find itself under assault by German commandos who were still garrisoned at Jersey. The Germans left 20 dead before making off with coal and GI prisoners.

ESSENTIAL INFORMATION

TOURIST OFFICE // Granville (☎ 02 33 91 30 03; www.granville-tourisme.fr; 4 cours Jonville; ⊗ 9am-12.30pm & 2-6pm Mon-Sat)

ORIENTATION

Granville is built on a peninsula with the ports to the south and the beach to the north. Between the two, the modern lower town contains most of the shops and services. The train and bus stations are east of the town centre. La Pointe du Roc at the southwestern tip of the upper town has a lighthouse (1869), a signal post and several blockhouses built by the Germans occupiers.

EXPLORING GRANVILLE

Cruises around the nearby Îles Chausey can be made from Granville (see p160).

❤ **MUSÉE & JARDIN CHRISTIAN DIOR // A CLIFF-TOP SHRINE FOR FASHION PILGRIMS**
☎ 02 33 61 48 21; www.musee-dior-granville.com; rue d'Estouteville; museum/gardens €6/free; ⊗ museum 10am-6.30pm May-Sep, gardens 9am-5pm Oct-Mar, to 8pm Apr, May & Sep, to 11pm Jun-Aug

Pretty in pink, the childhood home of the great French fashion designer is surrounded by exquisite gardens overlooking the ocean. Inside, Dior's evolution as a designer is traced through designs, watercolours and, *naturellement,* some fabulous frocks. Temporary exhibits each summer illuminate other aspects of the revolutionary changes he wrought to women's fashion.

❤ **LE ROC DES HARMONIES // WANDER A WONDERFULLY WHIMSICAL FANTASY WORLD**
☎ 02 33 50 19 83; www.aquarium-du-roc.com; Pointe du Roc; adult/child €8/4.50; ⊗ 10am-noon & 2-6.30pm Oct-May, 10am-7pm Jun-Sep

Even though it's targeted at kids, imaginative grown-ups will get a kick out of this window into a world where obsessive hobbies have been given full flight. The first room is devoted to butterflies, beetles and spiders, mounted in artistic patterns. The aquarium that follows might seem the most restrained part of the exhibition, until you remember the two huge sea lions (born in captivity) in

GRANVILLE'S CARNIVAL

Granville's annual Mardi Gras celebration is the biggest event in the region. For four days before Ash Wednesday, floats, bands and majorettes file down the narrow streets, while kids head to the Ferris wheel and grown-ups head to the bars. The festivities culminate on the final day of 'intrigue', when all the townspeople put on masks or disguises and try to surprise their friends and acquaintances. Finally the 'carnival man' mascot is burnt on the beach and the party's over.

The festival dates back several centuries when most of the town's male population was employed on fishing boats bringing cod back from Newfoundland. Before leaving on their eight months of hard labour, the fishermen partied hard for three or four days, spending money like, well, drunken sailors. Often they borrowed money from the shipowner against their wages and dressed up in disguises. The children made it into a game, pulling off the fishermen's masks and taunting them: *'Il a mangé ses 400 francs; il s'en ira le cul tout nu au Banc'.* (He ate up his 400 francs; he'll go bare-assed to the fishing banks.)

the outside tank. A collection of fossils leads into rooms full of back-lit paintings and sculptures composed of crystals and semi-precious stones. There are dragons, goddesses, zodiac signs – a veritable New Age pantheon. The final rooms are devoted to elaborate shell sculptures – mermaids, pythons, famous buildings, a family of chimpanzees – each of which took months to create.

♥ MUSÉE D'ART MODERNE RICHARD ANACRÉON // BRINGING ART AND LITERATURE TOGETHER

☎ 02 33 51 02 94; www.ville-granville.fr/culture/musee dartmodernerichardanacreon.html; place de l'Isthme; adult/child €2.60/1.40; ☺ 11am-6pm Tue-Sun Jun-Sep, 2-6pm Wed-Sun Oct-May

This eclectic collection of modern art was a donation from Granville resident Richard Anacréon, who owned a bookshop for many years in Paris' Latin Quarter. Artists displayed include Picasso Vlaminck, Utrillo, Signac and Derain. The window of Anacréon's bookshop has been recreated and contains mementos from Colette, Cocteau, Genet and other Parisian literary figures.

♥ MUSÉE DU VIEUX GRANVILLE // NAUTICALIA, AND HEADDRESSES THAT COULD SUBSTITUTE AS SAILS

☎ 02 33 50 44 10; www.ville-granville.fr/culture/musee duvieuxgranville.html; 2 rue Lecarpentier; adult/child €1.70/1; ☺ 10am-noon & 2-6pm Wed-Mon Apr-Sep, 2-6pm Wed, Sat & Sun Oct-Dec, Feb & Mar

Granville's maritime history is the focus of this little museum displaying painted and ceramic seascapes, model boats, posters, postcards and photographs. There are also rooms of local furniture and traditional Norman costumes, including some truly ridiculous *koefs* (or *coiffes;* women's headdresses).

GASTRONOMIC HIGHLIGHTS

For inexpensive crêperies and cafés, try rue Notre Dame in the upper town and rue St-Sauveur in the lower town.

♥ LA CITADELLE €€

☎ 02 33 50 34 10; 34 rue du Port; menus €23-29; ☺ Thu-Sun

Even the saltiest of sea dogs would feel at home in this port-side restaurant, decorated with knots, nautical photos, wooden seagulls and doomed lobsters in tanks. While seafood is understandably the focus, the meat dishes are equally inspiring. For proof, try the pork in bilberry sauce, served with four different vegetable creations – but save room for the delicious desserts.

TRANSPORT

TRAIN // From Granville's **station** (av de la Gare) there are trains to Paris-Montparnasse, Coutances, Villedieu-les-Poêles and St-Lô. Change at Folligny for travel between Rennes and Caen via Bayeux and Dol-et Bretagne.

BUS // Several buses head to Avranches and Coutances, while the 302 continues north to Valognes and Cherbourg-Octeville.

FERRY // Manche Îles Express (p320) ferries head from the **ferry terminal** (rue des Îles) to Jersey and on to Sark.

BOCAGE COUNTRY

· · · · · ·

WWII veterans remember with a shudder the bocage country that stretches from the Cotentin Peninsula southeast to Vire (in Calvados) and the Suisse Normande. The many zigzagging hedgerows that lend the region its distinctive character were used to devastating effect by the defending Germans, who were able to launch surprise attacks from their leafy hideouts.

From low bushes to higher trees, the bocage was designed to delineate small or irregular parcels of land and has existed for centuries. Its green patchwork carpets the low hills and gentle valleys formed by the Rivers Soulles and Sienne. Small towns and hamlets dot this region, which is predominantly agricultural.

ESSENTIAL INFORMATION

TOURIST OFFICES // Villedieu-les-Poêles (☎ 02 33 61 05 69; www.ot-villedieu.fr; 43 place de la République; ☽ 9am-7pm Jul & Aug, 9am-noon & 2-5.30pm Mon-Sat Sep-Jun); Coutances (☎ 02 33 19 08 10; www.coutances.fr; place Georges Leclerc; ☽ 10am-12.30pm & 2-5pm Mon-Sat); St-Lô (☎ 02 33 77 60 35; www.saint-lo.fr; place du Général de Gaulle; ☽ 9.30am-12.30pm & 2-6pm Mon-Fri, 10am-1pm Sat)

VILLEDIEU-LES-POÊLES & AROUND

♥ VILLEDIEU-LES-POÊLES // WHERE GOD BUYS HIS PANS

The 'city of God' *(villedieu)* and 'pans' *(poêles)* was founded in 1130 by the Hospitallers of St John of Jerusalem, who eventually became the Knights of Malta. The origins of Villedieu-les-Poêles' famous copper industry remain obscure, but it seems that the religious character of the town in the 12th century gave rise to various tax breaks that favoured artisans. Workshops began to produce church ornaments and eventually developed an expertise in kitchen implements.

After a decline in the 19th century, the industry has once again flowered to feed a demand for luxury kitchenware. Atel-ier du Cuivre (☎ 02 33 51 31 85; www.atelier ducuivre.com; 54 rue du Général Huard; adult/child €5/3.50; ☽ 9am-noon & 1.30-6pm Mon-Sat) is one of the oldest copper workshops in town. The admission price gets you an interesting short film (English headphones available) and the chance to wander around the workshop and watch the artisans bang out beautiful but fantastically expensive saucepans (available for purchase in the shop).

♥ MANOIR DE L'ACHERIE // DEVELOP A TASTE FOR COUNTRY LIFE

Well signposted from the road to Caen, 3km east of Villedieu-les-Poêles, this country manor (☎ 02 33 51 13 87; menus €18-39; ☽ Tue-Sun) sits amid bucolic farmland. An on-site boutique sells regional produce, while the restaurant is a celebration of the endeavours of Norman farmers. Only beef from the Normande breed of cow is served and the *menus* are filled with country favourites: home-made terrines, charcuterie platters, crusty bread, smoky barbecued meat and apple tart (served plain, with ice cream or flambéed in Calvados).

COUTANCES & ST-LÔ

♥ COUTANCES // A CHARMING TOWN WITH A SOARING CATHEDRAL

The medieval hilltop town of Coutances was once the capital of the Manche *département,* but since it lost that role in 1796 it has resigned itself to serving as a market for local agricultural products. Still, its remarkable cathedral recalls the days when it was an influential episcopal centre. The contours of the cathedral are visible from afar and its lofty towers and steeples dwarf the modest structures surrounding them. Religious life in Coutances reached its apogee in the 16th century, attracting wealthy and powerful people to set up residences in the town.

The town centre is compact and confined by bd Alsace-Lorraine in the northwest and bd Jeanne Paynel to the east. At the centre of town, the cathedral and town hall face the main square where the market is held on a Thursday morning. Look for the delicious local Coutances cheese with its creamy centre.

The Jazz Sous les Pommiers festival (p161) is held here in mid-May.

Cathédrale Notre Dame

Coutances' creamy limestone **cathedral** (🕙 9am-7pm) is one of France's finest, prompting Victor Hugo to call it the prettiest he'd seen after the one at Chartres. Initially erected in the 11th century, it was transformed by the wave of Gothic architecture that accompanied Philippe-Auguste's takeover of Normandy in the 1200s. A new layer of stone created soaring Gothic towers over the original Romanesque structure.

A rare octagonal lantern tower is the focal point of the light, bright interior and a series of parallel arches makes the cathedral look higher than it is. The dizzying sense of verticality was meant to create the impression that the church was rising to the floors of heaven. Look for the 13th-century stained-glass window in the north transept, which shows scenes from the lives of St Thomas à Becket, St George and St Blaise. In the Chapel of St-Lô is one of the cathedral's oldest windows, dating from the early 13th century. In the south transept, notice the 14th-century window depicting a frightening *Last Judgment*. **Tours** (adult/child €6.50/5.50; 🕙 11.45am Tue mid-Jul–mid-Aug) in English are available, which include access to the galleries in the lantern tower.

Jardin des Plantes

Conceived by a civil engineer and painter, this grand 19th-century landscape **garden** (🕙 9am-5pm Oct-Mar, to 8pm Apr-Jun & mid-Sep–Oct, to 11.30pm Jul–mid-Sep) tastefully blends symmetrical French lines with Italianesque terraces, English-style copses, a hedge maze and fountains. Its varied stock of ornamental trees includes a giant redwood, a Lebanese cedar, a Bhutan pine and a Canadian nut. There's also a labyrinth here. Like the cathedral, the gardens are illuminated on summer nights.

🌿 BEACHES // LOW-KEY OPTIONS FOR SEASIDE LAZING

The beaches of Agon-Coutainville, Gouville and Pirou lie a short distance west of Coutances. The beach at Agon-Coutainville was the first to be developed and remains the most popular; Pirou has the longest beach and a remarkable château that's surrounded by an artificial lake.

🌿 LESSAY // CELEBRATE THE HOLY CROSS FESTIVAL

Benedictine monks founded Lessay's **Foire de Sainte-Croix** (www.canton-lessay .com) in the 1100s and it's still going strong. It features spit roasts, livestock shows and a traditional country-fair atmosphere.

🌿 ST-LÔ // ART, HORSES AND UGLY BUILDINGS

Totally razed during the Allied bombing of 1944, St-Lô rose from the ashes to reclaim its place as the principal administrative and transport hub of Manche. Possibly qualifying as the most charmless city in Normandy, it can nevertheless be an interesting stop for lovers of art or horses.

The **Musée des Beaux-Arts** (☎ 02 33 72 52 55; Centre Culturel Jean-Lurçat, place du champ-de-Mars; admission €1.50; ⌚ 2-6pm Wed-Sun) is a fine regional museum, containing work by Boudin and Moreau. **Le Haras Nationaux** (National Stud Farm; ☎ 02 33 55 29 09; www.haras-nationaux.fr; 437 rue du Maréchal-Juin; adult/child €5/3; ⌚ guided tours 2.30pm, 3.30pm & 4.30pm Jun-Sep, 11am, 2.30pm, 3.30pm & 4.30pm Jul & Aug) houses over 60 stallions and specialises in breeding Norman Cob horses and the French saddle horses. In summer, the **Jeudis du Haras** (Stud Thursdays; ⌚ 3pm Thu Jul & Aug) involve colourful parades of horses and carriages.

TRANSPORT

TRAIN // Villedieu-les-Poêles is on the Granville–Paris line. Coutances and St-Lô both have direct trains to Caen, Bayeux, Granville, Avranches, Dol-de-Bretagne and Rennes.

BUS // All of these towns are well connected to each other and the rest of Manche.

HAUT-COTENTIN

The Cotentin Peninsula traces its name to 4th-century Roman emperor Constantius Chlorus. Its northwestern corner is especially captivating, with unspoilt stretches of rocky coastline sheltering tranquil bays and quaint villages – and the odd nuclear power station. Due west of the peninsula lie the Channel Islands of Jersey (25km from the coast) and Guernsey (45km), accessible by ferry from St-Malo and the Manche towns of Carteret and Granville. The peninsula's rugged tip is Cap de la Hague, the westernmost point of Normandy.

BARNEVILLE-CARTERET

Like Deauville-Trouville (p208) cast in extreme miniature, Barneville-Carteret is a pair of linked holiday towns separated by a river estuary. Carteret is the smaller and more fashionable of the two, while Barneville has the main town centre and a beach running into a sandy spit jutting into the estuary. It's extremely tidal – the river narrows to practically nothing at low tide, when it's a long trek to the shoreline.

Carteret is also home to Manche's best restaurant. At Michelin-starred **La Marine** (☎ 02 33 53 83 31; rue de Paris; menus €36-89; ⌚ lunch Tue, Wed & Fri-Sun, dinner Tue-Sat Mar-Nov), a parade of black-suited waiters welcome you and escort you into an elegant dining room with panoramic water views. In the kitchen, subtly flavoured sauces tango with fresh produce – especially locally caught fish – while intense reductions provide bursts of flavour. Save room for the desserts – the apple rice pudding with orange-blossom ice cream is divine.

You'll find the **tourist office** (☎ 02 33 04 93 24; www.barneville-carteret.fr; 10 rue des Ecoles; ⌚ 9.15am-12.30pm & 2-6pm Mon-Sat) near the main road in Barneville. Buses 103 (Cherbourg-Octeville) and 105 (Valognes) stop nearby. Ferries depart Carteret for Guernsey and Alderney (p320).

VALOGNES

pop 7800

The architectural unity of Valognes creates a surprising effect. From the banks of the narrow river to mansions, townhouses and bridges, everything is constructed from the same beige-grey granite. At first glance the town centre seems to be all angles, corners and walls, but closer examination reveals elaborate decoration on the sober facades.

TOP CAMPING

* **Camping La Vague** (☎ 02 33 50 29 97; rte de Vaudroulin; d €17; ♥ May-Sep) Two kilometres south of Granville town centre and 200m from the beach, this camping ground has 145 places.

* **Camping Les Vignettes** (☎ 02 33 45 43 13; rte de St-Malo-de-la-Lande; adult/site €3.20/3.40; ⌨) On the northwest outskirts of Coutances, the site has lots of flowering trees and views of the cathedral.

* **Camping le Bocage** (☎ 02 33 53 86 91; fax 02 33 04 35 98; rue du Bocage, Carteret; adult/child €6.20/4.50; ♥ Apr-Sep) A trim site delineated by tidy hedges.

* **La Blanche Nef** (☎ 02 33 23 15 40; www.camping-barfleur.fr; rue du Puit; low/high season s €4.75/7.05, d €7.90/13.70) Next to Barfleur's seaside promenade, this camping ground offers plenty of beach activities.

* **Camping de Collignon** (☎ 02 33 20 16 88; camping-collignon@wanadoo.fr; adult/site €4.50/6.40; ♥ May-Sep) On the coast in Tourlaville, 5km northeast of Cherbourg. There's a large indoor swimming pool nearby and a kayak club.

MANCHE

In the late 17th and early 18th centuries many noble families with chateaux in the countryside constructed opulent winter quarters in Valognes. With its new burst of money and prestige, Valognes became known as the 'little Versailles of Normandy'. Its moment of glory ended abruptly with the Revolution of 1789, but the town continued to prosper, turning out porcelain for a while, then butter and now material for the nearby nuclear industry.

Proud of its heritage, Valognes was rebuilt with style after WWII, and recovered a considerable part of its aristocratic allure.

ESSENTIAL INFORMATION

TOURIST OFFICE // Valognes (☎ 02 33 40 11 55; www.mairie-valognes.fr; place du Château; ♥ 9.30am-noon & 2.30-6pm)

ORIENTATION

At the centre of town is place du Château and the main thoroughfare is bd Division-Leclerc, which becomes bd

Félix Buhot in the northwest and bd de Verdun in the southeast.

EXPLORING VALOGNES

❦ **HÔTEL DE BEAUMONT // POKE AROUND A PRIVATE PALACE**
A fine columned facade and wrought-iron balcony front this elegant 18th-century **mansion** (☎ 02 33 40 12 30; cnr rue Barbey d'Aurevilly & rue Petit Versailles; adult/child €5/3; ♥ 10.30am-12.30pm & 2.30-5pm Mon-Sat, 2.30-5pm Sun Jul–mid-Sep), still inhabited by a count and countess. In the summer months they give guided visits to a set of rooms furnished in various historic styles, along with a stroll around the manicured gardens.

❦ **MUSEUMS // CELEBRATE THE UNION OF APPLES AND ALCOHOL**
A two-part **museum** (adult/child €4/2; ♥ 10am-noon & 2-6pm Mon & Wed-Sat, 2-6pm Sun Apr-Sep) is devoted to Normandy's most famous thirst-quenchers – cider and Calvados. **Musée Régional du Cidre** (☎ 02 33 40 22 73; rue du Petit Versailles) has three

floors of cider tools and equipment, plus a video explaining the production process. Up the street, **Musée de l'Eau-de-Vie et des Vieux Métiers** (☎ 02 33 40 26 25; rue Pelouze) is in a 17th-century mansion that functioned as a lace factory, barracks and fire station before it became a museum displaying the barrels, pipes and casks used to make Calvados. The stone, iron and leather trades are also described here.

TRANSPORT

BUS // Buses 1 (Cherbourg-Octeville/St-Lô), 101 (Barfleur), 105 (Barneville-Carteret), 106 (Coutances), 300 (Cherbourg-Octeville/Coutances/Avranches) and 302 (Cherbourg-Octeville/Coutances/Granville) all stop at place du Château.

TRAIN // The **station** (rue Henri-Cornat) is a stop on the Cherbourg–Paris line (via Bayeux and Caen).

AROUND VALOGNES

♥ **STE-MÈRE-ÉGLISE // THE TOWN INFATUATED WITH PARACHUTES**
In perhaps the most celebrated image of D-Day, John Steele, an American paratrooper, drifted down from the skies on the night of 6 June 1944 and entangled himself on the church steeple in Ste-Mère-Église. The episode was featured in the film *The Longest Day*, and Steele became something of a local celebrity, returning every so often to re-enact the drama. Since his death, a mannequin has taken his place on the church roof. Stained-glass windows inside the 12th-century church depict the Madonna and Child surrounded by parachutists and St Michael, the patron saint of paratroopers.

The **Musée Airborne** (☎ 02 33 41 41 35; www.musee-airborne.com; 14 rue Eisenhower; adult/

HAVE STILL, WILL TRAVEL

It was a sad day in Basse-Normandie (Lower Normandy) when the government decided to phase out home-brewed spirits. Until 1960 most households had the inherited right to distil about 20L annually (tax-free) for their personal consumption. In these parts, that liquor was likely to be Calvados. Rather than abruptly terminating production of the firewater (and possibly risking mass DTs), it was decided that the 'privilege' could only be passed on to a surviving spouse.

The immediate effect of the law was an explosion in the black-market trade of soon-to-be-scarce home-made Calvados. For a few years, it was Chicago-on-the-Orne as the gendarmeries, often tipped off by spiteful neighbours, battled a new network of gangsters. Local newspapers had a field day recounting tales of clandestine meetings, car chases and midnight busts.

The criminality gradually simmered down, but a centuries-old tradition went into long-term decline. Very few families could afford their own still, so most used the services of a *distillateur ambulant* (travelling moonshine maker). From October to December, the *distillateur ambulant* took his still from town to town to transform the local apple stock into precious liquor. His arrival was a festive occasion, celebrated with – *bien sur!* – lots of Calvados.

There are still a few old folk out there brewing up their spirits, but artisanal Calvados is extremely difficult to find. Old Norman families are bound to have a few bottles stashed away, but you'll probably have to marry into the family in order to taste it.

child €7/4; ⏰ 9am-6.45pm Apr-Sep, 9.30am-noon & 2-6pm Feb, Mar, Oct & Nov) tells the story of the landings through films, documents and photos. Jeeps, tanks and even a C47 transport plane help convey the intensity of the experience.

Ste-Mère-Église was the first village to be liberated on D-Day. It is now point zero for La Voie de la Liberté (Liberty Way), the route marked out by white milestones that follows the march of General Patton's Third Army across Normandy in 1944 (for more, see p185).

South of Ste-Mère-Église is the fine **PNR Marais du Cotentin et du Bessin** (see p161).

Bus 1 (Cherbourg-Octeville/Valognes/St-Lô) stops by the town hall.

☙ ÎLE TATIHOU // DEFENDED BY WALLS AND WATER

In 2008 this **fortified island** (☎ 02 33 23 19 92; www.tatihou.com; adult/child €7.80/3.20; ⏰ 10am-4pm daily Apr-Sep, 2-5pm Sat & Sun mid-Feb–Mar & Oct), was placed on the Unesco World Heritage list, joining 11 other forts designed by Sébastien Le Prestre de Vauban (1633–1707), scattered all over France. The complex includes a restaurant, a maritime museum, gardens, a bird reserve and, of course, the fort itself. Climb up the tower for terrific views.

Access is by an amphibian vehicle that leaves from St-Vaast-la-Hougue, a cute marina town 18km northeast of Valognes. Take bus 101 from Valognes or 102 from Cherbourg-Octeville.

☙ BARFLEUR // A FISHING PORT WITH A FRAGILE BEAUTY

Little more than a cluster of granite houses on a finger of land, Barfleur was once the most important commercial harbour on the Cotentin Peninsula with a population of 9000. The sea has been creeping up on the town for centuries, turning it into a scenic but relatively minor fishing port. Dykes have been erected on the northern shore, but the town still seems on the verge of disappearing under the waves. There's a small beach, but Barfleur is mainly attractive for its laid-back, village-on-the-sea ambience.

In its heyday under the Norman dukes, Barfleur was involved in two pivotal events. It was a local, Étienne, who built and piloted the ship – the *Mora* – that carried William the Conqueror to England in 1066. A stele across from the tourist office commemorates the fact.

Less happily, it was from Barfleur that the infamous *Blanche Nef* was launched in 1120. William the Conqueror's son, Henry I of England, was returning to England and entrusted a local seaman with the boat carrying his son, daughter-in-law and 300 courtiers. King Henry's vessel set out and began to outpace the *Blanche Nef*. Considerably intoxicated, the sailors of the *Blanche Nef* tried to outmanoeuvre the king's boat, but were swept away by currents and crashed onto the offshore rocks. All the nobles were drowned, ending the line of William the Conqueror and giving rise to the Plantagenet dynasty. The site is marked by a lighthouse, visible from the town centre.

The **tourist office** (☎ 02 33 54 02 48; www .ville-barfleur.fr; quai Henri Chardon; ⏰ 9.30am-12.30pm & 2.30-6.30pm Mon-Sat Apr-Jun & Sep, daily Jul & Aug) is at the tip of the port near a monument to William the Conqueror and a simple 17th-century church, **Église St-Nicolas**, clearly built to withstand maritime gusts. You can pay €2 to turn the church lights on, but then you'd miss the otherworldly golden glow cast over the sanctuary from the stained-glass windows.

MANCHE

The same buses that service the departure point for Île Tatihou stop here; see p171.

CHERBOURG-OCTEVILLE

pop 42,100

Cherbourg has a small old town huddled behind the sprawl of maritime installations radiating out from its immense port, but the city is not nearly as romantic as that portrayed in Jacques Demy's 1964 classic film *Les Parapluies de Cherbourg* (The Umbrellas of Cherbourg). The shops, cafés and sights might keep you occupied for a day, but the main reasons to visit are the excellent sailing and kayaking opportunities (p160) or as an entry point to the Cotentin Peninsula by ferry.

In 2000 Cherbourg was officially merged with its neighbour Octeville, which it had already effectively gobbled, and the hyphenated name was adopted. There are markets on Tuesday and Thursday until about 5pm at place Général de Gaulle and place Centrale.

ESSENTIAL INFORMATION

TOURIST OFFICES // Main Tourist Office
(☎ 02 33 93 52 02; www.otcherbourgcotentin.fr; 2 quai Alexandre III; ◷ 9am-6.30pm Mon-Sat Jul & Aug, 9am-noon & 2-6pm Mon-Sat Sep-Jun); **Tourist Office Annexe** (☎ 02 33 44 39 92; ferry terminal) Open for ferry arrivals.

ORIENTATION

Most places of interest are immediately west of the central waterway, the Bassin du Commerce. The train and bus station are at its southern end and the ferry terminal is to the northeast, connected to the city centre by buses.

EXPLORING CHERBOURG-OCTEVILLE

❦ MUSÉE D'ART THOMAS HENRY // TAKE A FREE SHOT OF ART

This wonderful **gallery** (☎ 02 33 23 39 30; www.ville-cherbourg.fr; 4 rue Vastel; admission free; ◷ 10am-noon & 2-6pm Tue-Sat, 2-6pm Sun & Mon May-Sep, 2-6pm Wed-Sun Oct-Apr) has a varied collection of 15th- to 19th-century art and stages regular contemporary exhibitions. Highlights include works by Fra Angelico and Poussin, and rooms devoted to three local artists: Jean-François Millet, Felix Bohut and Guillaume Fouace.

❦ CITÉ DE LA MER // DELVE THE DEPTHS, IN MORE WAYS THAN ONE

A combined aquarium, museum and amusement park, Cherbourg's big **attraction** (☎ 02 33 20 26 29; www.citedelamer.com; Allée du Président Menut; adult/child €18/13; ◷ 10am-6pm) could keep you, and especially the kids, entertained for half a day – and at these prices, you'd certainly want it to. The most interesting part is the audio-guided tour of the decommissioned nuclear submarine *Redoutable*. Visits to both the cramped crew quarters and the ballistic missile room are unsettling experiences. The other centrepiece is the Tahitian atoll recreated in an 11m-high cylindrical aquarium holding 350,000 cu metres of water – the biggest fish tank in Europe. Tickets include admission to a 'virtual adventure' that is lame beyond belief – although you may find it unintentionally hilarious.

❦ CHERBOURG HARBOUR // EXPLORE THE SMALL MAN'S HUGE PORT

It was Napoleon's idea to build a port here, in preparation for the invasion of

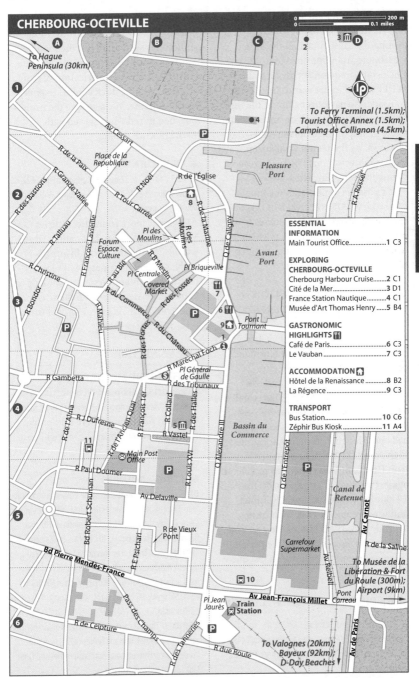

CHERBOURG-OCTEVILLE

MANCHE

To Hague Peninsula (30km)

To Ferry Terminal (1.5km);
Tourist Office Annex (1.5km);
Camping de Collignon (4.5km)

Pleasure Port

Avant Port

Place de la République

Forum Espace Culture

Pl des Moulins

Covered Market

Pl Centrale

Pl Briqueville

Pont Tournant

Pl Général de Gaulle

Bassin du Commerce

Main Post Office

Carrefour Supermarket

Canal de Retenue

To Musée de la Libération & Fort du Roule (300m); Airport (9km)

Pl Jean Jaurès

Train Station

To Valognes (20km); Bayeux (92km); D-Day Beaches

ESSENTIAL INFORMATION
Main Tourist Office.....................1 C3

EXPLORING CHERBOURG-OCTEVILLE
Cherbourg Harbour Cruise......2 C1
Cité de la Mer.............................3 D1
France Station Nautique...........4 C1
Musée d'Art Thomas Henry 5 B4

GASTRONOMIC HIGHLIGHTS
Café de Paris..............................6 C3
Le Vauban...................................7 C3

ACCOMMODATION
Hôtel de la Renaissance 8 B2
La Régence 9 C3

TRANSPORT
Bus Station..............................10 C6
Zéphir Bus Kiosk 11 A4

MANCHE

England he never got around to launching. Napoleon III completed the project around the same time that the Paris–Cherbourg train line opened in 1831. Enclosing 15 sq km, it's the largest artificial harbour in the world. It welcomed transatlantic passenger ships at the turn of the century and took on an enormous strategic importance during the D-Day landings. As the region's only deep-water harbour, it was indispensable in resupplying the Allied invasion forces.

It's possible to take an hour-long cruise (☎ 02 33 78 19 29; adult/child €12/8) out to the fortifications. The boat leaves from in front of the Cité de la Mer, which is where you can enquire about departure times and purchase tickets.

☘ MUSÉE DE LA LIBÉRATION // GREAT VIEWS AND INTERESTING DISPLAYS

Devoted to the role played by Cherbourg's port in the Battle of Normandy, this attention-grabbing museum (☎ 02 33 20 14 12; www.ville-cherbourg.fr; adult/child €3.40/1.85, 1st Sun of month free; ⊙ 10am-noon & 2-6pm Tue-Sat, 2-6pm Sun & Mon May-Sep, 2-6pm Wed-Sun Oct-Apr) is housed in the strategically positioned Fort du Roule, located high above the town. Built under Napoleon III, the fort was intended to defend against an English attack. On 19 June 1940 it fell to Field Marshal Rommel and was occupied by German troops until 26 June 1944. Photos, posters and audiovisual aids document the period of occupation and Cherbourg's subsequent liberation.

GASTRONOMIC HIGHLIGHTS

☘ CAFÉ DE PARIS €

☎ 02 33 43 12 36; 40 quai de Caligny; menus €19-37, 2-course lunch €16; ⊙ lunch & dinner Tue-Sat, dinner Mon

It's not the place for a romantic tête-à-tête, with the constant crowds and sometimes surly staff, but the food in this plum-hued brasserie is excellent. There's always a selection of fresh seafood, and the duck cooked in *pommeau* is divine. We also love the prunes poached in red wine, served with Armagnac ice cream.

☘ LE VAUBAN €€

☎ 02 33 43 10 11; 22 quai de Caligny; menus €22-60, 2-course lunch €17; ⊙ lunch Sun, lunch & dinner Tue-Fri, dinner Sat

Altogether more romantic, little Le Vauban has modern decor and a large window facing the port. Unsurprisingly, seafood dominates, with lobster, crabs, scallops and oysters all making an appearance, depending on the season. The 'trio of fish' is a treat, served with a creamy, buttery sauce.

TRANSPORT

TO/FROM THE AIRPORT

Aéroport Cherbourg-Maupertis (☎ 02 33 88 57 60; www.aeroport-cherbourg.com) is about 9km east of the city. There's no public transport into town and a taxi will cost around €20.

GETTING AROUND

BUS // Manéo services stop at the bus station (av Jean-François Millet). Routes include 1 (Valognes/St-Mère-Église/St-Lô), 100 (Hague Peninsula), 102 (Barfleur/St-Vaast-la-Hougue), 103 (Barneville-Carteret), 300 (Valognes/Coutances/Avranches) and 302 (Valognes/Coutances/Granville). There's also an extensive local network operated by Zéphir Bus (☎ 08 10 81 00 50; www.zephirbus.com), with its main hub on bd Schuman.

FERRY // Three ferry companies have regular services across the channel: Brittany Ferries (p321) heads to Poole and Portsmouth, and both Irish Ferries and Celtic Link (p321) sail to Rosslare.

TRAIN // The **train station** (av Jean-François Millet) has direct services to Paris-St-Lazare via Valognes, Bayeux, Caen and Lisieux.

HAGUE PENINSULA

The wild landscape on the northwestern tip of Normandy has often been compared to Ireland. Pastures, demarcated by stone walls, roll up to the edge of cliffs, while below an ice-blue sea pounds lonely coves.

Perhaps it was the remoteness of the site that inspired the French government to turn a hunk of it over to the nuclear-power industry. The eerie constellation of white tanks, tubes, towers and offices at the sprawling and controversial AREVA plant are devoted to the storage and reprocessing of spent nuclear fuel. Further down the coast there's a massive nuclear-power station at Flamanville.

At 128m, the sea cliff at **Nez de Jobourg** is the highest in continental Europe and is a sanctuary for sea birds. On a clear day you can see the Channel Islands. The majestic curve of the **Baie d'Ecalgrain** is a few kilometres north. Windswept skies, tossing waves and low cliffs capped with meadows create a romantic vista.

Near the tip of the peninsula, **Auderville** is a tiny village with an artful arrangement of stone houses built to withstand the gusty winds. The road ends 1km further at **Goury**, a world's-end hamlet hunkered around a tiny harbour. One of the world's most powerful and dangerous currents, the Raz Blanchard, runs just offshore, and a 150m lighthouse (1837) stands sentinel on a rocky outcrop just out to sea. The UK island of Alderney (Aurigny) is only 15km offshore.

The **Auberge de Goury** (☎ 02 33 52 77 01; menus €26-29, 2-course lunch €18; ⏰ lunch & dinner Tue-Sat, lunch Sun) is as atmospheric an establishment as you could hope for. An open fire blazes in the main dining room, where the ebullient owner barbecues whatever you order (lamb, whole fish, lobster) to a deliciously smoky effect.

From Goury you can walk a scenic circuit along the coast to the rustic hamlet of **La Roche**, where there's a covered well and *lavoir* (wash house), before cutting across to Auderville and following the main road back.

Bus 100 heads out from Cherbourg-Octeville as far as Auderville.

CLAMEUR DE HARO

Norman tradition allows someone who has been wronged to invoke their rights by raising *la clameur*. In front of two witnesses, the injured party sinks to their knees, recites the Lord's Prayer in French and cries *'Haro! Haro! À l'aide, mon Prince, on me fait tort!'* (Haro! Haro! Help me, my Prince, someone is wronging me!). The accused must then stop the offending acts and wait for the legal system to run its course. 'Haro' is thought to derive from the cry of 'Ha' and 'Roi' or 'Rollo', the first duke of Normandy. Although the custom has fallen out of use in Normandy, it survives in parts of the Channel Islands.

CALVADOS & ORNE

3 PERFECT DAYS

❦ DAY 1 // THE LONGEST DAY

Begin with a D-Day overview at the excellent Mémorial de Caen (p191) before heading to the beaches where the action took place. All of the major sites – Pointe du Hoc (p186), Batterie-de-Longues (p187), and the beaches themselves – can be seen in one day, but you'll need to be judicious with the museums you visit. Allow time for Arromanches 360 (p188), the American Military Cemetery (p187) and the Bayeux War Cemetery (p183) at a minimum.

❦ DAY 2 // CONQUER WILLIAM'S LEGACY

At Bayeux, brush up on the history of the Norman Conquest by viewing the famous tapestry (opposite). Head back to Caen (p191) you'll find one of William's castles and the abbeys where he and his wife were buried. Continue south to Falaise (p196) and tour the fortress where William was born. Spend the rest of the day exploring the beautiful Suisse Normande (p194).

❦ DAY 3 // GASTRONOMIC GOODIES

First stop, Camembert (p204) – if only for a photo in front of the road sign. Continue through the heart of the Pays d'Auge to Livarot (p204) and a tour and tasting at the cheese factory. Convince your travelling partner that it's their turn to be the designated driver and head to the Distillerie Christian Drouin (p180), just outside of Pont l'Évêque, to see how Calvados and cider are made. Hit Deauville-Trouville (p208) for lunch and a look around, and continue on to Honfleur (p211) where there are many wonderful restaurants to choose from for dinner.

BAYEUX

• • • • • •

pop 15,000

The first city to be liberated after the D-Day landings, Bayeux is one of the few towns in Calvados to have survived WWII largely unscathed. The River Aure still turns the paddles of watermills as it cuts through ancient streets lined with elegant stone mansions and the occasional rickety half-timbered medieval house. Rue St-Malo (which becomes St-Martin and then St-Jean) has been the main street since Gallo-Roman times, when the town was known as Augustodurum. Behind the cathedral you can see remnants of Bayeux's 3rd-century walls.

The town may be synonymous with its World Heritage–listed tapestry (see below) but it's also a wonderfully picturesque base from which to explore the D-Day beaches.

The **Fêtes Médiévales de Bayeux** is held here in July, and the **Calvadose de Rock** is held in August (see p181 for details).

ESSENTIAL INFORMATION

TOURIST OFFICE // Bayeux (☎ 02 31 51 28 28; www.bessin-normandie.com; Pont St-Jean; ⌚ 9am-6pm Jul & Aug; 9am-12.30pm & 2-5.30pm Mon-Sat Sep-Jun)

EXPLORING BAYEUX

❦ BAYEUX TAPESTRY // **READ THE WORLD'S MOST FAMOUS CARTOON STRIP**

They say that it's the prerogative of the victors to write history – and if they decide to embroider it onto 68m of linen, then who's to argue. The world-famous

Tapisserie de Bayeux (☎ 02 31 51 25 50; www.tapisserie-bayeux.fr; 13 bis rue de Nesmond; adult/child €7.80/3.80; ⌚ 9am-6.30pm mid-Mar–mid-Nov, 9.30am-12.30pm & 2-6pm mid-Nov–mid-Mar, last admission 45min prior) recounts the Norman take on their invasion of England. The Norman Conquest was the military epic that defined the 11th century, in much the same way as the D-Day landings defined the 20th century – which makes the tapestry the *Saving Private Ryan* of its time.

The cloth itself has had a turbulent history. In 1792 it was narrowly saved from use as a wagon cover, and in 1794 it was almost cut up into decorative sections. Napoleon displayed it in Paris for a few years to drum up support for an invasion of England, but the tapestry was eventually returned to Bayeux, where the priceless work underwent a careful restoration. In 1939 it was placed in an air-raid shelter and then in 1944 it was sent to Paris and hidden in a cellar of the Louvre.

An excellent free audioguide will walk you along the tapestry at a cracking rate (hit pause if you want to linger), providing plenty of detail but conveniently ignoring the sexually explicit images in the borders. For more on the tapestry, see the boxed text, p183. A separate room contains interesting bilingual displays about Norman life, the Conquest and the history of the tapestry. The visit culminates in a 16-minute film that brings the embroidered scenes to life with recreations and a commentary (English and French screenings alternate).

A tapestry ticket gets you free entrance into the **Musée Baron Gérard** (☎ 02 31 92 14 21; 6 rue Lambert Leforestier; adult/child €3.50/1.50; ⌚ 10am-12.30pm & 2-6pm), where a small collection of archaeological artefacts, paintings, local lace and porcelain is housed in the mansion, Hôtel du Doyen.

(Continued on page 182)

CALVADOS & ORNE

CALVADOS & ORNE

GETTING AROUND

Caen sits at the centre of a web of autoroutes, including the A13 heading east to Rouen and Paris, the A84 southwest to Rennes and the N158, which joins the A88 heading south. Orne is served by the **CapOrne** (☎ 02 33 81 61 95; www.orne.fr) bus network and Calvados by **busverts** (☎ 0810 214 214; www.busverts.fr), which has routes extending as far as Le Havre. The main train routes cut west–east through Bayeux, Caen and Lisieux, and south from Caen to Alençon.

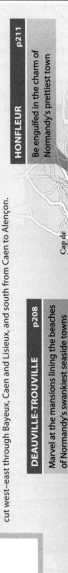

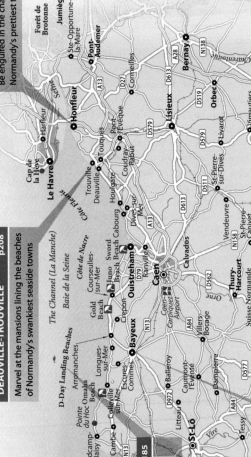

HONFLEUR p211

Be engulfed in the charm of Normandy's prettiest town

DEAUVILLE-TROUVILLE p208

Marvel at the mansions lining the beaches of Normandy's swankiest seaside towns

D-DAY BEACHES p185

Honour the fallen at the places where they fell

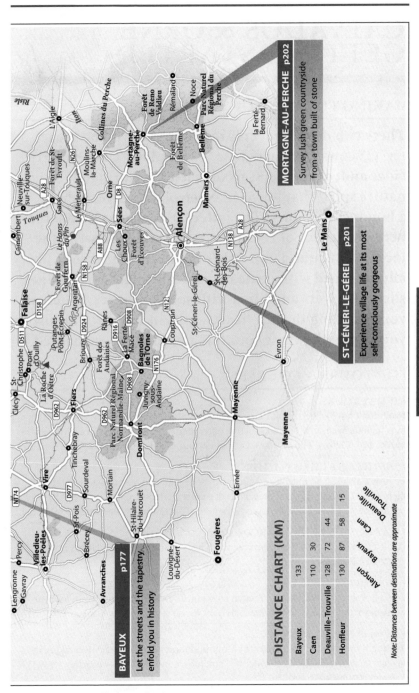

CALVADOS & ORNE

MORTAGNE-AU-PERCHE p202

Survey lush green countryside from a town built of stone

ST-CÉNERI-LE-GÉREI p201

Experience village life at its most self-consciously gorgeous

BAYEUX p177

Let the streets and the tapestry, enfold you in history

DISTANCE CHART (KM)

	Alençon	Bayeux	Caen	Deauville-Trouville
Bayeux	133			
Caen	110	30		
Deauville-Trouville	128	72	44	
Honfleur	130	87	58	15

Note: Distances between destinations are approximate

CALVADOS & ORNE
GETTING STARTED

MAKING THE MOST OF YOUR TIME

These two *départements* are brought to you by the letter 'C': cows, cream, cheese (particularly Camembert), cider and, of course, Calvados itself – Normandy's signature spirit that burns like petrol but leaves behind a bouquet of apples. The letter 'D' is also written large here: the legacy of D-Day is inescapable. Between the local produce and war sights is a lush countryside, liberally seasoned with châteaux and chocolate-box villages, sliced by rivers and lined with sandy beaches. Whether you're hitting the big-ticket sights in Calvados or losing yourself in the Orne countryside, you'll be enchanted.

TOP TOURS & COURSES

♥ D-DAY TOURS
If you don't have wheels, a tour is the best option for exploring the D-Day sites. Options include Mémorial de Caen (p191), **Normandy Sightseeing Tours** (www.normandy webguide.com), **Victory Tours** (www.victorytours.com) and **Overlordtour** (www.overlordtour.com).

♥ DISTILLERIE CHRISTIAN DROUIN
See how Calvados, *pommeau* and cider are made with a tour and tasting at this distillery in a 17th-century farm; free, with the expectation of a purchase. (☎ 02 31 64 30 05; www.coeur-de-lion.com; rte de Trouville, Coudray-Rabut (north of Pont l'Évêque); ⊙ 9am-noon & 2-6pm Mon-Sat)

♥ KAYAK CLUB THURY-HARCOURT
Kayak 14km down the Orne from Clécy to Thury-Harcourt. (☎ 02 31 79 40 59; www.kcth.fr; equipment & minibus €28)

♥ OUICHEF!
A village-based introduction to French cooking, as a day course or live-in four- or seven-day stint. (☎ 02 33 36 55 32; www.ouichef.co.uk; Neuville-sur-Touques; day/4-day/week €140/730/1285)

♥ NORMANDY SAFARIS
Five-night boutique tours including accommodation in the Pays d'Auge, taking in Bayeux, Giverny, Falaise, Les Andelys, Camembert and the D-Day beaches. (☎ 02 33 35 31 98; www.normandysafaris.co.uk)

GETTING AWAY FROM IT ALL

* **Parc Naturel Régional Normandie-Maine** Spilling from Basse-Normandie (Lower Normandy) into the Pays de la Loire, this large protected area includes the Forêt des Andaines around Bagnoles de l'Orne and the pretty villages of the Sarthe Valley (p201 and p197). (www.parc-naturel-normandie-maine.fr)

* **Parc Naturel Régional du Perche** Much of this 2035-sq-km park is fields and forests – there are no cities, no autoroutes and just a few towns. The Percheron horse (p203) originated here, as did a substantial proportion of French Canadians. Over 1000km of hiking, cycling and horse-riding trails are marked, and some fine villages can be visited (p202)

ADVANCE PLANNING

Deauville is the events capital of Normandy and can quickly fill up during these times.

* **Festival of American Film** (www.festival-deauville.com; day/festival pass €30/150) Hollywood stars join the crowds in Deauville in early September.

* **Fêtes Médiévales de Bayeux** (www.mairie-bayeux.fr; admission free) Held on the first weekend in July to commemorate the end to the Hundred Years' War. Expect costumes, song, dance, parades and street theatre.

* **Calvadose de Rock** (www.myspace.com/Calvadosederock; 1/2 days €10/15) Two-day rock festival held in Bayeux in early August.

* **Equi'days** (www.equidays.com) A three-weekend, two-week horse festival.

TOP RESTAURANTS

❦ LE P'TIT RESTO
Fusion French in hip surroundings (p185)

❦ LE BOUCHON DU VAUGUEUX
Hearty serves of homespun cooking (p194)

❦ LE RELAIS DE LA POSTE
An inventive take on game and seafood (p195)

❦ L'EDEN
Freshness is almost an obsession (p208)

❦ L'ORANGERIE
Revelling in the flavours of Normandy (p211)

❦ LA TERRASSE & L'ASSIETTE
Traditional French cooking, perfectly executed (p215)

❦ LE BRÉARD
A gastronomic journey par excellence (p215)

RESOURCES

* **Calvados Tourisme** (www.Calvados-tourisme.com) Practical information about the *département*'s sights and activities.

* **Orne Tourisme** (www.ornetourisme.com) As above, but for Orne.

* **D-Day-Overlord** (www.dday-overlord.com) Information about the Battle of Normandy.

* **Caen Tourisme** (www.tourisme.caen.fr) Accommodation, sights and events in the region's biggest city.

* **Bessin** (www.bessin-normandie.com) Bayeux and the D-Day beaches.

CALVADOS & ORNE

(Continued from page 177)

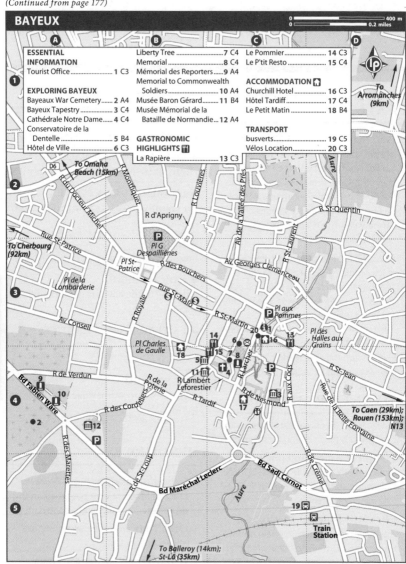

BAYEUX

| | | 0 — 400 m |
| | | 0 — 0.2 miles |

ESSENTIAL INFORMATION
Tourist Office 1 C3

EXPLORING BAYEUX
Bayeux War Cemetery....... 2 A4
Bayeux Tapestry 3 C4
Cathédrale Notre Dame..... 4 C4
Conservatoire de la
  Dentelle 5 B4
Hôtel de Ville 6 C3

Liberty Tree 7 C4
Memorial 8 C4
Mémorial des Reporters......9 A4
Memorial to Commonwealth
  Soldiers 10 A4
Musée Baron Gérard.......... 11 B4
Musée Mémorial de la
  Bataille de Normandie... 12 A4

GASTRONOMIC HIGHLIGHTS
La Rapière 13 C3

Le Pommier 14 C3
Le P'tit Resto 15 C4

ACCOMMODATION
Churchill Hotel 16 C3
Hôtel Tardiff....................... 17 C4
Le Petit Matin 18 B4

TRANSPORT
busverts............................... 19 C5
Vélos Location.................... 20 C3

Map labels:
To Arromanches (9km)
D6 To Omaha Beach (15km)
R.du Docteur Michel
R.Montfiquet
R d'Aprigny
R.Louviers
Av de la Vallée des Prés
R St-Quentin
Rue St-Patrice
To Cherbourg (92km)
Pl G Despailliènes
Pl St-Patrice
R.des Bouchers
Av Georges Clémenceau
R St-Laurent
Pl de la Lombarderie
R.Royale
Rue St-Malo
R St-Martin
Pl aux Pommes
Av Conseil
Pl Charles de Gaulle
Pl des Halles aux Grains
R de Verdun
R de la Poterie
R Lambert Leforestier
R.Larcher
R de Nesmond
R St-Jean
R aux Coqs
Rue de la Belle Fontaine
R Tardif
To Caen (29km); Rouen (153km); N13
Bd Fabien Ware
R des Cordeliers
R des Marettes
R de St-Loup
To Ballery (14km); St-Lô (35km)
Bd Maréchal Leclerc
Bd Sadi Carnot
Azure
R de Crémel
Train Station

♥ CATHÉDRALE NOTRE DAME & SURROUNDS // A BEAUTIFUL HODGE-PODGE OF ARCHITECTURAL STYLES

Most of Bayeux's spectacular **cathedral** (rue du Bienvenu; ⏰ 9am-6pm) is a fine example of Norman Gothic architecture, dating from the 13th century. However, the crypt, the arches of the nave and the lower portions of the towers on either side of the main entrance are 11th-century Romanesque. The central tower was added in the 15th century; the copper dome dates from the 1860s.

Next to the cathedral, the former bishop's palace became the **Hôtel de Ville** (Town Hall) following the Revolution. The massive plane tree in place de la Liberté is one of France's last remaining **Liberty Trees**; in 1797 the Revolutionary government decreed that one be planted in every commune in France. During WWII, the Nazis occupied the town hall and used part of it as a gaol. A harrowing **memorial** on place des Déportées commemorates those sent from here to the death camps.

❧ CONSERVATOIRE DE LA DENTELLE // WITNESS AN AGE-OLD LOCAL TRADITION

At the **Lace Conservatory** (☎ 02 31 92 73 80; http: // dentelledebayeux.free.fr; 6 rue du Bienvenu; admission free; ☉ 9.30am-12.30pm & 2.30-6pm Mon-Sat) you can watch some of France's most celebrated lace-makers create intricate designs using dozens of bobbins and hundreds of pins. At its height, the local lace industry employed 5000 people. The conservatory, dedicated to the preservation of traditional Norman lace-making, inhabits a wonderful late 15th-century half-timbered building called Adam and Eve House after the carvings on the top storey.

❧ BAYEUX WAR CEMETERY // THE SONS OF MANY NATIONS, UNITED IN DEATH

This tenderly cared-for **cemetery** (bd Fabien Ware) is the largest of the 18 Commonwealth military cemeteries in Normandy. Most of the nearly 5000 soldiers buried here were British, which explains the poignant inscription (in French) on the memorial: 'We, who were conquered by William, have liberated the homeland of the conqueror'. However there are also Canadians, Australians, New Zealanders, South Africans, Poles, Russians, French, Czechs and Italians buried here. Many of the 466 Germans were never identified

CALVADOS & ORNE

THE BAYEUX TAPESTRY

The story of the history-changing Norman conquest of England (p198) is presented cartoon-style, with 58 scenes, briefly captioned in Latin, and a cast of hundreds. The main narrative fills up the centre of the canvas, while Norman daily life unfolds in the top and bottom edges. Like many modern blockbusters, it's a man's story – there are only five female figures – with men's labours, animals, weapons, feasts and battles rendered in startling detail.

From the tapestry we have learned that 11th-century Saxons wore moustaches and had long hair, while the Normans were clean-shaven. Halley's Comet is depicted, along with a menagerie of mythical creatures.

The epic moves to a thrilling climax at the Battle of Hastings. The artist's conception of battle seems curiously modern: there is more death than glory on this battlefield. Finally King Harold falls, the battle is over and the tapestry ends with the fleeing English soldiers.

Although once called 'Queen Matilda's tapestry', in the erroneous belief that William the Conqueror's wife was responsible for it, scholars now believe that it may have been made in Canterbury. It was probably commissioned by Bishop Odo of Bayeux (William's half-brother, who features prominently in the scenes) for the opening of the cathedral in 1077.

and the headstones are simply marked 'Ein Deutscher Soldat' (A German Soldier).

The large **monument** across the boulevard commemorates the 1807 Commonwealth soldiers missing in action. Nearby is the **Mémorial des Reporters**, a garden dedicated to reporters killed in the line of duty since WWII. Depressingly, the 2006 and 2007 names are too numerous to fit on a single plinth.

♥ MUSÉE MÉMORIAL DE LA BATAILLE DE NORMANDIE // BAYEUX REMEMBERS ITS WARTIME PAST

Using photos, personal accounts, dioramas and wartime objects, this bilingual **museum** (☎ 02 31 51 46 90; bd Fabien Ware; adult/child €6.50/3.80; ☯ 9.30am-6.30pm May-Sep, 10am-12.30pm & 2-6pm Oct-Apr) offers an account of WWII in Normandy that will be most interesting to military enthusiasts. A 25-minute film on the Battle of Normandy is screened in English three to five times a day.

♥ CHÂTEAU DE BALLEROY // A SUMPTUOUS RESIDENCE FOR FRENCH AND US NOBILITY

Fourteen kilometres southwest of Bayeux, Balleroy is a humble village with a grand avenue leading to a grandiose **château** (☎ 02 31 21 60 61; www.chateau-balleroy.com; adult/child €6.50/5.50; ☯ 10am-6pm Jul & Aug, 10am-noon & 2-6pm Wed-Mon mid-Mar–Jun & Sep–mid-Oct).

In 1631 one of Louis XIII's top advisors commissioned François Mansart, the most prestigious architect of the day, to construct a magnificent residence, complete with a moat, *colombier* (see opposite), France's first suspended stone stairways and formal gardens. For the next several centuries the counts of Balleroy presided here, but in 1970 the late press prince Malcolm Forbes bought the property and restored it. He also installed a small **museum** (adult/child €4.50/3.50, combined ticket adult/child €8/6) devoted to ballooning, a hobby he pursued avidly in his time away from running *Forbes* magazine.

Far more interesting than the museum are the guided tours of the château. Forbes' children still keep apartments on the top floor but the grand rooms below are filled with antiques, art, oak panelling and some whimsical features such as a ceiling painted with balloons. Bring a picnic to enjoy in the 118-hectare grounds.

Only school-bus services head to Balleroy.

GASTRONOMIC HIGHLIGHTS

♥ LA RAPIÈRE €€

☎ 02 31 21 05 45; 53 rue St-Jean; 2-course lunch €15, menus €27.50-33.50; ☯ Fri-Tue

The entire family pitches in to make you feel welcome at this ancient house, composed of stone walls and big wooden beams, which you'll find secreted down a little laneway. Expect Normandy staples such as terrines, oysters, duck and veal with Camembert, served with considerable *savoir faire*.

♥ LE POMMIER €€

☎ 02 31 21 52 10; 38-40 rue des Cuisiniers; 2-course lunch €19, menus €23-37; ☯ closed Sun Nov-Mar; Ⓥ

A celebration of all things Norman, Le Pommier's 'Discovery' and 'Flavours of Normandy' *menus* include such classics as Caen-style tripe and pork with Neufchâtel cheese. A bland vegetarian menu is also available. The restaurant has a romantic setting, with bare stone walls,

OF PEASANTS AND PIGEONS

The unique cylindrical *colombiers* (pigeon lofts or dovecotes) dotting the Normandy countryside were once a major status symbol for Norman nobility. In pre-Revolutionary France the right to erect a *colombier* was a rare privilege that the law awarded to the most important landholders. With only one *colombier* permitted for each fiefdom, the lords tried to outdo each other in their construction. Brick and stone were often arranged in geometrical patterns, and halfway up the cylinder a stone band prevented rodents from reaching the top cone. The cone was usually topped with a small ornament in shiny metal or ceramic that pigeons on the wing could easily spot. Inside, a ladder led to the pigeon loft where the birds lived in thousands of niches.

The *colombiers* were a bitter source of grievance for the local peasantry, who watched in fury as pigeons ate their freshly sowed grain. For decades they agitated to close the *colombiers*, at least during the sowing season. It's significant that one of the Revolutionaries' first acts was to abolish the right to *colombiers*.

warm feature walls and large French doors opening on to the street.

❤ LE P'TIT RESTO €€

☎ 02 31 51 85 40; 2 rue du Bienvenu; menus €20-30; ⊙ Mon-Sat

Très hip, this little dining room serves up wonderfully inventive French fusion dishes with *menus* that allow you to pick and mix from the *à la carte* options. In summer the tables spill out onto the street facing the cathedral – a strange contrast to the New York scene on the walls inside. The service is friendly and first rate.

TRANSPORT

BIKE // Bikes can be rented from **Vélos Location** (☎ 02 31 92 89 16; Impasse de l'Islet; per half/full day €10/15), opposite the tourist office.

BUS // **Busverts** (☎ 08 10 21 42 14; www.bus verts.fr) services stop near the train station but they are infrequent and often timed around school hours. Catch bus 30 for Caen; 70 for Omaha Beach; and 74 for Arromanches, Gold and Juno beaches.

TRAIN // Bayeux's **train station** (bd Sadi Carnot) has direct services to Paris-St-Lazare, Évreux, Caen, Cherbourg, Granville and Rennes.

D-DAY BEACHES

· · · · · ·

Also known as the Côte de Nacre (Mother of Pearl Coast), this 80km stretch of broad golden-sand beaches was the staging point for the largest military operation in history, code-named Operation Overlord but better known as D-Day. Early on the morning of 6 June 1944, swarms of landing craft – part of a flotilla of almost 7000 boats – hit the shore, and tens of thousands of soldiers from the UK, Canada, USA and other nations began pouring onto occupied soil.

These beaches north of Bayeux are now better known by their operational code names: (from west to east) Utah and Omaha (in the US sector), and Gold, Juno and Sword (in the British and Canadian ones). While summer holiday-makers still come here to enjoy the sun and sand, many more come to pay their respects to the thousands who died.

The Allied landings on D-Day – known as Jour-J in French – were

CALVADOS & ORNE

followed by the Battle of Normandy, which would lead to the liberation of Europe from Nazi occupation (see p265). In the 76 days of fighting, the Allies suffered 210,000 casualties, including 37,000 deaths. German casualties are believed to be around 200,000, and another 200,000 German soldiers were taken prisoner.

There are dozens of battle sites, cemeteries and war museums scattered around these beaches and throughout Normandy. If you're planning to visit a few, pick up the **Normandie Pass** (www .normandiepass.com; adult €1) from the first participating museum you visit, which provides information and discounted admission to 40 of them.

ESSENTIAL INFORMATION

TOURIST OFFICE // Arromanches (☎ 02 31 22 36 45; www.arromanches.com; 2 rue Maréchal Joffre; ☺ 10am-6pm summer, reduced hrs in winter); **Longues-sur-Mer** (☺ 10am-8pm Apr-Oct, 10am-4pm Fri-Sun Nov-Mar)

EXPLORING THE D-DAY BEACHES

❦ POINTE DU HOC // VISIT A SITE OF EXTREME HEROISM

At 7.10am on D-Day (6 June 1944), 225 US Army Rangers scaled the 30m cliffs at Pointe du Hoc, where the Germans had emplaced a battery of huge artillery guns capable of pounding both Utah and Omaha beaches (to the west and east respectively). The guns, as it turned out, had been removed during the prior aerial bombardment, but the Americans captured the gun emplacements (the two huge circular cement structures) and the German command post (next to the two flagpoles), and then fought off German

counter-attacks for two days. By the time they were relieved on 8 June, 81 of the rangers had been killed and 58 more had been wounded.

Today the site, which France turned over in perpetuity to the US government in 1979, looks much as it did half a century ago. The ground is still pockmarked with massive craters. Visitors can walk among and inside the fortifications but coastal erosion has meant that you can't get near the cliff or the Ranger Memorial.

❦ OMAHA BEACH // VISUALISE THE ENORMITY OF THE D-DAY TASK

The most brutal fighting on D-Day took place 15km northwest of Bayeux along 7km of coastline centred on Colleville-sur-Mer and known as Omaha Beach. As you stand on the gently sloping sand, try to imagine how the US soldiers must have felt running inland towards the German positions on the nearby ridge. At the time of the landings the beach was covered with shingle, which was cleared by bulldozers and never replaced. A memorial marks the site of the first US military cemetery on French soil, where the soldiers killed on the beach were buried. As per US military custom, their remains were later repatriated or re-interred at the main military cemetery built nearby. Other Allied (and Axis) troops remain buried near where they fell.

These days Omaha Beach is lined with holiday cottages and little evidence of the war remains apart from a single concrete boat used to carry tanks ashore and, 1km further west, the bunkers and munitions sites of a German fortified point (look for the tall obelisk on the hill).

❧ NORMANDY AMERICAN MILITARY CEMETERY & MEMORIAL // COME ARMED WITH TISSUES

Nothing brings home the scale of the carnage that occurred here as much as this vast **cemetery** (☎ 02 31 51 62 00; www .abmc.gov; Colleville-sur-Mer; ☉ 9am-5pm). Set on a hill in the town of Colleville-sur-Mer overlooking Omaha Beach, the immaculately tended expanse of lawn contains the graves of 9386 American soldiers, each marked by a white cross or Star of David. The remains of an additional 14,000 soldiers were repatriated to the USA. Behind the white colonnaded memorial is a wall inscribed with the names of 1557 more whose remains were never found.

Start your visit at the excellent visitor centre, where there are displays and a continuous screening of *Letters,* a moving short film based on letters written home by soldiers who are buried here as well as interviews with their loved ones. In another room a voice continually recites the names of the dead. The staff can help you to locate specific graves, and veterans are invited to sign a register.

Overlooking the beach, an orientation table illustrates the landing sites of the invasion forces. Consider timing your visit for the end of the day, when the American flag is lowered and *Taps* is played.

Even more sombre is **La Cambe cemetery** (☎ 02 31 22 70 76; ☉ 9am-7pm summer, 9am-5pm winter), 15km west just off the N13, where 21,222 German soldiers are interred. The mound in the centre, surmounted by a black basalt cross, is a mass grave containing 300 bodies. A peace garden (Friedenspark) has been planted outside.

❧ BATTERIE-DE-LONGUES // WHERE THE BIG GUNS REMAIN

The massive 152mm German guns on the coast near Longues-sur-Mer were designed to hit targets 20km away, which included both Omaha and Gold beaches. Half a century later, the mammoth artillery pieces are still sitting in their colossal concrete emplacements. (In wartime they were covered with camouflage nets and tufts of grass.)

Parts of an American film about D-Day, *The Longest Day* (1962), were filmed here and at Pointe du Hoc. On clear days, Bayeux's cathedral, 8km away, is visible to the south.

❧ ARROMANCHES // MARVEL AT THE SCALE OF PORT WINSTON

In June 1944 this low-key resort town – with a sandy beach but no natural harbour – found itself one of the world's busiest ports. To make it possible to unload the quantities of cargo necessary for the invasion, Winston Churchill came up with the idea of creating two prefabricated ports that were manufactured on the Thames and floated into place. The Omaha Beach harbour was completely destroyed by a ferocious storm, days after being constructed, but the one built at Arromanches was a success. You can still see its remains today; the best views are from the cliffs overlooking the town.

The huge harbour (the size of 1000 football fields) consists of 146 massive cement caissons, sunk to form a semicircular breakwater in which floating bridge spans were moored. In the three months after D-Day, 2.5 million men, four million tonnes of equipment and 500,000 vehicles were unloaded here. It's all well explained at the **Musée du Débarquement** (☎ 02 31 22 34 31; www.musee-arromanches.fr; place du 6 Juin;

CALVADOS & ORNE

adult/child €6.50/4.50; ⊙ 9am-7pm May-Aug, 10am-5pm Feb-Apr & Sep-Dec).

Perhaps the best overview of the Battle of Normandy in the entire region is **Arromanches 360** (☎ 02 31 22 30 30; www .arromanches360.com; Chemin du Calvaire; adult/child €4.20/3.70; ⊙ 10.10am-4.40pm Feb-May & Sep-Dec, ⊙ 9.40am-6.40pm Jun-Aug, screenings at 10 & 40 mins past the hr), where the affecting 30-minute movie *The Price of Freedom* is projected all around you on a circular screen. It cleverly intersperses archive footage with shots of the locations today.

♥ JUNO BEACH // A LANDMARK FOR BOTH CANADA AND FREE FRANCE

Dune-lined Juno Beach, 12km east of Arromanches at Courseulles-sur-Mer, was stormed by Canadian troops on D-Day. A Cross of Lorraine marks the spot where General Charles de Gaulle came ashore a week later, on 14 June. Winston Churchill had preceded him on 12 June and King George VI followed on 16 June.

The area's only Canadian museum, **Centre Juno Beach** (☎ 02 31 37 32 17; www .junobeach.org; Courseulles-sur-Mer; adult/child €6.50/5; ⊙ 9.30am-7pm Apr-Sep, 10am-5pm Feb, Mar & Oct-Dec) has multimedia exhibits on Canada's history and role in the war (45,000 Canadians were killed). Guided tours of the beach (€3.50) are available from April to October.

♥ OUISTREHAM // STOCK UP AT OYSTERVILLE

Sandwiched between the mouth of the Orne and the eastern end of Sword Beach, a D-Day landing site for British and Free French troops, is the unassuming town of Ouistreham. If you're arriving by ferry from Portsmouth, your first impressions will be of a small **funfair, fish market** and numerous signs in English reminding you to drive on the right side of the road. The *Gare Maritime* (ferry terminal) has ATMs where you can stock up on euro.

Ouistreham means 'oyster village', so if you can't wait to get a feed of fresh Normandy seafood, turn right at the first big roundabout on the way out of town and stop in at **La Mare Ô Poissons** (☎ 02 31 37 53 05; 30-68 rue Émile Herbline; 2-/3-course lunch €15/20, menus €25-35; ⊙ lunch Tue-Sun, dinner Tue-Sat). This big modern establishment, guarded by metal cow sculptures, combines a speciality food store with an accomplished restaurant.

TRANSPORT

BUS // This stretch is difficult to explore by public transport as buses are infrequent, making taking a tour (p180) a good option if you don't have a car. Bus 3 from Caen heads to Gold, Juno and Sword beaches; see p185 for services from Bayeux.

FERRY // Brittany Ferries (☎ in UK 0871-244 1400, per minute €0.10, in France 08 25 82 88 28; www .brittanyferries.com) operates vessels from Ouistreham, 14km northeast of Caen, to Portsmouth.

CAEN

· · · · · ·

pop 110,400
Caen, Basse-Normandie's capital, is a bustling university city built in the shadow of an 11th-century château. Only a fraction of its medieval heritage remains following the pummelling it received during the Battle of Normandy. It's been rebuilt in a utilitarian, although not entirely unpleasing, style and at least the wide boulevards have been able to accommodate the traffic that accompanied the city's rapid postwar expansion.

CAEN

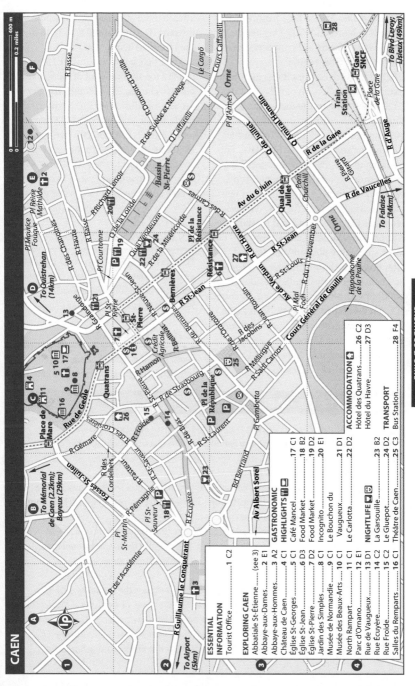

Caen makes a good base from which to explore Normandy's D-Day beaches and has good transport connections to other towns in the region.

Until the 11th century it was little more than a ragtag collection of villages scattered around the confluence of the Rivers Orne and Odon. Its fortunes changed in 1050 upon the marriage of William the Conqueror and Matilda of Flanders. This wedding of cousins displeased the Pope and in order to receive a dispensation each spouse promised to build an abbey in Caen. William built the Abbaye-aux-Hommes (Men's Abbey) and Matilda the Abbaye-aux-Dames (Ladies' Abbey). The town apparently pleased William and, after becoming king of England in 1066, he made Caen his secondary residence, building a fortified castle on a rocky spur.

Caen flourished under William's rule. The city's intellectual tradition was born and creamy Caen limestone was used to build Westminster Abbey and Canterbury Cathedral. The city's prosperity attracted the attention of England's King Edward III, who sacked it in 1346 during the Hundred Years' War.

The English returned under Henry V in 1417 for another bout of looting and pillage. The English occupied the city for 33 years during which the monarchy established a university in 1432 that currently attracts some 30,000 students. In 1850 Caen was linked to the sea by a canal running parallel to the River Orne, which aided the growth of the steel industry that is now at the heart of its economy.

ESSENTIAL INFORMATION

TOURIST OFFICE // Caen (☎ 02 31 27 14 14; www.tourisme.caen.fr; place St-Pierre; ⌚ 9.30am-6pm Mon-Sat Oct-Mar, 9.30am-6.30pm Mon-Sat, 10am-1pm Sun Apr-Jun & Sep, plus 2-5pm Sun Jul & Aug)

ORIENTATION

Caen's modern heart is made up of a few pedestrianised shopping streets and

THE BATTLE OF CAEN

Caen was a thriving centre when on 6 June 1944 the first Allied bombs began raining down. Although brutal, the bombing was intended to block German Panzers from reinforcing their divisions on the Cotentin beaches. Caen went up in flames and burned for 11 days, reducing the medieval quarters to ruins.

Having been told to evacuate the city, many residents fled south to the quarries of Fleury-sur-Orne, while others took refuge in the Abbaye-aux-Hommes. Thousands more were entombed in the rubble.

Although planning had called for a rapid occupation, the Germans quickly launched a counter-offensive that blocked Allied troops just outside the city. The stalemate continued for three weeks, but Caen had to be wrested from the Germans in order to allow a clear advance south.

On 7 July the northern part of the city was targeted, but the actual bombing pushed further into the centre, which received 2500 tonnes of explosives. More than 80% of the city was destroyed and some observers felt that the operation achieved dubious results. The heaps of rubble impeded the Allied advance through the city and it didn't delay the transfer of German divisions from the British to the American sectors as intended.

some busy boulevards. The largest, av du 6 Juin, links the centre, which is based around the southern end of the château, with the canal and train station to the southeast. Bassin St-Pierre, east of av du 6 Juin, is the city's pleasure port; its quays serving as favourite promenades in mild weather.

EXPLORING CAEN

❤ MÉMORIAL DE CAEN //
A VIVID EXPLORATION OF WAR AND PEACE

Caen's **Mémorial** (☎ 02 31 06 06 45; www .memorial-caen.fr; esplanade Général Eisenhower; adult/child €17/15; ⏱ 7am-7pm Feb-Oct, 9.30am-6pm Wed-Mon Nov-Dec) provides a comprehensive treatment of the Battle of Normandy, but its intention is not merely to commemorate the liberation of Europe but to promote peace. It packs a powerful punch, although the emotional effect can be diluted by hordes of noisy kids on school outings; try to visit on weekends or during school holidays. Some Caen hotels provide vouchers for a discounted entry (€13) and it's possible to combine your visit with a guided tour of the D-Day beaches (€75, four to five hours).

Visitors enter through a jagged crack in the stark white facade, meant to symbolise the broken city of Caen and the Allied breach of the German juggernaut. The French inscription across the wall reads: 'I was crushed by grief, but fraternity revived me, and from my wound there sprang a river of freedom.'

The museum's multilingual exhibits are divided into distinct parts. A **tunnel** spiralling downwards shows Europe's descent into war. Documents, posters and photos trace the failure of the Versailles agreement that ended WWI, leading to the rise of fascism in Germany and the fear of Bolshevism in France. Vichy France is recalled as well as the Resistance. Photos of concentration camps and Hitler's voice booming over the loudspeakers convey the sense of urgency facing Allied leaders. The war itself is comprehensively covered, including archival footage of the siege of Stalingrad. A concluding section dealing with the establishment of the UN and global conflicts since WWII ends on a note of cautious optimism. Another series of rooms deals with the Cold War.

Two **theatres** on the entrance level screen short movies, including the affecting 20-minute *Espérance* (Hope). The other deals with the Battle of Normandy (35 minutes) using un-narrated film footage taken from both sides. Most startling are the split-screen clips of D-Day from both viewpoints, enlivened by scenes from the fictional film *The Longest Day*.

An exhibit on Nobel Peace Prize laureates is housed in the former German command post underneath the main building. Within the extensive park surrounding the complex are separate British, Canadian and American memorial gardens. The **Centre de Documentation** above the main hall has an extensive library of books (some in English) covering WWII as well as a film archive that can be viewed for free.

The mémorial is 3km northwest of the tourist office. Take bus 2 or, by car, follow the numerous signs. Allow about 2½ hours for a visit.

❤ CHÂTEAU DE CAEN //
ART FLIRTS WITH HISTORY BEHIND STONE WALLS

This large **fortress** (www.chateau.caen.fr; admission free; ⏱ 10.30am-4.30pm) was begun by William the Conqueror in 1060 and extended by his son Henry I. It was a royal residence until the reign of Richard the Lion-Heart and then turned into a garrison when Normandy became part of France in 1204. Eventually it became a town within a town, containing residences, workshops, a church, a prison and a cemetery. From the Revolution until WWII it served various military functions. Until 1944 a nest of houses pressed up against the fortress, but the bombardment had the salutary effect of revealing the entire structure.

A walk around the **ramparts** is an excellent way to appreciate the layout of reconstructed Caen and its many church steeples. The north rampart gives a good view over the inaccessible keep. Temporary exhibitions are held in the **Salles du Remparts** and the 12th- to 16th-century **Église St-Georges**. Of particular interest is the **Jardin des Simples**, a garden of medicinal and aromatic herbs that were cultivated during the Middle Ages – some of which are poisonous.

The small **Musée de Normandie** (☎ 02 31 30 47 60; www.musee-de-normandie.fr; admission free; ☻ 9.30am-6pm Wed-Mon Oct-May, daily Jun-Sep) is devoted to life in Normandy through the ages and has a terrific Gallo-Roman section.

Nearby, a striking modern building houses **Musée des Beaux-Arts** (☎ 02 31 30 47 70; www.ville-caen.fr/mba; admission free; ☻ 9.30am-6pm Wed-Mon), an extensive collection of paintings and engravings dating from the 15th to 20th centuries, all well laid out. Normandy is well represented by Eugène Boudin's *La plage de Deauville,* Claude Monet's *Nymphéas* (Water Lilies) and *Étretat Manneporte* and local lad Nicolas Poussin's *Vénus pleurant Adonis* (Venus Mourning Adonis). Other big-hitters include Veronese, Tintoretto and Rubens.

Attached to the gallery, **Café Mancel** (☎ 02 31 86 63 64; 2-/3-course menu €17/23; ☻ lunch Tue-Sun, dinner Tue-Sat) is a great spot for a cocktail or a well-executed bistro-style meal.

❦ ABBEYS & CHURCHES //
TWIN-SET ABBEYS AND PEARLER CHURCHES
Abbaye-aux-Hommes

'When St-Étienne comes tumbling down, the kingdom of England will perish', wrote 12th-century Norman poet Robert Wace, and it seems nothing short of miraculous that the church and its abbey remained standing after the fearsome 1944 bombardments.

The church, the **Abbatiale St-Étienne** (rue Guillaume le Conquerant; ☻ 8.15am-7.30pm) was built relatively quickly – from 1066 to 1077 – which explains the unity of its style. The austere Romanesque facade creates an impression of sobriety and grandeur, accentuated by towers topped with Gothic steeples which became a model for churches around the region. Inside you can clearly see where the minimalist Romanesque nave gives way to the more intricate Gothic choir.

Its founder, William the Conqueror, chose this as his final resting place but now only his thigh bone remains here (buried in front of the altar). His tomb was desecrated during the 16th-century Wars of Religion but his corpse was badly treated even before he was buried. His thieving servants stripped him almost naked and the funeral procession caught fire. Finding him too large for the funeral bier, the pallbearers tried to fold him in half, causing his stomach to burst open. As a final indignity, a peasant launched the ancient cry of 'Haro' at his tomb (see p175), claiming that the grave was on his land. The peasant was hastily paid off and William was finally laid to rest amid a haze of incense to mask the smell.

Alongside the church are the majestic abbey buildings (now the town hall – the monks were ejected during the Revolution). Very little remains of the original abbey, which was rebuilt by the 18th-century monk-architect Guillaume de la Tremblaye in a classical style. A **tour** (☎ 02 31 30 42 81; www.ville-caen.fr; adult/child €2.40/free, free Sun; ⊙ 9.30am, 11am, 2.30pm & 4pm) takes you through the sumptuous interior, outfitted in sculpted oak panelling, classical paintings and stone staircases that seem suspended in midair.

Abbaye-aux-Dames

An even starker church than St-Étienne, the **Abbatiale de la Trinité** (place Reine Mathilde) has finely sculpted capitals and the tomb of Queen Matilda behind the main altar. William and Matilda's daughter, Cécile, was one of the first nuns at the convent but its most famous boarder was Charlotte Corday. In July 1793, she got a pass from the abbess, headed to Paris and stabbed revolutionary extremist Marat in his bath. She was guillotined within a week. Access to the abbey, which houses regional government offices, is by free **guided tours** (☎ 02 31 06 98 98; ⊙ 2.30pm & 4pm). Behind is the 5¼-hectare **Parc d'Ornano** (⊙ 8am-nightfall), which was once part of the abbey grounds.

Other churches

Also worth exploring are the **Église St-Pierre** (place St-Pierre) and **Église St-Jean** (rue St-Jean). Both have been painstakingly restored to their ornate Flamboyant Gothic and Renaissance splendour after having been badly damaged during the war.

♥ **OLD NEIGHBOURHOODS // GET A TASTE FOR WHAT WAS LOST**
The most popular old neighbourhood in Caen is **rue du Vaugueux** and its offshoots. The tiny neighbourhood can be overrun with tourists but the cobblestone streets and creaky houses convey the charm of working-class Caen. Most of the stone houses date from the 18th century, although a couple of half-timbered houses were built in the 16th century. Edith Piaf's grandparents had a bistro here.

Less touristy **rue Froide** also escaped the bombing and has fine examples of 17th- and 18th-century bourgeois architecture. Behind the elegant facades there are often courtyards with dormer windows and stone staircases. Although these apartments are private residences, there's usually not a problem opening the outside door for a look around. **Rue Écuyère** also contains some interesting old buildings. Notice the facade of No 9, the string of interior courtyards at No 32 and the 15th-century courtyard of No 42.

GASTRONOMIC HIGHLIGHTS

Restaurants and cafés line quai Vendeuvre and the old lanes around rue du Vaugueux. For food markets head to place St-Sauveur on Friday, bd Leroy (east of the train station) on Saturday and place Courtonne on Sunday.

♥ **INCOGNITO €€€**
☎ 02 31 28 36 60; 14 rue de la Courtonne; menus €29-77; ⊙ lunch Mon-Fri, dinner Mon-Sat
Michelin-starred chef Stéphane Carbone is at the helm of Caen's best restaurant. Expect a lively menu of seafood and meat dishes, with great care taken in the balancing of flavours. The lunch *menus*

are considerably cheaper (main with wine and coffee €20, two courses €26, three courses €29).

😋 LE BOUCHON DU VAUGUEUX €€
☎ 02 31 44 26 26; 12 rue Graindorge; menus €20-26, lunch €14-18; ☯ Tue-Sat

A crowd of regulars keeps this place humming, returning for hearty serves of homespun cooking. The menu is a celebration of all things meaty, particularly beef. Try the home-made terrines and so-tender-they-fall-apart beef cheeks.

😋 LE CARLOTTA €€
☎ 02 31 86 68 99; 16 quai Vendeuvre; menus €23-36; ☯ Mon-Sat

Decked out in a very Parisian *belle-époque* style (backlit stained glass, tiled floors and murals), this is a good spot to tuck into the local speciality, *tripes à la mode de Caen* (Caen tripe); otherwise go for a heaping platter of fresh shellfish or a delicious *cassoulet* (slow-cooked bean and meat casserole).

NIGHTLIFE

It's a universal truth that university towns have the liveliest bars, and Caen is no exception. Pick up a copy of *Allez-y, c'est gratuit* ('Let's go, it's free'), which lists free live music, DJ nights, cinemas, exhibitions and lectures; it too is free from the tourist office, bars and cafés.

Try La Garsouille (☎ 02 31 86 80 27; 11-13 rue Arcisse de Caumont) for hip surrounds, clientele and music, with the surprising bonus of reasonably priced drinks. Le Gluepot (☎ 02 31 86 29 15; 18 quai Vendeuvre) has an English-pub vibe and hosts live bands. You'll find plenty of other bars clustered in the vicinity of each of these two and on rue Écuyère.

Located in the centre of town, the **Théâtre de Caen** (☎ 02 31 30 48 00; www .theatre.caen.fr; 135 bd du Maréchal Leclerc) offers a season of theatre, opera, dance, jazz and classical concerts that run from October to May.

TRANSPORT

TO/FROM THE AIRPORT

Caen's **airport** (☎ 02 31 71 20 10; www.caen .aeroport.fr) is 5km west of town in Carpiquet. Bus No 8 to the bus station stops nearby, with up to nine services on weekdays.

GETTING AROUND

BUS // The bus station, next to the train station, is the hub for **busverts** (☎ 08 10 21 42 14; www .busverts.fr), which serves the entire Calvados *département*. Useful lines include 1 (Ouistreham), 3 (eastern D-Day beaches), 20 (Côte Fleurie & Le Havre), 34 (Clécy), 35 (Falaise), 36 (Pont l'Évêque) and 39 (express to Le Havre). Many also stop at place Courtonne, which is the hub of the city bus service.

CAR // A well-labelled ring route encircles Caen, with exits numbered counter-clockwise starting from the east.

TRAIN // Caen's busy **station** (place de la Gare) has direct services to Paris-St-Lazare, Rouen, Évreux, Alençon, Bayeux, Cherbourg, Granville and Rennes.

TRAM // A tram runs from the stations through the centre of town, along av du 6 Juin.

SUISSE NORMANDE & PAYS DE FALAISE

· · · · · ·

Although it couldn't really be mistaken for Switzerland, this attractive area straddling the Calvados and

Orne *départements,* due south of Caen, has more contour than most of pastoral Normandy. The jagged cliffs and forested slopes that rise above the River Orne are a magnet for outdoorsy types, attracting battalions of kayakers, canoeists, hang-gliders, cyclists and walkers. It was into this rugged environment that William the Conqueror was born.

ESSENTIAL INFORMATION

TOURIST OFFICE // Clécy (☎ 02 31 69 79 95; 4 place du Tripot; ☷ 10am-12.30pm & 2.30-6.30pm Mon-Sat, 10am-12.30pm Sun Jul & Aug, closed Mon Apr-Jun & Sep, mornings only Apr & Sep); **Falaise** (☎ 02 31 90 17 26; www.falaise-tourisme.com; bd de la Libéra-tion; ☷ 9.30am-5.30pm Mon-Sat Sep-Jun, 10.30am-12.30pm & 2-4pm Sun Jul & Aug); **Pont d'Ouilly** (☎ 02 31 69 29 86; bd de la Noë) This kiosk by the river has sporadic hours but posts details of accommodation and a swag of outdoor activities outside. **Thury-Harcourt** (☎ 02 31 79 70 45; www.ot-suisse -normande.com; 2 place St-Sauveur; ☷ 10am-12.30pm Tue-Sat, 2.30-5pm Wed-Fri)

SUISSE NORMANDE

❦ THURY-HARCOURT // IF NOTHING ELSE, STOP FOR A MEMORABLE MEAL

On the northernmost edge of Suisse Normande, this little town with an evocatively war-ruined château is built along a hill rising up from the Orne. Le **Relais de la Poste** (☎ 02 31 79 72 12; 7 rue de Caen; menus €27-63, lunch €18-23; ☷ lunch Mon-Thu & dinner Sat-Thu Oct-Apr, lunch Sat-Thu & dinner daily Apr-Oct) offers an inventive menu using local cheeses, seafood and game meats such as guinea fowl served with a deli-cate coffee sauce.

See p180 for details on kayaking trips.

❦ CLÉCY // PREPARE FOR A BIG DOSE OF PRETTY

The self-proclaimed capital of Suisse Normande, Clécy is an engaging town of narrow streets, granite houses and wooden shutters that is also set on a hill with views over the Orne Valley. Below, the leafy riverbanks are lined with *gu-inguettes* – cafés with riverside terraces.

CALVADOS & ORNE

TOP CAMPING

This region's rural environs provide plenty of peaceful spots to hitch a tent; for details of other accommodation options, see p299.

★ **Camping de la Vallée du Traspy** (☎ 02 31 79 61 80; www.campingtraspy.com; rue du Pont Benoit, Thury-Harcourt; adult/site €4.60/4.60; ☷ Apr-Sep) Well situated by the river, next to an aquatic centre and small lake.

★ **Camping de Pont d'Ouilly** (☎ 02 31 69 80 20; fax 02 31 69 80 70; rue du Stade, Pont d'Ouilly; site per s/d €6/8; ☷ mid-Apr–Sep) On the edge of the village, near the river.

★ **Camping du Château** (☎ 02 31 90 16 55; camping@falaise.re; rue du Val d'Ante, Falaise; adult/ site €3.30/4; ☷ May-Sep; ☷) A lovely location at the foot of Château Guillaume-le-Conquerant, near tennis courts and a pool.

★ **Camping du Phare** (☎ 02 31 24 22 12; bd Charles V, Honfleur; adult/site €4.70/2.90; ☷ Apr-Sep) A hedge-lined site well located between the old town and beach.

★ **Les Rochers des Parcs** (☎ 02 31 69 70 36; www.ocampings.com/campingclecy; Clécy; adult/site €4.25/5.20; ☷ Apr-Sep) An extremely beautiful location on the banks of the Orne.

With its natural charms and array of outdoor activities, it's not surprising that Clécy is packed with tourists on sunny weekends and during summer holidays.

Canoeing and kayaking are major attractions in Clécy. Rental places are scattered among the *guinguettes*. Across the River Orne the 205m Pain de Sucre (Sugar Loaf) massif looms over the valley. Several paths lead to the top.

♥ PONT D'OUILLY // A GOOD PLACE TO GET ACTIVE

At the confluence of the Rivers Orne and Noireau, Pont d'Ouilly is an inconspicuous little village known for its water sports. The centre is an unremarkable postwar reconstruction but the serene river banks, overhung with trees and rising to gentle slopes on either side, create a lovely setting for a stroll or drive.

Base de Plein Air (☎ 02 31 69 86 02; www .pontdouilly-loisirs.com), on the river, rents out canoes (per hour €12) and kayaks (per hour €8) and organises trips down the Orne. It also organises competitions in kayak polo, a sport unique to the area. You can hire mountain bikes from the **service station** (☎ 02 31 69 80 35; bd de la Noë; per day €16). Fishing enthusiasts can try their luck at Les Sources de la Here pond, north of Pont d'Ouilly at St-Christophe.

♥ LA ROCHE D'OËTRE // ENJOY THE VIEW WITH A STONY-FACED GIANTESS

Rising 120m over the gorge of the River Rouvre, this craggy outcrop looks down on forested slopes and steep valleys. A large **discovery centre** (☎ 02 31 59 13 13; www .roche-doetre.fr; ☯ 10am-6pm Apr-Oct, 2-5pm Nov-Mar), complete with a **geology museum** (adult/child €4/2), café, boutique and toilets has been built at the top. Walking tracks, ranging from 600m to 9km, loop down

and across the cliff, but be careful – after rainfall the rocks get slippery. Look for the profile of a human face that the wind has carved into the rock below the centre.

TRANSPORT

BUS // **CapOrne** (☎ 02 33 81 61 95; www.orne .fr/orne-reseau-caporne.asp) bus 10 heads from Pont d'Ouilly to Flers, which is on the Paris–Granville train line. **Busverts** (☎ 08 10 21 42 14; www.busverts.fr) line 34 links Caen to Flers via Thury-Harcourt and Clécy.

FALAISE

The strategic importance of this rocky promontory overlooking the Ante Valley was obvious to the earliest Norman dukes, although it's the scenic positioning that matters more today. In 1027 the castle on the hill was the birthplace of William the Conqueror (see p198). Falaise later emerged as a prosperous trade and crafts centre in the early Middle Ages, known throughout France for its trade fairs. Although disrupted during the Hundred Years' War, the fairs returned in full force in the 16th century and were the basis of the local economy until the 19th.

Falaise was devastated during WWII. Canadian forces liberated the city on 16 August 1944 and then joined other Allied forces intending to encircle remnants of the German army south of the city in the 'Falaise Pocket'. The Allied failure to close off the German retreat has been one of the more controversial subjects of WWII military history. Eighty-five percent of Falaise was destroyed in the fighting but it has been tidily rebuilt.

♥ CHÂTEAU GUILLAUME-LE-CONQUERANT // VISIT BILL THE BASTARD'S BIRTHPLACE

With its thick, square walls and circular tower, this sturdy **castle** (☎ 02 31 41

61 44; www.chateau-guillaume-le-conquerant.fr; adult/child €7/3; ⏰ 10am-6pm Feb-Dec) cuts a striking figure. Although it was fortified since the 9th century, it wasn't until the 11th century that Duke Robert of Normandy built the château that served as the birthplace of his son, William. Little remains of the 11th-century structure, which was probably the oldest castle in Normandy. In 1123 Henry Beauclerc, William's son, built the square keep and chapel, and later in the century Henry II Plantagenet built a small keep on the western side. When Normandy fell to the forces of Philippe-Auguste in 1204, the French king built the round Talbot Tower. After suffering a siege by Henry IV in 1590 during the Wars of Religion, the castle fell into disuse and was left to moulder for several centuries.

In 1986 architect Bruno Decaris was hired to restore the castle and completed his work in 1997 to a storm of criticism. His concrete and steel entryway sits alongside the ancient walls, echoing the shape and adding to the sense of impregnability. Inside, glass floors allow visitors to gaze down at the remains of the 11th-century castle.

Visits take the form of a self-guided multimedia tour, with headsets triggering sight and sound displays as you enter each room. It can be a little frustrating as inevitably you'll walk in halfway through a display that someone else has triggered, and the chessboard analogy gets a little laboured. Still, the structure itself is fascinating and the views from the tower wonderful.

In the valley below the castle is **La Fontaine d'Arlette**, which commemorates the meeting between Robert and Arlette (William's father and mother). Legend has it that Robert, son of the duke of Normandy, spotted Arlette, daughter of a successful tanner, washing clothes by the river. Struck by her beauty, Robert invited her to spend the night in his château. Arlette agreed but rather than slink in secretly she entered through the front gate on horseback, dressed magnificently. Nine months later, little William the Bastard entered the world. A bas-relief tells the story of their encounter next to an old wash house.

TRANSPORT

BUS // Busverts (☎ 08 10 21 42 14; www.bus verts.fr) line 35 heads between Caen and Falaise.

SOUTHERN ORNE

· · · · · ·

BAGNOLES DE L'ORNE

pop 900

Hugging the banks of the River Vée and its lake, genteel Bagnoles is the most attractive spa town in Normandy. The Forêt des Andaines (part of a *parc naturel*) presses around it and avenues of *belle-époque* buildings line the streets, dating from the time when wealthy city dwellers concocted various ailments in order to send themselves to Bagnoles for a relaxing 'cure'. It's a lovely place to relax in, even if you're not planning on getting pummelled by water jets in the pricy spa.

If you prefer to be active, there are plenty of hikes in the area as well as tennis, golf, horse-riding, rock-climbing, a casino, tourist train and a packed schedule of concerts and shows during the summer season.

FROM BASTARD TO CONQUEROR

As one version of history goes, Edward the Confessor, king of England and William's cousin, promised William that upon his death the throne would pass to the young Norman ruler, known at the time as Guillaume-le-Batard (William the Bastard). He apparently got a similar assurance from the most powerful Saxon lord in England, Harold Godwinson of Wessex, after he was shipwrecked on the Norman coast.

When Edward died in January 1066, Harold was crowned king, supported by the nobles of England (and very likely the majority of the Saxon people). He immediately faced several challengers, William being the most obvious. While William was preparing an invasion fleet, an army consisting of an alliance between Harold's estranged brother Tostig and Harold Hardrada of Norway landed in the north of England. Harold marched north and defeated them in battle.

Meanwhile, William had crossed the Channel unopposed with an army of about 6000 men, including a large cavalry force. Harold quickly returned south and faced them at Hastings with about 7000 men. He was killed on the battlefield and the victorious William immediately marched to London, ruthlessly quelled the opposition and was crowned king.

William, now ruler of England and Normandy, entrenched England's feudal system under the control of Norman nobles. He spent most of his time in Normandy, leaving much of the governance of England to his bishops. In 1087 he was injured during an attack on Mantes, near Paris. He died at Rouen a few weeks later and was buried at Caen.

ESSENTIAL INFORMATION

TOURIST OFFICE // Bagnoles de l'Orne
(☎ 02 33 37 85 66; www.bagnolesdelorne.com; place du Marché; ◷ 9.30am-6.30pm Mon-Sat Oct-Apr, plus 10am-12.30pm & 2.30-6.30pm Sun May-Sep) Has internet access, and maps for hikes, including a *belle époque* walking tour taking in the town's architecture.

EXPLORING BAGNOLES DE L'ORNE

❧ LES THERMES // LEAD A TIRED HORSE TO REVITALISING WATER

According to a local legend, the underground spring that feeds the **spa centre** (☎ 02 33 38 99 78; www.thermes-bagnoles.com; rue du Professeur Louvel) was discovered by a local landholder who noticed that his tired old horse gained vitality after daily swims. The elderly gentleman began bathing in the spring and found himself blessed with a youthful vigour. The water comes from a granite pocket about 5m deep and is lightly radioactive. Doctors prescribe it for circulatory troubles, skin disorders and, naturally enough, stress.

The French healthcare system pays for extended, prescribed treatments, meaning that it's not so easy just to pop in for a soak (and there's no information in English). Also, you'll need to commit to a complete afternoon of hydro and beauty treatments, and despite it costing a whopping €110, you'll need to bring your own towel, bathing costume (no board shorts please), flip-flops and swimming cap.

❧ TOUR DE BONVOULOIR // SEEK OUT RAPUNZEL

Once upon a time there was a squat tower in the woods with an elegant minaret rising up from it. This picturesque set of ruins sits precisely in the middle of nowhere, signposted off the road heading west to Juvigny-sous-Andaine. It was built at the end of the 15th century by Guyon Essirard, counsellor to the Duke of Alençon. You'll also find a *colombier* (p185), well and an old grindstone.

GASTRONOMIC HIGHLIGHTS

♥ LE MANOIR DU LYS €€€

☎ 02 33 27 80 69; rte de Juvigny; menus €40-119; ☽ closed Mon, dinner Sun & Jan–mid-Feb

Franck Quinton's Michelin-starred baby is attached to his family-run hotel (p301). He promises 'true Normandy, through and through' and delivers it with dishes such as duck with chestnuts, bacon and truffles. If you come in the autumn, chances are you'll be sampling wild mushrooms that he's personally gathered from the forest.

♥ NOUVEL HÔTEL €

☎ 02 33 30 75 00; www.nouvel-hotel-bagnoles.fr; 8 av du Docteur-Pierre-Noal; menus €18-32; ☽ Mar-Nov; Ⓥ

With its tiled floors and high ceilings, the dining room of this amiable hotel is the kind of place where you might expect to run into a pair of maiden aunts or a down-at-heel dowager duchess. The food is excellent, traditional and terrific value, with dishes such as home-smoked trout and duck with cider sauce. Unusually, it also offers a full vegetarian *menu*.

♥ Ô GAYOT €€

☎ 02 33 28 44 01; www.ogayot.com; 2 av de la Ferté Macé; lunch 2-/3-courses €15/19, menu €23; ☽ closed Thu, also dinner Sun, lunch Mon

Quinton's also the supervising chef at this restaurant-café–cocktail bar and

speciality food store in the centre of town. Interesting art and red chandeliers adorn the chichi dining room and the food is exceptional. It shares its name with a *pommeau*-flavoured gateau, created by Quinton to capture the flavours of Normandy.

TRANSPORT

TRAIN // The nearest train station is 13km north at Briouze.

BUS // Buses to Briouze are coordinated with the times of the trains to/from Paris-Montparnasse; buy your tickets at the **SNCF boutique** (☎ 02 33 37 80 04; place du Marché; ☽ 10am-12.30pm Tue-Sat, 2.30-7pm Mon-Fri) next to the tourist office. **Cap-Orne** (☎ 02 33 81 61 95; www.orne.fr) buses stop near the tourist office. Bus 20 heads to Alençon. There's also a free local bus that circles the town.

ALENÇON

pop 29,700

In the far south of Normandy lies the capital of the Orne *département*. From the 17th to 19th centuries, Alençon supplied fashionable women everywhere with astonishingly intricate lace, and grew prosperous in the process. With the Rivers Sarthe and Briante meandering through a town centre largely composed of pedestrianised shopping streets, Alençon makes a pleasant if unexciting base from which to explore the Orne.

ESSENTIAL INFORMATION

TOURIST OFFICE // Alençon (☎ 02 33 80 66 33; www.paysdalencontourisme.com; place de la Magdeleine; ☽ 9.30am-6pm Mon-Sat Sep-Jun, also 10am-12.30pm & 2.30-5pm Sun Jul & Aug) In the turreted Maison d'Ozé; check out the peaceful gardens behind. Pick up a free walking-tour map or hire an audioguide to the town (€3).

CALVADOS & ORNE

ALENÇON

CALVADOS & ORNE

0 400 m
0 0.2 miles

To Mortagne (34km);
Paris (195km)

To Sées (22km);
Caen (101km);
Rouen (144km)

To St-Céneri-
le-Gérei (13km)

To Le Mans
(49km)

EXPLORING ALENÇON

❦ HISTORIC ALENÇON // WALK STREETS TRODDEN BY DUKES, SAINTS AND NAZIS

The old town, especially along **Grand Rue**, is full of atmospheric Second Empire houses with forged iron balconies. Built between the 14th and 16th centuries, **Église Notre Dame** (Grande Rue; ⊗ 8.30am-noon & 2-5.30pm) has a stunning Flamboyant Gothic portal and some superb stained glass in the chapel where St Thérèse (p206) was baptised; you can also visit her **birthplace** (☎ 02 33 26 09 87; 58 rue St-Blaise).

With crenulated towers looking like a pair of chessboard rooks, the creepy **Château des Ducs** (rue du Château), built from 1361 to 1404, was the Gestapo headquarters during WWII and still serves as a prison.

❦ MUSÉE DES BEAUX-ARTS ET DE LA DENTELLE // VIEW FLEMISH FACES AND ALENÇON LACES

The **Fine Arts & Lace Museum** (☎ 02 33 32 40 07; cour Carrée de la Dentelle; admission €3.60; ⊗ 10am-noon & 2-6pm daily Jul & Aug, Tue-Sun Sep-Jun) is housed in a restored Jesuit school. It displays a so-so collection of Flemish, Dutch and French artworks from the 17th to 19th centuries, and an exhaustive exhibit on the history of lace-making and its techniques. There's also an unexpected section of Cambodian artefacts – including Buddhas, spears and tiger skulls – donated by a former (French) governor of Cambodia.

❦ AU PETIT VATEL // WHERE AGE BEGETS DELICIOUSNESS

There's an old-fashioned ambience at this, one of Alençon's oldest and certainly its best **restaurant** (☎ 02 33 26 23 78; 72 place du Commandant-Desmeulles; lunch €17, menus €20-39; ⊗ lunch Thu-Tue, dinner Thu-Sat & Tue). The cuisine is as classic as the decor, including such tasty titbits as *beignet de Camembert* (Camembert fritters) and chicken fettuccine with a creamy Normandy sauce. Order the *chariot* and practically a whole ice-cream shop will be wheeled up to you.

❦ BAR'JO // WINE AND SNAILS – LIFE'S LITTLE PLEASURES!

With its claret-coloured walls and bare stonework, this neighbourhood **wine bar** (☎ 02 33 29 70 03; 33 rue de Sarthe; ⊗ noon-2pm & 5pm-1am Thu-Sat, 5-10pm Sun) is a stylish but welcoming place for a tipple. Ask for a wine recommendation and enjoy it with a platter of cheese, chartucerie or snails.

TRANSPORT

TRAIN // Alençon's **station** (rue Denis Pepin) has direct services to Paris-Montparnasse and Caen via Sées and St-Pierre-sur-Dives.

BUS // CapOrne (☎ 02 33 81 61 95; www .orne.fr) buses stop in front of the train station. Bus 20 goes to Bagnoles de l'Orne, 40 to Sées and 70 to Mortagne-au-Perche.

AROUND ALENÇON

❦ ST-CÉNERI-LE-GÉREI // IS THIS NORMANDY'S PRETTIEST VILLAGE?

Following the Sarthe River southwest of Alençon takes you through an enchanting landscape of steep forested hills and fairy-tale villages. The most extravagantly pretty is **St-Céneri-le-Gérei**, officially classified as one of France's most beautiful villages. The impossibly romantic stone village is enfolded in a loop of the Sarthe and gives the impression of just holding its own against the encroaching greenery.

The highlight is a sweet Romanesque **church** built between 1089 and 1124. Original frescoes are still visible, uncovered from beneath a layer of whitewash in 1842. They make a wonderful counterpoint to a set of ultramodern metallic Stations of the Cross. Continue down to the smaller 15th-century chapel (usually locked), picturesquely placed by the river. Just across the sluggish water, a tiny shrine completes the set of Russian dolls.

There's no public transport but the back roads make a great 13km bike ride from Alençon. Bikes can be rented from **Bayi Cycles** (☎ 02 33 29 65 13; 104 bd de la République) in Alençon.

✿ SÉES // MEANDER MEDIEVAL STREETSCAPES

It's no surprise that director Luc Besson chose Sées, 17km north of Alençon, as the setting for several scenes in his movie *Jeanne d'Arc*. The town centre is crammed with medieval buildings, mostly religious structures dating from the days when Sées was the seat of the archbishop.

Of the churches, convents and abbeys, the most outstanding building is the 13th-century **cathedral** whose 70m towers dwarf the town centre. Badly damaged in the Hundred Years' War, Wars of Religion and the Revolution, nearly every carving has been, quite literally, defaced. Passing through the elaborate central doorway, you're faced with a cavernous interior marked by splendid 13th-century rose windows in the transepts. The northern one is unusual in that it's shaped like a snowflake.

Enquire at the **tourist office** (☎ 02 33 28 74 79; sees.tourisme@wanadoo.fr; place Charles de Gaulle; 🕑 9.30am-12.30pm Tue-Fri, plus 2-6pm Mon-Fri, 9am-12.30pm Sat) for dates for the spectacular 45-minute **lightshow** (www

.musilumieres.org; adult/child €12/5) that casts projections onto the interior of the cathedral, usually held during the summer months.

This transcendental affair stands in stark contrast to Sées other big event, it's annual turkey festival in December.

Sées is connected to Alençon by bus and to Alençon, St-Pierre-sur-Dives and Caen by train.

✿ LE HARAS DU PIN // A PALATIAL RESIDENCE FOR REGAL STEEDS

Called 'the Versailles for horses', the **national stud** (☎ 02 33 36 68 68; www.haras-national-du-pin.com; tour adult/child €9/7; 🕑 10am-6pm Apr-Sep, 2-5pm Sat & Sun Mar & Oct) near the town of Le Pin was founded by Louis XIV to preserve France's great breeds. Designed in the same sumptuous style as Versailles, the château and gardens provide a magnificent setting for the stallions and broodmares kept there to breed. In addition to a stroll in the grounds and the stables, the tour (in French, ask for English notes) includes a peek at the collection of buggies and the saddlery, and entry to a multimedia discovery centre. From June to September there are horse and carriage **parades** (admission €5; 🕑 3pm Thu & some Tue). You'll need wheels to get here.

✿ MORTAGNE-AU-PERCHE // EXPLORE THE ARISTOCRATIC TOWN PERCHED ABOVE THE PERCHE

Every other house seems to have a turret in this town, built on a rise overlooking the lush green Perche region. The narrow streets are lined with a wonderful assortment of centuries-old stone mansions and the occasional half-timbered one. Grab a walking-tour map (€1, French only) from the **tourist office** (☎ 02 33 85 11 18; www.ot-mortagneauperche.fr, in French; place du

FROM A TROT TO A GALLOP

Some 70% of French thoroughbreds and trotters are raised in Basse-Normandie, bred in the national stables of St-Lô and Le Pin as well as private stud farms. Horses that don't make the cut for a racing career are pressed into service for weekend riders at hundreds of local stables.

Normandy's most famous horse breed is the Percheron, named after the Perche region where they originated. These grey or black horses are immensely powerful and were once indispensable on the farm. Although the breed may extend back to the Middle Ages, all of today's Percherons are descended from one (busy) 19th-century stallion, Jean Le Blanc.

Their docility and strength made them the workhorse of choice a century ago, but modern farming has less need of them. For a while it looked as though the Percherons were going from harvesting dinner to being dinner, but Percheron appreciation associations emerged around the world to save the breed from the butcher's knife. Their strong backs, easy stride and adaptability, whether pulling carriages, sleighs or prancing in a parade, have ensured the breed's survival.

Général de Gaulle; ⊙ 10am-12.30pm & 3-6pm Tue-Sat mid-May–Sep) in the 19th-century Halle aux Grains (grain market) on the bustling main square. Of particular note is the beautiful 15th-century **Église Notre Dame**.

While no longer the key commercial centre it once was, the town remains an important marketplace for the agricultural products of the region. If blood sausage (black pudding; *boudin noir)* is to your taste, this is the place to sample it, particularly at the Lent **boudin fair**. Otherwise you can try it along with delectable dishes (such as cod flavoured with bergamot) at the restaurant attached to **Hôtel du Tribunal** (p301, menus €23-45).

Mortagne-au-Perche makes an excellent base for exploring the 2035-sq-km **Parc Naturel Régional du Perche** (see p181), a great place for hiking and horse riding. To get started, call into the **Maison du Parc** (☎ 02 33 25 70 10; www.parc -naturel-perche.fr; ⊙ 10.30am-6pm) housed in the wonderful Manoir de Courboyer, 19km southwest of Mortagne-au-Perche, near the village of Noce.

Bus 70 from Alençon stops at Mortagne-au-Perche.

PAYS D'AUGE

· · · · · ·

If a French person gets a faraway look at the mention of the Pays d'Auge, chances are they're fantasising about cheese…or possibly Calvados…or even Camembert soaked in Calvados. This luscious green landscape of hills, pastures and apple trees is home to three of France's finest and most famous *fromages:* Camembert, Pont l'Évêque and Livarot.

Apart from Lisieux, the biggest city, the region is entirely composed of the kinds of small towns and villages that make French people sentimental about rural life. The landscape is dotted with half-timbered family farms that usually contain a dairy, an apple barn and a cider press. The Risle, Dives and Touques water the lowlands, sprouting streams and brooks that add to the visual allure.

CALVADOS & ORNE

ESSENTIAL INFORMATION

TOURIST OFFICE // Lisieux (☎ 02 31 48 18 10; www.lisieux-tourisme.com; 11 rue Alençon; ◷ 8.30am-noon & 1.30-6pm Mon-Sat Oct–mid-Jun, also 10am-12.30pm & 2-5pm Sun mid-Jun–Sep) Rents audioguides (€5); **Pont l'Évêque** (☎ 02 31 64 12 77; www .pontleveque.com; 16 bis place Jean Bureau; ◷ 10am-12.30pm & 2-6pm Mon-Sat Oct-Apr, also 10am-1pm Sun May-Sep); **St-Pierre-sur-Dives** (☎ 02 31 20 97 90; www.mairie-saint-pierre-sur-dives.fr; 19 rue St-Benoit; ◷ 9.30am-5.30pm Mon-Fri mid-Oct–mid-Apr, also 10am-12.30pm & 2.30-5pm Sat mid-Apr–mid-Oct)

EXPLORING PAYS D'AUGE

❦ CAMEMBERT // AN ESSENTIAL PIT STOP ON A FOODIE PILGRIMAGE

For such a famous name, this really is a very tiny village. There's little to do here but visit the **Maison du Camembert**

(☎ 02 33 12 10 37; ◷ 9.30am-12.30pm & 2-5.30pm Fri-Sun Feb, Thu-Sun Mar, Wed-Sun Apr & Sep, 10am-6pm daily May-Aug) for a tasting. More interesting is a visit to one of the local farms. Turn right at the bottom of the hill and after 2km you'll come to **Fromagerie Durand** (☎ 02 33 39 08 08; ◷ 9.30am-12.30pm & 3-6pm Mon-Sat), a working cheesemakers, where they have information boards, videos and offer tastings (€4).

Camembert is attributed to Marie Harel. In 1791 she obtained the technique from a priest from Brie whom she briefly sheltered here following the Revolution. You'll need wheels to visit the village.

❦ LIVAROT // THE BIG CHEESE TOUR

Although not as famous internationally as Camembert, Livarot is a big deal in France. The town where it originated is home to the best cheese tour in Normandy. **Le Village Fromager** (☎ 02 31 48 20 10; www.graindorge.fr; 42 rue du Général

THE TROUT OF THE TOUQUES

More than their first taste of Calvados, even more than Maman's *tarte tatin,* any man born in the Pays d'Auge will remember the first *truite de mer* (sea trout) he reeled in from the Touques River; catching one is a rite of passage for local boys. The season begins in May just after the fish swim up the river from Deauville, but locals know that the good fishing probably won't start until July. As the sunlight fades, the banks of the Touques fill up with fly-fishing anglers. After passing their days in the cool, relatively deep reaches of the river, the trout head to the shallows to spend the nights, occasionally darting out of the water with a soft splash.

Until the season ends in October, everyone has trout mania. The pinkish flesh has a distinctive and delectable flavour. The trout eat little during their sojourn along the river, but fatten up all winter on tasty little sea shrimp that impart their aroma. If you want to sample this delicacy, though, you'll have to catch a trout yourself or become very good friends with a very skilled angler. The sale of sea trout in restaurants or markets is strictly forbidden.

After a summer spent cleverly dodging hooks, the trout set about the business of reproducing, leaving behind legions of frustrated anglers and a few happy diners. While the new trout families enjoy the frigid open water of the North Atlantic, local fly-fishing aficionados plan their attack for the following summer.

Leclerc; 10-noon & 2-5pm Mon-Fri, 9.30am-noon Sat Nov-Mar, 9.30am-5.30pm Mon-Fri, 9.30am-noon Sat Apr-Jun, Sep & Oct, 9.30am-5.30pm Mon-Sat, 10.30am-1pm & 3-5.30pm Sun Jul & Aug) offers a free tour and tasting at the Graindorge factory, the biggest cheese producer in the area. A self-guided tour accompanied by multimedia displays leads through a series of whiffy viewing rooms where you can watch Livarot, Camembert and Pont l'Évêque being made. The French are the world's biggest cheese consumers, downing an average of 24.6kg per annum each.

☙ ST-PIERRE-SUR-DIVES // FANCY SOME MACAROONS OR A HEIFER? HIT THE MARKET

Formed around a powerful 11th-century Benedictine abbey that endured until the Revolution, this small town remains a commercial centre for the local farming communities. The bustling Monday market affords an indelible glimpse of rural Norman life. It's amazing to think that stallholders have been flogging local produce in the impressive **Halles** since the 13th century. Although it was burned in 1944, it was faithfully restored using the 290,000 original handmade wooden pegs. The first Sunday of the month is given over to the **Marché aux Antiquaires** (antiques market; 8am-6pm).

The **abbey** (rue de l'Église; 9.30am-12.30pm & 2.30-6pm) was founded in 1012 by William the Conqueror's great-aunt on the site of the martyrdom of St Wambert, who was killed by Vikings in 867. The church is still in use but the other abbey buildings have been converted into shops and offices. You can get into the cloister from rue St-Benoit where you'll find the restored chapter room, which now displays works by the painter André Lemaître.

If you're heading on to nearby Vendeuvre, look out for the **Château de Carel** on the right, just out of town. It's privately owned, but you can get a good view of this elegant moated 17th-century mansion from the road.

☙ CHÂTEAU DE VENDEUVRE // LIFESTYLES OF THE RICH AND DECAPITATED

Set in magical countryside 5km south of St-Pierre-sur-Dives, this 18th-century **château** (02 31 40 93 83; Vendeuvre; adult/child gardens €6.90/5.30, château & gardens €8.90/6.90; 11am-6pm daily May-Sep, 2-6pm Sun Apr & Oct–mid-Nov) testifies to the enviably luxurious life of pre-Revolutionary aristocrats. The manor presides over spectacular gardens including a marvellous water garden with a shellfish grotto. The interior recreates the 18th-century lifestyle with period furniture and *objets d'art*.

Displayed in the orangery is a collection of miniatures created between the 16th and 19th centuries. Made with the same materials as standard furniture, these exquisite pieces served as models for larger items and were sometimes created simply as a hobby by artisans. Among other wonders, look for the bed made for the cat of Louis XV's daughter.

TRANSPORT

BUS // From Lisieux, busverts services go to St-Pierre-sur-Dives (No 52) and Livarot (No 53).

TRAIN // St-Pierre-sur-Dives is on the Caen–Alençon train line.

LISIEUX & AROUND

Any Catholic of a certain age will have heard of Lisieux (population 24,500), associated as it is with one of the 20th century's most popular saints, Ste-Thérèse (p206). After 13 bombardments between 6 June and 31 July 1944, very little remains of the town's medieval centre. Postwar reconstruction was graceless, replacing the sinuous streets with straight wide roads and squat nondescript buildings.

The city was inhabited by an ancient Gallic tribe that succumbed to the Romans in the 1st century BC. Traces of the Roman occupation are visible in excavations on the place de la République. Lisieux became the seat of a bishopric in the 6th century and controlled most of the Pays d'Auge by the 12th century. Henry II and Eleanor of Aquitaine were married here in 1152 (or so it's thought), and the town remained important until the triple troubles of the 14th century – war, famine and plague – reduced its influence.

The town's association with Ste-Thérèse, which has been assiduously promoted, has made it one of the top pilgrimage destinations in Europe, attracting hundreds of thousands of pilgrims each year.

The Saturday morning **market** on place de la République is replete with local food products, and there's a Wednesday **market** from 4pm in July and August that offers more elaborate gastronomic adventures accompanied by music.

The train station is 1km south of the town centre; follow Rue de la Gare north, where you'll find the tourist office after about 400m.

♥ CATHÉDRALE ST-PIERRE //
INDULGE IN SOME NAVAL GAZING
Begun in 1170 and largely completed by the mid-13th century, **Cathédrale St-Pierre** (place François Mitterrand; 9.30am-6.45pm) is marked by an elegant sobriety characteristic of early Gothic architec-

ture. Pierre Cauchon, who became bishop of Lisieux after presiding over the trial and sentence of Joan of Arc, is buried to the left of the altar. Behind the cathedral, the **Jardin de l'Evêché** was designed by Le Nôtre, who also designed the gardens of Versailles.

♥ BASILIQUE STE-THÉRÈSE //
A BLINGED-UP BASILICA FOR A LOCAL SAINT
While Thérèse went about her humble life unnoticed, her grandiose **basilica** (www.therese-de-lisieux.com; av Jean XXIII; 9am-6.30pm) is hard to miss. Work commenced on this striking stone-and-concrete Romanesque- and Byzantine-influenced church in 1928 and wasn't completed until after the war, in 1954. The interior, which can accommodate 4000 people, is covered with exquisite mosaics.

You'll recognise Thérèse's shrine by the blaze of candles. It's only her right arm that's displayed here; the rest of her is entombed in the **Carmelite monastery** (37 rue du Carmel) where she lived.

STE THÉRÈSE

Ste Thérèse (1873–97), a Carmelite nun, died in Lisieux of tuberculosis at age 24. Unknown in her lifetime, her memoirs were released posthumously, quickly becoming a hit with their simple, direct approach to spirituality, including frank discussions of doubt. Among other miracles attributed to her, Edith Piaf is said to have been cured of blindness while praying at her grave as a little girl. Thérèse was canonised in 1925 and is now the patron saint of florists, the missions and people with AIDS and, along with St Joan of Arc, a co-patroness of France.

Head down to the crypt for more rainbow-hued mosaics. In July and August it's possible to climb to the 100m dome (🕐 2-6pm).

🍴 PONT L'ÉVÊQUE // COMPLETE THE HAT-TRICK OF CHEESE TOWNS

Since the 13th century this unpretentious little town with rivers meandering through its centre has been known for its eponymous cheese. Although two-thirds of the town was destroyed in the 1944 bombings, a careful reconstruction has preserved much of its layout. Half-timbered buildings still line the main street and 1960s stained glass bathes the 15th-century **Église St-Michel** (place de l'Église) in coloured light. A wonderful 16th-century convent has been converted into **Espace Culturel les Dominicaines** (☎ 02 31 64 89 33; www.espace lesdominicaines.over-blog.com; place du Tribunal; adult/child €3/1; 🕐 2.30-6pm Wed-Sun Oct-Mar, 10.30am-12.30pm Wed-Sun Apr-Jun & Sep, 10.30am-7pm Jul & Aug), which holds temporary exhibitions.

Cheese-lovers won't want to miss the **Fête du Fromage** (cheese festival) in the second weekend in May, where there are prizes for the best cheese and displays of regional products.

Tours of a Calvados distillery are possible nearby (see p180).

TRANSPORT

BUS // Lisieux is the region's hub, with busverts services to St-Pierre-sur-Dives (No 52), Livarot (No 53) and Le Havre via Pont l'Évêque (No 50). Bus 36 heads from Pont l'Évêque to Caen.

TRAIN // Pont l'Évêque is on the line that links Deauville-Trouville to Paris-St-Lazare via Lisieux. Lisieux also has direct connections to Rouen, Caen, Bayeux, Valognes, Cherbourg and Coutances.

CÔTE FLEURIE
······

The floral coast, lying between the Orne and Seine river mouths, is a lovely but highly developed string of beach resorts along a sandy coast. Glamorous Deauville-Trouville attracts the chic set from Paris; Cabourg is more sedate; and Honfleur retains its medieval charm amid the summer hoopla. The landscape is gentle, with low cliffs and dunes rising behind wide swathes of sand.

CABOURG, DIVES-SUR-MER & HOULGATE

pop 3500, 5800 & 1900

Given the rarefied ambience further up the coast, this trio of contiguous towns is surprisingly low-key. Of the three, **Cabourg** is the most genteel – coming across as the retirement-age version of Deauville. Its main claim to fame is as the inspiration for Balbec, a town appearing in Proust's *Du Côté de Chez Swann*. The novelist stayed at the *belle époque* Grand Hôtel, which opens directly on to the surf-battered beach.

Dives-sur-Mer has historical interest but no beach. The harbour from whence William set out to conquer England has since silted up, leaving the town removed from the sea. Try to visit the Saturday morning market, held beneath a medieval wooden canopy in the main square. Nearby, the **Village Guillaume le Conquérant** (cnr rue d'Hastings & rue Gaston Manneville) is a set of ancient buildings sporting intriguing wooden and stone sculptures that have been converted into a touristy complex of galleries and restaurants.

Although it's retained much of its 19th-century elegance, the prices in

Houlgate are more reasonable than other Côte Fleurie beach resorts, making it a popular spot for family holidays.

ESSENTIAL INFORMATION

TOURIST OFFICE // Cabourg (☎ 02 31 06 20 00; www.cabourg.net, in French; Jardins de l'Hôtel de Ville; ⊗ 9.30am-7pm Jul & Aug, 10am-12.30pm & 2-5.30pm Mon-Sat, 10am-noon & 2-4pm Sun Sep-Jun); **Houlgate** (☎ 02 31 24 34 79; www.ville-houlgate.fr; 10 bd des Belges; ⊗ 10am-6.30pm Jul & Aug, 10am-6pm Mon-Sat, 10.30am-4pm Sun Easter-Jun & Sep, closed Sun Oct-Easter).

GASTRONOMIC HIGHLIGHTS

❦ CHEZ LE BOUGNAT // DIVES-SUR-MER €€

☎ 02 31 91 06 13; 27 rue Gaston Manneville; lunch €17, menus €23-27; ⊗ lunch daily, dinner Thu-Sat
The eclectic decor of this buzzy bistro comprises a ceramics collection, vintage lottery posters, a stuffed fox and a metre-long spitfire suspended from the ceiling. Foodwise, it's seasonal classics all the way: an award-winning terrine, *boudin*, fish soup and a hearty beef salad being indicative of the fare.

❦ L'EDEN // HOULGATE €€

☎ 02 31 24 84 37; 7 rue Henri Fouchard; lunch €20, menus €26-42; ⊗ Wed-Sun
Predominantly but not exclusively a seafood restaurant, L'Eden doesn't waver in its commitment to serving only the freshest food that can be sourced at the market each day. Try the *poisson du marché* (market fish): the type of fish and seasonal accompaniment may vary from day to day, but it's unlikely to ever disappoint.

TRANSPORT

BUS // Busverts bus 20 stops at all three towns (as well as Deauville-Trouville and Honfleur) en route between Caen and Le Havre.

TRAIN // Cabourg and Dives-sur-Mer share a train station and Houlgate has one of its own, but services are limited to the holiday period and they all terminate at Deauville-Trouville, which has connections to Paris via Lisieux.

DEAUVILLE-TROUVILLE

pop 4600 & 5500

About midway along the Côte Fleurie lie the non-identical twin seaside resorts of Deauville and Trouville-sur-Mer, which are only separated by a bridge but maintain distinctly different personalities. Chic Deauville couldn't be more impressed with itself. With designer boutiques, an upmarket casino, a racetrack and the yearly Festival of American Film, the town is clearly comfortable with world-class shoppers, gamblers and film stars. Trouville is more down-to-earth. Hotels and restaurants are less expensive and the town is proud of the 19th-century artists and writers that once flocked to its picturesque port. Both towns boast a wide, sandy beach lined with mansions and hotels.

The town of Trouville developed before Deauville. When painter Paul Huet and writer Alexandre Dumas first came here in 1826, Trouville was merely a small fishing village. Its proximity to Paris (200km) attracted a set of painters and writers at a time when the concept of therapeutic bathing was gaining popularity. Gustav Flaubert came in 1836 when he was still a teenager and the landscape painter Charles Mozin produced several Trouville paintings. In the 20th century, writer-director Marguerite Duras was inspired to make several films in the town.

Deauville became fashionable in the early 20th century after construction of a racetrack and casino. Designer Coco Chanel opened a boutique in 1913 that was soon patronised by the fashionable set fleeing WWI for their secondary residences. Throughout the 1920s and 1930s, Deauville glittered with international royalty, industrialists and political heavyweights such as Winston Churchill. The Festival of American Film (see p181) arrived in 1975, bringing a parade of stars and added glamour. Events revolving around horses, polo and film attract the highest rungs of Parisian society, who sometimes refer to the town as Paris' 21st *arrondissement* (district).

ESSENTIAL INFORMATION

TOURIST OFFICE // **Deauville** (☎ 02 31 14 40 00; www.deauville.org; place de la Mairie; ☺ 10am-5pm); **Trouville** (☎ 02 31 14 60 70; www.trouvillesurmer.org; 32 quai Fernand Moureaux; ☺ 10am-6pm Jul & Aug, 9.30am-6pm Mon-Sat, 10am-1pm Sun Sep-Jun); **Point Info** (rue des Bains, Trouville; ☺ 10.30am-1pm & 3.30-6.30pm Jul & Aug)

ORIENTATION

The two towns are separated by the River Touques, with Deauville on the western bank. The combined train and bus station is on the Deauville side of the bridge.

EXPLORING DEAUVILLE-TROUVILLE

❤ MUSÉE VILLA MONTEBELLO // HANG OUT IN NAPOLEON III'S BEACH HOUSE

This former summer residence of Napoleon III was built at the height of Trouville's popularity in 1865 for the marquise of Montebello. There are panoramic views over the beach and a small **collection** (☎ 02 31 88 16 26; 64 rue du Général Leclerc; adult/concession €2/1.50, Wed free; ☺ 11am-6pm May-Sep, 2-5.30pm Wed-Mon, 11am-1pm Sat & Sun Apr & Oct–mid-Nov) of posters, drawings

and paintings that recounts the history of the town.

❤ CASINOS // ORDER A SHAKEN-NOT-STIRRED MARTINI, GO ON!

The French love their casinos, particularly at seaside towns. It's thought that the grand 1912 **Casino Barrière Trouville** (☎ 02 31 87 75 00; www.lucienbarriere .com; place Maréchal Foch; ☺ 9.30am-3am) may have been the inspiration for *Casino Royale* in the first James Bond novel (as opposed to the film, which was set in Montenegro). However, if you're looking for Bond-esque glamour, you may be disappointed to find that casinos are basically the same all around the world – lots of flashing lights and disappearing cash. You'll need a passport and tidy clothes to get in, but sharp suits and bow ties certainly aren't required. However, both the Trouville casino and its sister, the more upmarket **Casino Barrière Deauville** (☎ 02 31 98 66 00; www .lucienbarriere.com; rue Edmond Blanc; ☺ 10am-3am), boast lovely *belle époque* architecture, multiple bars and restaurants, and host a busy program of concerts, shows and movies.

❤ VILLA STRASSBURGER // POKE AROUND A POSH PAD

One of Deauville's grandest mansions, the **Villa Strassburger** (☎ 02 31 88 20 44; av de Strassburger; adult/child €3/2) was built by the Rothschild family and then given to the town. The exterior is an eye-pleasing mixture of towers and gables coalescing within a unique Alsatian-Norman style, and the interior is furnished in its original 1950s American style. Guided visits are conducted at 3pm on Wednesday and Thursday in July, and from Wednesday to Friday in August; bookings are essential.

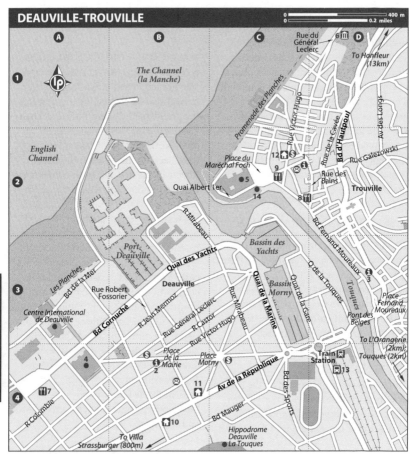

DEAUVILLE-TROUVILLE

CALVADOS & ORNE

GASTRONOMIC HIGHLIGHTS

Trouville's river-facing bd Fernand Moureaux is lined with cafés and eateries.

❤ LES MOUETTES €

☎ 02 31 98 06 97; 11 rue des Bains; menus €14-27

Painted seagulls *(mouettes)* circle the ceiling while the tightly seated punters below tuck into big serves of local treats: Trouville mussels, salmon and steaks with creamy sauces, and tasty apple tarts. It's hard to tell who's having more fun, the customers or the staff.

❤ L'ETRIER €€€

☎ 02 31 98 66 33; bd Cornuché; menus €65; ☉ dinner daily, lunch summer only

Deauville may attract plenty of movie stars but (at the time of research anyway) it has snagged only one Michelin star, and that's firmly affixed to the firmament of the Royal Barrière hotel. Chef Eric Provost waves his magic spatula over this intimate and elegant dining room, offering an imaginative and extravagant eight-course degustation (€105). Other quality *menus* are also available.

♥ L'ORANGERIE €€

☎ 02 31 81 47 81; 12 quai Monrival, Touques; menus €27-45; ☙ Fri-Tue

About 2km along the river the cutesy village of Touques has some great restaurants. While the 'quai' faces a motorway, you'll forget about it in the romantic wood-beamed dining room, especially when the food arrives. The flavours of Normandy abound: chicken accompanied by apples, veal with Calvados and oysters.

♥ PATISSERIE CHARLOTTE CORDAY €

☎ 02 31 88 11 76; place du Maréchal Foch; croissant €1

Only in France could a cake shop and *salon de thé* be named after a political assassin, but then again the mouth-watering array of pastries and chocolates might be enough to raise Marat out of his bath (see p193). Enjoy a morning coffee and *tarte Normande* at the sunny outdoor tables.

TRANSPORT

BUS // Busverts bus 20 stops en route between Caen and Le Havre via Honfleur.

BIKE // Hire bikes, tandems, pedal cars and rollerblades from **Les Trouvillaises** (☎ 02 31 98 54 11; place du Maréchal Foch; per hr/2hr/24hr/week €5/8/18/50).

TRAIN // Trains to/from Paris-St-Lazare also stop at Pont l'Évêque and Lisieux. There are occasional services to Houlgate and Dives/Cabourg, mainly in summer.

HONFLEUR

pop 8200

In its strategic coastal position at the mouth of the Seine, Honfleur is a relic of an era when fishermen, pirates and explorers set sail from its harbour to seek their fortunes. Its wood and stone buildings, constructed at the height of its glory, survive in a warren of streets around an amazingly picturesque old harbour. Even though Parisian weekenders sometimes outnumber residents, and cruise ships can be more plentiful than fishing boats, it remains an active maritime centre dispatching prawns, scallops and mackerel to the interior. While Honfleur may still have a commitment to the sea, the sea has less of a commitment to it, constantly edging away from the town with the build-up of silt dumped from the Seine.

Honfleur's seafaring tradition dates back over a millennium. After the 1066 invasion of England, goods bound for the conquered territory were shipped from the port. During the Hundred Years' War, Charles V fortified the town, but it was conquered by the English and remained in English hands until 1450. With the return of peace, the town was rebuilt and re-established its commercial links. The creation of Le Havre as a rival port in 1517 spurred the town on to developing trade relations with the New World.

In 1608 Samuel de Champlain set sail from here to found Quebec City. More than 4000 people migrated to Canada in the 17th century, working as fishermen, merchants and fur traders. In 1681 Cavelier de la Salle started out from Honfleur and reached the mouth of the

CALVADOS & ORNE

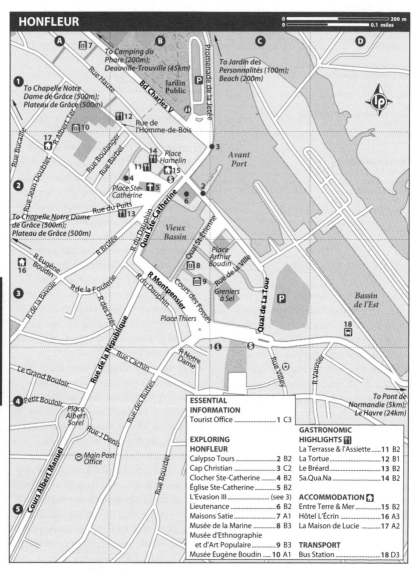

Mississippi, naming the area Louisiana in honour of King Louis XIV.

During the 17th and 18th centuries, Honfleur achieved prosperity through trade with the West Indies, the Azores and the colonies on the western coast of Africa. In order to accommodate the growing maritime traffic, Louis XIV's minister Colbert ordered the construction of a sheltered port, now the Vieux Bassin (old harbour), completed in 1684. It was followed by the construction of the Bassin de l'Est in the 18th century, but the age of maritime adventure was passing as England assumed control of the seas. Honfleur's diminishing importance made it unnecessary to undertake any grand renovation projects, leaving the town much as it was when its moment in the spotlight had passed.

Every year on Pentecost, Honfleur's sailors stage the Fête de Marins, starting with a colourful blessing of the sea in front of the old harbour. The following day there's a procession up to Chapelle Notre Dame de Grâce, where an open-air mass is held.

ESSENTIAL INFORMATION

TOURIST OFFICE // Honfleur (☎ 02 31 89 23 30; www.ot-honfleur.fr; quai Lepaulmier; ⌚ 9.30am-noon & 2-6pm Mon-Sat Oct-Easter, also 10am-12.30pm & 2-5pm Sun Easter-Jun & Sep, 9.30am-7pm Mon-Sat, 10am-5pm Sun Jul-Aug)

ORIENTATION

Honfleur is centred on the Vieux Bassin. To the southeast is the heart of the old city, known as the Enclos because it was once enclosed by fortifications. To the north is the Avant Port (outer harbour). Quai Ste-Catherine fronts the Vieux Bassin to the west. The Plateau de Grâce, with the Chapelle Notre Dame de Grâce on top, is west of town. To reach the beach, walk up promenade de la Jetée and head west along the coast.

EXPLORING HONFLEUR

♥ PLACE STE-CATHERINE // THE HEART AND SOUL OF HONFLEUR'S OLD TOWN

On Saturday mornings a traditional market covers the cobbles of this lively square, lined with cafés, restaurants, boutiques and real-estate agents flogging 15th-century rural chateaux; on Wednes-day mornings the market's an exclusively *bio* (organic) affair.

A romantic backdrop is provided by the wooden **Église Ste-Catherine** (⌚ 9am-6.30pm). This unusual double-naved church has a vaulted roof that looks like overturned ships' hulls. Inside, the left-hand nave is the oldest, dating from the 15th century. It is thought that wood was used as it could be worked by local shipwrights, saving stone, which was needed for the town's fortifications. The result is a charmingly bright interior, although the effect is often disrupted by flocks of tourists.

The church's free-standing wooden bell tower, **Clocher Ste-Catherine**, dates from the second half of the 15th century. It was built apart from the church for structural reasons (so the church roof would not be subject to the bells' weight and vibrations) and for safety (a high tower was more likely to be hit by lightning). The former bell-ringer's residence is at the tower's base.

♥ HARBOURS // THE PLACE TO TAKE THAT POSTCARD-PERFECT SHOT

Although it may look like it was designed for a chocolate-box lid, the **Vieux Bassin**, was once a busy port. Now the only cargo being unloaded here are the trays full of beverages being served in front of the tall, narrow, 16th- to 18th-century houses lining **quai Ste-Catherine**. At the mouth of the old harbour, the **Lieutenance**, the former residence of the town's royal governor, is the sole remaining vestige of the fortifications that once completely encircled the town. It faces the **Avant Port**, which is home to Honfleur's fishing fleet and tour boats.

Public gardens line the waterfront to the west of the Avant Port. In the **Jardin des Personnalités** (⌚ 8am-sunset), north

CALVADOS & ORNE

of the centre, famous Honfleurais are each honoured in their own boat-shaped minigarden. Where the river meets the sea, a wall follows the fast-moving channel an extremely long way out, partially sheltering the sandy beach to the west. Lifeguards patrol in July and August but be prepared for a hike to the water at low tide.

An excellent way to explore the Seine estuary and get a closer look at the Pont de Normandie (opposite) is on a sightseeing cruise. Both **Cap Christian** (☎ /fax 02 31 89 21 10) and **l'Evasion III** (☎ /fax 02 31 89 41 80) offer 50-minute trips (adult/child €7.50/5), departing from near the Lieutenance, while the **Calypso** (☎ 02 31 89 07 77; www.joliefrance-calipso.com, in French; adult/child €6/4) has a 40-minute version.

♥ MUSEUMS // BRUSH UP ON LOCAL LUMINARIES AND HONFLEUR HISTORY

Named in honour of the influential painter, born here in 1824, **Musée Eugène Boudin** (☎ 02 31 89 54 00; rue de l'Homme de Bois; adult/child €4.80/3.10; ⏰ 10am-noon & 2-6pm Wed-Mon mid-Mar–Sep, 2.30-5pm Mon & Wed-Fri, 10am-noon & 2.30-5pm Sat & Sun Oct–mid-Mar) contains an impressive collection of paintings representing the local landscape, including works by Monet. An entire room is devoted to Boudin, whom Baudelaire called the 'king of skies' for his luscious skyscapes. There's also a small ethnographic section, sporting some gravity-defying bonnets, and a terrific view of the Pont de Normandie from the top gallery.

The spirit of another local lad is celebrated in the unusual **Maisons Satie** (☎ 02 31 89 11 11; 67 bd Charles V; adult/child €5.50/4.50; ⏰ 11am-6pm Wed-Mon mid-Feb–Dec). Erik Satie was known for his esoteric wit ('Like money, piano is only agreeable to those that touch it') as well as for his

starkly beautiful compositions. Visitors wander through the museum (located in the composer's birthplace) with a headset playing Satie's music and excerpts from his writings. Each room is a surprise. One features a winged pear, another has a light display around a basin, and a room called the Laboratory of Emotions has a whimsical instrument that you pedal.

Two fairly interesting smaller museums complete the set of four that can be visited on the Pass Musées (€9.30), which is cheaper than the combined price of the two main museums. The **Musée de la Marine** (☎ 02 31 89 14 12; quai St-Etienne; adult/child €3.40/2.20; ⏰ 10am-noon & 2-6.30pm Tue-Sun Apr & mid-Jul–Sep, 2-5.30pm Tue-Fri, 10am-noon & 2.30-5.30pm Sat & Sun Oct–mid-Nov & mid-Feb–Mar) displays nautical artefacts in a deconsecrated 14th-century church. **Musée d'Ethnographie et d'Art Populaire** (rue de la Prison; details as for marine museum) occupies a pair of houses and a former prison dating from the 16th and 17th centuries. Its rooms are furnished to represent the lives of Honfleur residents in different eras.

♥ CHAPELLE NOTRE DAME DE GRÂCE // A PEACEFUL REWARD FOR A CHALLENGING WALK

A steep track up the escarpment behind the old town (off rue Charrière) leads to the 100m-high Plateau de Grâce and great views over Honfleur and the Pont de Normandie. After a short, mercifully flat, stroll through verdant farmland you'll find this gorgeous early-17th-century **chapel** (⏰ 9am-6.15pm), set in a peaceful copse overlooking the beach. Vibrant stained glass lights the interior walls, which are covered with hundreds of thanksgiving plaques to Our Lady of Grace. Louis-Philippe and his queen spent their last few days up here before leaving France for exile in England.

PONT DE NORMANDIE

Straddling the mouth of the Seine, connecting Upper and Lower Normandy, the Pont de Normandie is a majestic feat of engineering. When completed in 1995 it was the world's longest cable-stayed bridge, with a total length of 2141m (in 1998 it was surpassed by the Tatara bridge in Hiroshima). A delicate web of cables connects its gently arched span with two soaring 214m towers, etching a bold silhouette against the sky. At night, theatrically placed lights create an even more dramatic effect.

The decision to construct a cable-stayed bridge was based in part upon the softness of the riverbed, which probably would not have supported a suspension bridge. The two towers descend to a depth of 50m to rest upon sufficiently solid bedrock. Also, one malfunctioning stay doesn't affect the entire bridge. Its aerodynamic design keeps the bridge stable even in tornado-level winds, and a battery of computers monitor its stress level.

GASTRONOMIC HIGHLIGHTS

This town loves prawns (it even hosts an annual prawn festival in mid-October). There are many places around town to snack out on this local delicacy.

❧ LA TERRASSE & L'ASSIETTE €€
☎ 02 31 89 31 33; 8 place Ste-Catherine; menus €32-54; ✆ closed Mon, also Tue Sep-Jun

For the indecisive, the first hurdle comes before you even pick up a menu: whether to sit on the gorgeous square or head into the atmospheric wooden interior. Chef Gérard Bonnefoy earned his Michelin star by doing traditional dishes exceptionally well – his delicious lamb shank with ratatouille is a case in point.

❧ LA TORTUE €
☎ 02 31 81 24 60; 36 rue de l'Homme de Bois; 2-course lunch €14, menus €19-36; Ⓥ

Orange lampshades and lime-green trim bring flashes of colour into this cute little dining room. The menu is traditional French with a distinctly Norman bent, such as fish in a creamy cider sauce, Auge-style pork and apple tart.

❧ LE BRÉARD €€
☎ 02 31 89 53 40; 7 rue du Puits; 2-course lunch €20, menus €28-38; ✆ lunch Thu-Sun, dinner Wed-Sun

Tackling an adventurous approach to the summit of Norman cuisine, Le Bréard travels with a well-stocked kitbag including the best quality local ingredients and exotic spices. For example, pork is allowed to ditch its usual companion, apple, and hit the slopes with orange and endive instead. Surely a Michelin star is close by.

❧ SA.QUA.NA €€€
☎ 02 31 89 40 80; 22 place Hamelin; degustation 5-/10-courses €50/80; ✆ lunch Sat & Sun, dinner Fri-Tue

The name, while a little pretentious, is a statement of intent – *Saveurs.Qualité.Nature* (flavours-quality-nature) and a play on *sakana*, the Japanese word for fish. But when you're Michelin-starred and you produce French-Japanese seafood dishes this well, a little flashiness can be forgiven.

TRANSPORT

BUS // Busverts line 50 from Le Havre to Lisieux via Pont l'Évêque stops at Honfleur's **bus station** (☎ 02 31 89 28 41; rue des Vases), as does line 20 between Le Havre and Caen (via the coastal road) and an express bus between the two cities.

SEINE-MARITIME & EURE

3 PERFECT DAYS

❦ DAY 1 // COASTAL CRUISING

At 150km, the coastal drive along the dramatic Côte d'Albâtre (opposite) can be done in a day. Spend the morning wandering around Eu's historic sights (p231) before continuing on to Dieppe for lunch (p231). Consider stopping at the gardens at Varengeville-sur-Mer (p228), Fécamp's spectacular Palais Bénédictine (p226) and the pretty seaside town of Étretat (p224). Head to Le Havre for dinner (p223) and a taste of World Heritage architecture (opposite).

❦ DAY 2 // ROAMING ROUEN

This fascinating city, with its medieval laneways and magnificent edifices, begs for a thorough exploration. The walking tour, p236, is a good way to get your bearings and get started. If it's a Sunday morning, head to the market (p240). Allow plenty of time for the Musée des Beaux-Arts (p240), the famous cathedral (p238) and the city's other Gothic glories (p239). With plenty of wonderful restaurants to choose from, a leisurely lunch and dinner are essential (p242).

❦ DAY 3 // CHÂTEAU AND ABBEY HOPPING

The Haute-Normandie countryside is littered with remarkable chateaux and abbeys, many complete with glorious gardens or museums. There are too many to visit in a day, but options include (circling Rouen clockwise) the Parc de Clères (p243), Château de Martainville (p244), Château de Vascœuil (p256), Abbaye de Mortemer (p256), Fortresse de Gisors (p257), Château-Gaillard (p254), Château de Beaumesnil (p248), Château du Champ de Bataille (p247), Abbaye Notre Dame du Bec (p247), Abbaye St-Georges (p245), Abbaye de Jumièges (p245) and Abbaye St-Wandrille (p246).

CÔTE D'ALBÂTRE

· · · · · ·

Stretching 120km from Le Havre to Le Tréport, the lofty white cliffs of the Côte d'Albâtre (Alabaster Coast) create the most dramatic coastal scenery in Normandy. Reminiscent of the southern coast of England, these chalky towers can reach 120m as they curve around stony beaches and crack open into river valleys. Fishing ports and resort towns compete for dominance along the coast, while fields and pastures cap off the cliffs.

LE HAVRE

pop 185,300

France's premier cargo port and Europe's fifth largest, Le Havre is also a bustling gateway for ferries to Britain and Ireland. As with most gateways, people tend to pass through it on the way to somewhere else, but to do so would be to miss out on a designated World Heritage Site.

Le Havre was created in 1517 by François I to replace the ports of Harfleur and Honfleur, which were silting up. With its two-hour high tides it became an important maritime centre. In the 17th century Cardinal Richelieu built a citadel and enlarged the ports just in time for the city to capitalise on emerging trade connections with the Americas. Ships loaded with cotton and coffee sailed into the port and, in the 18th century, sailed out with guns and supplies for American revolutionaries.

During WWI the Belgian government retreated to Ste-Adresse, an adjoining village that had been a fashionable seaside retreat for such luminaries as Sarah Bernhardt, Alexandre Dumas, Raoul Dufy and Claude Monet.

The Germans occupied Le Havre in 1940, turning it into an important garrison. From 2 to 12 September 1944, the city was subjected to a furious bombing campaign by the Allies, while the Germans, in a desperate last stand, blew up the port installations. By the time it was liberated, 85% of the city had been destroyed and 5000 civilians killed.

ESSENTIAL INFORMATION

TOURIST OFFICE // Tourist Office (☎ 02 32 74 04 04; www.lehavretourisme.com; 186 bd Clemenceau; ☽ 9am-6.15pm Mon-Sat, 10am-12.30pm & 2.30-5pm Sun Easter-Oct, same except closed 12.30-2pm Mon-Sat Nov-Easter)

ORIENTATION

A triumph in town planning, the major roads radiate from the place de l'Hôtel de Ville. Av Foch runs west to the sea and the Port de Plaisance recreational area; bd de Strasbourg goes east to the train and bus stations; rue de Paris cuts south to the quai de Southampton, where the cruise liners stop. Bd Albert leads along the beach 2km to the Ste-Adresse neighbourhood, which survived WWII with its grand turreted mansions intact.

EXPLORING LE HAVRE

♥ **WORLD HERITAGE ARCHITECTURE // DISCOVER THE BEAUTY OF CONCRETE; NO, REALLY!**

After the war the task of rebuilding an obliterated Le Havre fell to architect Auguste Perret. With a pressing need to shelter 80,000 suddenly homeless residents

(Continued on page 222)

SEINE-MARITIME & EURE

SEINE-MARITIME & EURE

SEINE-MARITIME & EURE

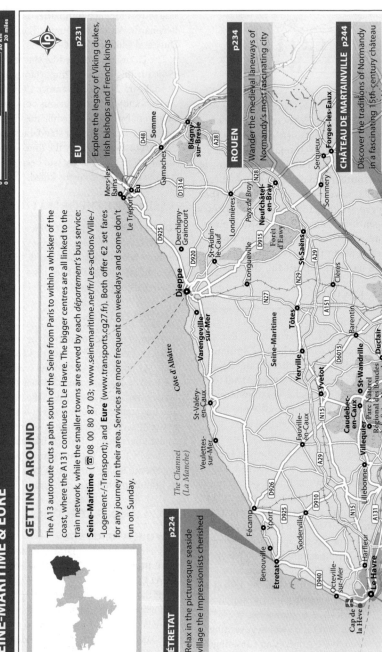

GETTING AROUND

The A13 autoroute cuts a path south of the Seine from Paris to within a whisker of the coast, where the A131 continues to Le Havre. The bigger centres are all linked to the train network, while the smaller towns are served by each *département's* bus service: **Seine-Maritime** (☎ 08 00 80 87 03; www.seinemaritime.net/fr/Les-actions/Ville-/-Logement-/-Transport); and **Eure** (www.transports.cg27.fr). Both offer €2 set fares for any journey in their area. Services are more frequent on weekdays and some don't run on Sunday.

ÉTRETAT p224

Relax in the picturesque seaside village the Impressionists cherished

EU p231

Explore the legacy of Viking dukes, Irish bishops and French kings

ROUEN p234

Wander the medieval laneways of Normandy's most fascinating city

CHÂTEAU DE MARTAINVILLE p244

Discover the traditions of Normandy in a fascinating 15th-century château

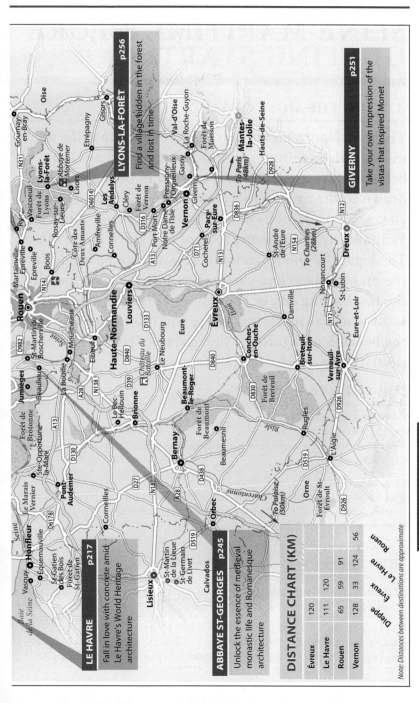

LYONS-LA-FORÊT p256

Find a village hidden in the forest and lost in time

GIVERNY p251

Take your own impression of the vistas that inspired Monet

LE HAVRE p217

Fall in love with concrete amid Le Havre's World Heritage architecture

ABBAYE ST-GEORGES p245

Unlock the essence of medieval monastic life and Romanesque architecture

DISTANCE CHART (KM)

	Dieppe	Évreux	Le Havre	Rouen
Évreux	120			
Le Havre	111	120		
Rouen	65	59	91	
Vernon	128	33	124	56

Note: Distances between destinations are approximate

SEINE-MARITIME & EURE GETTING STARTED

MAKING THE MOST OF YOUR TIME

The two *départements* that together compose the administrative region of Haute-Normandie have long been the favoured weekend escapes of bored Parisians, drawn to the lush countryside and genteel beach enclaves. Three famous names loom large over this land: William the Conqueror, Joan of Arc and Claude Monet. The legacy of the Norman duke-king can be found in the many abbeys and castles littering the countryside; the fascinating city of Rouen remains in thrall to the saint who was martyred there; and thousands flock to the beaches and gardens that gave birth to the Impressionist style of art.

TOP TOURS & COURSES

❧ FAITES-LE VOUS-MÊME

Learn how to make traditional pastries and chocolate in Rouen. (Map p235; ☎ 02 35 71 58 47; www.pastryclasses.blogspot.com; Passage de la Petite Horloge, 11 rue des Faulx, Rouen; day/weekend/week course €50/350/1500)

❧ ON RUE TATIN

Susan Loomis, an American expat and author of books on Norman life and cuisine, runs this cooking school in her fabulous half-timbered house in Louviers. (☎ 09 51 14 38 94; www.onruetatin.com; rue Tatin; 3-day course €1000)

❧ AVENUE VERTE

This 40km walking and cycling route follows a former rail route from St-Aubin-le-Cauf, near Dieppe, to just outside Forges-les-Eaux in the Pays de Bray (see boxed text, p232). Eventually it's hoped that this will become part of a green route linking London to Paris via the Newhaven–Dieppe ferry.

❧ 'VILLE DE FÉCAMP' BOAT CRUISES

This 63-passenger launch offers cruises from Le Havre (September to July) and Fécamp (August). (Map p222; ☎ 02 35 28 99 53; tim76@wanadoo.fr; 90min cruise €14, 4hr fishing trip €40)

GETTING AWAY FROM IT ALL

* **Forêt d'Eawy** Take one of the trails through the giant beeches in this 65-sq-km forest, west of Neufchâtel-en-Bray

* **Parc Naturel Régional des Boucles de la Seine Normande** Straddling the Eure and Seine-Maritime *départements,* this vast protected area includes the Forêt de Brotonne and the Marais Vernier, 45 sq km of bird-friendly wetlands (www.pnr-seine-normande.com)

* **Giverny** Stay at one of the excellent local *chambres d'hôtes* to experience the after-hours tranquillity of this daytime tourist trap (p251)

* **Forêt de Lyons** Base yourself in atmospheric Lyons-la-Forêt to explore the depths of the forest (p256)

ADVANCE PLANNING

Outside of the July and August peak season you shouldn't need to arrange too much in advance, unless there's something special on.

* **Fêtes de Rouen** This 10-day arts festival culminates in religious parades and street events to commemorate Joan of Arc's martyrdom (closest Sunday to 30 May).

* **Rouen Armada** (www.armada.org) Held every five years (the next one's in July 2013), this 10-day festival attracts millions of spectators to its parade of tall ships, sailing races and associated concerts and fireworks displays.

* **Étretat** Last-minute weekend accommodation is hard to come by at any time of the year.

TOP RESTAURANTS

♥ JEAN LUC TARTARIN
Innovative gastronomy in stylish surrounds (p224)

♥ LA PETITE AUBERGE
A romantic setting for seafood and more (p224)

♥ LE VICOMTÉ
Old-fashioned bistro atmosphere and quality food (p227)

♥ GILL
Normandy's finest, with two Michelin stars to prove it (p242)

♥ LES NYMPHÉAS
Traditional Norman setting for adventurous cuisine (p242)

♥ AUBERGE DU MOULIN
Sophisticated regional cuisine in tiny Le Tôt (p244)

♥ LE BISTRO
The perfect informal bistro experience (p253)

RESOURCES

* **Seine-Maritime Tourisme** (www.seine-maritime-tourisme.com) Practical information about the *département's* sights and activities

* **Eure Tourisme** (www.eure-tourisme.fr, in French) As above, but for Eure

* **Le Havre Tourisme** (www.lehavretourisme.com) Sights, events and accommodation guide for Le Havre

* **Rouen Tourisme** (www.rouentourisme.com) As above, for Rouen

SEINE-MARITIME & EURE

(Continued from page 217)

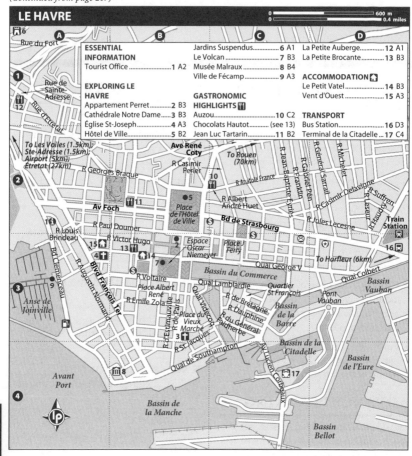

SEINE-MARITIME & EURE

and little money to work with, he created a brand-new, custom-built city out of reinforced concrete in his signature style, structural classicism. While some dismiss the result as sterile, the detractors have largely been silenced since the inner city was added to the Unesco World Heritage list in 2005 – the first modern European city to be so honoured.

Perret's (literally) towering achievement is the 107m-high **Église St-Joseph** (bd François 1er; ☺ 10am-6pm). Anyone who smirks at the idea of concrete being beautiful should kiss this wonderful

church's pebblecreted derrière. Visible all over the city, its skyscraper design was intended to greet sea passengers from New York as they neared Le Havre. The interior space is filled by muted light filtering through 12,768 glass panels in 50 colours.

Another highlight is the classically proportioned **Hôtel de Ville** (Town Hall), placed at the end of a large park-like square filled with dancing fountains. The facade is lined with fluted columns tapering elegantly towards the ground.

However, Perret's achievements weren't just monumental; six apartment blocks he personally designed (dozens of the others were by his protégés) face the Hôtel de Ville and are now Le Havre's most sought-after flats. The **Appartement Perret** (adult/child €3/free; ☺ tours 2pm, 3pm, 4pm & 5pm Wed, Sat & Sun) is a showcase flat, furnished in impeccable 1950s style, that can be visited on a guided tour (meet at 1 place de l'Hôtel de Ville).

The other famous architect to leave his mark on Le Havre was Brazilian Oscar Niemeyer, the designer of Brasilia. He's responsible for **Le Volcan** (The Volcano; ☎ 02 35 19 10 10; www.levolcan.com; espace Oscar Niemeyer), the city's premier cultural venue, comprising concert halls and an arthouse cinema. At a glance you'll see how it got its name, although it bears more than a passing resemblance to a nuclear cooling tower.

♥ MUSÉE MALRAUX // TUCK INTO A BIG SERVE OF IMPRESSIONISTS

Among other artistic treasures, this modern **museum** (☎ 02 35 19 62 62; http://musee-malraux.ville-lehavre.fr; 2 bd Clemenceau; adult/child €5/free, 1st Sat of month free; ☺ 11am-6pm Wed-Mon) houses a truly fabulous set of Impressionist and fauvist works – perhaps the finest in France outside Paris. Four Monets are a highlight of a collection that includes such luminaries as Pissarro, Renoir, Sisley, Delacroix, Constable, Manet, Gauguin and Matisse. Locals Eugène Boudin and Dufy are well represented.

♥ JARDINS SUSPENDUS // TAKE IN THE VIEWS FROM THE 'HANGING GARDENS'

Built from 1854 to 1856, partly by Russian POWs from Crimea, this large fortress overlooking Ste-Adresse and the town centre was occupied by the Germans in 1940 and the Americans after the war but was completely abandoned by the French military in 1972. Rather than let it fall into ruin, it was opened to the public in September 2008 with a rather more peaceful purpose.

Although they're still quite young, these interesting **gardens** (rue du Fort; admission free; ☺ 1-8pm Mon-Fri, 10.30am-8pm Sat & Sun May–mid-Jun, 10.30am-8pm daily mid-Jun–Sep, 1-5pm Mon-Fri, 10.30am-5pm Sat Oct-Apr) celebrate the impact of explorers – the kind that have set out from Le Havre over the centuries – on the French landscape. Three of the corners of the earthen ramparts are themed by region: Asia, North America and Austral (Australia, Chile and, especially, New Zealand). The last corner is an experimental planting of flora recently introduced to France by contemporary explorers; the views from here are exceptional. In the centre there are tropical **greenhouses** (admission €1; ☺ 10.30am-5pm mid-Jun–Sep, Sat & Sun only Oct–mid-Jun) and formal flower beds.

♥ CATHÉDRALE NOTRE DAME // CATCH A GLIMPSE OF OLD LE HAVRE

Built mainly between 1575 and 1610, the **cathedral** (place du Vieux-Marché) is a rare survivor from pre-war Le Havre. Although it was severely damaged during 1944, clever restoration has preserved the church's unusual mixture of Gothic and Renaissance styles. The magnificent 17th-century organ was a gift from Cardinal Richelieu.

GASTRONOMIC HIGHLIGHTS

The Quartier St-François is a good place for a cheap eat and there are cafés scattered throughout the central city. For a sweet treat, try the branches of **Auzou** (1 rue Albert André Huet) and **Chocolats Hautot** (69 rue Louis Brindeau).

♥ JEAN LUC TARTARIN €€€

☎ 02 35 45 46 20; 73 av Foch; menus €40-145, 2-course lunch €29; ⊗ Tue-Sat

Complimentary appetisers are de rigueur at finer establishments, but when five fascinating, fiddly creations arrive – accompanying even the two-course lunch special (€29, weekdays only) – you know you're in for an experience. The modern art-festooned dining room and, yes, even the slightly snooty staff add to the effect. By the time the *petits fours* roll out, their volume and inventiveness rivalling the appetisers', your taste buds will be singing.

♥ LA PETITE AUBERGE €€

☎ 02 35 46 27 32; 32 rue de Ste-Adresse; menus €23-43, 2-course lunch €18; ⊗ lunch & dinner Tue & Thu-Sat, dinner Wed, lunch Sun

The cosy, low-beamed dining room whispers of romance, even if you're dining alone. Seafood features prominently on an interesting menu that is nonetheless rooted in the traditions of the *terroir*. Leave room for the lush chocolate mousse and mint sorbet. At €18, the weekday lunch special (two courses with a glass of wine) is terrific value.

♥ LA PETITE BROCANTE €€

☎ 02 35 21 42 20; 75 rue Louis Brindeau; menu €25; ⊗ Mon-Sat

The buzz doesn't let up in this tiny bistro where the locals are happy to wait for a table if the need arises – as it frequently does. You're best to come with an empty stomach as the serves are massive. Everything is double what you'd expect: two thick slices of delicious homemade terrine, two large crispy-skinned duck legs. You may need to be wheeled out.

TRANSPORT

TO/FROM THE AIRPORT

AIR // The **airport** (☎ 02 35 54 65 00; www.havre .aeroport.fr) is 6km north of town in Octeville-sur-Mer. There's no public transport; a taxi will cost about €12.

GETTING AROUND

FERRY // LD Lines (p321) car ferries from Portsmouth and Rosslare (Ireland) dock at Terminal de la Citadelle.

TRAIN // Le Havre's **train station** (cours de la République) has frequent services to Rouen (€14, one hour), Vernon and Paris-St-Lazare (€29, 2¼ hours). A secondary line heads north to Fécamp.

BUS // The bus station is immediately next to the train station. Seine-Maritime buses head to Étretat and Fécamp. Calvados' busverts services include routes 20 (Honfleur-Deauville-Trouville), 39 (express to Honfleur and Caen) and 50 (Honfleur/Pont l'Évêque/Lisieux). **Bus Océane** (☎ 02 35 22 34 00; www.bus-oceane .com; ticket per hr/day/week €1.50/3.50/11.90) provides an efficient local bus service.

BIKE // The local bus company also runs **Vélo Océane** (per 2hr/half-day/day/week €2/3/7/25), renting bikes from seven locations around the city including the tourist office, bus station, beach and Hôtel de Ville.

ÉTRETAT

Sweet little Étretat has no port and never amounted to much until painters and writers immortalised its beauty in the 19th century. Guy de Maupassant spent part of his youth here and the dramatic scenery made it a favourite of painters Camille Corot, Boudin, Gustav Courbet and Monet. With the vogue for sea air at the end of the 19th century, fashionable Parisians came and built extravagant villas. Étretat has never gone out of style and swells to bursting point with visitors every weekend.

Étretat's most famous features are the white cliffs that bookend the town, the **Falaise d'Amont** to the northeast and

Falaise d'Aval to the southwest. The latter is accessible via signposted stairs from place du Général de Gaulle. The cliff descends to the water in a delicate arch, the **Porte d'Aval**, which reminded writer Guy de Maupassant of an elephant dipping its trunk into the water. Behind the arch is the 70m-high **l'Aiguille** (the Needle), which rises from the water like an obelisk. **Le Trou à l'Homme** grotto lies on the other side of the arch and can be reached on foot at low tide. Beyond the grotto is the stunning **La Manneporte** rock arch.

Serious walkers might enjoy continuing north of the arch on the GR21 from Falaise d'Amont to Benouville for the splendid coastal views. Do *not* try to explore the base of the cliffs outside low tide. Ask the tourist office for the tide tables.

The Falaise d'Amont is accessible by car, taking rue Jules Gerbeau, or on foot from the signposted path at the northeastern end of the promenade.

A sign, perhaps, of the town's awareness of its own cuteness, the handsome wooden **covered market** at its centre was only built in 1926. It now houses various arts and crafts shops.

The 17th-century decor of **Le Galion** (☎ 02 35 29 48 74; bd René Coty; menus €25-39; ☺ closed Tue & Wed), filled with beams and style, creates a serious atmosphere in which to partake of such specialities as salmon with Muscadet sauce. **La Salamandre** (☎ 02 35 27 17 07; 4 bd René Coty) is a congenial place to drink and snack, cloistered within ancient wooden walls.

The **tourist office** (☎ 02 35 27 05 21; www .etretat.net; place Maurice Guillard; ☺ 10am-noon & 2-6pm Mon-Sat) posts information about the bus times to Le Havre and Fécamp on its window. Bus is the only way to get to Étretat by public transport.

FÉCAMP

pop 19,900

At the foot of the highest cliffs in Normandy (126m), Fécamp is a sturdy fishing town with a busy port and a stretch of rocky beach. The town's dramatic setting and neat rows of brick houses have made it a popular summer resort and there are fascinating reminders of its history scattered throughout the town.

Fécamp was little more than a village until the 6th century, when a few drops of Christ's blood miraculously found their way here and it became a pilgrimage centre.

Until the mid-1970s, Fécamp was the fourth-largest fishing port in France, with local fishermen setting sail for the cod-filled waters of Newfoundland. In recent decades the boats stay closer to home, bringing the daily catch to nearby freezing, drying and salting factories. Ship repair and net making are also important industries.

ESSENTIAL INFORMATION

TOURIST OFFICES // Tourist Office (☎ 02 35 28 51 01; www.fecamptourisme.com; quai Sadi Carnot; ☺ 9am-6pm Mon-Fri Sep-May, 9am-6pm Mon-Fri, 10am-6pm Sat & Sun Apr-Aug) There's also an information kiosk on the beach during the summer months.

ORIENTATION

The town centre lies southwest of a series of ports and basins. Quai de la Vicomté and quai Bérigny along the Port de Plaisance and Bassin Bérigny form a busy road packed with shops and restaurants. The pedestrianised streets between St-Étienne church and place Charles de Gaulle are also good for shopping. Most places of interest are in the oldest part of town, east of rue du Président Coty.

SEINE-MARITIME & EURE

EXPLORING FÉCAMP

❦ PALAIS BÉNÉDICTINE //
PARTAKE IN SPIRITUAL ART AND AN ARTFUL SPIRIT

In the early 16th century a Benedictine monk concocted a 'medicinal elixir' from a variety of plants. Although the recipe was lost during the Revolution, it was rediscovered in the 19th century and produced commercially. Today, Bénédictine is one of the most widely marketed *digestifs* in the world – although strangely it's less ubiquitous at home than overseas.

The **Palais Bénédictine** (☎ 02 35 10 26 10; www.benedictine.fr; 110 rue Alexandre Le Grand; adult/child €6.50/3; ☆ 10am-7pm mid-Jul–Aug, 10.30am-12.45pm & 2-6pm Feb–mid-Jul & Sep-Dec) is a wonderfully ornate building (1900) inspired by the 15th-century Hôtel de Cluny in Paris. Here you'll discover everything about the history and manufacture of the aromatic liqueur – except the exact recipe.

Visits start in the art museum, which houses the private collection of founder Alexandre Le Grand. This rich merchant loved medieval art and the display includes carved ivory and wood, religious paintings, statues, manuscripts, wrought iron and a stained-glass window of the man himself, commissioned by his son. A separate gallery is devoted to modern art exhibitions. In the fragrant Plant & Spice Room, you can smell the ingredients used to make the potent drink and then continue through the distillery and cellars. Admission includes a shot of Bénédictine.

❦ ABBATIALE DE LA STE-TRINITÉ //
JOIN A QUEST FOR HOLY BLOOD

Built from 1175 to 1220 at the instigation of Richard the Lion-Heart, this large Benedictine **abbey church** (place des Ducs Richard; ☆ 9am-7pm Apr-Sep, 9am-noon & 2-5pm Oct-Mar)

was the most important pilgrimage site in Normandy until the construction of Mont St-Michel. Pilgrims would come to venerate a drop of Christ's blood that was believed to have floated to Fécamp in the trunk of a fig tree (housed in a tabernacle directly behind the main altar). The abbey remained influential until the Revolution but now has a neglected air. Many of the statues have lost their heads and some of the paintings are torn.

The exterior is a combination of primitive Gothic and a classical style dating from an 18th-century reconstruction. Among the treasures inside is a late-15th-century polychrome bas-relief *Dormition de la Vierge* (Assumption of the Virgin). Nearby is the *Pas de l'Ange* sculpture, which represents the footprint of the angel that reputedly descended upon the church during its consecration, demanding that it be named after the Holy Trinity.

Across from the abbey are the remains of the **fortified château** built by the earliest dukes of Normandy in the 10th and 11th centuries.

GASTRONOMIC HIGHLIGHTS

Fécamp is a good place to sample *sole normande*.

❦ LA MARÉE €€

☎ 02 35 29 39 15; 77 quai Bérigny; menus €28-33; ☆ closed Tue & dinner Sun & Thu

An extension of a fish shop, this 1st-floor restaurant offers views over the harbour and the freshest, tastiest fish in town. Try the bouillabaisse or, depending on the season, the pan-fried *coquilles St-Jacques* (scallops).

❦ LA PYRAMIDE DE MACARONS €

☎ 02 35 28 17 95; 5-7 rue Andre Paul Leroux; ☆ 9am-noon Tue-Sun, 3-6.30pm Tue-Sat

This branch of Chocolats Hautot – there are others in Le Havre (p223) and Étretat (4 rue Doctor Fidelin) – stocks an irresistible array of pastries, chocolates and, of course, macaroons, stacked in delectable pyramids. Best of all, there's a *salon de thé* (tearoom) attached, so you can justify it as a breakfast stop.

☙ LE VICOMTÉ €

☎ 02 35 28 47 63; 4 rue du Président Coty; menu €17.50; ☙ closed Sun & Wed

With its blackboard *menu,* moustachioed owner and cosy dining room, Le Vicomté could be a movie set for a typical French bistro. With the scene in place, prepare for the perfect Norman meal. Choices are limited and ever-changing, so be prepared to go with the flow.

TRANSPORT

TRAIN & BUS // The bus and train **stations** (bd de la République) are side by side near the port, just down the hill from the Gothic Église St-Etienne. Trains head to Le Havre and buses to Étretat and Le Havre.

VARENGEVILLE-SUR-MER

A country village 8km west of Dieppe, **Varengeville-sur-Mer** is so small that you hardly know you've been there until you leave it. Little more than a cluster of houses along the side of the road, Varengeville charmed painters such as Monet, Dufy, Miró and Georges Braque.

Buses from Dieppe's station head here at least three times daily from Monday to Saturday (25 minutes).

EXPLORING VARENGEVILLE-SUR-MER

☙ ÉGLISE ST-MARGUERITE // A TOMB WITH A VIEW

Braque's grave, marked by a mosaic of a white dove, is in the cemetery of this

TOP CAMPING

Camping is popular in these *départements*; for details of other accommodation options, see p302.

★ **Camping de l'Aulnaie** (☎ /fax 02 32 55 43 42; Dangu; per site & 1 person €6.10, additional person €3.60; ☙ Apr-Oct) In an idyllic location on the banks of a lake near the River Epte, this memorable camping ground is 6km southwest of Gisors in the tiny village of Dangu.

★ **Camping de l'Île des 3 Rois** (☎ 02 32 54 23 79; www.camping-troisrois.com; Les Andelys; s/d €15/20; ☙ mid-Mar–mid-Oct; ☙) Blissfully located on an island in the Seine directly under the castle.

★ **Camping de Reneville** (☎ 02 35 28 20 97; www.campingdereneville.com; Chemin de Nesmond, Fécamp; sites per d €11.30; ☙ Easter–mid-Nov) Dramatically situated on the western cliffs overlooking the beach.

★ **Camping La Source** (☎ 02 35 84 27 04; www.camping-la-source.fr; 63 rue Tisserands, Petit-Appeville; per adult/site/car €4.70/5.50/1.50; ☙ mid-Mar–mid-Oct; ☙) This rural camping ground is 3km southwest of Dieppe in a lovely creek-side location, well signposted just off the D925.

★ **Camping Municipal** (☎ /fax 02 35 86 20 04; Parc du Château, Eu; per d/site/car €2.30/2.30/2.30; ☙ Apr-Oct) A terrific spot for a camping ground, in a forested glade within the grounds of the former royal palace.

clifftop church for which he designed a set of vivid stained-glass windows. Step down into the church, where the filtered light through the windows and the flickering candles create a moody atmosphere.

♣ PARC DU BOIS DES MOUTIERS // EXPLORE ONE OF FRANCE'S FINEST PRIVATE GARDENS

These splendid **gardens** (☎ 02 35 85 10 02; Jul-Apr adult/concession €6/2.50, May & Jun adult €7; ☺ 10am-noon & 2-6pm mid-Mar–mid-Nov) consist of a series of walled spaces leading to a 12-hectare park that winds down to the sea. British architect Sir Edwin Lutyens designed the Arts and Crafts–style house at the turn of the 20th century and the English landscape gardener Gertrude Jekyll collaborated with him on the gardens. Come in March and April for the flowering magnolias, in May and June for the azaleas and rhododendrons (some of which are 10m high), in the summer for roses and hydrangeas, and in October and November for the Japanese maples. The house can only be visited by appointment.

♣ MANOIR D'ANGO // THE ITALIAN RENAISSANCE COMES TO NORMANDY

Built by the shipbuilder and privateer Jehan Ango in the 16th century, this **manor** (☎ 02 35 83 61 56; www.manoirdango .fr; adult/child €5/3; ☺ 10am-12.30pm & 2-6pm mid-Apr–Sep) has a stunning *colombier* (pigeon loft; see p185) with an unusual domed top and an Italian loggia decorated with frescoes from the school of Leonardo da Vinci. The manor is fit for a king and, in fact, Ango received François I here in 1523. Despite his successful expeditions on behalf of the crown, Ango died in his manor almost penniless, still waiting for repayment of money he had lent to the treasury years earlier.

DIEPPE

pop 34,700

Built in the shadow of a medieval castle and limestone cliffs, Dieppe balances the seaside with the gritty appeal of an old-fashioned port. It's the closest Channel port to Paris and, like most Norman port cities, it was a coveted prize for invading armies down the centuries.

The Vikings came in the 7th and 8th centuries, followed by Philippe-Auguste of France, who seized it from Richard the Lion-Heart in the 12th century. It changed hands several times in the Hundred Years' War and was invaded by Prussians in the war of 1870.

The port and wide sweep of beach have always defined Dieppe's culture and economy. Privateers made Dieppe their lair of choice as early as 1338 when they pillaged Southampton. Explorers launched expeditions from Dieppe, most notably Giovanni da Verrazano, who sailed in 1524 to found New York. In the 16th and 17th centuries, the town flourished as the ivory and spice trade brought new wealth to its coffers. Protestants fleeing persecution left from here in the 17th century when the Edict of Nantes was revoked; many ended up in Canada. A bout of plague and the bombardment of the city by the English and Dutch put an end to Dieppe's prosperity in the late 17th century.

It rebounded in the 19th century when aristocrats discovered the health benefits of sea bathing. With the construction of a railway link to Paris in 1848, fashionable Parisians began to spend weekends in Dieppe, whereas the British came for longer periods. Parisians deserted Dieppe following WWII in favour of glamorous Deauville, but Dieppe still keeps Paris well supplied with fish and seafood.

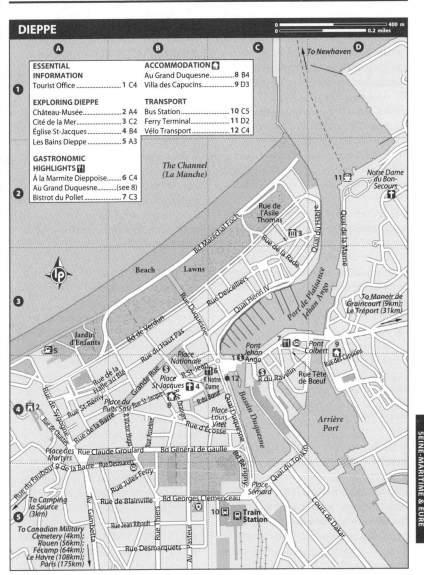

DIEPPE

| | 0 | 400 m |
| 0 | | 0.2 miles |

ESSENTIAL INFORMATION
Tourist Office 1 C4

EXPLORING DIEPPE
Château-Musée........................ 2 A4
Cité de la Mer........................... 3 C2
Église St-Jacques..................... 4 B4
Les Bains Dieppe 5 A3

GASTRONOMIC HIGHLIGHTS 🍴
Á la Marmite Dieppoise........ 6 C4
Au Grand Duquesne............(see 8)
Bistrot du Pollet 7 C3

ACCOMMODATION 🏠
Au Grand Duquesne.............. 8 B4
Villa des Capucins.................. 9 D3

TRANSPORT
Bus Station.............................. 10 C5
Ferry Terminal......................... 11 D2
Vélo Transport........................ 12 C4

To Newhaven

The Channel (La Manche)

Notre Dame du Bon-Secours

Rue de l'Asile Thomas

Bd Maréchal Foch

Rue de la Rade

Quai du Hâble

Quai de la Marne

Beach   Lawns

Rue Desceliers

Quai Henri IV

Port de Plaisance Jehan Ango

To Manoir de Graincourt (9km); Le Tréport (31km)

Jardin d'Enfants

Bd de Verdun

Rue du Haut Pas

Rue Duquesne

Place Nationale

Pont Jehan Ango

Pont Colbert

Rue des Capucins

Rue Tête de Bœuf

R du Ravelin

Rue de la Halle au Blé

Grande Rue

R St-Jean

Place St-Jacques

R Notre Dame

Rue St-Rémy

Place du Puits Salé

Rue St-Jacques

R Drangel

R du Bœuf

Rue de Sygogne

Rue de la Barre

R Victor Hugo

Rue Asseline

Place Louis Vitet

Rue d'Ecosse

Quai Duquesne

Bassin Duquesne

Arrière Port

Place des Martyrs

Rue Claude Groulard

Bd Général de Gaulle

Bd Périgny

Rue de la Barre

Rue Desmarets

Rue du Faubourg de la Barre

Av Gambetta

Rue Jules Ferry

Rue de Blainville

Bd Georges Clemenceau

Place Sémard

Quai du Tonkin

Cours de Dakar

To Camping la Source (3km)

To Canadian Military Cemetery (4km); Rouen (56km); Fécamp (64km); Le Havre (108km); Paris (175km)

Rue Jean Ribault

Rue Thiers

Av Pasteur

Rue Desmarquets

Train Station

SEINE-MARITIME & EURE

ESSENTIAL INFORMATION

TOURIST OFFICE // Dieppe (☎ 02 32 14 40 60; www.dieppetourisme.com; Pont Jehan Ango; ⊙ 9am-7pm May-Sep, 9am-noon & 2-6pm Mon-Sat Oct-Apr)

EXPLORING DIEPPE

♥ **CHÂTEAU MUSÉE // A TOWER OF IVORY, ART AND NAVAL MEMORABILIA**
Offering sweeping views over the city and sea, this 15th-century **castle** (☎ 02

35 06 61 99; rue de Chastes; adult/child €3.50/2; ☺ 10am-noon & 2-6pm Jun-Sep, 10am-noon & 2-5pm Wed-Mon Oct-May) served as a residence for the governors of Dieppe until the Revolution, receiving François I, Henri IV and Louis XIV as visitors. It was a prison and a barracks before the city purchased it in 1906 and turned it into a museum. The museum is devoted to Dieppe's maritime and artistic history, a significant portion of which depended upon the separation of elephants from their tusks.

The craft of ivory carving reached extraordinary heights in Dieppe during the 17th century and the results are on display in a series of rooms. At one time, some 350 artisans were working ivory in the town, with skills so finely honed it was rumoured that they had found a way to soften the ivory before carving it.

The collection of paintings favours views of Dieppe. There's also a room of prints by Braque, who periodically resided in Dieppe, and memorabilia of composer Camille St-Saëns, whose family was from Dieppe.

❦ BEACH & BATHS // TAKE TO THE WATERS, WHATEVER THE WEATHER

Dieppe's pebbly beach is framed by white cliffs and a vast lawn, laid out in the 1860s by that seashore-loving imperial duo Napoleon III and his wife, Eugénie. If the winds are too high or the water too cold, head to the neighbouring Les Bains Dieppe (☎ 02 35 82 80 90; www .lesbainsdieppe.com; 101 bd de Verdun; adult/child €5.60/4.60; ☺ 10am-8pm Mon-Fri, to 6pm Sat & Sun), an impressive new aquatic and spa centre complete with large indoor and outdoor pools.

❦ CANADIAN MILITARY CEMETERY // A PLACE OF PILGRIMAGE FOR CANADIAN VISITORS

In 1942 a mainly Canadian force of 6086 men landed in Dieppe in a show of force against the German occupiers. Nearly two-thirds of them were killed, wounded or captured in one day, but valuable lessons were learnt for the eventual D-Day invasion. This sobering cemetery, in farmland 4km towards Rouen, is the resting place for 955 Canadian and other Commonwealth soldiers. To find it, take av des Canadiens (the continuation of av Gambetta) and follow the signs.

❦ ÉGLISE ST-JACQUES // SAVOUR STAINED GLASS AND THE SCALLOP SAINT

Dominating the main square, this impressively large Norman Gothic church (place St-Jacques) has been reconstructed several times since the early 13th century. It still has just enough stained glass remaining to send coloured light dancing onto the pillars of the choir. On the facade you'll recognise St Jacques (St James) by the scallop on his hat. Pilgrims on the way to Santiago de Compostela in Spain, the saint's reputed burial place, adopted the scallop as their emblem – hence the local name for scallops, *coquilles St-Jacques*.

❦ CITÉ DE LA MER // DELVE INTO THE DIEPPE BLUE SEA

If you want to learn more about what Dieppe takes from – and gives back to – the sea around it, visit this small maritime museum (☎ 02 35 06 93 20; http://estrancitedela mer.free.fr/; 37 rue de l'Asile Thomas; adult/concession €5.80/3.50; ☺ 10am-noon & 2-6pm). Those with an interest in boating will enjoy the 1st floor, which traces the evolution of boat building and navigation. Fishing techniques are the subject of the upper-floor exhibits. Curious about cliffs? The formation, erosion and utility of Dieppe's cliffs are explained in detail. The visit ends with five large aquariums filled with much of the seafood that is often found on French plates: octopus, sole, lobsters, turbot and cod. Most of the signage is in French; ask for the English explanatory folder.

GASTRONOMIC HIGHLIGHTS

☙ À LA MARMITE DIEPPOISE €€
☎ 02 35 84 24 26; 8 rue St-Jean; menus €29-43; ⟨⟩ lunch & dinner Tue-Sat, lunch Sun
If you really want to taste Dieppe's *fruits de la mer* at their best, head for this intimate establishment in the old city. Its speciality is *marmite Dieppoise* (see boxed text, p233), but save room for the apple tart served with caramel Calvados sauce and apple sorbet.

☙ AU GRAND DUQUESNE €
☎ 02 32 14 61 10; 15 place St-Jacques; menus €14-40; Ⓥ
It's rare to find such reasonable prices for cuisine that's both *traditionelle* and *créative* and served in such a chic setting. It's even rarer to find one offering a full alternative *menu* for vegetarians (€19). Seafood features prominently, and other specialities include *crêpiau dieppois* (a thick, pear-filled crêpe).

☙ BISTROT DU POLLET €€
☎ 02 35 84 68 57; 23 rue Tête de Boeuf; mains €25-40, lunch menu €16; ⟨⟩ Tue-Sat
Away from the tourist crowds in the old fishermen's quarter is this gem for fish lovers. The à la carte offerings might include *lotte* (monkfish) marinated in wine or *daurade* (sea bream) with herbs. The dining room is small, so it's best to reserve.

TRANSPORT

TRAIN // From Dieppe's **train station** (☎ 02 35 06 69 33; bd Georges Clemenceau) there are direct services to Rouen (via Clères) and Paris-St-Lazare.

BUS // The bus station is next to the train station and has services to Le Tréport, Neufchâtel-en-Bray and Gisors.

FERRY // The first ferry service from Dieppe to the UK began in 1790. Nowadays LD Lines (p321) runs car ferries to/from Newhaven. The terminal is east of the town at the end of quai de la Marne.

BIKE // **Vélo Transport** (☎ 06 24 56 06 27; hire per 1hr/2hr/4hr/day/week €1/2/3.50/5.50/15; ⟨⟩ 9.30am-5.30pm) hires bikes from a bus parked outside the tourist office.

LE TRÉPORT & EU

pop 6000 & 7800
These twin towns sit 3km apart along the River Bresle, right on the border between Normandy and Picardy. Like many towns along the coast, Le Tréport was a fishing port that became fashionable with holidaymakers in the 19th century. It's not particularly fashionable now, very crowded only in summer. The beachfront has been developed to death, but the wide, pebbly beach has its charms and the towering cliffs rising above the southwestern end provide a striking backdrop. If the summer craziness gets too much, the quieter Mers-les-Bains village lies just northeast of the port.

Eu was one of the earliest Norman towns, founded by the first Duke of Normandy in 996. It was here in 1051 that Guillaume le Batard (William the Bastard, later the Conqueror) married his cousin Mathilde. A labyrinth of tight streets still conceals numerous flint and half-timbered houses, alongside some grand historic sights. There's a chance that during the lifetime of this book Eu will be renamed, possibly as Ville

SEINE-MARITIME & EURE

d'Eu or Eu-le-Château. It's not because the name, when pronounced correctly, sounds reminiscent of a vomit to English speakers. The official reason is that the town is losing out on business, as an internet search on Eu brings up a deluge of European Union websites. We wonder if the *maire d'Eu* (mayor of Eu) may have an ulterior motive – her current title sounds virtually indistinguishable from *merde* (shit).

ESSENTIAL INFORMATION

TOURIST OFFICES // Le Tréport (☎ 02 35 86 05 69; www.ville-le-treport.fr; quai Sadi Carnot; ☉ 10am-7pm Jul & Aug, 9am-noon & 2-6.30pm Apr-Jun & Sep, 10am-noon & 3-5pm Mon-Sat Oct-Mar); Eu (☎ 02 35 86 04 68; www.ville-eu.fr; place Guillaume-le-Conquérant; ☉ 9.30am-12.30pm & 2-5.30pm Mon-Sat Oct-Apr, 9.30am-12.30pm & 2-5.30pm Mon-Sat, 10am-1pm Sun May-Sep) Stocks a fascinating heritage trail brochure.

ORIENTATION

Le Tréport is separated from Mers-les-Bains by the canalised River Bresle, which opens into a port at the Channel. The restaurant-packed quai François 1er runs along the port to the seafront. Eu is 3km to the southwest along the Bresle. In both towns the train station is north of the town, across the River Bresle.

EXPLORING LE TRÉPORT & EU

♥ CHÂTEAU-MUSÉE LOUIS-PHILIPPE // ENJOY THE ROYAL LIFESTYLE WITHOUT LOSING YOUR HEAD

Royalty may not be popular in France generally, but Eu plays up its regal connections regardless. Dominating the town, this wonderful **château** (☎ 02 35 86 44 00; www.louisphilippe.eu; place d'Orléans; adult/child €4/2; ☉ 10am-noon & 2-6pm Sat-Mon, Wed & Thu, 2-6pm Fri mid-Mar–Oct) was built in 1578 by Catherine of Clèves and Henry of Lorraine, the Duchess and Duke of Guise, who played a leading role on the Catholic side of the Wars of Religion; you'll find their wonderful white marble mausoleums in the **Chapelle du Collège des Jésuites** (rue du College; ☉ 10am-noon & 2-6pm Mon-Sat, 3-6pm Sun), which they founded.

The château became the palace of Louis-Philippe, who took the throne in 1830. He entertained Queen Victoria here in an historic rapprochement between France and England. In 1848, faced with another revolution, he scarpered off to Newhaven, where he managed to keep his head until the end of his natural days.

The palace is in the process of being restored to the glory of those times, with the intention of giving it a lived-in feel. You'll find some gorgeous carriages, a magnifi-

SEINE-MARITIME & EURE

～ WORTH A TRIP ～

The **Pays de Bray** is a fertile buttonhole of land, 70km long and 15km wide, marked by rolling hills, meandering rivers and lush pastures. Sparsely populated, the area has always relied on dairy farming as its economic mainstay. The famous heart-shaped Neufchâtel cheese is available everywhere, from local markets to family farms. Try to hit the town of **Neufchâtel-en-Bray** on a Saturday morning, when the market spreads over the square in front of the impressive Flamboyant Gothic porch of the **Église Notre Dame** (☉ 8.30am-12.15pm & 1.30-6.30pm).

Buses link Neufchâtel-en-Bray with Dieppe (50 minutes) and Gisors (80 minutes), where they connect with trains to Paris-St-Lazare.

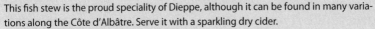

MARMITE DIEPPOISE

This fish stew is the proud speciality of Dieppe, although it can be found in many variations along the Côte d'Albâtre. Serve it with a sparkling dry cider.

    700g mussels in shells
    2 onions, peeled and chopped
    5 tablespoons butter
    1L cider
    assorted fish heads and bones
    2 leeks, washed and chopped
    2 celery stalks, cut into rounds
    1 bay leaf
    3 stalks of fresh thyme or 1 teaspoon dried
    900g firm-fleshed white fish
    250mL crème fraîche
    2 tablespoons chopped fresh parsley
    salt and pepper to taste

Scrub the shells under cold running water. Put half of the onions in a large saucepan with half the butter, 200mL of cider and then the mussels. Cover and cook on high heat for a few minutes until the mussels open.

Shell the mussels, discarding any that have not opened, and set aside. Strain the cooking liquid and reserve.

Put the fish heads and bones in a saucepan. Add leeks, remaining chopped onions, celery, bay leaf and thyme. Add the remaining cider, 250mL of water and the cooking liquid from the mussels. Cook uncovered over medium heat for 30 minutes.

Season the fish and place it into another saucepan. Then pour the strained broth over it. Add the remaining butter, cut into pieces, and the crème fraîche. Bring back to a simmer and cook over low heat for 15 minutes. Adjust seasoning to taste.

Add the mussels and reheat for two minutes. Pour into a large serving bowl and garnish with parsley; serves four.

Voilà!

cent golden bedroom and an extravagantly set dining room. The lovely formal gardens are open to the public all year long.

♥ **COLLÉGIALE NOTRE DAME ET ST-LAURENT // AN UNLIKELY IRISH CONNECTION COMMEMORATED IN STONE**
Lawrence O'Toole may seem an unlikely name for a saint venerated in a French town (Lorcán Ua Tuathail, to give him

his Irish propers, even more so), but this erstwhile bishop of Dublin is the patron of a grand Norman Gothic **church** (place Guillaume-le-Conquérant; ⊙ 9am-noon & 2-5pm) begun six years after his death in Eu in 1180. Devout Dubliners still make pilgrimages here to pay their respects. Look for his recumbent effigy in the crypt and the Celtic cross to the north of the church, transported from his home town of Castledermot. From the cross there

SEINE-MARITIME & EURE

are wonderful views over Eu and the Bresle valley.

❦ CLIMB THE CLIFF // SWEAT YOUR WAY TO SPECTACULAR VIEWS

By far the easiest way up to the views provided by Le Tréport's towering white cliff is via the recently revived, free **funicular** (7.45am-2.45am Jul & Aug, 7.45am-8.45pm Sun-Thu, 7.45am-12.45am Fri & Sat Sep-Jun), dating from 1908. Otherwise you can tackle the 350 steps leading from quai François 1er. On your way, take a breather at the 15th-century **Église St-Jacques** (rue Alexandre Papin) and reward yourself with a beverage at the café at the top.

❦ SAVOUR THE SEAFOOD // FIND YOURSELF A FISHY FEAST

Le Tréport's quai François 1er is lined with festive seafood restaurants serving fresh local produce derived, presumably, from the **Poissonerie Municipal** (Municipal Fish Market; 9am-12.30pm & 2.30-7pm Wed-Mon) at the end of the quay. Reputable options include **Le St-Louis** (☎ 02 35 86 20 70; 43 quai François 1er; menus €19-60) and **La Matelote** (☎ 02 35 86 17 02; 34 quai François 1er; menus €16-52).

TRANSPORT

TRAIN // Trains stopping at both Le Tréport (quai Albert Cauët) and Eu (av de la Gare) head to Abbeville, Abancourt or Beauvais (towns in Picardy), where they're timed to meet connections to Rouen or Paris-Nord.

BUS // There are regular buses between Le Tréport and Eu (15 minutes), as well as buses to Dieppe (about an hour). In Eu they stop in front of the Collégiale.

PARKING // Part of the reason that Le Tréport's funicular is free is to encourage drivers to leave their cars in the parking stations at the top of the cliff and avoid the town's narrow streets.

ROUEN

· · · · · ·

pop 110,000

Wonky half-timbered houses, narrow lanes and soaring spires make the medieval heart of Rouen one of the most atmospheric city centres in France. As the capital of both the Haute-Normandie region and the Seine-Maritime *département*, the city has the political and economic muscle to support a thriving cultural scene, excellent restaurants and lively street life.

Strategically positioned at the place where the Seine's fresh waters meet the tidal flows from the sea, Rouen's importance is linked to its two ports: an upstream river port and a major ocean-facing port. While postwar recovery has encircled it in ugly suburban and industrial sprawl, every effort has been made to restore the city's ancient centre to its former glory. Around 2000 half-timbered houses have been preserved alongside Rouen's famous Gothic edifices. It's here that visitors can lose themselves in streets once traversed by Joan of Arc (Ste Jeanne d'Arc), Gustave Flaubert and Monet.

One of the oldest towns in Normandy, the settlement became known as Rotomagus from around 50 BC following the Roman invasion. St Mellon Christianised the town in the 3rd century, but little else is recorded about Rouen until the 9th century, when the Vikings arrived, repeatedly pillaging it for 50 years. The great Viking leader Rollo was baptised here. He made Rouen his capital and it became an important religious, political and administrative centre. The city expanded in importance and gained a substantial degree of autonomy under King Henry II of England until the French king Philippe-Auguste seized it in 1204 as the culmination of his conquest of Normandy. Once again the city flourished, its great cathedral being erected with money earned from a flourishing textile business and bustling port.

The 14th century saw a trio of troubles: famine, plague and the Hundred Years' War. Rouen fell into the hands of the English in 1419 and was, infamously, the place where Joan of Arc was burnt at the stake (see boxed text, p236). The 16th-century Renaissance brought a

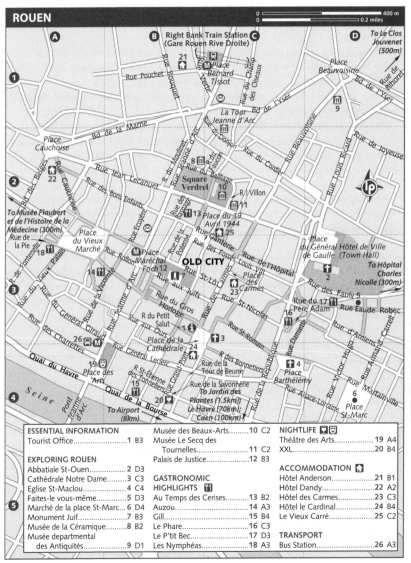

ROUEN

SEINE-MARITIME & EURE

THE WARRIOR SAINT

Nowhere is Joan of Arc more venerated than in Rouen, the place of her death. In 1412, when she was born, the Hundred Years' War had been raging for over 70 years and a demoralised France was being ruled by an English king.

Joan claimed that she began receiving visions when she was 12 years old. Their simple admonishments soon evolved into a more specific message: she was to save France and put the French dauphin Charles on the throne. When she was 17 she rode to Charles' court at Chinon and somehow convinced him to give her command of his army.

With a retinue of 4000 men Joan headed to Orléans, which the English had besieged for six months. She chose the time if not the manner of the attack and fought alongside her men with strength and courage. Her example inspired the troops and led to a great victory that paved the way for the English to be pushed out of the Loire valley and for Charles to be crowned as king of France.

The following year Joan was captured at Compiègne while defending the town from attack. Threatened by her enormous popularity, the English brought her to their stronghold at Rouen and tried her for heresy. Joan defended herself with panache, displaying tremendous stamina and mental agility, but the result was a foregone conclusion.

She was convicted and, on 30 May 1431, the 19-year-old was led to place du Vieux Marché, tied to a stake and burnt alive. Twenty-four years later the pope reversed the court's decision and in 1920 she was declared a saint.

flurry of magnificent new construction, some of which still survives. The city expanded again in the 19th century when the southern bank of the Seine was developed for manufacturing.

German troops set fire to Rouen in 1940 as part of their push into France, and the Allies bombed it ferociously in 1944.

Rouen's big annual event is the Fête de Rouen (see p221), while every five years the Rouen Armada floats by on a sea of visitors.

ESSENTIAL INFORMATION

EMERGENCIES // SOS Médicins (☎ 02 35 03 03 30) Will send a doctor to your hotel if necessary. Hôpital Charles Nicolle (☎ 02 32 88 89 90; 1 rue de Germont)

TOURIST OFFICE // Rouen (☎ 02 32 08 32 40; www.rouentourisme.com; 25 place de la Cathédrale; ☺ 9am-7pm Mon-Sat, 9.30am-12.30pm & 2-6pm Sun May-Sep, 9.30am-6pm Mon-Sat Oct-Apr) Assists with hotel reservations for a €3 fee.

ORIENTATION

The historic heart of the city is on the Rive Droite (right bank), north of the Seine. The main thoroughfare, rue Jeanne d'Arc, runs from the train station (Gare Rouen Rive Droite) to the river.

WALKING TOUR

Distance: 3km
Duration: 1 hour
This walk traces the path of Joan of Arc from her incarceration to her execution. La Tour Jeanne d'Arc (1; ☎ 02 35 98 16 21; rue du Donjon; admission €1.50; ☺ 10am-12.30pm &

2-5pm Mon & Wed-Sat, 2-5.30pm Sun) is the sole survivor of eight towers that once ringed a huge château built by Philippe-Auguste from 1204 to 1210. Joan was imprisoned and tortured here before her execution. It now holds a collection devoted to her life.

Next to the tower on rue du Donjon a **plaque (2)** and an ash-filled urn commemorate those deported to the concentration camps during the Nazi occupation. Continue uphill to rue du Cordier, which features a good mix of half-timbered and stone buildings. There are some particularly lovely ones lining **place de la Rougemare (3)**.

Turn right onto rue de la République, where you'll pass the **Hôtel de Ville (4)**, a large **equestrian statue of Napoleon (5)** and the **Abbatiale St-Ouen (6; p239)**. Continue down the road, turning left at rue d'Amiens and right at place du Lieutenant Aubert and head along **rue Damiette (7)**, one of Rouen's most atmospheric cobbled lanes – lined with antique and art shops in ancient half-timbered buildings. The lane ends at the impressive **Église St-Maclou (8; p240)**.

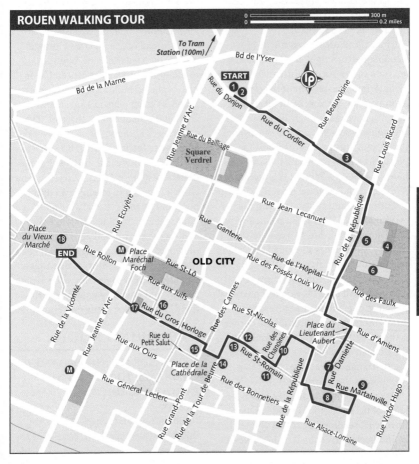

Follow alongside the church and pop into the **Aître St-Maclou (9**; 186 rue Martainville; admission free; 8am-8pm), a rare example of a medieval charnel house, which now houses the arts college. From 1348 until 1781, victims of the plague were buried here. A curious ensemble of 16th-century half-timbered buildings carved with skulls, crossbones, gravediggers' tools and hourglasses line the courtyard. It's eerily beautiful in winter when the bone-bare trees cast lattice shadows onto the walls. The cat's carcass displayed in a case near the entrance was discovered in a wall. It was probably an unlucky black cat, believed to embody the devil, which was entombed in order to keep evil spirits at bay.

Circle the church, cross rue de la République, turn right and take the first left onto rue St-Nicolas. Just after number 27 duck into **rue des Chanoines (10)**, an impossibly narrow medieval alley that would be exceedingly handy if you ever found yourself being chased around Rouen by someone on horseback. Opposite the end of the lane imposing walls hide the **Bishop's Palace (11)**, the site of Joan's trial and eventual rehabilitation.

Turn right and continue along rue St-Romain. **No 74 (12)** is a particularly handsome Gothic house from the 16th century, with niches showing St Nicolas reviving three children, the Madonna and Child, and St Romain crushing a gargoyle. **No 11 (13)** is a typical medieval structure of overhanging storeys that dates from 1466. Just around the corner is the **cathedral (14**; right). Facing it is the **Bureau des Finances (15)** – a striking Renaissance structure (1509) that now houses the tourist office.

As you walk up rue du Gros Horloge look for the harmonious facade of the **former Hôtel de Ville (16)** on your right at numbers 60 to 66, built in 1607. Nearby is an icon of the city, the **Gros Horloge (17)**. The clock's mechanism dates from the 14th century, when it was lodged in the adjacent belfry, but the citizens demanded a more conspicuous location. In 1529 it was given a flamboyant Renaissance facade and placed over its current arch. Its single hand points to the hour and, under the numeral VI, the day of the week appears in the form of the divinity associated with each day. Over the clock, a globe indicates the phases of the moon. The result was considered so admirable that the gender of the clock was 'elevated' from feminine to masculine. (In French, *horloge* is a feminine noun; the proper formulation should be *'grosse horloge'*.)

At the end of rue du Gros Horloge is place du Vieux Marché, bounded to the south by a striking ensemble of half-timbered buildings. It was here that Joan was burnt alive in 1431; a towering cross and a plaque mark the spot. The centrepiece of the square is the remarkable **Église Jeanne d'Arc (18**; 10am-noon & 2-5.30pm), constructed in 1979 after the designs of architect Louis Arretche. The church is meant to resemble an upturned boat, and its roofs sprawl over most of the square. An older church, Église St-Vincent, once stood here, but it was destroyed in the bombing of 1944. Fortunately, its 16th-century stained-glass windows were removed for safe keeping in 1939 and now they grace the surprisingly lofty interior of the new church.

EXPLORING ROUEN

♥ CATHÉDRALE NOTRE DAME // COME FACE TO FACE WITH A FAMOUS FACADE
History
Begun in 1201 and completed in 1514, this mighty **cathedral (** 2-6pm Mon, 7.30am-

SEINE-MARITIME & EURE

noon & 2-6pm Tue-Sat, 8am-6pm Sun) spans
the entire period of French Gothic
architecture.

An early Christian sanctuary built by
St Victrice stood here at the end of the
4th century. A Romanesque cathedral
followed, consecrated in the presence
of William the Conqueror in 1063. As
part of a 12th-century expansion the
Tour St-Romain was built in the Gothic
style, which was considered innovative
at the time. A fire in 1200 destroyed the
entire church, leaving only the Tour St-
Romain, two doors – Portes St-Jean and
St-Etienne – and the **crypt**. Reconstruction was begun almost immediately and
much of the basic structure was finished
by 1250. A period of expansion and em-
bellishment followed that lasted for three
centuries.

Huguenots pillaged the cathedral in
1562, and 18th-century revolutionaries
turned it into a Temple of Reason, after
destroying the tomb of Charles V. Then,
on the night of 19 April 1944, bombs
rained down on the cathedral causing
severe damage.

Architecture
Notice the contrast between the austere
early Gothic Tour St-Romain on the left
side and the Flamboyant Gothic **Tour
de Beurre** on the right of the cathedral's
exterior. Built between 1485 and 1506,
the latter tower was paid for by donations from members of the congregation
who wanted to eat butter during Lent.
(Given the liberal use of butter in Norman cuisine, its absence must have been
an intolerable hardship.) The **central
doorway** is surrounded by statues of
patriarchs and prophets and topped by a
sculpted Tree of Jesse. The central **spire**
dates from 1822, replacing an earlier one
that was destroyed by lightning.

Monet immortalised the facade of the
cathedral in some 30 canvases. In the
evenings of July and August the frontage
is cloaked in a spectacular light show.

The overall impression of the 135m-
long interior is one of grace and har-
mony. The earliest part of the church is
the **choir**, dating from the 13th century
and notable for the simplicity and purity
of its design. In the ambulatory on either
side of the choir are the **tombs** of Rollo,
the first duke of Normandy, and King
Richard I of England. Only the Lion-
Heart's heart was ever buried here (it's
now in the cathedral's treasury); the rest
of him is in Fontevraud Abbey in the
Loire.

In the **Chapelle de Ste-Jeanne** in the
south transept there's a post-WWII
statue of St Joan at the stake and an interesting dedication in the stained glass
from the nation that executed her: 'from
the English in homage'.

Free guided tours (in French only) that
include the crypt take place at 2.30pm
on the weekends and daily during school
holidays.

❦ OTHER GOTHIC GLORIES // STUDY A DEFINING STYLE OF NORMAN ARCHITECTURE
The **Abbatiale St-Ouen** (rue de la République;
🕙 10am-noon & 2-5.30pm Tue-Thu, Sat & Sun) is a
jewel of Rayonnant Gothic architecture.
This 14th-century church was part of
a powerful Benedictine abbey (active
until the Revolution) established in the
mid-8th century on the site of St Ouen's
grave. Inside, the imposing size (137m
long, 26m wide) and relative lack of decoration focuses the eye onto its sweeping
vertical lines and balanced proportions.
Vast stained-glass windows bathe it in an
ethereal light that filters through a forest
of slim columns. Its famous pipe organ is

often used for concerts and recordings of classical music.

Église St-Maclou (place Barthélémy; 10am-noon & 2-5.30pm Fri-Mon) was built between 1437 and 1521 in the later Flamboyant Gothic style. Its facade is an unusual arrangement of five pointed arches over a richly decorated Renaissance porch. Badly bombed in 1944, the church has an elegant interior with an interesting mix of modern and antique stained glass.

The ornate **Palais de Justice** (Law Courts; rue aux Juifs) is typical of the Flamboyant Gothic style. The architects move your eye upwards from a relatively sober ground floor to increasingly elaborate upper levels, topped by spires, gargoyles and statuary. The oldest part is the west wing, the Palais du Neuf Marché, begun in 1499. Since the end of WWII the building has been painstakingly restored, although the 19th-century facade facing rue Jeanne d'Arc still displays extensive bullet and shell damage. It was during construction of the city's subway that archaeologists discovered a 3rd-century Gallo-Roman settlement at this site.

Under the courtyard of the Palais de Justice is Rouen's only reminder of its ancient Jewish community. Until their expulsion by Philippe Le Bel in 1306, Jews composed up to 20% of the town's population. The **Monument Juif** (tours €6.50; 3pm Tue) was discovered by accident in 1976 as the courtyard was being repaved. Although this impressive two-storey stone building is in the heart of the former Jewish ghetto and the presence of Hebrew graffiti confirms that it belonged to the Jewish community, its exact function is unknown. It may have been a *yeshiva* (religious college), a synagogue or the home of a rich merchant. Dating from around 1100, it's the oldest

Jewish monument in France. It can only be visited by guided tours (in French) run by the tourist office (see p236); bookings are essential.

🍴 **MARCHÉ DE LA PLACE ST-MARC // PARTAKE IN LOCAL LIFE AT THE SUNDAY MARKET**
Every Sunday morning at place St-Marc, Rouen turns into a big country village when its residents descend en masse to the weekly market. You'll find everything here from antiques to flowers, but it's the food section that's the most interesting. There's cheese, charcuterie, chickens with their heads still attached, even Chinese takeaways, and a spectacular array of produce. When you're reaching sensory overload, recharge at a café in one of the grand buildings lining the square.

🍴 **MUSÉES DE LA VILLE DE ROUEN // ADMIRE ART IN MANY AND VARIED FORMS**
Rouen's three city-run **museums** (www.rouen-musees.com; combined pass €5.35, 1st Sun of month free) make strange bedfellows. If you've got eclectic tastes the combined ticket is great value.

Allow a least a couple of hours to explore the wonderful **Musée des Beaux-Arts** (Fine Arts Museum; ☎ 02 35 71 28 40; 26 bis rue Jean Lecanuet; adult/child €3/free; 10am-6pm Wed-Mon). One of the finest regional galleries in France, it samples all the major movements in European painting from the 15th to the 20th century. The collection has important works by artists such as Rubens, Caravaggio, Poussin, Delacroix, Duchamp, Degas, Renoir and Modigliani. Delacroix himself maintained that viewing *St-Barnabé Guéris-sant les Malades* (St Barnabas Healing the Sick) by Italian master Veronese was enough to justify a visit to Rouen. Naturally, painters who lived and worked in Rouen are well represented. One of Monet's famous studies of Rouen's cathedral is a highlight of the small but excellent Impressionist collection. There's also a whole wall devoted to images of Joan of Arc, including a photograph by contemporary local lad Charles Fréger.

The **Musée Le Secq des Tournelles** (☎ 02 35 52 00 62; 2 rue Jacques Villon; adult/child €2.30/ free; ☺ 10am-1pm & 2-6pm Wed-Mon) is much more interesting than a museum devoted exclusively to ironwork has any right to be. The collection fills a deconsecrated 16th-century church with thousands of utensils, belt buckles, items of jewellery and tools from various professions like gardening, dentistry, carpentry and surgery. Most interesting are the lock and key mechanisms, some of which are so exquisitely crafted that they include religious scenes hidden on the inside where only the object's creator would ever see them.

Rouen is known for its fine ceramics, dating back to the 16th century when Italian artisans were imported into the court of François I. The craft flourished until the end of the 18th century when competition from English Wedgwood and a growing taste for porcelain sent it into decline. The **Musée de la Céramique** (☎ 02 35 07 31 74; 1 rue du Faucon; adult/child €2.30/ free; ☺ 10am-1pm & 2-6pm Wed-Mon) has a large collection from the height of the city's artistry in the 17th and 18th centuries and samples of Delft, Sèvres, Wedgwood and oriental works. If ceramics aren't your thing it's still worth visiting for the chance to poke around the fine 17th-century mansion the museum inhabits.

♥ OTHER MUSEUMS // PURSUE THE ANCIENT AND THE STRANGE

If you're at all interested in history, the University of Rouen's **Musée depart-mental des Antiquités** (☎ 02 35 15 69 11; 198 rue Beauvoisine; admission €3; ☺ 10am-noon & 1.30-5.30pm Mon & Wed-Sat, 2-6pm Sun), housed in a 17th-century convent, is a must see. A beautiful 3rd-century mosaic is the highlight of the Gallo-Roman exhibit, along with some raunchy Greek vases. There's also a splendid collection of glassware, jewels, gold and silver, carvings and tapestries dating from antiquity to the Renaissance.

The quirky **Musée Flaubert et d'Histoire de la Médecine** (☎ 02 35 15 59 95; 51 rue de Lecat; admission €3; ☺ 10am-noon & 2-6pm Tue-Sat) inhabits the house where the famous novelist's family lived when his father was a surgeon at the neighbouring hospital. The displays include an Egyptian mummy, shrunken heads, death masks and a terrifying collection of surgical and medical instruments. Anyone contemplating pregnancy would do well to avoid the childbirth section. Explanations are in French only.

♥ JARDIN DES PLANTES // JOIN THE PROMENADE ON A SUNNY DAY

On a sunny day this attractively landscaped 9.5-hectare **park** (☎ 02 32 18 21 30; rue des Martyrs de la Résistance; admission free; ☺ 8.30am-sunset) fills up with teenagers playing ball games, parents pushing prams, and dapper elderly couples taking a promenade. The formal gardens and greenhouses are filled with exotic plants, and there's a carousel, sports courts, a children's playground and a shallow basin for kids to splash about in or sail model boats.

The park is 2km south of the river (cross Pont Pierre Corneille and keep going). By public transport, catch bus 7 from outside the Hôtel de Ville.

SEINE-MARITIME & EURE

GASTRONOMIC HIGHLIGHTS

Cafés and eateries line place du Vieux Marché, the car-free streets north of the *cathédrale* and the lanes surrounding Église St-Maclou.

☺ AU TEMPS DES CERISES €

☎ 02 35 89 98 00; 4-6 rue des Basnage; lunch €13, menus €17.50-22; ☺ Mon-Sat

It's big and gimmicky, but it's only the menu that's actually cheesy at this temple to *fromage*. A great waft of the stuff greats you as you open the door. Chicken with Camembert, *oeufs en cocotte* (eggs cooked in ramekins and topped with a cheese sauce) and, of course, fondue are well prepared at reasonable prices. If three courses of cheese seems excessive, there are à la carte options such as crêpes and omelettes for less than €10.

☺ AUZOU €

☎ 02 35 70 59 31; 163 rue du Gros Horloge; large macaroons €2.70; ☺ 2-7.15pm Mon, 9.15am-7.15pm Tue-Sat, 9.15am-12.45pm Sun

Jean-Michel Auzou is the vice-president of the Artisans Chocolatiers de France, so it takes an iron will to walk past his shop without succumbing to some sweet morsel. Try *les larmes de Jeanne d'Arc* (Joan of Arc's tears) – roasted almonds coated with caramel and chocolate – or, better still, one of the 18 flavours of exquisitely soft macaroons. There are branches in Évreux (p249) and Le Havre (p223).

☺ GILL €€€

☎ 02 35 71 16 14; 8 quai de la Bourse; menus €35-92; ☺ Tue-Sat

The only restaurant in Normandy that can boast two Michelin stars, Gill is quite simply the region's finest. Let chef Gilles Tournadre and his team seduce you with

langoustine in a divinely inspired sauce, or pigeon *à la rouennaise*. Even the cheaper lunch *menu* (€35) is exquisite, but it may wipe you out for the rest of the day.

☺ LE PHARE €

☎ 02 35 07 00 00; 5 rue du Père Adam; mains €7-13; ☺ Tue-Sat

A bumper selection of galettes and crêpes (including vegetarian versions) are cheerfully served at this brightly coloured place adorned with stuffed seagulls and a miniature lighthouse. The Made in Normandy galette is filled with cheese, naturally, and best attacked with a cider at the ready.

☺ LE P'TIT BEC €

☎ 02 35 07 63 33; 182 rue Eau de Robec; menus €13-15.50; ☺ lunch Mon-Thu, lunch & dinner Fri & Sat

Those looking for an escape from heavy cream sauces can find sanctuary in a down-to-earth menu stuffed with salads, *tartes,* terrines, poached fish and steamed vegetables. *Belle époque* posters decorate the stone walls of the bright dining room.

☺ LES NYMPHÉAS €€€

☎ 02 35 89 26 69; 7 rue de la Pie; menus €30-70; ☺ Tue-Sat

Chef Patrice Kukurudz is one of the stars of Norman cuisine, showcasing local produce and specialities in the elegant surrounds of a traditional half-timbered house near the main square. Apples in their various Norman forms (including cider and Calvados) make an appearance, as does a variation on the city's speciality *canard sauvageon* (wild duck) *à la rouennaise.*

NIGHTLIFE

Rouen has bars scattered all around its historic centre. While a little touristy, place du Vieux Marché has some nice

GAY & LESBIAN ROUEN

While it's no Paris, Rouen has a better gay scene than anywhere else in Normandy, with venues including bars, clubs, saunas and cruise clubs. A good place to start is XXL (☎ 02 35 88 84 00; 25 rue de la Savonnerie; ☺ 7pm-2am Tue-Thu, to 4am Fri & Sat), a busy bar with a dance floor that's one of a cluster of venues in the blocks immediately north of the river. For other venues, pick up a copy of *Wag!,* a free gay magazine (in French) covering Normandy and Brittany, the free *Wag! Map* or visit www.gaynormandie.com/rubrique/rouen.

options that allow you to spill out onto the square in the warmer months.

Culture vultures will find plenty to keep them entertained, although the action quietens down during the summer and comes to a complete halt in August. Pick up a copy of the free fortnightly *Rouen Magazine* (available from the tourist office, cafés, bars and hotels), a night-by-night guide to clubbing, live music, cinema, theatre, opera and dance. Regular classical-music concerts are held in Abbatiale St-Ouen (p239) and Église St-Maclou (p240).

♥ THÉÂTRE DES ARTS

☎ 08 10 81 11 16; www.operaderouen.com; place des Arts

While home to the Opéra de Rouen, the city's premier theatre also presents classical concerts and ballet. Standby tickets start from €10 for the back row and €5 for students with a relevant ID.

TRANSPORT

TO/FROM THE AIRPORT

AIR // Aéroport Rouen Vallée du Seine (☎ 02 35 79 41 00; www.rouen.aeroport.fr) is only 9km southeast of central Rouen, so a taxi is the best option. Bus 13 passes by but only stops outside the police station in nearby Boos hourly; in Rouen it stops outside the Hôtel de Ville.

GETTING AROUND

TRAIN // There are frequent trains to/from Gare Rouen Rive Droite (☎ 08 92 35 35 35; 1 place Bernard Tissot) via Vernon to Paris-St-Lazare (€19.80, 70 minutes). Other major routes head to Le Tréport (via Eu), Dieppe (via Clères), Fécamp, Le Havre and Caen (via Lisieux and Bernay).

BUS & METRO // Buses to most corners of Seine-Maritime leave from the bus station (☎ 08 25 07 60 27; 9 rue Jeanne d'Arc). Tcar (www.tcar.fr) operates Rouen's extensive local bus network as well as its metro (subway) line. Tickets, valid for an hour of unlimited travel, cost €1.40. You can buy them from dispensing machines (click on the English option) or directly from the bus driver; either way, be sure to validate them in the machines in the bus or metro carriage.

BIKE // Cy'clic (☎ 08 00 08 78 00; http://cyclic .rouen.fr) provides bikes at 17 self-service racks for short trips around the city. Once you've paid your access fee (€1/5 per 1/7 days) the first half-hour of every trip is free, but you'll be hit with a sharply increasing fee for each additional half-hour you keep the bike (from €1 to €4). Instructions are in French only.

AROUND ROUEN

♥ CLÈRES // WANDER THE PARK AND IDYLLIC COUNTRYSIDE

Surrounded by picturesque farmland 28km due north of Rouen, Clères is an attractive large village with a stream tinkling through its centre. Its main attraction is the Parc de Clères (☎ 02 35 33 23 08; www.parcdecleres.net; 32 av du Parc; adult/child €5.50/4; ☺ 1.30-5pm Feb & Nov, 10am-6.30pm Mar-Oct), just steps away from the 18th-century covered marketplace in the main square. Established in 1920 around a ruined 9th-century castle, a 15th-century Flamboyant Gothic château and a

SEINE-MARITIME & EURE

16th-century half-timbered manor house, Le Parc is a mainly free-range zoo with beautiful grounds. Antelopes, wallabies, deer, peacocks, flamingos and cranes wander about under a wide variety of exotic trees, while a colony of gibbons rules an island in the middle of the lake.

In the hamlet Le Tôt, 2km to the south, **Auberge du Moulin** (☎ 02 35 33 62 76; 2-course lunch €17.50, menus €27-47; ☺ dinner Tue, lunch & dinner Wed-Sat, lunch Sun) serves sophisticated regional cuisine with a light touch.

The Clères **tourist office** (☎ 02 35 33 38 64; www.ot-cleres.fr; 59 av du Parc; ☺ 2-5pm Mon, 10am-noon & 2-5.30pm Tue-Fri) can help with accommodation and details of walks in the area.

There are regular trains from Clères to Rouen (€4.20, 20 minutes) and Dieppe.

❤ CHÂTEAU DE MARTAINVILLE // EXPLORE NORMAN TRADITIONS IN A STATELY COUNTRY MANOR

Built for a wealthy shipbuilder in 1485, this turreted brick manor is an impressive combination of Renaissance and traditional Norman styles. It now houses the fascinating **Musée des Traditions et Arts Normands** (☎ 02 35 23 44 70; adult/child €3/free; ☺ 10am-12.30pm & 2-5pm Mon & Wed-Sat, 2-5.30pm Sun). The 1st floor progresses through rooms richly decorated in different styles from the Renaissance through to Louis XV. There's a wonderful collection of armoires; these beautifully carved cupboards were created to hold a daughter's trousseau (a dowry of household linen). Upstairs, the rooms are designed to represent the dwellings of ordinary people living in different parts of Normandy. The top floor is devoted to the once-important local textile industry, costumes and music.

Martainville-Epreville is 17km east of Rouen; bus 73 departs hourly from outside Rouen's train station.

❤ RY // WALK IN EMMA BOVARY'S FOOTSTEPS

Flaubert's *Madame Bovary* was based on a real-life drama that occurred in Ry in the mid-19th century. Emma Bovary's adulterous prototype was Delphine Couturier Delamare, wife of Eugène Delamare, who was a student of Flaubert's father when he was teaching at the medical school in Rouen. As in the novel, Madame Delamare committed suicide after running up enormous and unpayable debts. Her husband died shortly afterwards.

The pretty village of Ry offers incessant reminders of its connection with Flaubert's ground-breaking novel. The small **Galerie Bovary Musée d'Automates** (☎ 02 35 23 61 44; adult/child €5/3; ☺ 2.30-6pm Sat & Sun May-Oct) presents scenes from the novel, animated by mannequins. An English translation of the scenes provides a good summary of the novel for those who haven't read it, can't remember it or haven't seen any of the Bovary movies. It also has a reconstruction of the pharmacy where Madame Delamare bought her lethal poison. You can visit the Delamare graves behind **Église St-Sulpice**, built between the 12th and 16th centuries. The elaborately carved Renaissance wooden porch is unique in the region.

The **tourist office** (☎ 02 35 23 19 90; www.ot-ry-troisvallees.com; place Gustave Flaubert; ☺ 10am-12.30pm & 2-5pm Mon-Fri) has a list of local accommodation and free maps of suggested scenic walking, cycling and driving routes through the region.

Ry is 4km past Martainville-Epreville on the same bus route (73) from Rouen.

❦ MOULINEAUX // **STROLL PAST HISTORIC SITES AND ENJOY THE VIEWS**

In the shade of a creepy castle, the village of Moulineaux is worth the dreary trip past Rouen's port installations. A 3km loop leads past a 13th-century church, up to the castle and back down to an historic *lavoir* (open-air laundry basin) beneath a gurgling spring.

Château de Robert-le-Diable dates to the earliest Norman dukes, but Gallo-Roman wells in the courtyard indicate a long presence on the site. Robert the Devil was a mythical figure who could communicate with demons and ghosts. The character was probably inspired by William the Conqueror's father, Robert, and over the centuries his name became attached to the château. At the time of research the castle was closed for reconstruction, but it's still worth the trek up here for the panoramic views of the Seine and some magnificent mansions dotted around the valley.

There are frequent bus services (line 31) from Rouen's quai de la Bourse.

❦ LA BOUILLE // **A PICTURESQUE PIT STOP**

Easily combined with a visit to Moulineaux (it's 3km further on the same bus route), La Bouille's flower-bedecked houses gather around a pretty square and riverside promenade. In the 15th century it was an important port, and later painters and poets fell in love with the village. If you bring a bike, you can pedal up the river about 6km to Beaulieu. Otherwise, there's not much to do except eat, stroll and eat again, which is not a hardship since there are some excellent restaurants.

Restaurant Le Bellevue (☎ 02 35 18 05 05; 13 quai Hector Malot; 2-course lunch €15, menus €20-42; ☯ lunch & dinner) has a charming old-world ambience and serves up reasonably priced local specialities (salmon in a creamy sauce, veal head, duck hotpot, fish soup). The two-course lunch menu (€15) is great value.

SEINE VALLEY ABBEYS

Following the Seine valley west of Rouen, the D982 road winds through little towns, occasionally following the banks of the Seine as it climbs and descends. The **PNR Boucles de la Seine Normande** (p221) is also found around here. The minor resort towns such as Duclair, Caudebec-en-Caux and Villequier are pleasant places to have a snack or stroll along the river, but the real highlights are three extraordinary abbeys.

Only 10km west of Rouen, the first abbey downstream is the **Abbaye St-Georges** (☎ 02 35 32 10 82; www.abbaye-saint -georges.com; adult/child €5.50/4; ☯ 9am-6.30pm Apr-Oct, 2-5pm Nov-Mar) in the village of St-Martin-de-Boscherville. Founded in 1113 on the site of a Gallo-Roman temple, its sober but elegant church showcases Norman Romanesque architecture at its finest. The geometric motifs that adorn the facade seem curiously modern. Its light, bright nave is supported by massive pillars forming majestic arcades. This still-functioning church is free to visit, but it's well worth stumping up the admission fee and taking the audio-guided tour of the abbey buildings and restored gardens.

With its ghostly white stone set off by a backdrop of trees, **Abbaye de Jumièges** (☎ 02 35 37 24 02; adult/child €5/free; ☯ 9.30am-6.30pm mid-Apr–mid-Sep, 9.30am-1pm & 2.30-5.30pm mid-Sep–mid-Apr) is one of the most evocative ruins in the region. It's easy to imagine the former majesty of the structure

SEINE-MARITIME & EURE

from the sheer size of the remaining fragments, especially the church's imposing facade and 46m-high towers. The church was begun in 1020 on the site of a 7th-century abbey destroyed by the Viking invasion. William the Conqueror attended its consecration in 1067 and the abbey soon took its place at the forefront of the spiritual and intellectual development of the age. It declined during the Hundred Years' War and then enjoyed a renaissance under Charles VII, who stayed there with his mistress Agnes Sorel. It continued to flourish until the 18th-century revolutionaries booted out the monks and allowed the buildings to be mined for building materials. To get to Jumièges take the D65 south from the D982.

Returning to the D982, the next abbey you come to is **Abbaye St-Wandrille** (☎ 02 35 96 23 11; www.st-wandrille.com; ◷ 5.15am-1pm & 2-9.15pm), 19.5km west of Rouen, which still houses a community of 50 Benedictine monks. Founded in 649 by St-Wandrille, the original structure was destroyed by the Vikings in the 9th century. A new abbey church was consecrated in 1031 and donations from William the Conqueror enlarged the abbey's property. The abbey flourished along with other Norman abbeys in the 11th century until the church was destroyed by fire in the mid-13th century. By the time a new church was completed, the Hundred Years' War ended the monastic life of St-Wandrille. The abbey reopened in the 16th century, but, with little revenue, it wasn't until the 17th century that buildings were improved and expanded. Most of the structure dates from the 17th and 18th centuries, when the Revolution caused another suspension of monastic life. A Benedictine community moved in again in 1931 and began its restoration.

Guided tours (€3; ◷ 11.30am Sun, 3.30pm Wed-Mon Easter-Oct) include the refectory, the cloister, the chapel and the ruins of the Gothic abbey church. The latter two are freely open to the public; Mass is at 10am on Sunday and 9.45am Monday to Saturday. The abbey's excellent boutique sells religious knick-knacks, local products and various traditional lotions concocted at the abbey for everything from killing bugs to cleaning floors.

Bus 30 runs 17 times on weekdays from Rouen to Caudebec-en-Caux, stopping at St-Martin de Boscherville and St-Wandrille; it stops at Jumièges five times a day.

PAYS D'OUCHE & RISLE-CHARENTONNE

· · · · · ·

The Eure *département* begins with forested vales in the northwest and the humid hills of the Ouche country in the southwest. The Pays d'Ouche is a sparsely populated, forested plateau, well watered by rivers. With harsh winters and chalky soil, neither industry nor agriculture has taken root, but mysteries and tales of sorcerers have flourished in the evocative mists wafting through the valleys.

LE BEC-HELLOUIN & AROUND

This peaceful little village buried in the lush Becquet valley seems custom-built to rest the eyes of weary tourists. The ivy-covered half-timbered houses cluster around an ancient abbey and a little river bubbles between tree-shaded banks. Except for paved roads, cars and a few art galleries, everything looks about the same as it must have around 900 years ago when the abbey was built.

♥ ABBAYE NOTRE DAME DU BEC // THE ABBEY OF A VILLAGE FROZEN IN TIME

The **abbey** (☎ 02 32 43 72 60; www.abbayedubec .com; ☺ tours 10.30am, 3pm & 4pm Mon & Wed-Sat, noon, 3pm & 4pm Sun) was founded in 1035 and soon became a highly influential intellectual centre. Its first abbot, Lanfranc, was one of the most learned men of the age and was summoned by William the Conqueror to straighten out the pope's opposition to his marriage to Mathilde. Lanfranc and his successor, Anselm, became archbishops of Canterbury. The monastery remained a powerful force until the Revolution, when the monks were chased out and the invaluable library was vandalised. In 1948 a new community of monks revived the abbey and began restorations. The on-site boutique sells the monks' ceramics, jams and traditional cleaning products. Try to time a visit for Mass, held in the vaulted refectory (11.45am Monday to Saturday, 10.30am Sunday), when the monks' Gregorian chants filter through clouds of incense.

Bus 380 stops here four times on weekdays on its run between Évreux and Honfleur. The nearest train station is at Le Neubourg, 25 minutes away on the same bus line.

♥ CHÂTEAU DU CHAMP DE BATAILLE // SURROUND YOURSELF WITH PRE-REVOLUTIONARY OPULENCE

This sumptuous **château** (☎ 02 32 34 84 34; www.chateauduchampdebataille.com; apartments & gardens incl audioguide adult/child €24/15; ☺ 3.30-5.30pm Jul & Aug, weekends only Easter-Jun, Sep & Oct), 5km northwest of Le Neubourg, contains an exquisite collection of 17th- and 18th-century furniture and objets d'art. Built in the 17th century, the château was purchased by French designer Jacques Garcia, who decorated the interior in opulent 18th-century style. Some of the items on display belonged to the royal family of Louis XVI before revolutionaries looted the palaces at Versailles and Tuileries. Panelled walls, chandeliers, Flemish tapestries, Chinese porcelain, portraits, busts and vases have been arranged with impeccable taste in order to evoke the royal lifestyle in pre-Revolutionary France.

The vast **gardens** (adult/child €12/8; ☺ 10am-6pm Jul & Aug, 2-6pm May-Jun & Sep, 2-6pm Sat & Sun Apr & Oct) are also in a French classical style, with Italian statuary, lawns and a maze. The overall effect is eye popping, but it's a shame that admission to the entire château is a whopping €60 (10 people minimum, by appointment only; the more affordable €24 admission fee allows access to some apartments only).

BERNAY TO ÉVREUX

♥ BERNAY // WANDER MEDIEVAL STREETS ALONGSIDE ANCIENT WATERWAYS

A thick layer of cloud is all that spared Bernay from being bombed to rubble in WWII, like so many other towns in Normandy. Instead, it has kept its ramshackle medieval street plan, with branches of the Rivers Charentonne and Cosnier meandering through streets littered with ancient half-timbered houses. The town originally coalesced around an 11th-century abbey and owed its early prosperity to a now-defunct textile industry.

It's still a thriving regional centre, boasting a population in excess of 11,000.

The best time to stroll the ancient streets is on a Saturday morning, when an extensive market provides additional colour. The **tourist office** (☎ 02 32 43 32 08; www.ville-bernay27.fr; 29 rue Thiers; ☽ 9.30am-noon & 2-5.30pm Mon-Sat mid-Sep–mid-Jun, 9.30am-noon & 2-5.30pm Mon-Sat, 10am-1pm Sun mid-Jun–mid-Sep) dispenses free brochures for a 'Water, Stone & Wood' walking tour of the town centre.

Remains of the abbey complex now serve as the town hall, courthouse, public gardens and the **Musée des Beaux-Arts** (☎ 02 32 46 63 23; place Guillaume de Volpiano; adult/child €3.60/free; ☽ 2-5.30pm Tue-Sun mid-Sep–mid Jun, 10am-noon & 2-7pm mid-Jun–mid-Sep), which houses a small collection of paintings, furniture, pottery and antiquities. Admission to the museum includes the key to the **Église Abbatiale Notre Dame**, a large, empty Romanesque church commenced in 1017. Ravaged by fire in the 13th century, and again during the Hundred Years' War, the Wars of Religion and peasant revolts in 1589, the abbey finally met its end in the Revolution. Since then the church has been used as a warehouse and a granary, with sections sliced off to make way for roads. Restoration is a work in progress, but the great columned arcades of the nave and the high windows recall the building's ancient majesty.

Bernay is on the busy train line between Caen and Rouen (via Lisieux) and between Caen and Paris-St-Lazare (via Conches-en-Ouche and Évreux).

♥ CHÂTEAU DE BEAUMESNIL // VISIT NORMANDY'S ANSWER TO VERSAILLES

Dubbed the 'Normandy Versailles', the exterior of the **Château de Beaumesnil** (☎ 02 32 44 40 09; www.chateaubeaumesnil.com; château/park €7/3; ☽ 10am-noon & 2-6pm Wed-Mon Jul & Aug, 2-6pm Fri-Mon Easter-Jun & Sep) is almost as marvellous as that other château outside Paris, albeit on a much smaller scale. This baroque manor seems to float in the middle of an artificial pond that opens onto a magnificent 80-hectare landscaped park. Built by an obscure architect between 1633 and 1640, the ornate brick-and-stone facade is decorated with a profusion of sculpted heads, making it one of the finest examples of baroque style in Normandy. Don't miss the maze of privet bushes alongside the castle and take time to appreciate the park designed by a student of Le Nôtre, the landscaper of Versailles. The interior contains a museum of bookbinding, displaying hundreds of intricately decorated leather-bound books, and an unusual staircase suspended between two floors, but it's not as interesting as the castle's exterior.

The château is 13km southeast of Bernay in a little village on the D140; there is no public transport.

♥ CONCHES-EN-OUCHE // ENIGMATIC RUINS, HALF-TIMBERED HOUSES AND VALLEY VIEWS

This little town perched on a spur above the River Rouloir is a popular destination for weekending Parisians, just as it was once a prestigious stop on the pilgrimage to Santiago de Compostela in Spain. The **Église Ste-Foy** (rue Ste-Foy; admission free; ☽ 9am-7pm) is the town's proudest monument. This 16th-century Flamboyant Gothic church is notable for its vivid ensemble of Renaissance stained-glass windows and its intricate stonework.

Conches-en-Ouche was tossed back and forth during the Hundred Years'

SEINE-MARITIME & EURE

War, with fighting centred on its **11th-century castle**. It's now little more than an artful collection of ruins with trees sprouting at strange angles. The interior can't be visited, but the park is agreeable and a woodsy path circles it. Facing the park, the **Maison des Arts et du Tourisme** (☎ 02 32 30 76 42; www.conches-en-ouche.fr; place Aristide-Briand; ☼ 10am-12.30pm & 2-6pm Tue-Sat) houses both a friendly tourist office and an excellent gallery featuring local contemporary artists.

The town's best eatery faces a large fountain, a block north of the main street. **La Grand'Mare** (☎ 02 32 30 23 30; 13 av Croix de Fer; menu €13-28, 2-course lunch €11; ☼ lunch Tue & Sun, lunch & dinner Wed-Sat) presents sophisticated and imaginative cooking in both a relaxed bistro setting and a more formal dining room. It's extremely good value for the quality.

Conches is an easy day trip from Évreux by bus or train.

EASTERN EURE

· · · · · ·

ÉVREUX

pop 53,300

The capital of the Eure *département* hovers somewhere between a city and a large country town. The centre offers a modicum of hustle and bustle, but from many streets you can still look up to green hills and see livestock grazing.

These tranquil glimpses belie Évreux's extremely turbulent past. Entering recorded history as the Gallo-Roman town Mediolanum, Évreux has been a battleground for every conquering army in Normandy. The Vandals destroyed the ancient city in the 5th century, the Normans destroyed it again in the 9th century and Henry I burnt it in the 12th century. It was burnt again by French king Philippe-Auguste later that century after John Lackland (brother of Richard the Lion-Heart) invited 300 French soldiers garrisoned in Évreux for dinner and massacred them. During the 14th century Évreux was caught in the struggle between the French and English and burnt once more, this time losing its episcopal palace and priceless archives. It became part of France in 1441 but suffered again in 1791 when revolutionaries razed six churches, two convents and two abbeys.

German bombs devastated the town in 1940 and Allied bombs rained down on it in 1944. Phoenix-like, Évreux has risen again. Careful reconstruction has created a warm, liveable centre with plenty of green spaces. Although there's not enough in Évreux to keep most people engrossed for more than a day, it makes an interesting overnight stop or base for exploring other towns in Eure.

ESSENTIAL INFORMATION

TOURIST OFFICE // Évreux (☎ 02 32 24 04 43; www.ot-pays-evreux.fr; 1 place du Général de Gaulle; ☼ 9.30am-6pm Mon-Sat)

EXPLORING ÉVREUX

If you've a sweet tooth, don't miss the chocolates and macaroons at the branch of **Auzou** (34 rue Chartraine).

♥ RIVER ITON // STROLL ALONG THE RIVER AND DISCOVER THE CITY

The banks of the River Iton, which runs through central Évreux, are graced with tree-lined promenades and half-timbered houses. Where the river meets place du Général de Gaulle, you'll find the 44m-high **Tour de l'Horloge**, a

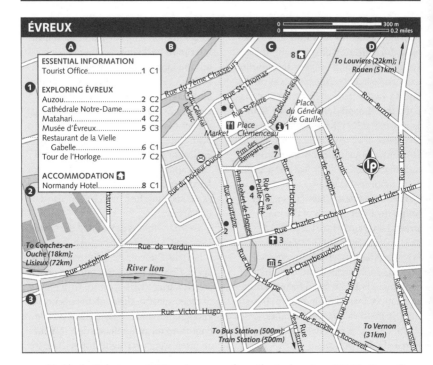

ÉVREUX

ESSENTIAL INFORMATION
Tourist Office.........................1 C1

EXPLORING ÉVREUX
Auzou...................................2 C2
Cathédrale Notre-Dame........3 C2
Matahari..............................4 C2
Musée d'Évreux...................5 C3
Restaurant de la Vieille
    Gabelle.............................6 C1
Tour de l'Horloge.................7 C2

ACCOMMODATION
Normandy Hotel...................8 C1

grand belfry built between 1490 and 1497 on the site of the former city gates.

Further downstream you'll pass the busy terrace of one of Normandy's coolest bars. Inside **Matahari** (☎ 02 32 38 49 88; 15 rue de la Petite Cité) there's an industrial-chic aesthetic, with a large dining and drinking space and secluded corners with comfy couches. Acoustic musicians perform regularly.

✦ MUSÉE D'ÉVREUX // DISCOVER GREEK GODS AND NAUGHTY ANTIQUES

Spread throughout the 15th-century bishop's palace, the **Musée d'Évreux** (☎ 02 32 31 81 90; 6 rue Charles Corbeau; admission free; ⏰ 10am-noon & 2-6pm Tue-Sun) presents an excellent overview of the town's history. Highlights include a remarkable pair of statues of Jupiter and Apollo dating

from the 2nd century BC. Vestiges of the ancient Gallo-Roman rampart that enclosed the city in the 3rd century AD have been excavated and form one wall of the basement. Also look out for some extremely risqué pocket watches on the 1st floor, one depicting a Franciscan friar graphically breaking one of his vows.

✦ CATHÉDRALE NOTRE DAME // AN INTERSECTION OF ARCHITECTURAL IDEAS

Évreux's **cathedral** (rue Charles Corbeau; ⏰ 8am-noon & 2-7pm) has been destroyed and rebuilt so many times it has become a temple to changing architectural styles. You'll find examples of Romanesque (the 12th-century arcades in the nave), Rayonnant Gothic (the 13th-century choir and 14th-century stained glass) and Flamboyant Gothic (the transept, lantern

SEINE-MARITIME & EURE

tower, north door and Mother-of-God chapel). It's only fitting then that the new organ, unveiled in 2006, was built in a similarly contemporary style. The ultra-modern structure resembles a giant lunar landing craft. Its weight balances on six thin metal legs, while metallic fabric wafts around like the smoke from take-off.

💗 **RESTAURANT DE LA VIELLE GABELLE //** SAVOUR INNOVATIVE CUISINE IN TRADITIONAL SURROUNDS
Picture a half-timbered house and a beamed dining room filled with Norman furniture and you'll think tradition. Nothing could be further from the truth at this **restaurant** (☎ 02 32 39 77 13; 3 rue de la Vielle Gabelle; menu €29, midweek lunch €18; ☻ lunch & dinner Tue-Fri, dinner Sat, lunch Sun). The cuisine is wonderfully imaginative and is permeated with influences from every region of France.

TRANSPORT

TRAIN // Évreux's **train station** (bd Gambetta) is on the line between Paris-St-Lazare and Caen, which includes Bernay and Lisieux.
BUS // Évreux is the hub for Eure's bus network. Route 200 heads to Gisors via Les Andelys; 300 to Gisors via Vernon; 370 to Conches-en-Ouche; 380 to Honfleur via Le Bec-Hellouin; and 390 to Rouen via Louviers. The bus station is next to the train station. Fares are €2 (€4 to Rouen).

VERNON & GIVERNY

pop 25,000 & 520
Although it's an ancient city with roots stretching back to the earliest Viking settlements, Vernon's main drawcard is as a jumping-off point for Giverny, 3km to the southeast.

Synonymous with Monet, this small village gets swamped by visitors queuing to visit the artist's famous gardens and to pay their respects at his resting place in the little churchyard. Despite 400,000 visitors teeming down its one main street annually, once the last bus has departed Giverny becomes an idyllic country village.

ESSENTIAL INFORMATION

TOURIST OFFICE // Vernon (☎ 02 32 51 39 60; www.cape-tourisme.fr; 36 rue Carnot, Vernon; ☻ 9am-12.30pm & 2-5.30pm Tue-Sat Oct-Apr, 9am-12.30pm & 2-5.30pm Tue-Sat, 10am-noon Sun May-Sep) Provides maps of suggested hikes in the region and cycling routes that take in Giverny.

EXPLORING VERNON & GIVERNY

💗 **FONDATION CLAUDE MONET //** SEE MONET'S WATER LILIES COME TO LIFE
From 1883 to 1926, this was Monet's **home and garden** (☎ 02 32 51 28 21; www.fondation-monet.com; 84 rue Claude Monet, Giverny; full admission/garden only €6/4.50; ☻ 9.30am-6pm Tue-Sun Apr-Oct) and constant source of inspiration. Here he painted some of his most famous series of works, including *Nymphéas* (Water Lilies).

The artist's **studio** is now the entrance hall and shop. It's here that you can pick up those water-lily ties, mugs and T-shirts to inflict on your family back home. Monet's love of colour is demonstrated inside his pretty pink **house**. His extensive collection of Japanese prints is on display, as well as faithful reproductions of his work.

Monet planted the **Clos Normand garden** in front of the house shortly after moving in, converting an orchard into a lawn scattered with Japanese cherry and flowering crab-apple trees. An arbour of climbing roses leads down to it, surrounded by symmetrical flower beds.

From the Clos Normand's far corner, a tunnel leads under the D5 to the

Jardin d'Eau (Water Garden). Having bought this piece of land in 1895 after his reputation had been established, Monet installed a pond, planted water lilies and constructed the wisteria-draped Japanese bridge. In contrast to the orderly Clos Normand, the Jardin d'Eau has a dreamy, mysterious ambience.

The seasons have an enormous effect on the gardens at Giverny. From early to late spring, daffodils, pansies, tulips, rhododendrons, wisteria and irises appear, followed by poppies and lilies. By June, nasturtiums, roses and sweet peas are in flower. Around September, there are dahlias, sunflowers and hollyhocks.

Avoiding the camera-clicking crowds isn't easy, but first thing in the morning or late in the afternoon are your best bets.

❦ MUSÉE DES IMPRESSIONNISMES // ORIGINAL IMPRESSIONIST ART IN THE MASTER'S HOME TOWN

Working with famous institutions such as Paris' Musée d'Orsay, this modern museum (☎ 02 32 51 94 65; www.mdig.fr; 99 rue Claude Monet, Giverny; adult/concession €5.50/3; ⊙ 10am-6pm May–mid-Jul, 10am-6pm Tue-Sun mid-Jul–Oct) stages exhibitions devoted exclu-

CLAUDE MONET

One of the most important figures in modern art, Monet was the undisputed leader of the Impressionists. Born in Paris in 1840, he grew up near Le Havre. It was here that he started painting nature in the open air, a practice that was to greatly influence his work.

At 17 Monet was studying in Paris at the Académie Suisse with such artists as Pissarro. His studies were interrupted by two years of military service in Algiers, where the intense light and colours planted the seeds of his future painting style. Returning to Le Havre, Monet painted Étretat, Fécamp and Trouville, aiming to capture the immediate impression of the scene before him, rather than precise detail.

During the Franco-Prussian War of 1870–71, Monet travelled to London, where he discovered the works of Turner and Constable. Consequently, painting from his houseboat on the Seine at Argenteuil, he focused on the effects of air and light, and in particular on the latter's effect on the water's surface. He also began using the undisguised, broken brush strokes that best characterise the Impressionist style.

It was in the late 1870s that Monet first began painting series of canvases in order to study the effects of changing light. The best known of these include the Rouen cathedral series, which were painted in the 1890s. In 1883, four years after the death of his first wife, Camille, he moved to Giverny with Alice Hoschedé, his two sons and her five children from a previous marriage. Using his wealth to turn Giverny into the exact setting he required for his art, Monet planted his property with a variety of flowers to ensure he would have something to paint nearly all year. With the first morning light, Monet was before his lily pond with an easel capturing the reflection of sun and sky in the water. He sometimes worked on a dozen canvases at a time.

Alice died in 1911, followed three years later by Monet's eldest son, Jean. Soon after, the portly, bearded artist started painting the Nymphéas series. The huge dimensions of some of these works, together with the fact that the pond's surface takes up the entire canvas, meant the abandonment of composition in the traditional sense and the virtual disintegration of form. Monet completed the series just before his death in 1926.

SEINE-MARITIME & EURE

sively to Impressionist art. Like the Fondation Claude Monet just up the road, the fabulous gardens are an integral part of the experience.

♥ VERNON SELF-GUIDED TOUR // A QUICK ROUND-UP OF VERNON'S SURVIVING SIGHTS

Although WWII bombs destroyed most of Vernon's medieval centre, the city has lavished attention on the few crooked streets and half-timbered houses that remain, creating an agreeably cosy feeling. One such wonky 15th-century building contains the tourist office (p251), where you can pick up a pamphlet listing 14 interesting stops in the immediate vicinity. The starting point is **Collégiale Notre Dame**, a stately Gothic church dating from the 12th century but incessantly restored since. The 15th-century facade contains an exceptional rose window and the central tower dates from the 13th century. Highlights of the interior include a 15th-century sculpted organ loft, a Louis XVI altar and a mixture of stained glass from the 16th to the 20th century.

♥ MUSÉE AG POULAIN // MONET PAINTINGS AND OTHER BITS AND PIECES

Vernon's **museum** (☎ 02 32 21 28 09; www.vernon27.fr/musee; 12 rue du Pont; adult/child €2.80/free, Wed free; ☷ 10.30am-12.30pm & 2-5.30pm Tue-Fri, 2-5.30pm Sat & Sun Apr-Sep, 2-5.30pm Tue-Sun Oct-Mar) is a grab bag of antiquities, sculpture and paintings displayed in a 16th-century mansion. The highlights are two works by Monet, *Falaises à Pourville* (Cliffs at Pourville) and *Nymphéas* (Water Lilies).

GASTRONOMIC HIGHLIGHTS

♥ LE BISTRO €
☎ 02 32 21 29 19; 73 rue Carnot, Vernon; menus €18-35; ☷ Tue-Sat

Using the name as a statement of intent, this friendly establishment ticks off every item on your bistro wish list: a cosily atmospheric dining room, attentive staff, a great wine list and an ever-changing blackboard menu featuring a small selection of bistro classics at reasonable prices.

♥ LES FLEURS €€
☎ 02 32 51 16 80; 71 rue Carnot, Vernon; menus €27-53, 2-course lunch incl drinks €20-29; ☷ lunch & dinner Tue-Sat, lunch Sun

Directly next to Le Bistro, Les Fleurs is the more formal of the two and Vernon's main sense-of-occasion restaurant. While the decor doesn't quite gel, the well-crafted cuisine certainly does.

TRANSPORT

TRAIN // Vernon is on the busy line between Paris-St-Lazare and Rouen, making for an easy day trip from either city.

BUS // Bus 300 stops in Vernon en route between Gisors and Évreux, and bus 220 heads to Les Andelys. From April to November, buses meet the trains for the trip to Giverny (€4 return).

BIKE // Opposite the station there are two places that rent bikes for around €12 per day.

LE VEXIN NORMAND & AROUND

· · · · · ·

Normandy and France haven't always been the best of buddies, aptly demonstrated by the impressive castles that define this border region. As the Seine was the main highway between Rouen and Paris, this northeastern corner of the Eure *département* was more heavily fortified than most.

In the midst of these crumbling ruins and now peaceful villages lies the Forêt de Lyons, a magical beech forest spreading over 105 sq km that was once a favourite hunting turf for the Merovingian kings.

LES ANDELYS

Les Andelys is set at the confluence of the mighty River Seine and modest River Gambon, bordered by forested hills and high, white bluffs. As the name indicates, there are in fact two Andelys: modern Grand Andely, the commercial heart of the duo, and the older, more scenic Petit Andely, on the banks of the Seine. Most visitors gravitate to the riverside Andely for the winding streets of half-timbered houses and the pretty 12th-century church, and to scramble up the hill to the château. There are also some excellent restaurants (see La Chaîne d'Or, p306).

By 1196, Richard the Lion-Heart's territory was coming under increasing pressure from French king Philippe-Auguste, who was pushing west from Paris along the Seine. Sensing that Rouen, his prize possession, was under threat, Richard looked for a position that would definitively lock the French out. On the promontory rising more than 100m above the Seine, he built the magnificent Château-Gaillard, intending it to be an impenetrable bulwark against French expansion. The fortress lasted only seven years before falling to Philippe-Auguste, but the little village of Petit Andely took root and expanded northeast to Grand Andely. The bombs that fell on Grand Andely in 1940 destroyed a large chunk of the town, but it is still worth visiting for the 13th-century Église Notre Dame.

The tiny tourist office (☎ 02 32 54 41 93; www.ville-andelys.fr; 24 rue Philippe-Auguste, Petit Andely; ☉ 2-6pm Mon-Fri, 10am-1pm & 2-5pm Sat) is at the foot of the cliffs that form the base of the château. Bus 200 stops at Grand Andely en route between Évreux and Gisors; bus 220 heads to Vernon.

EXPLORING LES ANDELYS

♥ CHÂTEAU-GAILLARD // A MIGHTY CASTLE IN A RIVERSIDE GEM

The château (☎ 02 32 54 04 16; adult/child €3/2.50; ☉ 10am-1pm & 2-6pm Wed-Mon mid-Mar–mid-Nov) was built with extraordinary speed between 1196 and 1197 according to the latest ideas in military architecture and engineering. Workers rerouted tributaries of the Seine, leaving the mammoth clifftop structure tenuously connected to the plateau by a narrow and easily defensible ridge, which was divided into two parts separated by a deep moat. The northern structure was the *châtelet* (the heart of the castle), protected by five towers, while the *fort principal* opposite featured a three-storey keep at its heart protected by a series of concentric circular 4m walls. The defensive system included iron chains that reached across the Seine, blocking all river traffic.

Richard the Lion-Heart merrily pronounced it *gaillard,* a word that translates as saucy or gallant, reflecting its impregnability, to mock French pretensions to the region. It's said that Philippe-Auguste defiantly shouted, 'If its walls were made of solid iron, yet would I take them!', to which Richard cried back, 'By the throat of God, if its walls were made of butter, yet would I hold them!'

After Richard's death in 1199, Philippe-Auguste laid siege to the château. A population of about 400 terrified civilians joined the English garrison, but when supplies dwindled they were abruptly ejected into the winter snow, resorting to cannibalism in a desperate attempt to survive. The siege dragged on for eight months, until a cavalryman noticed that the mighty fortress had one unprotected opening: the latrine. The French soldiers squirmed in and the battle for Château-Gaillard – and Normandy – was over in hours.

The château is now mostly in ruins thanks to Henri IV, who ordered its destruction in 1603, but the ghostly white walls still cut a dramatic silhouette against the sky and enough remains to give a reasonably good idea of its former majesty. You can walk a loop around the ruins taking in the impressive views over the Seine without paying the admission charge to enter the main keep. The viewing platform just north of the castle has interesting information boards in English; there aren't any inside the castle.

The château is a stiff 20-minute climb via a signposted path, which begins about 100m north of the tourist office.

LOUVIERS & AROUND

♥ LOUVIERS // EXPLORE A TRADITIONAL MARKET AND HISTORIC RIVERSIDE
Halfway between Rouen and Évreux, Louviers has retained much of its original grace, despite ruinous bombardment in 1940. Several branches of the Eure cut through the town centre, making it a pleasant place for a stroll, particularly on a Saturday morning when the market takes over the streets. Some carefully restored half-timbered houses survive from the days when Louviers was renowned for its wool industry and cloth manufacturing.

The **tourist office** (☎ 02 32 40 04 41; www .tourisme-seine-eure.com; 10 rue du Maréchal Foch; 🕑 10am-12.30pm & 2-5.30pm Mon-Sat) produces (in English) a free map listing 22 interesting buildings, as well as a pamphlet

about **Église Notre Dame**, the wonderful Flamboyant Gothic church that dominates the town centre. While the church's underlying structure dates from the 13th century, much of its extravagant decoration belongs to the 16th century.

The town's cloth-making history is on display in the **Musée de Louviers** (☎ 02 32 09 58 55; www.ville-louviers.fr/ville/musee/musee.htm; place Ernest Thorel; admission free; 🕑 2-6pm Wed-Sun), along with a collection of ceramics, paintings and furniture from the 16th to 19th centuries and regular temporary exhibits of contemporary art.

La Maison-en-Vaisselle Cassée (80 rue du Bal-Champêtre) is one of the most eccentric residences in Normandy. For over 40 years the owner has amassed pieces of broken crockery and shells and arranged them in whimsical, swirling designs on his house, garage and wall, in his garden – and even on his dog's kennel. Although it's a private house, you can peek over the gate for a closer look. Take bd du Maréchal Joffre from place Ernest Thorel, continue along rue de la Citadelle, then turn right into rue du Bal-Champêtre.

There are regular buses between Rouen's quai du Havre and Évreux's bus station that stop a block up from the tourist office on rue Gustave Bertinot.

♥ CÔTE DES DEUX AMANTS // STOP FOR SWEEPING RIVER VIEWS
There are some excellent scenic viewpoints on the road heading up the cliffs on the east bank of the Seine close to Amfreville-sous-les-Monts. The first is marked only by a parking sign but provides sumptuous views down the valley between the Seine and the Eure. Much better signposted is **Côte des Deux Amants**, a 150m-high limestone spur behind an historic convent. The view is a little more industrial here, but an indicator

table (partly vandalised when we visited) lets you know what you're looking at. According to legend, Two Lovers' Hill got its name from the tragic tale of Edmond and Calliste. They fell in love when Edmond rescued her from a wild boar, but her father wouldn't consent to the marriage until Edmond proved his strength by running to the top of the hill with Calliste in his arms. He tried but collapsed and died at the summit, and Calliste immediately expired from a broken heart.

FORÊT DE LYONS

♣ LYONS-LA-FORÊT //
WALK INTO A FAIRY TALE

In the middle of Forêt de Lyons and on the banks of the River Lieure, Lyons-la-Forêt is the most postcard-perfect village in Haute-Normandie. The brick and half-timbered houses clustered around the central square have survived nearly intact since the 17th century, and look like a film set. In fact, it was a film set, for Jean Renoir's and Claude Chabrol's film versions of *Madame Bovary*. It's easy enough to imagine women in long dresses sweeping down the streets to meet illicit lovers, even though you're more likely to meet Parisians on their way to their weekend mansions in the woods. The composer Maurice Ravel found the village a peaceful spot, coming here to reflect and compose (his fairy-tale house is marked by a plaque on rue d'Enfer). Fortunately, WWII bombing spared the town, which is now classified as a national historic monument.

Once the location of a Gallo-Roman settlement, Lyons-la-Forêt coalesced around the castle built by Henry I in the 12th century. The king died in his fortified castle in 1135 (supposedly from eating eels fished from the Lieure), but the village thrived until it was destroyed by a fire in 1590. It was rebuilt in the 17th century and reached its commercial heyday in the 18th century when the thatched **Les Halles** marketplace was built.

On the other side of the River Lieure, the 12th-century **Église St-Denis** (rue de l'Église) is constructed of silex (flint) and contains a 16th-century wooden statue of St Christopher. Opening hours are irregular; check with the **tourist office** (☎ 02 32 49 31 65; www.lyons.tourisme.free.fr; 20 rue de l'Hôtel de Ville; ☒ 10am-noon & 2-5pm Tue-Sat mid-Oct–Easter, 10am-noon & 2-5pm Tue-Sun Easter–mid-Oct) near the main square. It can also supply you with information about forest walks.

Lyons-la-Forêt has some memorable sleeping options (see p306) that also offer good food.

There are three to four buses a day Monday to Saturday to and from Rouen.

♣ CHÂTEAU DE VASCŒUIL //
A GARDEN, AN OPEN-AIR
GALLERY AND A MUSEUM

On the northwestern edge of the Forêt de Lyons is the **Château de Vascœuil** (☎ 02 35 23 62 35; www.chateauvascoeuil.com; Vascœuil; adult/child €8/5.50; ☒ 11am-6.30pm Jul & Aug, 2.30-6pm Wed-Sat Easter–Jun, Sep & Oct), a stately manor built between the 14th and 16th centuries. In addition to impressive sculpture gardens and a well-preserved *colombier* (see boxed text, p185), the château contains a museum dedicated to the historian of the French Revolution, Jules Michelet. There are often excellent temporary art exhibitions.

Bus line 73 (Rouen, Martainville-Epreville, Ry) stops here.

♣ ABBAYE DE MORTEMER //
HUNT FOR GHOSTS AMONG
HISTORIC RUINS

About 6km south of Lyons-la-Forêt, this former Cistercian **abbey** (☎ 02 32 49

54 34; www.mortemer.fr; adult/child €6/4; ☺ 2-6pm)
was founded in 1134 by Henry I, son
of William the Conqueror. After the
Revolution, stones from the abbey were
removed and used to construct the village of Lisors. The remains are slowly
disintegrating in the middle of their large
grounds, but a remarkable 934-niche
colombier is still standing. There is also
an 18th-century château in the grounds,
which has been transformed into a **museum**. Audiovisual equipment and wax
figures are used to vividly recreate scenes
from monastic life and there's also a
small doll museum.

It's said that the abbey is haunted.
Mathilde, wife of the German emperor
Henry V, was imprisoned here and cries
out her anguish whenever there's a full
moon. Other ghosts include the last four
monks of the abbey, whose throats were
cut by revolutionaries. You might catch
them floating around the *colombier*.

In addition to visits from beyond, the
abbey hosts a **medieval fair** on 15 August, which includes a light show, costumes and re-enactments. Guided visits
(€3 extra) take place from 2pm to 6pm
daily between May and September, and
only on weekends for the rest of the
year.

GISORS

Situated at the confluence of three rivers
and surrounded by verdant farmland,
Gisors doesn't initially strike you as a
frontier town. Yet its defining feature,
the **Fortresse de Gisors**, is symbolic of
centuries of Norman-French conflict.
Built on Normandy's far eastern border,
yet only 63km from central Paris, this
imposing castle was raised as a physical
barrier to the aspirations of the kings of
France.

It was begun by Guillaume le Roux
(William Rufus), son of William the
Conqueror, in 1097. Originally a mound
topped by a two-storey wooden keep, it
was added to and strengthened in stone
by his successors, Henry I and Henry II
of England. Despite this, French king
Philippe-Auguste took the castle in
1193 and built new defences. The round
Prisoners Tower dates from this time, so
called because of ancient graffiti on the
walls scribbled by prisoners incarcerated
there. Despite its increased strength, the
castle was retaken by the English during the Hundred Years' War, returned
to the French when hostilities ceased,
and seized by Henri IV during the Wars
of Religion. It was finally abandoned
in the 16th century and slowly fell into
disrepair.

Nowadays there's a popular **park** (admission free; ☺ 8am-7.30pm Apr-Sep, to 5pm Oct-Mar)
within the outer fortifications. Entry to
the castle proper is by **guided tour** (☎ 02
32 55 59 36; adult/child €5/3; ☺ 10.30am, 2.30pm &
4pm Sat & Sun). The castle's office has a good
stash of tourist information.

Just down the hill, **Église St-Gervais
St-Protais** (rue Vienne; ☺ 9am-7pm Wed-Mon)
is an interesting combination of Gothic
and Renaissance styles, built between the
12th and 16th centuries. Its pure Renaissance facade has a noble arch and a rich
profusion of carvings flanked by classic
Gothic towers. Inside, the Gothic structure houses a series of fine Renaissance
chapels.

Gisors is connected by train to Paris-
St-Lazare and by bus to Dieppe (via
Serqueux – change here for Rouen – and
Neufchâtel-en-Bray) and Évreux (via Les
Andelys or Vernon).

SEINE-MARITIME & EURE

BACKGROUND

HISTORY
· · · · · · ·

ARRIVAL OF THE ANCIENTS

Humans have been living along the Breton and Norman coastline for at least 100,000 years, but the first hard evidence of settlement emerges from around the end of the last ice age in around 10,000 BC. The melting of the great ice sheets raised the sea level by around 100m, flooding large areas of land and creating the region's distinctive coastline, including the deep coastal inlets known as *rias* or *abers*. As northern Europe warmed, Neolithic tribes slowly migrated north, clearing areas of forest for settlement and establishing rudimentary arable farms and cattle enclosures.

By around 5000 BC, Neolithic communities were well established across Brittany and Normandy. Around this time prehistoric settlers began to construct a series of dramatic stone monuments such as cairns (stone burial mounds), dolmens (burial chambers consisting of a capstone supported by menhirs), *cromlechs* (stone circles), menhirs (single standing stones), and the strange arrow-straight arrangements known as *alignements*. The exact purpose of many of these monuments is still a mystery, although the consensus is that they probably served a spiritual or religious function. Normandy has relatively few Stone Age sites, but the Breton landscape is littered with them, including the monumental Alignements de Carnac (p122). By the dawn of the Bronze Age (2500 BC), Normans and Bretons had also established trading links with several areas of Europe and the British Isles, especially in precious metals such as tin and copper.

CELTS, ROMANS & CHRISTIANS

Around 500 BC, Celtic settlers spread across northern Europe from their heartland in present-day Germany. They settled between the Seine and Loire rivers, christening their new homeland Armor, meaning 'the land by the sea'. There were five principal tribes, whose ancient territories roughly mirror Brittany's present *départements*: the Namneti (Loire-Atlantique), Veneti (Golfe du Morbihan), Rhedoni (Ille-et-Vilaine), Osismi (western Finistère) and Coriosolites (Côtes d'Armor). Other Celtic tribes settled in Normandy around Lisieux, Évreux, Carentan and Bayeux, while the powerful Veliocasses founded their capital in Rouen.

The Celts were a skilled and cultured people, with a complex society governed by warrior kings, religious mystics (known as Druids) and an elaborate pantheon of

» 5000–2500 BC	» 500–56 BC	» 5TH CENTURY AD
Neolithic people begin construction of Brittany's major stone monuments, including the great burial cairn of Barnenez and the Alignements de Carnac.	Celts settle widely throughout Brittany and Normandy. Many hill forts and fortified villages are built before the Celts' subjugation by the Romans, completed by 56 BC.	A new wave of Celtic settlers arrive from Cornwall, Wales and Ireland. Missionaries begin the process of Christianisation and found small churches, abbeys and chapels.

BACKGROUND

natural deities. Archaeologists have uncovered many stunning examples of Celtic art, including fine jewellery and pottery decorated with the Celts' trademark curved, interlaced designs – you can see fine examples at the Musée Départemental Breton (p104) and the Musée Thomas Dobrée in Nantes (p145).

The Celts' heyday was cut short by the arrival of a new wave of invaders – the Romans, who marched into France around 125 BC and rapidly defeated most of the major tribes, culminating with the defeat of the Venetis in 56 BC and the annihilation of the last Celtic king, Vercingetorix, in 52 BC. Four centuries of Gallo-Roman rule followed; with typical efficiency the Roman rulers set about constructing new roads, forts and provincial towns including Condate (present-day Rennes), Condevincum (Nantes) and Rotomagus (Rouen). Despite their enforced Romanisation many Gaulish tribes held on to their traditional customs, which they then slowly reasserted following the collapse of the Roman Empire in the early 4th century AD.

Around the 5th and 6th centuries a new wave of Celtic immigrants sailed across the English Channel from Wales, Cornwall and Ireland, probably to escape the advance of Anglo-Saxon invaders from strongholds in the southeast. Among these invaders were Christian monks and missionaries who promptly set about converting the pagan Gauls: the names of many of these early evangelists live on across the region, including Brieuc (St-Brieuc), Tugdual (Tréguier), Pol Aurelian (St-Pol de Léon), Corentin (Quimper) and Maclow (St-Malo). But they brought with them more than a new religion; they also brought a new Celtic language and a new name for their adopted homeland – Brittany, meaning little Britain.

THE RISE OF THE KINGS

By the end of the 8th century, Normandy and Brittany had fallen under the auspices of the powerful Frankish kings, who had wrested control of much of the country following the Romans' departure. Charlemagne was the first to subjugate the region, but the Breton warrior-king Nominoë subsequently led his armies to victory against Charles le Chauve (the Bald) in 845, leading to a peace treaty which guaranteed the survival of a strong and independent Brittany – at least for a while.

Within a few decades both kingdoms faced a new threat: the arrival of a wave of Viking invaders from Scandinavia, dubbed the Norse-men (men of the north, later shortened to Normans). These merciless raiders rampaged their way across the region throughout the 9th century, sacking regional centres and monastic communities in

» 8–9TH CENTURY	» 1100S	» 1204
Viking invaders begin attacks on the Breton and Norman coastline, conquering large areas of territory, but are finally driven from Brittany by Alain Barbe-torte in AD 937.	Construction begins on the great abbey of Mont St-Michel to replace an earlier 8th-century chapel. Construction continues periodically for the next three centuries.	Philip II confiscates the Duchy of Normandy and the region officially becomes part of the kingdom of France. The act is ratified by the Treaty of Paris in 1259.

Rouen, Évreux, Bayeux, Sées, Rennes and Nantes. They were eventually stopped at Dol de Bretagne in 936 and driven out of Brittany by Alain Barbe-Torte, the first Duke of Brittany; the invaders subsequently put down roots east of the Couesnon River, establishing the boundaries for the new region of Normandy.

A century of Norman power struggles followed until a new king, Guillaume, assumed the throne in 1035, aged only seven. As the illegitimate son of Robert I, duke of Normandy, and Arlette, a tanner's daughter, Guillaume le Batard (William the Bastard) was hardly blessed with an auspicious start, but he was a formidable leader: he united the rebellious Norman barons and steadily expanded his territory and influence, culminating in his landmark defeat of the English king Harold at the Battle of Hastings in 1066.

Despite a series of power struggles and skirmishes, Brittany meanwhile remained an independent duchy, but was plunged into bloody civil war following the death of Jean III, in 1341. The subsequent War of Succession lasted almost a quarter of a century, contested by the English-backed Jean IV de Montfort and Charles de Blois, who was supported by the French king. The war eventually ended with the death of Charles at the Battle of Auray in 1364, and Brittany's dukes entered a period of great influence and prosperity, effectively ruling the region as an independent kingdom from their newly built château at Nantes.

The region endured further instability during the Hundred Years' War, when the English monarch Edward III landed on Normandy's shores in pursuit of the French crown. After a century of bloody conflict, Edward's descendant Henry IV laid claim to be the King of France, until the French armies were galvanised by a young firebrand by the name of Jeanne d'Arc (Joan of Arc), who inspired Charles VII to defeat the English armies at the crucial Siege of Orléans in 1429. Unfortunately for Joan, she was subsequently betrayed by the Burgundians and was burnt at the stake in Rouen just two years later. The English armies were eventually driven from France in 1453.

Flush with victory, the new French king, Charles VIII, sought to expand his power, and before too long he began to develop designs on the Breton dukedom. He launched a series of unsuccessful attacks on Brittany before enforcing a shotgun marriage to the young Breton duchess, Anne de Bretagne. When Charles died, in 1498, Anne (still aged only 23) married his successor Louis XII, on the condition that Brittany would retain its rights of independence. Her efforts ultimately came to naught; her daughter Claude subsequently married François d'Angoulême (later François I), and the two kingdoms were irrevocably joined in a Treaty of Union in 1532.

» 1341	» 1491	» 1675
The Breton War of Succession begins, and ends with the death of Charles de Blois, in 1364. Peace is formally declared at the Treaty of Guérande in 1365.	Anne de Bretagne marries Charles VII in an attempt to ensure Brittany's independence, but her daughter, Claude, later cedes Brittany to France in 1532.	Brittany is rocked by the 'Stamped Paper' Riot (opposing duties on legal documents) and the 'Bonnets Rouges' riots against feudal rule. Both uprisings are bloodily suppressed.

A NEW WORLD

Under the edicts of the new treaty, Brittany retained control of many of its laws and statutes, and was ruled by its own regional parliament, based in Rennes (p52), while the French monarchy consolidated its control over its Norman neighbour. Following another bloody period of conflict during the Wars of Religion in the late 16th century, the French monarchy imposed a series of punitive new taxes (especially on tobacco and legal papers) which met with widespread opposition and a string of violent revolts, all of which were put down in bloody fashion.

But while trouble was brewing at home, overseas the news was better. Following in the footsteps of Jacques Cartier's landmark expeditions to Canada between 1534 and 1542, the region's sea ports had established lucrative trading links all across the New World: exotic goods were flowing into the expanding ports of Nantes, Brest, St-Malo, Le Havre and Lorient, generating huge profits for the cities' sea captains and merchants, and prompting the construction of many lavish villas, châteaux and country estates. In order to protect their coastal interests from plunder (especially from the hated English), the pioneering military architect Vauban oversaw the construction of a string of defensive forts, most notably at Brest (p92) and St-Malo (p38).

The increasing gap between rich and poor, coupled with the autocratic attitudes and ever-greater excesses of the ruling elite, meant it was only a matter of time before things boiled over. The Revolution of 1789 heralded a new reign of terror which saw the execution of thousands of aristocrats and the wanton destruction of anything and everything relating to the *ancien régime* – manors were torched, statues were defaced, churches and abbeys were sacked, and estates were confiscated in the headlong rush towards the bright new republic. Crucially for Brittany, the self-appointed Revolutionary Convention had little truck with regional divisions; Brittany's age-old rights of self-governance were abolished, its parliament was dissolved, its clergy were stripped of power and its young men were conscripted into the revolutionary army.

Enough was enough. Headed by their passionate leader Jean Cottereau, a counter-revolutionary group known as the Chouans (their name, which comes from the Breton word for owl, is said to stem from their use of hooting calls to communicate in darkness) led a series of uprisings against the Convention. They paid a heavy price for their opposition; Cottereau and other Chouan leaders were guillotined in 1794, and over 10,000 people in Nantes were beheaded or drowned during bloody reprisals. It's a period that remains deeply engrained in the Breton consciousness; many academics maintain it established deep rifts between Brittany and the rest of France that endure

BACKGROUND

» 1790S	» 1800S	» 1940
The region is plunged into strife following the French Revolution in 1789. Antirevolutionary plots led by the aristocrat Rouërie, the Chouan rebels and others all fail.	The region enjoys major industrial and economic expansion. Naval ports are founded in Brest and Cherbourg, and railways are laid between Paris, Brest and Rouen.	Germans invade Brittany and Normandy. U-Boat harbours are established in St-Nazaire and Lorient, and major fortifications are built along the Norman coast.

to this day. Order was eventually restored by Napoléon Bonaparte, the genius Corsican general who led the nation to a string of military victories, re-establishing France's sense of national pride and laying the foundations for a more stable French republic, though his wars were to prove disastrous in the short term.

Following the Napoleonic wars, France soon entered a period of relative stability. Industry and economy began to flourish: the region's ports developed rapidly, factories and warehouses sprang up in many cities, and the first stretches of France's national railway network were laid, including the Paris–Rouen line in 1843 and the Paris–Brest line in 1865. Beyond the city suburbs, shrinking maritime trade, collapsing fish stocks, the advent of industrial-scale farming and a steady population drain towards the cities meant that many rural areas of Brittany and Normandy suffered increasing hardship as the century wore on. The region was rocked by a wave of industrial conflicts from the 1890s onwards, fought out in the dockyards of Nantes, the canneries of Finistère, the shoe factories of Fougères and the farms of the interior.

WORLD WARS

Normandy and Brittany both suffered heavy losses and great economic hardship during WWI, but the horrors of the Great War were soon eclipsed by those endured during WWII. In 1940, German troops launched their blitzkrieg assault on northern France, and within a few short months had an iron grip over Brittany, Normandy and the Channel Islands. For four years the region suffered all the indignities and cruelties of occupation: deportations, forced labour, arrests and summary executions. Many people fled across the Channel to join de Gaulle's Free French forces, while others stayed behind to join the Resistance. Some also chose to collaborate with the Nazi regime; many members of the Parti National Breton (PNB) were openly supportive of the Nazis, and the Bezenn Perrot (a Breton militia group) even fought in German uniform. Finally, on 6 June 1944, the D-Day landings along the beaches of Normandy heralded the end of the long Nazi occupation (see p265 for more details), but not before several months of vicious fighting razed many of the region's cities (including Brest, Caen, St-Malo, Lorient, St-Nazaire and Le Havre) to rubble.

The postwar era saw rapid reconstruction of the region's infrastructure and the modernisation of many of its ports, railways and shattered industries. By the mid-1950s, much of the rebuilding work had been completed, although speedy construction often took precedence over architectural aesthetics – St-Malo reconstructed its 18th-century architecture but Brest, Caen and many other cities were rebuilt in

» 1944	» 1978	» 2003
Allied Forces land at Normandy. Major bridges, towns and ports are destroyed. Cherbourg is liberated on 27 June, followed by Caen (9 July) and Rouen (1 September).	The oil tanker *Amoco Cadiz* runs aground off Portsall, spilling 1.5m barrels of crude oil onto the Breton coastline – France's worst oil disaster.	The largest passenger liner ever built, the RMS *Queen Mary* II, is launched from the historic shipyards in St-Nazaire.

functional concrete, while Le Havre took a bold leap into the brave new world of structural classicism.

TO THE PRESENT DAY

Since the war, Brittany has continued its steady integration with the rest of France, but has never quite lost sight of its own unique history and identity. Since the 1960s it's become a major player in telecommunications, car-making, shipbuilding and agriculture, as well as one of France's busiest tourist destinations – Brittany is the country's second most popular holiday region, topped only by Paris. There's been a simultaneous resurgence of interest in traditional culture and the Brezhoneg language, and while the spirit of Breton nationalism is certainly alive and well, the majority of Bretons retain a passionate bond with their homeland but do not belong to any separatist movement – no doubt deterred by the militant campaigns of organisations such as the Front de Libération de la Bretagne, which launched its first bombing campaigns in 1965. A recent poll suggested around 25% of Bretons had some sympathy with the nationalist cause, but the vast majority favour increased regional autonomy over complete separation from the state.

Normandy has never had an independence movement à la Brittany, although several prominent politicians are endorsing a movement to bring Basse-Normandie and Haute-Normandie into one unified region. Most people seem fairly content with the status quo: Normandy's a relatively prosperous region, with a thriving agricultural industry, some of the nation's busiest shipping ports and plenty of corporate clout thanks to its proximity to Paris – not to mention a higher concentration of AOCs (Appellation d'Origine Contrôlée) than practically anywhere else in France.

THE BATTLE FOR NORMANDY

· · · · · · ·

The Normandy coastline is inextricably linked with the events of 6 June 1944, when Allied troops launched the largest amphibious assault ever attempted in a desperate gambit to liberate Europe from Nazi occupation. Known to the troops as Operation Overlord, this epoch-making event is today known as D-Day (Jour-J in France). It signalled both the beginning of the end of the war in Europe and the ultimate downfall of the Nazi regime.

THE DECISION TO GO

As early as 1942, the Allies had contemplated an invasion of the European mainland. Stalin was a particularly strong advocate; following Hitler's invasion of Russia in 1941, Stalin desperately lobbied for a second European front to help divert German resources away from the Russian campaign. But in reality, mounting a full-scale invasion in 1942 was impossible – especially after the disastrous assault by Canadian forces on Dieppe in 1942, which ended with an estimated 65% of troops killed, wounded or captured. The invasion plans were shelved in favour of increased operations in North Africa and Italy, which would also buy the Allied commanders more time to assemble the massive quantity of *matériel* and human resources necessary for such a perilous undertaking.

The decision to go was eventually made in late 1943 at the Tehran conference, attended by the 'Big Three' leaders – Churchill, Stalin and Roosevelt. Hitler's devastating losses on the Russian front had left Germany vulnerable, but the question of where – and when – to attempt the landings wasn't so straightforward.

The most obvious choice was the shortest route, straight across the Pas de Calais, but the Germans had foreseen the danger and heavily refortified Calais as the strongest point in Hitler's 'Atlantic Wall', and the Dieppe raids had made Allied commanders wary of another direct assault on a heavily defended port. Holland and Belgium were too close for comfort to the Luftwaffe's German bases, while Norway and southern Brittany were too far away to ensure air supremacy. After much deliberation, the decision was made: the Allies would make their stand on the beaches of the Normandy coast. The preparations for D-Day had begun.

THE BUILD-UP

The plans for Operation Overlord entailed a frontal assault by two army groups (the US First Army and British Second Army) consisting of five

D-DAY DEBATE

D-Day: it's one of the most recognisable code names in the history of warfare, but rather oddly, no one can quite remember what the D was supposed to stand for. In a television interview years after the event, Dwight Eisenhower recalled that it signified 'Debarkation', others thought it stood for 'Designated' or 'Deliverance', while veterans often chillingly joked it signified 'Death' or 'Doom'. In fact, it probably didn't stand for anything at all – the D is simply the initial letter of 'day', signifying the first phase of a military campaign, just as 'H-Hour' represented the first hour of an assault.

seaborne divisions, 13,000 aeroplanes and 6000 vessels. Three paratroop divisions (the British 6th Airborne and US 82nd and 101st) would land in advance of the main landings to secure key objectives behind enemy lines. The initial force involved 45,000 troops; 15 further divisions were to follow once beachheads had been established. The proposed landing area stretched across five beach sectors (code named Sword, Juno, Gold, Omaha and Utah) covering 80km between Caen and Ste-Mère-Église.

Allied intelligence went to extraordinary lengths to encourage the German belief that the invasion would be anywhere but Normandy. Double agents, leaked documents and fake radio traffic suggested the invasion would centre on the Pas de Calais, reinforced by phoney airfields and even a fictitious American army group, supposedly stationed in the southeast of England. The Allies were further helped by the fact that the Germans' supposedly unbreakable Enigma code had been cracked at Station X (Bletchley Park in Buckinghamshire), enabling them to read the Germans' secret communications.

Because of the tides and unpredictable weather, Allied planners had only a few days each month in which to launch the invasion. On 5 June, the original date chosen, the worst storm in 20 years set in, unexpectedly delaying the operation. The weather had only marginally improved the next day, but General Dwight D Eisenhower, the Allied commander-in-chief, gave the go-ahead: 6 June would be D-Day.

D-DAY DAWNS

In the early hours of D-Day, the BBC World Service released coded messages to alert the French Resistance that the invasion was imminent, and demolition teams set about disrupting German communications, blowing up railway lines and cutting telephone wires. Just after midnight on 6 June, the first troops were on the ground. British commandos and glider units captured key bridges and gun emplacements, including Pegasus Bridge and the massive gun battery at Merville. The American 82nd and 101st Airborne regiments landed west of the invasion site around St-Mère-Église and Vierville. Although the paratroops' tactical victories were few, they caused enormous confusion in German ranks (famously, fake paratroop divisions consisting of dummies, firecrackers and looped gramophone messages fooled the Germans into thinking the invasion force was much greater than it actually was).

'the Germans' supposedly unbreakable Enigma code had been cracked at Station X'

Just before 6am, waves of Allied bombers dropped high explosives onto the beaches, and naval ships opened up with a devastating artillery bombardment in an effort to destroy the Germans' positions and terrify the defenders into submission. Unfortunately, the Germans had constructed their bunkers and gun emplacements with customary efficiency – the vast majority of positions remained intact after the initial bombardment, with mortars and heavy machine guns pre-zeroed on practically every inch of beach. In addition, the German commander of the Atlantic Wall, Field Marshal Rommel, had laid antitank obstacles, underwater obstructions, several thousand miles of barbed wire and six million mines all along the five invasion beaches.

BACKGROUND

SWORD, JUNO & GOLD

These three beaches were assaulted by the British 2nd Army (which also included Canadian, Commonwealth, Free French and Polish troops) under General Bernard 'Monty' Montgomery, the legendary British commander who had defeated Rommel's forces at the Battle of Alamein in 1942.

At Sword Beach (Colleville), initial German resistance was quickly overcome and the beach was secured within hours. Infantry pushed inland from Ouistreham to link with paratroops around Ranville, but they suffered heavy casualties as their supporting armour fell behind, trapped in a massive traffic jam on the narrow roads. Monty was convinced he would be able to take Caen on the first day – by 4pm his troops were within 5km of the city's outskirts – but a determined German counterattack forced them to fall back and dig in.

At Juno Beach (Courseulles, Bernières and St-Aubin) Canadian battalions landed quickly but had to clear the Germans trench by trench. Mines took a heavy toll, but by noon the Canadians were south and east of Creuilly. Late in the afternoon the German armoured divisions that had halted the British coming from Sword Beach were deflected towards the coast. They held Douvres, threatening to drive a wedge between the Sword and Juno forces, but the threat of encirclement made them withdraw the next day.

At Gold Beach, the attack by the British forces was at first chaotic, as unexpectedly high waters obscured German underwater obstacles. By 9am, though, Allied armoured divisions were on the beach and several brigades pushed inland. By afternoon they had joined up with the Juno forces and were only 3km from Bayeux.

OMAHA & UTAH

The struggle on Omaha (Vierville, St-Laurent and Colleville) was by far the bloodiest of the day. Omaha stretched 10km from Port-en-Bessin to the mouth of the River Vire and was backed by 30m-high bluffs. From the outset the Allies' plans were thrown into chaos. The beach was heavily defended by three battalions of heavily armed, highly trained Germans, including the veteran 352nd Infantry Division, which had recently been moved into the area for training exercises. Even worse, the naval and air bombardments had largely overshot their targets and strong winds blew many landing craft far from their carefully planned landing sectors.

The 1st US Infantry Division (the 'Big Red One') launched the attack on Omaha

DON'T MISS...

D-DAY SITES

- ★ **The Caen Mémorial //** Immerse yourself in the events of D-Day at this world-class museum (p191)
- ★ **Omaha Beach and Military Cemetery //** Pay your respects on the sands of bloody Omaha (p187)
- ★ **Pointe du Hoc //** Marvel at the feats of the Texas Rangers (p186)
- ★ **Batterie-de-Longues //** The great 152mm guns still sit at this German emplacement (p187)
- ★ **Arromanches 360 //** Visit the excellent military museum and see the remains of one of the Mulberry Harbours (p188)

BACKGROUND

and immediately ran into a hail of murderous fire. Many troops, heavily overloaded with equipment, disembarked in deep water and drowned; others were cut to pieces by machine-gun and mortar fire from the cliffs. Only two of the 29 Sherman tanks made it to shore, equipment was scattered all over the beach, and it proved impossible to advance up the beach as planned.

By midday the situation was so serious that General Bradley, in charge of the Omaha beach forces, considered abandoning the attack; but eventually, soldier by soldier, metre by metre, the GIs began to gain a precarious toehold. Assisted by naval bombardment, the US troops blew through a key German strongpoint and at last began to move off the beach, but the statistics tell their own story: of 2500 American casualties sustained on Omaha on D-Day, more than 1000 were killed, mostly within the first hour of the landings.

> 'The struggle on Omaha was by far the bloodiest of the day'

Matters were little better over at Pointe du Hoc, where Colonel Earl Rudder's Texas Ranger Battalion was struggling straight up 30m cliffs in an attempt to seize a nest of huge German howitzers. Unfortunately, the guns had been moved from the position days earlier, and the Rangers were forced to hang on for two ferocious days of fighting before they were eventually relieved by troops breaking out of Omaha Beach.

In contrast to the events at Omaha, US forces at Utah Beach faced relatively light resistance, taking large tracts of territory to the west of the beach within hours of the invasion, hooking up with paratroopers who had already captured the strategic town of Ste-Mère-Église.

THE BATTLE OF NORMANDY

Four days after D-Day, the Allies held a coastal strip 100km long and 10km deep. Montgomery's forces drew the Germans towards Caen, where fierce fighting continued for more than a month and reduced the city to rubble.

The prized port of Cherbourg eventually fell to the Allies on 27 June after a series of fierce battles, but not before the retreating Germans had sabotaged many of its vital harbour facilities. To overcome such logistical problems, the Allies had devised the remarkable 'Mulberry Harbours', huge temporary ports that were set up off the Norman coast.

Meanwhile, US troops pushed northwards into the Cotentin Peninsula, but were hampered by the area's extensive *bocages* (hedgerows), which provided ready-made defensive positions for the retreating Germans. After fierce fighting, the Americans captured the vital communications centre of St-Lô, and by the end of July had smashed through to the Breton border.

By mid-August, two German armies had been surrounded near Argentan and Falaise (the so-called 'Falaise Pocket'). Sensing the trap, German commanders ordered an immediate retreat, but not before more than 10,000 troops had been killed and another 50,000 taken prisoner. On 20 August, US forces crossed the Seine at several points around Paris. Symbolically lead by General Charles de Gaulle, France's leader-

HOBART'S 'FUNNIES'

British forces used a range of bizarre mechanical contraptions in their D-Day assault, which were nicknamed 'Funnies' by troops on account of their weird and wonderful designs. They were dreamt up by the British Major-General, Percy Hobart, as a response to some of the problems faced during the Canadians' ill-fated assault on Dieppe in 1942. Among the more outlandish contraptions were the Crab, a Sherman tank with a flail to detonate mines; the ARK, which featured extendable ramps to span ditches and tank-traps; the Crocodile, a Churchill tank capable of spitting out 100m jets of superheated flame; and the AVRE, which fired 40lb projectiles (nicknamed 'Flying Dustbins') powerful enough to knock out a concrete bunker.

in-exile, the first French troops arrived on the streets of Paris on 25 August, and by that afternoon the city – and effectively the entire French nation – had been liberated.

The Battle of Normandy was over, but it came at a terrible price. During the course of the campaign, the Germans lost 200,000 soldiers, with an equal number taken prisoner. Some 53,000 Allied soldiers were killed, more than 150,000 were wounded and nearly 20,000 were listed as missing in action. Statistics for civilian deaths are harder to come by, but it's thought that Normandy's five *départements* lost between 15,000 and 35,000 lives in the fierce battle for liberation.

THE AGE OF IMPRESSIONISM

• • • • • • •

During the mid- to late 18th century, some of the greatest painters of the age pitched up along the shores of Brittany and Normandy in search of fresh scenery, new subjects and unpainted skies, attracted by the area's unspoilt scenery and unique quality of light. Their experiments with colour, movement, light and form were a reaction against the strictures of classical French painting, and ultimately developed into one of the most influential movements in the history of art – but they certainly weren't the first artists to draw inspiration from the Norman landscape.

THE EARLY YEARS

Normandy's earliest art can be found in the *enclos paroissiaux* (parish enclosures) of the Élorn Valley and the medieval churches of Kermaria-an-Iskuit (p70) and St-Gonéry (p73). Two early artists, Jean Jouvenet (1644–1717) and Jean Restout (1692–1768), both concentrated predominantly on religious subjects, but it was the classical painter Nicolas Poussin (1594–1665), born near Les Andelys in 1594, who put the region on the artistic map. Voltaire wrote that French painting began with Poussin. Strongly influenced by Titian and Raphael, Poussin's striking composition, dramatic colours and mythological subjects set the benchmark for 'classical' French painting that endured for the next three centuries.

But in the century after Poussin's death, a new generation of artists, writers and thinkers across Europe became increasingly dissatisfied with academically defined notions of order and beauty, and began to move away from classical scenes in favour of more contemporary subjects. Painters such as Rouen-born Théodore Géricault (1791–1824) and Eugène Délacroix (1798–1863) led the way, drawing inspiration from recent French history and prominent people of the day, while other artists experimented with the drama of the natural landscape – cloud-capped mountains and lonely hilltops, peaceful meadows and pastoral countryside. These shifts, coupled with a growing preoccupation with light, colour and expressive brushwork rather than carefully modelled subjects, underpinned the development of the Romantic movement and proved an important inspiration for the artists who followed.

The great English landscape artist Joseph Turner (1775–1851) was an early convert to the Norman coastline. His dreamy depictions of Dieppe and Rouen, bathed in hazy light and watery colours, prefigured many of the presiding concerns of the Impressionists. Gréville-born Jean-François Millet (1814–75) emerged as another key figure. After studying art in Cherbourg and Paris, he joined the 'Barbizon School', a group of French painters based on the Île-de-France known for their naturalistic depictions of real people and everyday scenes, and their doctrine of painting on location to capture the immediacy of a scene.

Another influential figure was the Swiss-born artist Gustave Courbet (1819–77), who courted controversy by depicting supposedly 'vulgar' subjects, especially pastoral peasants and the working poor – not to mention some highly provocative nudes, the most famous of which, *L'Origine du Monde*, still caused a major stir when it was acquired by the Musée d'Orsay in Paris in 1995. Many of Courbet's works were a direct reaction against the classical aesthetics advocated by the French Academy; he sought beauty in strange, sometimes shocking places, treating his subjects in an unromanticised and often confrontational ways.

For Courbet and the Realists, the immediacy of the artist's experience was everything. As his work developed, Courbet increasingly favoured loose, spontaneous brushstrokes over carefully observed elements of line and form. A visit to the Norman coastline in 1869 inspired a series of wild seascapes (including the famous *La Mer Orageuse*, known in English as *The Wave*), in which he painted and repainted the same scene in an attempt to capture the ocean's raw, feral quality and explore the interplay between light, sea and landscape. As a creative endeavour, it clearly struck a chord with the young Claude Monet, who was just beginning his own artistic experiments along the Normandy coastline around the same time.

MONET & THE IMPRESSIONISTS

Courbet and Monet weren't the only painters exploring the artistic possibilities of northern France. The area's proximity to Paris (along with the newly invented railway) enabled many famous artists to make artistic sojourns to the Norman coastline: Étretat's cliffs attracted Delacroix and Corot, Manet headed for Cherbourg, Pissarro chose Rouen, and Degas and Whistler 'discovered' Dieppe in the 1880s.

For most 19th-century painters the coast was a part-time subject, a convenient opportunity to escape the smog and society of the big city, but for the Honfleur-born painter Eugène Boudin (1824–98) it became a lifelong obsession. The new craze for seaside holidays provided him with a wealth of subjects; his canvases shimmer with the light and optimism of the *belle époque,* depicting elegant gents and crinoline-dressed ladies strolling along the seafront promenades of Normandy's fashionable *stations balnéaires* (seaside resorts).

But while Boudin's canvases certainly provide an evocative insight into the fashions of France's golden age, they're actually more interesting for their fascination with atmosphere. In his best works, you can almost feel the salty tang of the sea air, the hazy beach light and the soft tug of the ocean breeze oozing from the canvas, while his figures are often blurred,

DON'T MISS...

ART MUSEUMS

★ **Musée des Beaux-Arts //** Highlights of the region's pre-eminent arts institution include Poussin's *Venus Presenting Arms to Aeneas* (1639) and Monet's *La Cathédrale de Rouen, temps gris* (1894; p240)

★ **Musée Malraux //** Monet, Gaugin, Renoir and Delacroix are just some of the big names at Le Havre's art museum (p223)

★ **Musée de Pont-Aven //** Get the low-down on the Pont-Aven artists (p112)

★ **Musée Eugène Boudin //** Reconsider the work of the forgotten father of Impressionism (p214)

★ **Musée des Impressionismes //** Giverny's art museum has a new Impressionist focus (p252)

BACKGROUND

hazy impressions, designed to reflect a world in a perpetual state of motion. It didn't yet have a name, but the spirit of Impressionism was clearly already at work in Boudin's imagination.

Boudin's work interested many young artists, including Camille Pissarro, Frédéric Bazille, Alfred Sisley, Berthe Morisot, Mary Cassatt and Paul Cézanne, but his most passionate pupil was a gifted young artist by the name of Claude Monet. Born in Paris in 1840, Monet was initially educated at the Secondary School of Arts in Le Havre, but met Boudin during a painting expedition to the Normandy coast in 1857. The two quickly became friends, and Boudin introduced Monet to the possibilities of oils and *plein-air* (outdoor) painting. Together this loose group of artists staged their first joint exhibition in Paris in 1874, having had their work rejected by the stuffy French Academy on several occasions. The reaction was mixed, but over the coming years their work gained public and critical acceptance, and they staged another eight shows during the late 1870s and early 1880s. While they certainly weren't a great financial success, the exhibitions helped define the fundamental principles of a new artistic movement – Impressionism, which took its title from one of Monet's seminal early paintings, *Impression, Soleil Levant* (Impression, Sunrise), painted in 1872.

> '*Boudin's canvases shimmer with the light and optimism of the belle époque*'

Monet spent the next few years travelling widely throughout France and Europe. Following periods in Paris, London and Holland (interrupted by a short-lived stint in the African Light Cavalry), Monet returned to Normandy following the death of his wife Camille from tuberculosis in 1879. Stricken by grief and unsure of his artistic future, he rediscovered the delights of the Normandy landscape, producing several famous paintings of the Seine, the cliffs of Étretat (p224) and the rugged shoreline of Belle-Île-en-Mer (p127).

But it was deep in the Norman countryside where Monet rediscovered his creative muse. He fell in love with an old farmhouse near the quiet village of Giverny and set about converting it into an ideal artistic haven, adding greenhouses, studios and gardens laid out according to his own exacting designs. Here he lived with his two sons, his second wife, Alice Hoschedé, and her five children from her previous marriage to the retail magnate and art collector Ernest Hoschedé.

> '*Monet's Nymphéas paintings have come to represent the zenith of the Impressionist movement*'

Encouraged by his new domestic stability and an increasing commercial interest in his work, Monet created some of the most iconic works of the Impressionist movement at Giverny over the next 43 years, including his celebrated 'Series' paintings, in which he repeatedly painted the same subject in order to capture the effect of the changing light and shifting colours on the scene. Often working on several canvases at once, Monet's series covered subjects as diverse as Rouen Cathedral, the River Seine, a field of haystacks and a poplar meadow, but it was his shimmering evocations of his Giverny gardens (particularly its lily ponds) that proved the most enduring. Later in life, Monet suffered from cataracts and underwent two major eye operations; many academics think the treatment permanently affected his perception, and might even have helped inspire the ethereal light and quasi-abstract forms of the later *Nymphéas* (Waterlilies) paintings, which have come to represent the zenith of the Impressionist movement.

Monet's most famous canvases are scattered throughout the world's major art institutions, but he's still on show at several of the region's museums (see p271), and, of course, you can also visit the gardens that so inspired him at his house in Giverny (p252). Make the most of the scenery – the same view cost one buyer a cool £41 million when one of Monet's *Nymphéas* paintings was sold at Christie's in London in June 2008.

BRETON CULTURE

· · · · · · ·

Brittany's history as an autonomous nation ended with the Act of Union in 1532, but the treaty certainly didn't mark the end of Breton culture. Arguments over independence, autonomy and the relationship between Brittany and the rest of France have continued to rumble for the last four centuries. In many ways it's the area's complex history, culture and regional identity that make it such a fascinating place to visit.

POLITICS

Following the abolition of the Breton parliament after the French Revolution, the first recognisable political movements emerged during the industrial expansion of the 19th century. Socialist campaigners and union movements found fertile ground among Brittany's blue-collar workers, who often felt exploited and neglected by the privileged political elite in Paris. This sense of estrangement was reinforced by the catastrophic losses of WWI; many young Breton men joined up in an effort to escape the poverty and hardship back home, only to find themselves plunged into infinitely worse conditions in the trenches of the Western Front. By the end of the war in 1918, casualties in Breton regiments were double the national average.

In the wake of these experiences, the Breton nationalist movement steadily gained ground during the early 20th century. The first openly pro-Breton movement, the URB (Union Régionaliste Bretonne), had been founded in 1898, followed two years later by the Gorsedd of Brittan, which aimed to preserve Brittany's native language and bardic traditions. In 1925 the political activist Morvan Marchal designed a new Breton flag, the Gwenn ha Du (see below), to help galvanise support for the independence cause.

As the century wore on, Brittany's political movements began to fracture along federalist and nationalist lines. Parties such as the LFB (Ligue Fédéraliste de Bretagne) proposed increased integration with the French state, while the hard-line

---

BRETON EMBLEMS

Brittany's oldest symbol is the **triskelion** (from the Greek *triskeles*, meaning 'three-legged'), a three-armed spiral used by the ancient Celts, and later revived as a Breton emblem during the 1920s (it's also used by the Isles of Scilly and the Isle of Man).

During the Middle Ages, Brittany's heraldic symbol was the **ermine**, a spiked triangle topped by three 'spots', representing a flattened ermine pelt. Traditionally used on Brittany's coat of arms, these days the symbol graces everything from town signs to biscuit boxes, but its most obvious incarnation is in the top-right corner of the **Gwenn ha Du**, Brittany's official flag. Taking its name from the Breton for 'white and black', the flag features nine stripes – five black (representing Brittany's five bishoprics of St-Malo, St-Brieuc, Dol, Nantes and Rennes) and four white (representing the four counties of ancient Brittany: Cornouaille, Trégor, Léon and Vannetais).

BACKGROUND

PNB (Parti Nationaliste Bretagne) advocated an independence-or-nothing agenda. The PNB's militant wing (also called the Gwenn ha Du), was responsible for the first terrorist act on Breton soil, when they blew up a statue commemorating the Act of Union in 1932. The party later allied itself with the occupying Nazi regime during WWII – an inconvenient truth that has left a lasting stain on the Breton nationalist cause.

After WWII, the decision to divide Brittany between two French administrative regions (Bretagne and Pays de la Loire) – which involved the 'loss' of the region's historic capital, Nantes – caused considerable resentment. But in a region reeling from the horrors and hardships of war, not to mention the harsh realities of militant nationalism, there was an increasing desire to define Brittany's cultural heritage within the context of the French state. Left-wing federalist parties such as the Union Démocratique Bretonne (UDB) gained a surge in support after the war, helped by the foundation of cultural festivals such as the Festival InterCeltique in Lorient and the Festival de Cornouaille in Quimper in the 1960s, and the development of the first Breton-language (Diwan) schools in the 1970s.

> ### DON'T MISS...
>
> Here are some ideas of how to get a feel for Breton culture by participating in the local customs.
>
> ★ Attending a lively *festou-noz* (night festival; p14)
> ★ Tucking into the hearty dish of *Kig Ha Farz* (p279)
> ★ Sipping a Breton beer in the historic cities of Rennes (p50) and Nantes (p144)
> ★ Bopping to the Breton beat at Lorient's Festival InterCeltique (p121)
> ★ Visiting the Musée Départemental Breton (p104) in Quimper

The UDB remains the major force in Brittany's political landscape, advocating increased autonomy for the Breton region, the protection of the Breton language, and ultimately the establishment of a devolved Breton parliament, after the Scottish and Welsh examples. The UDB's major opposition comes from the Parti Breton (Strollad Breizh), which argues for an 'emancipated and reunited Brittany' that can effectively represent itself independently from France within the European Union. The hard-line independence parties have haemorrhaged support in recent years; the Parti pour l'Organisation d'une Bretagne Libre imploded in 2002, leaving Emgann and a few other minor parties to pursue the nationalist agenda. Unfortunately, violence hasn't entirely disappeared from Breton politics: since the Front de Libération de la Bretagne launched its first attacks in the 1960s, various armed groups have continued sporadic terrorist campaigns, including the Armée Révolutionnaire Bretonne (ARB), whose most recent attack was in April 2000, when a bomb in a McDonald's restaurant in Quévert, near Dinan, left one person dead.

'few Bretons see the sense in completely divorcing themselves from the French state'

The vast majority of modern Bretons support cultural causes, particularly increased autonomy, the restoration of the 'lost' Loire-Atlantique *départmente* and

BACKGROUND

better teaching of the Breton language – opinion polls published in the regional newspaper *Le Télégramme* in 2000 revealed 23% of Bretons were sympathetic to some of the causes espoused by separatist parties and 49% were in favour of the compulsory teaching of the Breton language in schools. But very few Bretons see the sense in completely divorcing themselves from the French state, and in local elections, the separatist parties have never polled more than a few per cent of the vote.

THE BRETON LANGUAGE

If there's one issue guaranteed to get even the quietest Breton hot under the collar, it's Brezhoneg (the Breton language). First introduced by Celtic migrants from Britain in the 5th and 6th centuries, Brezhoneg has become a powerful symbol of Brittany's cultural revival.

Historically, Brezhoneg is a Brythonic language closely related to Cornish and Welsh. Until the French Revolution, it was widely spoken throughout Brittany, but the new republic banned its use in schools and punished children who spoke it. Like other Celtic languages, Brezhoneg became stigmatised as a language of the poor, uneducated and illiterate, and by the late 19th century it had become rare to hear the language spoken openly in public.

Numbers of native speakers declined by around 80% between 1880 and 1950, but during the 1960s a concerted effort was made to bring the language back from the brink. The old law prohibiting its use in schools was overturned, and many idealistic young Bretons rediscovered their native language during the radical years of the 1960s. But like many minority languages, Brezhoneg was more often spoken than written down, and the handful of medieval manuscripts that did exist bore little relation to the language as it was spoken by everyday people. Even more problematically, each of the four ancient Breton counties had their own distinct dialects, so deciding which one to champion as the 'standard' Breton language caused considerable problems.

But thanks to the dedicated work of academics and amateur linguists, a new form of 'standardised' Breton eventually began to emerge during the mid-20th century. The foundation of schools called Écoles Diwan (from the Breton for 'seed') in the 1970s, where pupils are taught entirely in the Breton language until they are aged seven or eight, was a major step forward; many state schools followed the example with their own bilingual approach (Div Yezh, 'Two Languages'), while Catholic schools developed their own Dihun ('Awakening') system.

By 2008, the Office de la Langue Bretonne counted 206,000 active Brezhoneg speakers, about 5% of the population. Bilingual road signs are now widespread, and the Breton language has its own radio stations, mobile network and television channel, TV Breizh. But despite the progress, the language is still in a precarious position. The number of Brezhoneg speakers continues to decline, and it's thought only 3% of people are actively engaged in passing the language on to their children. More worryingly, despite constant pressure from lobby groups, the French government still refuses to recognise Breton as an official language; according to the constitution, French is the only language of instruction allowed in state schools, a legal hangover from the days of the Revolution.

BRETON MUSIC

Swing by any Breton event, whether it's a *pardon* (religious procession) or a lively *fest-noz* (literally, 'night party'), and you're bound to catch a Breton band in full swing. Bretons are enormously proud of their musical traditions, and many of their instruments date back to the Middle Ages; the most common ones include the *biniou kozh*, a double-reeded bagpipe made of goat skin, known for its ear-splittingly shrill tone, and the *bombarde*, an early precursor of the oboe, usually made of ebony or fruitwood. Clarinets, accordions, harps and fiddles are also often used, and in some areas you might also hear instruments such as the *chalumeau* (hurdy-gurdy) and *veuze* (large bagpipes).

Nearly every town has its own *bagad* (marching band) consisting of bagpipes, *bombardes* and drums bashing out Breton melodies and Scottish-style reels. Lorient and Brest hold major *bagad* competitions, and there's an annual pipe-off at the Festival InterCeltique every August. Smaller duos known as *sonneurs* feature Scottish and Breton pipers playing together.

Singing is another important element of much Breton music, from salty *chants de marins* (sea shanties) to *gwerzioù* and *sonioù* (laments and ballads), usually sung unaccompanied, and inspired by melancholy events such as wars, deaths and unrequited love. *Kan ha diskan* is another traditional form of singing, involving two singers (the *kaner* and *diskaner*) who sing alternate phrases in a call-and-response style.

Since the 1960s, Brittany has had a buzzing contemporary music scene. The pioneering harpist and composer Alain Stivell has perhaps done the most to put modern Breton music on the map, with a string of 22 albums, starting with the landmark *Renaissance de la Harpe Celtique* (1971). The crooner and Brezhoneg campaigner Gilles Servat, the Nantes-based folk-rock band Tri Yann, Breton rockers Soldat Louis and the Celtic supergroup Skolvan are among the best-known bands, while singer-songwriters such as Nolwenn Korbell, Denez Prigent and Dom Duff have helped keep the spirit of Breton singing alive.

> '*Since the 1960s, Brittany has had a buzzing contemporary music scene*'

More recent Breton bands have experimented with other styles of music – Wig-a-Wag have a distinctive world flavour, while Manau have made major waves with their groundbreaking fusion of Celtic folk and French hip hop. Brittany also hosts some major music festivals – check out p10 for details.

BRETON COSTUME

Another highlight of *pardons* and other community events is the chance to see traditional Breton costume. A century ago *koefs* (lace headdresses), *chupenn* (short jackets) and *giletenn* (waistcoats) were still a common sight. Each individual region had its own colours, styles and variations; it was possible to tell where someone came from (and often their wealth, age and status) simply from the cut of their jacket, the colour of their waistcoat or the style of their headdress.

BACKGROUND

Every occasion demanded its own outfit. For women, the standard garb consisted of a black dress, an embroidered bodice covered by a lacy white apron, and a lace bonnet, while men generally wore a white shirt, *bragou-braz* (baggy trousers), a black felt hat and a lavishly embroidered waistcoat. Outfits were livened up by ornaments: men often donned blingy belt-buckles, velvet hat ribbons or coloured waistcoats for special occasions, while women wore decorative 'pardon pins' made of copper, glass or silver. Waterproofed duffel coats known as *kabigs* were used by farmers and fishingfolk to protect them from the worst of the winter weather.

Perhaps the most outlandish piece of Breton costume is the *koef*, the hand-sewn lace bonnets worn by Breton women, which varied in style depending on where they were made. Most Breton women had two: one small one for everyday use, and another tall one reserved for special events. The most extravagant are those of the Pays Bigouden in southern Finistère, which could tower up to 36cm. You can see lots of Breton costumes at the Musée Départemental Breton in Quimper (p104) and the Musée Bigouden in Pont l'Abbé (p107).

FOOD & DRINK

· · · · · · ·

Eating your way around the region is one of the great joys of visiting Brittany and Normandy. Each region has its own culinary pleasures and peculiarities: in general, Norman cuisine tends to be richer and more elaborate, making ample use of the region's famous butters, creams and cheeses, while Breton cuisine tends to be more homely and down-to-earth. Seafood is the constant: each region takes full advantage of a huge coastline that brings in heaps and heaps of fresh fish and *fruits de mer*.

BRETON SPECIALITIES

Brittany's best known for its fresh produce and straightforward, no-nonsense *cuisine paysanne* (country cooking). Unlike its Norman neighbour, Brittany produces very little cheese, and its sole wine – Muscadet – slipped outside its borders when Loire-Atlantique was moved into the Pays de la Loire. Seafood, Guérande sea salt and *primeurs* (spring vegetables, especially cauliflower, carrots, artichokes, peas and pink onions) are the region's main exports, and of course Brittany is the spiritual home of the classic French fast food, the humble crêpe, and its savoury sister, the buckwheat galette.

FISH & SEAFOOD

Brittany is seventh heaven for fish fans. The region's lively *criées* (fish auctions) sell practically every fish and crustacean you can think of, but there are a few regional specialities to look out for. Cancale produces some of France's best oysters, while nearby St-Brieuc is renowned for its *coquilles de St-Jacques* (scallops) and *oursins* (sea urchins). Crabs from St-Malo and lobsters from Camaret, Concarneau and Quiberon are also highly prized by crustacean connoisseurs.

Most fish is presented simply to bring out its flavours, often in a *beurre blanc* (butter sauce). Other dishes on the Breton menu include *cotriade* (known as *godaille* in Loire-Atlantique), a hearty soup of fish and shellfish, sometimes called the 'bouillabaisse of the north', and *bar de ligne au sel de Guérande* (line-caught sea bass baked in a salt crust); the best bass is still caught by hand around the Pointe du Raz.

Brittany's most famous seafood dish is *homard à l'armoricaine* (lobster flambéed in cognac and simmered in a tomato, herb and garlic sauce). The origins of the name are a source of considerable debate – some chefs claim it stems from Brittany's ancient name, Armor ('land by the sea'), while others think it's a corruption of '*homard à l'Américaine*', and that the dish was invented by a chef who trained in Chicago.

MEAT & CHARCUTERIE

Brittany's meat dishes include *andouille* (smoked pork-tripe sausage, usually eaten cold), *andouillette* (tripe sausage) and *boudin* (black pudding), but the top cut is *agneau de pré-salé* (salt-marsh lamb), raised on the shores of the Baie du Mont St-Michel and prized for its salty, gamey flavour.

BACKGROUND

Kig ha farz, a rich stew of beef, pork and vegetables, is another Breton speciality, especially on winter menus. Its name comes from the Breton words *kig* (meat), *ha* (and) and *farz* (buckwheat flour), and it's usually served as a shared dish accompanied by buckwheat dumplings.

CRÊPES & GALETTES

Brittany's culinary superstars are crêpes and galettes, large thin pancakes made by spreading batter on a hot griddle (known as a *bilig* in Breton). Crêpes are made with ordinary wheat flour *(froment)*, while galettes are made using buckwheat flour *(sarrasin* or *blé noir)*. The classic galette filling is ham, egg and cheese, but you can choose anything from just a smear of butter to scallops in a champagne sauce. Crêpes are often eaten as a sweet dessert or snack, slathered in jam, stuffed with fruit or drowned in ice cream and chocolate sauce. *Crêpes dentelles* are the most indulgent version, rolled, dusted with sugar and baked until crispy.

CHEESE COUNTRY

If you like your cheese soft and smelly, Normandy is definitely the place for you. Monks first began experimenting with cheese-making in the Pays d'Auge in the 11th century, and Normandy is now home to some of the most celebrated names in French *fromage* (most protected by their own AOC – Appellation d'Origine Contrôlée – to prevent unauthorised copying).

Normandy's oldest cheese is **Pont l'Évêque**, a strong, soft cheese that gets its flavour from the rich pastureland between Deauville and Lisieux. **Livarot** (known as the 'colonel' because of the five stripes on its rind) is the most complicated to make, requiring frequent washing and a good month of ageing to develop its complex flavour. Other cheeses include the heart-shaped **Neufchâtel** and the **pavé d'Auge**, but the real superstar is **Camembert**, which two-thirds of French cheese buyers consider an essential element of any cheeseboard.

The invention of Camembert is generally credited to Marie Herel, who was supposedly given the secret of soft-cheese-making by an abbot from Brie on the run from revolutionary mobs in 1790. Production quickly grew from a cottage industry into an international operation; between 10,000 and 15,000 tonnes of Camembert are now produced in Normandy every year. Camembert is traditionally made from unpasteurised cow's milk and requires two moulds, *Penicillium candida* and *Penicillium camemberti*, to mature, a process that takes around three weeks. The distinctive round wooden boxes that are used have been around since 1890; they were designed by a local engineer, Monsieur Ridel, to protect the cheese during long-distance travel.

If you're buying Camembert, remember to squeeze your cheese before buying it to test its ripeness – the texture should be soft but not runny. A good Camembert should have a white rind with a sprinkling of reddish spots, and the taste should be strong and fruity. Most importantly, don't put it in the fridge – it needs to be served at room temperature, ideally on warm crusty French bread.

BACKGROUND

CAKES, DESSERTS & PASTRIES

Brittany's teatime treats include the *kouign amann* (butter cake), a rich sweet cake made with leavened dough, butter and sugar, and the *far Breton*, a heavy, golden flan flavoured with vanilla and prunes. Other sweets to look out for are *galettes de Pont-Aven* (shortbread biscuits), *niniches de Quiberon* (cane-sugar lollipops) and *salidou* or *caramels au beurre salé* (salt-butter caramels).

NORMAN SPECIALITIES

Two ingredients sum up Norman cuisine: salted butter and soft cheese. Norman cows produce an average of 5 tonnes of milk annually, so it's hardly surprising that the region supplies around half of France's total quota of milk, butter, cream and cheese. Normandy's top butter comes from Isigny-sur-Mer and even has its own AOC.

You'll often see dishes served *à la normande* in Normandy, which basically means they'll be served with a sauce made with butter, cream or cheese (sometimes even a combination of all three). Whichever way it's served, the calorie count is guaranteed to be through the roof.

FISH & SEAFOOD

Normandy's seafood specials include oysters and turbot from the Cotentin peninsula, scallops from Dieppe, and crabs, clams, mussels and flat fish all along the coast. *Sole à la normande* is a common sight on many menus, but each area adds its own signature touch, such as mussels and mushrooms in Dieppe, or shrimp in Fécamp and Trouville.

Dieppe is known for a hearty fisherfolk's stew, *marmite dieppoise*, served piping hot in a cast-iron casserole pan and accompanied by chips or crusty bread.

MEAT & CHARCUTERIE

Meat, lamb and poultry are ever present on Norman menus, often served in cider and Calvados-based sauces – but you might need a strong stomach to handle some regional delicacies. Perhaps the most blood-curdling is *caneton Rouennais*, in which a duckling is strangled, roasted and pressed and then served in a sauce prepared from the duck's heart, liver and blood simmered in red wine. The dish is such a delicacy it even has its own chefs' association, L'Ordre des Canardiers.

'If you like your cheese soft and smelly, Normandy is definitely the place for you'

Other carnivorous treats include *tripes à la mode de Caen* (cow's intestines stewed in cider, Calvados and vegetables), *andouille de Vire* (a seasoned sausage made from pig tripe) and *boudin* (blood sausage made with one-third pig's blood, one-third onion and one-third pig fat), which has its own festival held yearly in its honour, in Montagne-au-Perche.

Vegetarians look away now…

BACKGROUND

CAKES, DESSERTS & PASTRIES

Puddings are rather more palatable. Top of the list is scrummy *tarte normande,* a kind of apple pie with no top crust. *Tergoule,* sometimes called *terrinée,* is an oven-baked concoction of rice, sugar, milk and cinnamon, often enjoyed with *falue,* an eggy bread. You might also find yourself tucking into *bourdelots* or *douillons* (apples or pears encased in pastry), *sablés* (a round, crumbly pastry), *fouaces* (hearth cake) and *sucres de pomme* (apple sweets).

DRINKS

CIDER

Brittany is one of France's main apple exporters, so it's no surprise that cider's one of the most popular drinks. The length of fermentation determines the sweetness of the cider: *cidre doux* (sweet) is 2.5% to 3% proof, while *brut* (dry) is about 4.5%. Most cider is bubbly and, like champagne, comes in corked bottles. Look for *sec* (at least a year old), *pur jus* (no added water), *mousseux* (carbonated) or *bouché* (cider fermented in the bottle).

WINE

Normandy has never had a wine industry, and even Brittany has had to give up the business now that Nantes' Muscadet vineyards belong to the Pays de la Loire. Nevertheless, most restaurants offer a good selection of wines from all across France.

BEER & MEAD

True to its Celtic roots, Brittany produces some excellent local ales. The beer business was supposedly started by John Facan, an Irish Catholic on the run from English persecution, who founded the region's first commercial brewery in Quimper in 1624. While most of the big breweries have been squeezed out of business, microbreweries are flourishing throughout Brittany: top brands include the light ale Coreff, the dark Telenn Du (brewed from fermented buckwheat flour), the rich honey-flavoured Cervoise Lancelot and the pale Blanche Hermine (made with wheat and malted barley).

NORMAN AOCS

The label Appellation d'Origine Contrôlée (AOC) is the highest honour that can be bestowed on a French product, and signifies that the product comes from a specific area and is made according to a strict set of officially sanctioned standards. Normandy's AOC products include cream and butter from Isigny, four cheeses (Camembert, Livarot, Neufchâtel, Pont l'Évêque) and several types of cider and Calvados (including Pays d'Auge cider, Pommeau, Calvados, Calvados Pays d'Auge and Calvados Domfrontais). New AOCs are in the pipeline for several more ciders, as well as salt-marsh lamb from Mont-St-Michel and Bringé beef.

BACKGROUND

You may occasionally see *chouchen* (mead, sometimes known in Brittany as *hydromel*) in bars and cafés. It's a rich and sweet drink halfway between beer and wine, with an alcohol content around the 18% mark. Made by fermenting diluted honey, its origins are thought to date back to the Celts and Druids.

APÉRITIFS & DIGESTIFS

Pommeau is the most popular Norman *apéritif*. Made from apple juice and Calvados, it should be served cold but without ice – and it's around 18% proof so you probably won't be too legless. Start with plain Calvados, on the other hand, and you'll need a designated driver just to get to the dinner table. With an alcohol content of around 55%, this apple brandy certainly takes the sting out of a rainy Norman winter. Calvados is essentially cider that's been allowed to age for at least a year, but it's a notoriously complicated process: 40 different apples can find their way into a good brew, and its eventual quality depends on how long it's allowed to age in the oak barrels. Top vintages are at least five years old, and sometimes substantially older.

Fécamp's plant-based liqueur, Bénédictine, is another *digestif* you might sometimes see served in Normandy.

TROU NORMAND

With even everyday meals stretching to four courses, it's hardly surprising that Normans take a break halfway through. The traditional *digestif* is a shot of Calvados, known as the *trou normand* (Norman hole), although it's often replaced these days by a serving of Calvados sorbet. According to nutritionists, there might even be some sense in the idea – Calvados supposedly dilates the stomach lining, eliminating the feeling of fullness and allowing you to eat even more.

BACKGROUND

FOOD & DRINK GLOSSARY

· · · · · · ·

THE BASICS

addition (f) **a·dee·syon** bill
assiette (f) **as·yet** plate
coûteau (m) **koo·to** knife
cuillière (f) **kwee·yair** spoon
déjeuner (m) **day·zher·nay** lunch
dîner (m) **dee·nay** dinner
fourchette (f) **foor·shet** fork
petit déjeuner (m) **per·tee day·zher·nay** breakfast

STAPLES

beurre (m) **ber** butter
blé (m) **blay** flour
confiture (f) **kon·fee·tewr** jam
fromage (m) **fro·mazh** cheese
fromage de chèvre (m) **fro·mazh der she·vrer** goat's cheese
huile d'olive (m) **weel do·leev** olive oil
lait (m) **lay** milk
œuf (m) **erf** egg
pain (m) **pun** bread
pâtes (f) **pat** pasta
poivre (m) **pwa·vrer** pepper
potage (m) **pot·arzh** thick vegetable-based soup
riz (m) **ree** rice
sel (m) **sel** salt
sucre (m) **sew·krer** sugar

DRINKS

bière (f) **byair** beer
boisson (f) **bwa·son** drink
boisson gazeuse (f) **bwa·son ga·zers** fizzy drink
cidre (m) **see·drer** cider
café (m) **ka·fay** espresso/coffee
café au lait (m) **ka·fay o lay** milky coffee/latte
chocolat chaud (m) **sho·ko·la sho** hot chocolate
eau (f) **o** water
eau gazeuse (f) **o ga·zers** sparkling mineral water
eau plate (f) **o plat** still mineral water
jus (m) **zhew** juice
thé (m) **tay** tea
vin (m) **vun** wine

FISH & SEAFOOD

anchois (m) **on·shwa** anchovy
bar (m) **bahr** sea bass
belons (m) **ber·lon** flat oysters
cabillaud (m) **ka·bee·yo** fresh cod
calmar (m) **kal·mar** squid
coquilles St-Jacques (f) **ko·keey san zhak** scallops
crabe (f) **krab** crab
crevettes (f) **krer·vet** shrimp/prawns
daurade (f) **doh·rard** sea bream
espadon (m) **es·pa·don** swordfish
homard (m) **o·mar** lobster
huître (f) **wee·trer** oyster
langouste (f) **lang·goost** crayfish/rock lobster
langoustine (f) **lang·goos·teen** langoustine/Dublin Bay prawn
lotte (f) **lot** monkfish
loup (de mer) (m) **loo/der·mayr** sea bass
maquereau (m) **ma·kro** mackerel
morue (f) **mo·rew** salted cod
moules (f) **mool** mussels
palourde (f) **pa·loord** clam
poisson (m) **pwa·son** fish
rouget (m) **roo·zhay** red mullet
saumon (m) **so·mon** salmon
St-Pierre (f) **san·pyar** John Dory
thon (m) **ton** tuna
tourteau (m) **toor·to** large crab
truite (f) **trweet** trout

MEAT

agneau (m) **a·nyo** lamb
bœuf (m) **berf** beef
boudin noir (m) **boo·dun nwar** black pudding
brochette (f) **bro·shet** kebab
canard (m) **ka·nar** duck

confit (m) **kon·fee** meat cooked and preserved in its fat
cuisse (f) **kwees** leg/thigh
dinde (m) **dund** turkey
entrecôte (f) **on·trer·kot** rib steak
escargot (m) **es·kar·go** snail
faisan (m/f) **fer·zon** pheasant
faux-filet (m) **fo·fee·lay** sirloin steak
foie gras (m) **fwa gra** goose liver
gibier (m) **zhee·byay** game
gigot (m) **zhee·go** leg of lamb
jambon (m) **zhom·bon** ham
lapin (m) **la·pun** rabbit
lardon (m) **lar·don** cubed bacon
lièvre (m) **lye·vrer** hare
magret de canard (m) **ma·gray der ka·nar** duck
breast
oie (f) **wa** goose
porc (m) **por** pork
poulet (m) **poo·lay** chicken
poussin (f) **poo·sun** baby chicken
rognons (m) **ron·yon** kidneys
saucisson (m) **so·see·son** large sausage
tournedos **toor·ner·do** thick beef fillet
veau (m) **vo** veal
viande (f) **vyond** meat
volaille (f) **vo·lai** poultry

VEGETABLES & HERBS

ail (m) **ai** garlic
artichaut (m) **ar·tee·sho** artichoke
asperge (f) **a·spairz** asparagus
aubergine (f) **o·bair·zheen** eggplant
avocat (m) **a·vo·ka** avocado
basilic (m) **ba·zee·leek** basil
carotte (f) **ka·rot** carrot
champignon (m) **shom·pee·nyon** mushroom
chou (m) **shoo** cabbage
chou-fleur (m) **shoo·fler** cauliflower
citrouille (f) **see·troo·yer** pumpkin
courgette (f) **koor·zhet** zucchini
épinards (m) **ay·pee·nar** spinach
fenouil (m) **fe·nooy** fennel
flageolets (m) **fla·zho·lay** type of kidney beans
haricots blancs (m) **a·ree·ko blong** white beans
haricots rouges (m) **a·ree·ko roozh** kidney beans

haricots verts (m) **a·ree·ko vair** green beans
laitue (f) **lay·tew** lettuce
légumes (m) **lay·gewm** vegetables
maïs (m) **my·ee** sweet corn
oignon (m) **on·yon** onion
olive (f) **o·leev** olive
persil (m) **pair·see** parsley
petits pois (m) **per·tee pwa** peas
poireau (m) **pwa·ro** leek
poivron (m) **pwa·vron** capsicum
pomme de terre (f) **pom der tair** potato
romarin (m) **ro·ma·run** rosemary
safran (m) **sa·fron** saffron
tomate (f) **to·mat** tomato
truffe (f) **trewf** truffle

FRUIT & NUTS

amande (f) **a·mond** almond
ananas (m) **a·na·nas** pineapple
banane (f) **ba·nan** banana
cacahuète (f) **ka·ka·wet** peanut
cerise (m) **ser·reez** cherry
chataigne (f) **sha·tay·nyer** chestnut
citron (m) **see·tron** lemon
fraise (f) **frez** strawberry
framboise (f) **from·bwaz** raspberry
marron (m) **ma·ron** chestnut
noix (f) **nwa** walnut
pamplemousse (m) **pon·pler·moos** grapefruit
pêche (f) **pesh** peach
pomme (f) **pom** apple
raisin (m) **ray·zun** grape

DESSERTS

douillon (m) **doo·yon** pear cooked in pastry
far (m) **far** flan with prunes
gâteau (m) **ga·to** cake
glace (f) **glas** ice cream
sucre de pomme (m) **sew·krer der pom** sweet apple
dessert
tarte normande (f) **tart nor·mond** apple tart
tarte tatin (f) **tart ta·tun** apple tart
vienoisseries (f) **vyen·wa·zree** pastries
yaourt (m) **ya·oort** yogurt

BACKGROUND

COOKING METHODS

à point a pwun medium-rare

à l'américaine a la·may·ree·ken cooked in brandy, white wine and tomatoes

à l'étouffée a lay·too·fay steamed or braised

à la meunière a la mer·nyair fried in butter, lemon juice and parsley

à la vapeur a la va·per steamed

au feu de bois o fer der bwa wood-fired

au four o foor baked

beárnaise bay·ar·nayz herby white sauce

bien cuit(e) (m/f) **byun kwee(t)** well-done

bleu(e) (m/f) **bler** very rare (meat)

brochette bro·shet kebab

cassoulet ka·soo·lay casserole

chaud(e) (m/f) **sho(d)** hot

cru(e) (m/f) **krew** raw

dieppoise dyep·waz stew of fish, shellfish, herbs and cider

dijonnaise dee·zho·nez mustard sauce

en croûte on kroot in pastry

farci(e) (m/f) **far·see** stuffed

florentine flo·ron·teen in a creamy spinach sauce

fricassée free·ka·say flash-fried food/meat in a thick creamy sauce

froid(e) (m/f) **frwa(d)** cold

fumé(e) (m/f) **few·may** smoked

grille(e) (m/f) **gree·yay** grilled

jus zhew gravy/sauce

lyonnaise lee·o·nez sauce of browned onions, wine, garlic and parsley

normande nor·mond with cream or butter sauce

poché(e) (m/f) **po·shay** poached

poêlé(e) (m/f) **pwa·lay** pan-fried

provençale pro·von·sal tomato and herb sauce

rôti(e) (m/f) **ro·tee** roast

saignant(e) (m/f) **sen·yon(t)** rare (meat)

sauté(e) (m/f) **so·tay** sautéed

sec/sèche (m/f) **sek/sesh** dry

ACCOMMODATION

FINDING ACCOMMODATION

Whether you plump for a seaside villa, a backcountry retreat or a rural *chambre d'hôte* (French equivalent of a B&B), you won't be short on places to stay in Brittany and Normandy. Both regions are awash with accommodation to suit all tastes and budgets.

Hôtels in France range from small family-run affairs to national chains such as Citôtel, Contact, Kyriad, Inter-Hôtel and Sofitel. Throughout this chapter we've concentrated on choosing independently run places with real charm and character. French hotels are rated from one to four stars, although this is a fairly arbitrary system based on factors such as the size of the entry hall and whether or not the hotel has a swimming pool. Many hotels – especially those outside the major towns – also have their own restaurant; *soirée étape* also known as *demi-pension* (half-board) stays can be really good value. The **Logis de France** (www.logis-de-france.fr) organisation collates lists of hotels known for their warm welcome and good-quality food; one, two or three chimney ratings give a rough idea of the standards you can expect.

A little pre-trip research will turn up some really fantastic *chambres d'hôtes* properties, from converted windmills to country manors; we've picked out a few of our favourites for this chapter. Choose carefully and you might well find facilities easily measure up to a much more expensive hotel, and the owners are usually a great resource for local restaurant tips, sights and secret spots. Best of all, breakfast is often included in the room price.

The last option offering a roof over your head is a self-contained *gîte* (holiday cottage). Generally these are rented by the week or month, and are a great way of cutting costs if you're travelling *en famille* and don't mind basing yourself in one area. There are hundreds of places throughout Brittany and Normandy – far too many for us to cover here. Check out the boxed text (p288) for useful suggestions or contact the **Fédération Nationale des Gîtes des France**

ACCOMMODATION

(☎ 01 49 70 75 75; www.gitesdefrance.fr), which has extensive online listings and produces an annual printed guide.

Camping in Brittany and Normandy (as in most of the rest of France) is enormously popular. French campsites are star-rated in a similar way to hotels: at the bottom end are simple municipal campsites (which are often just a field with simple toilet facilities), while at the other end are the full-blown four-star campsites equipped with swimming pools, restaurants, self-catering chalets, tennis courts and practically every other leisure facility you could wish for. Staying at a top-notch campsite can often work out much the same price as a mid-range hotel. For this guidebook we've picked out a few of our favourite sites for each of the destination chapters.

PRICES AND BOOKING

As throughout France, prices take a hefty upwards hike during the busy seasons – especially Christmas, Easter and July to August, when most of France shuts up shop and heads off for *les grandes vacan-*

RENT YOUR OWN

Check out these websites if you're looking for a home away from home.

★ **www.gites-brittany.com** Searchable listings from all over Brittany.

★ **www.gites-de-france-charme.com** Cottages with a charming edge.

★ **www.gites-de-france-bretagne .com** Brittany-specific listings from the Gîtes de France organisation.

★ **www.gites-de-france-normandie .com** As above but for Normandy.

★ **www.holiday-chateau.com** Castles for rent, searchable by region.

BOOK YOUR STAY ONLINE

For more accommodation reviews and recommendations by Lonely Planet authors, check out the online booking service at www.lonelyplanet.com/hotels. You'll find the true, insider low-down on the best places to stay. Reviews are thorough and independent. Best of all, you can book online.

---

ces. In popular towns and seaside resorts, you could find prices double for even the most average of rooms, and many places are booked out months in advance; a bit of judicious pre-planning will lessen the impact on your pocket and won't leave you out on the street. Prices also tend to shoot up to coincide with major festivals such as Quimper's Festival de Cornouaille and Lorient's Festival InterCeltique. Many hotels also shut for a couple of months during the off-season, generally around November, January or February.

Booking ahead is always worthwhile, and essential during the peak periods. Usually you'll be asked to give a credit card number to secure the booking. Many hotels shut for a couple of hours at lunchtime, so checking in before 3pm is the exception rather than the rule. Apart from the big chains and city hotels, very few establishments are staffed around the clock: you'll often be given a separate key or *code d'acces* (keycode) to let yourself through the front door after-hours. Check-out time is generally between 10am and noon.

Lastly, remember that breakfast is almost never included in French hotel prices: factor in an extra €6 to €10 per person if you're planning on eating in. What you get can vary wildly depending on the establishment: some places lay on full-blown continental buffets, while others scrape by with a bit of yesterday's baguette and a pot of jam. Ask what the deal is when you're checking in; breakfast is by no means compulsory and you can often find much better value at a nearby café.

Accommodation reviews are grouped by chapter and location, and then presented in alphabetical order.

ILLE-ET-VILAINE

For details of camping options in the *département,* see boxed text, p48.

ST-MALO & AROUND

♥ HÔTEL CARTIER // ST-MALO €€€
☎ 02 99 56 30 00; www.hotel-cartier.com; 13 rue St-Vincent; s €60-130, d €70-150, tr €80-160; 🛜
Sexy, super-central digs in St-Malo, offering spacious rooms decked out in beiges, golds and creams (the newspaper-print lampshades are a nice touch, too). It's a classy affair, smart but not snooty, and you couldn't ask for a better old-city position.

♥ HOTEL ELIZABETH // ST-MALO €€
☎ 02 99 56 24 98; www.st-malo-hotel-elizabeth .com; 2 rue des Cordiers; d €80-145; 🛜
Compact and bijou are the watchwords at this old city townhouse, but while the rooms are hardly spacious, they're well equipped and quietly elegant. The hotel

has two buildings: the 'Armateurs' rooms have the most character, but you might well find yourself plonked into the less attractive 'Skippers' annexe during busy times.

♥ HÔTEL LE CROISEUR // ST-MALO €
☎ 02 99 40 80 40; www.hotel-le-croiseur.com; 2 place de la Poissonnerie; s €55-65, d €60-72, tr €75-85; 🅿 🛜
Tucked away beside the old fish market, this 'zen-hotel' is a soothing escape from the St-Malo hubbub. City-chic rooms are small but perfectly formed, with flat-screens, neutral colours and modern furniture throughout; some have double windows overlooking the courtyard. The urban theme continues downstairs, where coffee, cakes and pâtisseries are served right on the cobbled square.

♥ HÔTEL ST-PEDRO // ST-MALO €
☎ 02 99 40 88 57; 1 rue Ste-Anne; d €50-71; 🕐 Mar–mid-Nov; 🛜
Occupying a *malouinière* mansion beside the ramparts, this hotel is one of the best old-city deals. The 12 rooms are compact, all with a vague maritime feel; insist on a sea view if you can. The breakfast is a real spoil, with different daily treats including *pain perdu* (French toast), vanilla pannacotta, chocolate crêpes and a 'potion magique'.

♥ LE MONT FLEURY // ST-MALO €€
☎ 02 23 52 28 85; 2 rue du Mont Fleury; d €75-105, tr €108-128; 🅿
Sick of the crowds? No sweat – there's peace aplenty at this 18th-century house on the eastern city outskirts, offering four luxury-laced *chambres d'hôtes*. Top choices are the Chambre Orientale for its floaty fabrics and Moroccan *objets d'art*, and the Chambre Chinoise, with its hot-pink futon and spiral mezzanine staircase.

PRICE GUIDE

Throughout this chapter, we've based our prices on double rooms with bathrooms and tried to include seasonal variations (or room variations for Normandy) in the price ranges where possible. Price ranges used in the book are as follows:

€	under €70
€€	€70-150
€€€	more than €150

ACCOMMODATION

✿ HÔTEL DUGUAY-TROUIN // CANCALE €€

☎ 02 23 15 12 07; www.hotelduguaytrouin.com; 11 quai Douguay-Trouin; r €85-115; 🛜

There are plenty of posh establishments to choose from in Cancale, but our tip's this refreshingly simple seven-roomer right on the harbour front. The layouts are a bit awkward, but the maritime aura is pleasant and all rooms have DVD players, king-size beds and hydromassage showers.

✿ HÔTEL DE LA REINE-HORTENSE // DINARD €€€

☎ 02 99 46 54 31; 19 rue de la Malouine; d €150, d with sea view €215-245, ste €305-385; 🅿

Dinard was once the English gentry's favourite getaway, and you'll be regally treated at this lavish *belle époque* mansion. Massive rooms brim with aristocratic splendour – vintage bathtubs, antique furniture, upholstered armchairs – and three rooms have private verandahs overlooking the plage d'Écluse. Afternoon tea is served in a Napoleon III–era lounge. Utterly extravagant.

✿ HÔTEL PRINTANIA // DINARD €€

☎ 02 99 46 13 07; www.printaniahotel.com; 5 av George V; s €60-65, d €70-125, ste €215-220

You keep expecting Hercule Poirot to pop his head around the corner of this charmingly old-world hotel. Modern and minimal it isn't, but if you're a sucker for antique dressers, gilded mirrors and richly patterned rugs, you'll be chuffed to bits. The 50 rooms vary in size and style; don't even consider one without a harbour view.

✿ LE MESNIL DES BOIS // LE TRONCHET €€

☎ 02 99 58 97 12; www.le-mesnil-des-bois.com; Le Tronchet; d €95-120; 🅿

In a 16th-century mansion surrounded by groomed grounds are five bedrooms named after trees. Chêne (Oak) is tucked up in the eaves; Frêne (Ash) is criss-crossed by beams and lit by doll's-house windows; Charme (Hornbeam) is all rough-stoned, chandeliered splendour.

RENNES & AROUND

✿ HÔTEL NEMOURS // RENNES €€

☎ 02 99 78 26 26; www.hotelnemours.com; 5 rue de Nemours; s €57, d €67-80, f €90; 🛜

Rennes is short on quality sleeps, but this townhouse hotel makes up for the shortfall. It's a perfect city base, decked out in creams and charcoals, offset by the odd black-and-white photo or boutique piece. Double-glazing shuts out the street noise, and the breakfast features homemade bread, luxury jams and mini-pâtisseries.

✿ CHÂTEAU DES TESNIÈRES // TORCÉ €€

☎ 02 99 49 65 02; www.chateau-des-tesnieres.com; r €110-160; 🅿 🖵

You'll sleep like a king (or queen) at this mid-19th century, turret-crowned pile surrounded by 6 hectares of parkland, oak trees and fishponds, located near Vitré. Four of the five rooms are (justifiably) designated as suites, complete with free-standing tubs and private drawing rooms: the South Suite is contemporary, while the Count's and Countess' rooms ooze old-fashioned extravagance. The château is about 3km from the village of Torcé, just off the N157 east of Rennes.

CÔTES D'ARMOR

For details of camping options in the *département,* see boxed text, p65.

EASTERN CÔTES D'ARMOR

💗 HÔTEL-MANOIR DE RIGOURDAINE // PLOUËR-SUR-RANCE €€

☎ 02 96 86 89 96; www.hotel-rigourdaine.fr; d €68-82; Ⓟ

This country estate north of Dinan makes a fine place to retire to when the coastal crowds get too hectic. Wander among ponds and terraces in the private grounds, take afternoon tea in the beamed dining room, or relax in rooms with a choice of estuary or countryside views.

💗 HÔTEL DE LA PORTE ST-MALO // DINAN €

☎ 02 96 39 19 76; www.hotelportemalo.com; 35 rue de St-Malo; s €46-51, d €54-62, tr €65-71; Ⓟ 🖳

Surprisingly, Dinan is light on good places to stay. The best hotel is this solid stone two-starrer in the town's oldest quarter. Rooms are plain and pleasant, and a great breakfast buffet is served in the stone-arched salon or a cute interior courtyard.

💗 MALIK // PLÉLAN-LE-PETIT €€

☎ 02 96 27 62 71; www.malik-bretagne.com; Chemin de l'Étoupe; d €72-82, f €104-122; ☽ Easter-autumn

Bored with Breton character? These three modern wood-clad chalets a little west of Dinan might be just the ticket. Take your pick from Tea, Coffee and Chocolate, set around an old pasture full of roses and cedar trees. The pastel colours and feminine fabrics might be too frippy for some, but they're ideal if country cosiness is your cup of tea.

💗 CHÂTEAU DU VAL // NOTRE-DAME-DE-GUILDO €€

☎ 02 96 41 07 03; www.chateauduval.com; r €90-140, cabins €115; Ⓟ

A short spin inland from the beaches of St-Cast-le-Guildo, this fine old manor covers every base. There are old-fashioned, château-style *chambres d'hôtes* in the main manor house (including a couple with their own private sitting rooms), and around the grounds you'll find tree-top cabins and a couple of self-catering cottages.

💗 LA VILLA MARGUERITE // PLÉNEUF VAL-ANDRÉ €

☎ 02 96 72 85 88; www.villa-marguerite.fr; 34 rue des Garennes; d €60-65; Ⓟ

Each of the four romantic B&B rooms here has a flowery name. Our choices are 'Iris', with its floaty canopy and sky-blue tones, and 'Marguerite', with its king-size screened bed and parquet floor. Three rooms have double doors leading onto little beach-view balconies.

WESTERN CÔTES D'ARMOR

💗 LA DEMEURE // GUINGAMP €€

☎ 02 96 44 28 53; www.demeure-vb.com; 5 rue du Gal de Gaulle; s €66, d €85-145; Ⓟ 📶

Eighteenth-century grace is offered near the ramparts in Guingamp, at this place where the *chambres d'hôtes* are of a standard that puts many top-class hotels to shame. The building's antique character has been lovingly preserved during refurbishment – ask for Anne de Bretagne with its period panelling and private salon, or Roi Morvan with its parquet floor, private terrace and Louis XVI–style decor.

💗 CHÂTEAU DE BRÉLIDY // BRÉLIDY €€

☎ 02 96 95 69 38; www.chateau-brelidy.com; Brélidy; s €82-96, d €102-128, ste €140-168; Ⓟ 🚣

There's history in spades at this country château, built in the Breton Renaissance style and reconstructed over the last 15 years by the present owner. It's a true feudal pile, dotted with gabled windows, creaky hallways and even the odd suit of armour, although the rooms are underwhelming considering the spiffy setting.

♥ MANOIR DE KERGREC'H // PLOUGRESCANT €€

☎ 02 96 92 59 13; www.manoirdekergrech.com; d €110, tr €130-150, ste €170; Ⓟ

Here you'll find super *chambres d'hôtes* in a 15th-century manor. Rooms are unashamedly floral: some have antique dressers, others marble fireplaces and half-tester beds. The manor runs its own plant nursery and the Plougrescant beaches are just a stone's throw away.

♥ L'AGAPA // PERROS-GUIREC €€€

☎ 02 96 49 01 10; www.lagapa.com; 12 rue des Bons-Enfants; d €160-220; Ⓟ 🛜 🖳

Perros-Guirec is a favourite getaway for the Parisian jet set, so if you're going to stay in town, you may as well do so in style. This sexy seaside barnstormer brings a dash of Riviera class to northern Brittany: think chrome, glass and industrial finishes, Philippe Starck-esque design, and an utterly indulgent spa overlooking the Sept-Îles.

♥ CASTEL BEAU-SITE // PLOUMANAC'H €€€

☎ 02 96 91 40 87; www.castelbeausite.com; Plage de St-Guirec; d €110-210; Ⓟ 🛜 ♿

The anonymous rooms might not set your pulse racing, but the location will, perched on the shoreline of St-Guirec beach in Ploumanac'h. It's a classic modern beach hotel, strong on facilities, short on character, but ideal if it's a smart, efficient seaside retreat that you're after.

FINISTÈRE

For details of camping options in the *département*, see boxed text, p87.

MORLAIX & ROSCOFF

♥ HÔTEL DE L'EUROPE // MORLAIX €€

☎ 02 98 62 11 99; www.hotel-europe-com.fr; 1 rue d'Aiguillon; d €88-150, tr €95, f €120-150

This Morlaix grandee has been a town institution for over a hundred years, and it still has turn-of-the-century cachet. Glittering chandeliers, original coving and a massive staircase set the tone, although most of the rooms have had a bland modern-day refit. Breakfast is served in an art nouveau–era salon.

♥ MANOIR DE COAT AMOUR // MORLAIX €€

☎ 02 98 88 57 02; www.gites-morlaix.com; rte de Paris; d €89-105, f €160; Ⓟ

Live out those aristocratic fantasies at this heart-melting manor house in outer Morlaix. There are six upper-crust *chambres d'hôtes* – our choices are the soothing blue 'Chambre de Dulong de Rosay', with its Toile de Jouy wallpaper and double-aspect, and the regal four-postered 'Chambre de Général Maxime de Weygand'. *Gîte* accommodation is offered in a converted stable and gardener's cottage.

♥ HÔTEL DU CENTRE 'CHEZ JANIE' // ROSCOFF €€

☎ 02 98 61 24 25; www.chezjanie.com; Le Port; d €66-99, sea view extra €25

You couldn't wish for a better Roscoff base than this airy hotel perched above Chez Janie's bistro. Rooms are simply finished in white, offset by the odd crimson throw or stripy cushion. Each has a different maritime-themed poem painted on the wall, and the bathrooms positively gleam. The harbour views are worth the outlay.

❤ LE TEMPS DE VIVRE // ROSCOFF €€

☎ 02 98 19 33 19; 19 place Lacaze Duthiers; d €140-170, seaside rooms €225-268; 🛜 ♿

Despite the granite-fronted setting, the inside of this Roscoff hotel is all sexy, modern minimalism: sharp edges and sculptures in reception; chrome, wood and contemporary furniture in the bedrooms; and picture windows looking out over the bay. The only drawback? The seaside *'pieds dans l'eau'* rooms command an eye-watering premium.

NORTHWEST FINISTÈRE

❤ BAIE DES ANGES // ABER WRAC'H €€€

☎ 02 98 04 90 04; www.baie-des-anges.com; 350 rte des Angesr; €115-295, apt per week from €945; 🅿 🛜 ♨

This place consists of three impeccably finished houses along the Aber Wrac'h port. The main hotel occupies a granite shipowner's mansion; self-contained studios and apartments can be found in the *villa* and *résidence*. The interior design is glossy-mag calibre and the sea views are splendid, but it's the thoughtful touches (cardboard pillow angels, wicker-basket breakfasts, Swedish sauna) that really make this place.

❤ LA VINOTIÈRE // LE CONQUET €€

☎ 02 98 89 17 79; www.lavinotiere.com; 1 rue du Lieutenant Jourden; d €85-125; 🅿 🛜 ♿

Medieval architecture meets 21st-century style in a 16th-century house in Le Conquet. Neutral greys, off-whites and beiges offset the elegant finishes: pale wooden furniture, elegant bathrooms in slate and stone, and shutters looking out onto the seafront. Spot the original 16th-century staircase spiralling to the upper floors.

❤ TI JAN AR C'HAFÉ // ÎLE D'OUESSANT €€

☎ 02 98 48 82 64; hoteltijan@wanadoo.fr; Kernigou; d €68-98

Just about the only hotel worth its stripes on Ouessant, offering 10 rooms near the island's main town at Lampaul. The decor could do with updating, but the rural setting and gorgeous garden are tough to top.

❤ HÔTEL DE LA PAIX // BREST €€

☎ 02 98 43 30 95; 32 rue Algésiras; s €69-80, d €85-145, f €169-260; 🛜

This smart hotel in central Brest caters for a businessy crowd, so it feels faceless in places, but the facilities are top-notch: flat-screen TVs, wi-fi, safes, work desks and a complimentary newspaper with breakfast. Flash fixtures and fabrics in orange, yellow and crimson liven up the otherwise boxy rooms.

❤ HÔTEL ST-LOUIS // BREST €

☎ 02 98 44 23 91; www.brest-hotel.com; 6 rue Algésiras; d €35-40; 🕒 reception closed noon-5pm; 🛜

This sassy hotel has a 'boutique-on-a-budget' feel. The spartan rooms are livened up by eccentric flourishes – pop-art prints and quirky textiles, big splashes of green, puce and magenta paint, retro bathrooms tucked away inside cupboards. Yes, really! Many have double windows offering fab city views. Cheap, but kinda cool.

DOUARNENEZ & QUIMPER

❤ L'AUBERGE DE KERVÉOC'H // DOUARNENEZ €

☎ 02 98 92 07 58; www.auberge-kerveoch.com; 42 rte de Kervéoc'h; d €56-93; 🅿

It's a country retreat inside an authentic Breton farmstead – beams, wonky floors and all. Rooms are in the old

ACCOMMODATION

stable block, overlooking a colonnaded courtyard and grassy garden; they're a bit cramped and the layouts are quirky, but chock-full of charm. For breakfast, tuck into warm crêpes and homemade honey.

♥ TY MAD // DOUARNENEZ €€€
☎ 02 98 74 00 53; www.hoteltymad.com; plage St-Jean, Tréboul; d €105-191; Ⓟ ☎

This chic hideaway behind Tréboul beach oozes class from every polished corner. Three floors scream style with a 1960s accent: exposed stone and boutique fabrics sit alongside retro furniture, dress-shop mannequins and abstract art. Eleven rooms have sea views: try No 11 for its double aspect, or the sky-lit attic room (No 19).

♥ HÔTEL GRADLON // QUIMPER €€
☎ 02 98 95 04 39; www.hotel-gradlon.fr; 30 rte de Brest; d €102-160; Ⓟ ☎ ♿

Country house style in downtown Quimper. The rooms are a riot of floral wallpapers, heavy drapes and brass bedsteads, so if you're allergic to clutter, you're best off looking elsewhere. Wi-fi and flat-screen TVs lend a contemporary touch, though, and the city's on your doorstep.

♥ HÔTEL KREGENN // QUIMPER €€
☎ 02 98 95 08 70; www.hotel-kregenn.fr; 13 rue des Réguaires; d €80-180; Ⓟ ☎

Yes, yes, we know it's a Best Western – but this place is more Parisian *pied-à-terre* than cookie-cutter chain. Forget the usual off-the-shelf furnishings; here the reception desk is a from-scratch composition of granite and glass, and the rooms are an enticing mix of old and new: Breton stone sits alongside swirly bedspreads, plasma tellies as well as chocolate-and-cappuccino colours.

SOUTHERN FINISTÈRE

♥ VILLA TRI-MEN // COMBRIT €€€
☎ 02 98 51 94 94; www.trimen.fr; 16 rue du Phare; r €115-270; Ⓟ ☎

Overlooking the beautiful Bénodet estuary, this indulgent pamper-pad is the place to really spoil yourself in southern Finistère. Built in 1913, it looks like it has dropped out of the pages of a Fitzgerald novel: all shuttered windows and smart gables, with grassy gardens tumbling down into the bay. There are 20 utterly contemporary rooms to choose from, plus a few garden cottages if you've got the kids in tow.

♥ HÔTEL DES HALLES // CONCARNEAU €
☎ 02 98 97 11 41; www.hoteldeshalles.com; place de l'Hôtel de Ville; s €43-49, d €54-84, f €79-90

Don't be put off by the charmless concrete exterior: inside, this hotel is crammed with nautical curiosities, from deckchairs and portholes to model boats, seaside pictures and buoy-shaped key-fobs. The rooms are simple and shipshape; some are panelled in wood for extra cabin character.

♥ CHATEAU DE KERMINAOUËT // TRÉGUNC €€
☎ 02 98 50 19 68; www.chateaukerminaouet .joelmalice.com; Trégunc; d €90-180, gîtes per week €350-850; Ⓟ

There aren't many *chambres d'hôtes* that can match this country manor for architectural class: the turret-topped edifice dates from the mid-19th century, and has been renovated by a pair of Breton artists. Five rooms are named after characters from Arthurian legend, and most have views over the castle's grounds. Old outbuildings have been converted into self-contained *gîtes* for families.

❦ HÔTEL VINTAGE // QUIMPERLÉ €€

☎ 02 98 35 09 10; www.hotelvintage.com; 20 rue Brémond d'Ars; s €60, d €87-130; 🛜

Quimperlé makes a peaceful base, and this art-deco beauty is the best place to stay in town. It offers 10 rooms, 10 characters, all with individual decorative features. Bumping up to 'Prestige class' buys space, character and a hand-painted mural. The hotel also runs the excellent Bistro de la Tour restaurant (see p114).

❦ MANOIR DE KERTALG // MOËLAN-SUR-MER €€€

☎ 02 98 39 77 77; www.manoirdekertalg.com; d €115-210; Ⓟ 🛜 ♿

Yearning to stay in your own country castle? This fabulous 17th-century château sits deep in the Finistère countryside southwest of Quimperlé. Puffy quilts and heritage fabrics predominate, but it's the *seigneurial setting* you're splashing out on here: landscaped grounds, family oils and a baronial hall for taking your breakfast.

MORBIHAN

For details of camping options in the *département*, see boxed text, p126.

CARNAC & AROUND

❦ PLUME AU VENT // CARNAC €€

☎ 06 16 98 34 79; www.plume-au-vent.com; 4 venelle Notre Dame; d €75-90

You'll need to book early to bag your spot at this delightful *maison d'hôte*. There's only one room, but it's a beauty: floored in oak, dotted with old chairs and arty knick-knacks, with a private next-door lounge stocked with books and a refurbished sea-captain's desk.

❦ LA VILLA MANE LANN // PLOUHARNEL €€

☎ 02 97 58 31 99; www.villamanelann.com; d €75-110, duplex per night €110-128, per week in summer €990; Ⓟ 🛋

Extravagance is the watchword at this villa complex, set back from the Carnac crowds in Plouharnel. The elegant villas feature teak flooring and private sundecks, all with views over pine-shaded gardens and a gorgeous heated pool. Families can plump for the super-sized duplex versions.

❦ LE LODGE KERISPER // LA TRINITÉ-SUR-MER €€€

☎ 02 97 52 88 56; www.lodge-kerisper.com; 4 rue du Latz; d €95-180, ste €155-290; Ⓟ 🛜 🛋

Beach shack meets boutique hotel at this seaside retreat. Lashings of distressed wood and sloping ceilings studded with skylights create the feel of a luxurious chalet, but you certainly won't be slumming it – top-notch finishes, 'atelier'-style bathrooms and a luminous wood-decked pool are just some of the spoils in store.

❦ DIHAN // PLOEMEL €

☎ 02 97 56 88 27; www.dihan-evasion.org; Kerganiet; r €40-60, cabins €110-220; Ⓟ

Bring out your inner Tarzan at these wood-panelled cabins, perched among the tree-tops in Ploemel (the highest is a full 10m off *terra firma*), west of Auray. All have balconies overlooking the peaceful grounds, and – get this – breakfast is hoisted up to you in a basket. Mongolian yurts and B&B rooms are available if you prefer your feet to be on solid ground.

❦ LE CLOS DES EVOCELLES // AURAY €€

☎ 02 97 56 42 03; www.evocelles.com; 26 rue du Pont Neuf; r €80-120; 🛋

This *maison d'hôtes* in Auray is full of treats: a wood-lined sauna, a Turkish-

ACCOMMODATION

tiled *hammam,* a heated outdoor pool and five fancy rooms, ranging from coquettish Coquine (garden views, wicker drawers) to deluxe Aubergine (leather desk, luxury shower) and sexy Cacao (twisted willow and wood-panelling).

VANNES & AROUND

♥ VILLA CATHERINE // VANNES €€
☎ 06 79 24 36 88; www.villa-catherine.fr; 89 av Edouard Herriot; d €85-98; Ⓟ 🛜

The villa offers five frilly *chambres d'hôtes* on the edge of Vannes, all christened after flowers: try cosy Camélia, marine-themed Magnolia or Rose Pompadour, with its writing desk and original hearth. The owners run a tight environmental ship: ecofriendly products, anti-allergenic pillows and locally sourced goodies on the breakfast table.

♥ VILLA KERASY // VANNES €€
☎ 02 97 68 36 83; www.villakerasy.com; 20 av Favrel et Lincy; d €97-150, ste €320

The spectre of the East hangs heavy over this luxurious villa, which commemorates Vannes' historical role as a centre in the spice trade. Balinese furniture, oriental china and countless Buddhas conjure the feel of a colonial mansion. Top 'Prestige rooms' have private patios, and the Indian Suite overlooks the hotel's *jardin japonais.*

♥ HÔTEL DE L'ISLE // ÎLE AUX MOINES €€
☎ 02 97 26 32 50; www.hotel-de-lisle.com; rue du Commerce; d €75-120; 🛜

This charming hotel makes a lovely island escape. The rooms are christened after local beauty spots: top of the heap is the Salzen suite, which boasts a grand bed, timber floors and a tiny private terrace, but the Anse du Guip isn't a bad

backup; we loved the fishy-themed bathroom and the sand-dipper tapestry above the bed.

INLAND MORBIHAN

♥ LE MANOIR DU RODOIR // LA-ROCHE-BERNARD €€
☎ 02 99 90 82 68; www.lemanoirdurodoir.com; d €85-130; Ⓟ 🛜 🖳

Every inch of this Roche-Bernard mansion is cloaked in ivy, but inside it's a haven of cool, uncluttered simplicity. Unfussy, country-tinged rooms in creams and smoky blues make for a soothing sleep, but the main attraction is that you won't need a designated driver for dinner: the formal restaurant and more relaxed brasserie are both fantastic. It's just southeast of town.

♥ LE ROHAN // PONTIVY €€
☎ 02 97 25 02 01; www.hotelpontivy.com; 90 rue Nationale; s €60-82, d €72-100, ste €140-150; Ⓟ 🛜

This Pontivy hotel's camp themes run the decorative gamut from Oriental boudoir to a cinematic shrine to Marilyn Monroe (although some aren't quite as fancy as the owners think). The 'Chambres Nuptiales' are the pick of the bunch, but for top value ask for one of the self-catering apartments in the garden annexe.

LOIRE-ATLANTIQUE

For details of camping options in the *département,* see boxed text, p152.

NANTES & AROUND

♥ HÔTEL DES COLONIES // NANTES €
☎ 02 40 48 79 76; www.hoteldescolonies.fr; 5 rue du Chapeau Rouge; s €56-75, d €63-75

Local art shows revolve in the lobby of this city-centre hotel, while upstairs you'll find a painter's palette of rooms decked out in dusky pinks, lime greens and plush purples. The rooms are a bit boxy, but a good bet considering the price.

♥ HÔTEL LA PÉROUSE // NANTES €€

☎ 02 40 89 75 00; www.hotel-laperouse.fr; 3 allée Duquesne; r €86-149; P 🛜

It's a striking modernist hotel, which scooped a major European award in 1995, so you can count on top-quality design: pale hardwood floors, 'zigzag' concept chairs and quite possibly the poshest all-glass sinks this side of Paris. It's on one of the city's busiest shopping streets, so rooms are sized like clothes (L, XL, XXL). If you like your threads to be designer, you'll be smitten.

♥ HÔTEL POMMERAYE // NANTES €€

☎ 02 40 48 78 79; www.hotel-pommeraye.com; 2 rue Boileau; s €54-94, d €59-124; P 🛜

The period facade of this downtown hotel conceals a fresh, funky interior. Pass through the lobby with its puce chairs, panels and palm tree en route to well-groomed rooms, most with power-showers, groovy interiors and dinky balconies overlooking the city streets. Light sleepers beware on weekend nights.

♥ HÔTEL ST-YVES // NANTES €

☎ 02 40 74 48 42; www.hotel-saintyves.fr; 154 av du Général Buat; d €47-49, tr €55-60; 🛜

This place has to be one of Brittany's best bargains. Despite the bottom-of-the-barrel price tag, it's packed with thoughtful touches, from the 10 cute, individually styled rooms to the complimentary wi-fi and a barnstorming breakfast of cheeses, croissants, hams and pastries.

♥ ABBAYE DE VILLENEUVE // VIAIS €€€

☎ 02 40 04 40 25; www.abbayedevilleneuve.com; rte de La Roche sur Yon; d €95-230; P

The Revolution took its toll on this superb 15th-century abbey, but it's been comprehensively polished up and deserves every one of its four stars. Stone staircases and echoing hallways lead to a pick-and-mix of plush period rooms: some come with hefty beams in medieval oak, others have bathroom mosaics and vintage tubs. Upmarket grub is served in the Épicurien restaurant in the old monks' cloister.

THE NORTHWEST & THE COAST

♥ LA MARE AUX OISEAUX // ST-JOACHIM €€

☎ 02 40 88 53 01; www.mareauxoiseaux.fr; 162 Île de Fedrun; r €145-160; P 🛜

You'll be woken by birds at this bewitching hideaway in the heart of the Brière nature reserve, surrounded by misty rivers and reed-filled marshes. Rooms are named after feathered friends – Héron and Aigrette (Egret) are panelled in wood, cosy Colvert has a four-poster, and Becassiné (Snipe) oozes boutique boudoir elegance. Several rooms have balconies overlooking nearby marshland, and chef-patron Eric Guérin cooks up a storm downstairs. One of our Breton faves.

♥ HÔTEL LE ST-PIERRE // LA BAULE €

☎ 02 40 24 05 41; www.hotel-saint-pierre.com; 124 av de Lattre de Tassigny; s €54-64, d €62-82, f €92-102; P 🛜

This is a trim little number in the beach resort of La Baule, lodged inside a characteristic turn-of-the-century villa. The 19 rooms have a sweet fin-de-siècle feel: curly cast-iron room keys, patterned wallpaper and plenty of puffy cushions.

♥ HÔTEL MONA-LISA // LA BAULE €€

☎ 02 40 60 21 33; www.hotelmonalisa-labaule.com; 42 av Georges Clemenceau; d €57-97; 🛜

Another recommendation in La Baule, modern, thoroughly renovated and dead handy for the beach. Rooms are finished in a choice of styles: cool sea-tones in some, opulent golds and regal blues in others. Bathrooms shine in slate and glass.

MANCHE

For details of camping options in the *département*, see boxed text, p169.

MONT ST-MICHEL & BOCAGE COUNTRY

♥ HÔTEL MONTGOMERY // PONTORSON €€

☎ 02 33 60 00 09; www.hotel-montgomery.com; 13 rue du Couësnon; r €55-225, ste €115-250; 🅿

Mont St-Michel's hotels are either tourist traps or faceless chains, which makes this 16th-century mansion in Pontorson all the more appealing. Its vine-covered Renaissance facade conceals creaky old rooms: the priciest have four-poster beds and hefty Renaissance furniture, although most are more modestly furnished.

♥ HÔTEL MICHELET // GRANVILLE €

☎ 02 33 50 06 55; www.hotel-michelet-granville. com; 5 rue Jules-Michelet; r €32-57; 🅿 🛜

Get rid of the stained carpet and this elegant old hotel with high ceilings would be downright grand. As it is, it offers simply furnished but handsome rooms at bargain prices. The cheaper ones share bathroom facilities.

♥ MANOIR DE L'ACHERIE // VILLEDIEU-LES-POÊLES €

☎ 02 33 51 13 87; www.manoir-acherie.fr; 37 rue Michel de L'Epinay; l'Acherie; s €45, d €55-110; 🅿

This charming stone farmhouse 3km east of Villedieu-les-Poêles has an excellent restaurant (p166) and a creaky wooden staircase leading to a set of simple but pleasant rooms of varying sizes and prices. The blissful gardens and surrounding farmland are the perfect tonic to city living.

♥ MANOIR DE L'ECOULANDERIE // COUTANCES €€€

☎ 02 33 45 05 05; www.l-b-c.com; rue de la Broche; s €100-110, d €120-130, tr €160; 🅿 🛜 🏊

Thoroughly romantic, this white 17th-century manor with pale-blue shutters looks through a fragrant garden to Coutances' medieval skyline. The delightful hostess may even offer you an aperitif in the heated indoor swimming pool.

♥ LA DUCRIE // LE HOMMET-D'ARTHENAY €€

☎ 02 33 55 75 33; www.la-ducrie.com; r €90-100; 🅿 🛜

Part country house and part moated castle, this austere stone edifice near St-Lô was built for the future Louis XI in 1437. Now it makes a homely B&B with only the odd suit of armour, arrow slit, secret compartment and tight spiral staircase to remind you of its regal past. The vivacious hosts counterbalance the building's sobriety with a well-stocked bar. Set in 11 hectares of hobby farm, tranquillity is assured.

HAUT-COTENTIN

♥ HÔTEL DES ORMES // CARTERET €€

☎ 02 33 52 23 50; www.hoteldesormes.fr; promenade Barbey-d'Aurevilly; Jan-Mar r €79-110, Apr-May & Oct-Dec €125-155, Jun-Sep €135-175; 🖳

This charming boutique hotel looks out from behind a curtain of ivy onto the river. Muted pinks and greys permeate the luxurious rooms and the back garden is a popular spot for a cocktail when the sun shines.

☙ CHÂTEAU DE L'ISLE-MARIE // PICAUVILLE €€€

☎ 02 33 21 37 25; www.islemarie.com; D70; r €170-185, apt €130-240; Ⓟ

Staying in this stately château is a little like staying in a museum, which isn't to say that it's not homely. The welcoming owner (whose family has lived here for 1000 years) invites you to make the grand drawing rooms and extensive grounds your own.

☙ MANOIR DE SAVIGNY // VALOGNES €€

☎ 02 33 68 37 75; www.manoir-de-savigny.com; Savigny; s €75-95, d €80-100, tr/q €115/120; Ⓟ 🛜

Set in farmland 2km from Valognes, this 15th-century manor has been eclectically decorated by its young owners. The themed bedrooms (African, French country, Moroccan, Egyptian) are charming and bright. Relax by the pond and stroll through the orchard.

☙ HÔTEL LE CONQUÉRANT // BARFLEUR €€

☎ 02 33 54 00 82; www.hotel-leconquerant.com; 18 rue St-Thomas Becket; r €69-106, tr €116; 🌣 mid-Mar–mid-Nov; Ⓟ

In a handsome 17th-century house with a flourishing rear garden, this hotel promises a quiet, contemplative holiday in prettily furnished rooms. Book well ahead.

☙ HÔTEL DE LA RENAISSANCE // CHERBOURG €

☎ 02 33 43 23 90; www.hotel-renaissance-cherbourg .com; 4 rue de l'Église; s €48-62, d €54-65

Friendly staff, reasonable rates, comfortably renovated rooms, a central location and port views make this hotel a highly desirable option. It's often booked out.

☙ LA RÉGENCE // CHERBOURG €

☎ 02 33 43 05 16; www.laregence.com; 42-44 quai de Caligny; r €55-105

The facade does a good impersonation of an upmarket London pub, with black paint and brass at street level and colourful window boxes above. Inside are 21 tasteful, well-kept rooms (most of modest size), some with terrific harbour views.

☙ HÔTEL DU CAP // AUDERVILLE €

☎ 02 33 52 73 46; www.hotelducap.org; r €48-90; Ⓟ

They build them sturdy in these parts – if they didn't they'd be blown into the sea. Within the characterful stone walls are simple but pretty rooms, some with views.

CALVADOS & ORNE

For details of camping options in these *départements*, see boxed text, p195.

BAYEUX

☙ CHURCHILL HÔTEL €€

☎ 02 31 21 31 80; www.hotel-churchill.fr; 14-16 rue St-Jean; s €100, d €108-128, tr €160; 🖥 🛜 ♿

With an elegance and good taste that would have made Winston proud, this sober structure offers friendly, first-rate service and comfortable rooms.

☙ HÔTEL TARDIF €€€

☎ 02 31 92 67 72; www.hoteltardif.com; 16 rue Nesmond; s €60-140, d €180-200; Ⓟ 🛜

Hidden behind high walls near the cathedral, this 18th-century mansion is chockfull of antiques and surrounded by lovely gardens. Best of all is the huge upstairs bedroom dripping with chandeliers that served as the mayor's reception room during WWII.

♥ LE PETIT MATIN €€

☎ 02 31 10 09 27; www.lepetitmatin.com; 2 bis rue Quincangrogne; s/d/tr €60/65/80

Tucked into a side lane in the historic centre, this little B&B offers three charmingly old-fashioned rooms in a dinky 15th-century house. The family-friendly 'pink' room has an adorable old-fashioned cot and a separate bed that would suit a small child.

AROUND BAYEUX

♥ MANOIR D'HÉROUVILLE // LITTEAU €€

☎ 02 31 21 89 22; www.herouville.biz; Litteau; s/d €55/110, apt per week €450; Ⓟ ⏦

For peace and quiet and a gargantuan breakfast, this 400-year-old rural manor is tops. Set on 7 hectares of farmland halfway between Balleroy and St-Lô, there's even a small lake for fishing. The *colombier* (pigeon house; see p185) has been converted into a self-contained apartment.

♥ LA CHENEVIÈRE // PORT-EN-BESSIN €€€

☎ 02 31 51 25 25; www.lacheneviere.com; D6, Escures-Commes; r Nov-Mar €202-382, Apr-Oct €242-462; Ⓟ

Luxury and sophistication are the hallmarks of this 18th-century château conversion, along with personable staff. Soak up the rarefied ambience as you wander from your mutely decorated room, along corridors wallpapered in rose-coloured velvet, to the grand dining room. Port-en-Bessin is just east of Arromanches.

♥ FERME DE LA RANÇONNIÈRE // CREPON €€

☎ 02 31 22 21 73; www.ranconniere.fr; rte de Creully-Arromanches; r €65-130, ste €175-260; Ⓟ ▢ ⏦

Enter the gateway of this 13th-century fortified farm, surrounded by crops, and be transported to another era. The rooms

are elegantly furnished, making the most of the pale stone walls and polished floors, and the restaurant is excellent.

CAEN

♥ HÔTEL DES QUATRANS // CAEN €€

☎ 02 31 86 25 57; www.hotel-des-quatrans.com; 17 rue Gémare; s/d/tr/q €56/65/70/75

Named after an historically prominent local family, this mid-20th-century *moderne* hotel has 47 comfy rooms, some with balconies. The decor has been freshened up with smartly tiled bathrooms, yellow walls and shimmery purple bedspreads and drapes.

♥ HÔTEL DU HAVRE // CAEN €

☎ 02 31 86 19 80; www.hotelduhavre.com; 11 rue du Havre; s €38-47, d €46-55, tr/q €67/72; Ⓟ ⏦

With efficient, friendly service and bright, comfortable rooms, this modern but modest hotel offers good value. The free first-come-first-serve parking is a bonus, as is the double-glazing.

SUISSE NORMANDE & PAYS DE FALAISE

♥ LE RELAIS DE LA POSTE // THURY-HARCOURT €€

☎ 02 31 79 72 12; www.hotel-relaisdelaposte.com; 7 rue de Caen; d €65-105, tr/ste €125/140; Ⓟ

Built as a pit stop for stage coaches, this hotel continues to provide respite to weary travellers within its stone walls and lush gardens. The rooms are nicely decorated, although the addition of en suites has rendered the cheaper ones a little cramped.

♥ FERME DU VEY // CLÉCY €

☎ 02 31 69 71 02; pbrisset@9online.fr; Le Vey; s/d €32/40; Ⓟ

Stay in one of three pretty little rooms in a working farm, idyllically located by the

River Orne. If you get thirsty, the farm sells its own cider, Calvados and *pommeau* (apple juice).

❤ DOMAINE DE LA TOUR // FALAISE €€

☎ 02 31 20 53 07; www.domainedelatour.fr; St-Pierre-Canivet; s/d/tr €55/60/80; Ⓟ 🛜

Take the kilometre-long private road, 4km northwest of Falaise, drive past a magnificent château and you'll find this wonderful B&B, housed in what was once the château's farmhouse (1774). Large rooms, country-chic decor, friendly young hosts and absolute rural tranquillity make this a memorable choice.

❤ HÔTEL DE LA POSTE // FALAISE €

☎ 02 31 90 13 14; hotel.delaposte@wanadoo.fr; 38 rue Georges Clemenceau; r €54-100; Ⓟ

The restaurant downstairs offers nicely presented, simple, good-value food with a dash of old-fashioned charm (*menus* €16 to €42), and the rooms upstairs share all the same virtues.

ORNE

❤ BOIS JOLI // BAGNOLES DE L'ORNE €€

☎ 02 33 37 92 77; www.hotelboisjoli.com; 12 av Philippe du Rozier; r Oct-Apr €74-102, May-Sep €88-122; Ⓟ 🛜

'Pretty wood' indeed, this late-19th-century house overlooking the lake is sweetness personified. The elegant old-world decor carries through the rooms, where you'll find chandeliers and tulip-shaped lampshades.

❤ LE MANOIR DU LYS // BAGNOLES DE L'ORNE €€

☎ 02 33 27 80 69; www.manoir-du-lys.fr; rte de Juvigny; r low season €80-190, high season €95-220; Ⓟ 🛜 🖳

Set on the edge of the woods a little out of town, any qualms about the slightly generic decor are dissolved by the peaceful setting and large pool/spa area. Best of all are the apartment-style stilt bungalows facing the garden (€250 to €300).

❤ Ô GAYOT HÔTEL // BAGNOLES DE L'ORNE €

☎ 02 33 28 44 01; www.ogayot.com; 2 av de la Ferté Macé; r €45-95; 🛜

The beautiful pale stone exterior may be strictly *belle époque* but on the inside this well-priced boutique hotel is chic, contemporary and extremely comfortable. Expect good modern bathrooms and lots of white, pale blue and earthy brown tones.

❤ HÔTEL DES DUCS // ALENÇON €

☎ 02 33 29 03 93; www.hoteldesducs-alencon.fr; 50 av Président Wilson; s €49-59, d €55-65; Ⓟ 🛜

Of the clump of budget hotels near the train station this one has the advantage of off-street parking, a private garden and smart, bright rooms.

❤ HÔTEL DU TRIBUNAL // MORTAGNE-AU-PERCHE €€

☎ 02 33 25 04 77; www.hotel-tribunal.fr; 4 place du Palais; r €65-110

It's the best place in town, spreading between several tastefully renovated 16th-century buildings. The historic ambience has been preserved while modern comforts have been added.

CÔTE FLEURIE

❤ 81 L'HÔTEL // DEAUVILLE-TROUVILLE €€€

☎ 02 31 14 01 50; www.81lhotel.com; 81 av de la République; r low season €139-310, high season €190-370; Ⓟ 🛜

As if this turn-of-last-century mansion wasn't glamorous enough, it's successfully shaken off the Deauville cobwebs with an uberstylish over-the-top makeover. Expect huge chandeliers, opulent silver mirrors, stripy carpets and Lichtenstein cartoon prints.

❤ HÔTEL LE CHANTILLY // DEAUVILLE-TROUVILLE €€

☎ 02 31 88 79 75; hchantilly@orange.fr; 120 av de la République; r low/mid/high season €65/73/95

As sweet as a button with its red awnings and window boxes, this is a good, moderately priced hotel with simple but smart rooms. The front ones get the afternoon sun but those at the rear are quieter.

❤ LE FER À CHEVAL // DEAUVILLE-TROUVILLE €€

☎ 02 31 98 30 20; www.hotel-trouville.com; 11 rue Victor-Hugo; s €51-64, d €75-87, tr/q/ste €90/132/147; P 🛜

Occupying three beautiful turn-of-the-20th-century buildings, this modern hotel has 34 comfortable rooms with big windows, horse-themed decor and bright bathrooms. The owner is a retired *boulanger* (baker) who loves to bake fresh croissants.

❤ ENTRE TERRE ET MER // HONFLEUR €€

☎ 02 31 98 83 33; www.hotel-centre-honfleur.com; 29 place Hamelin; r €98-105, ste €120; 🛜

A juxtaposition of up-to-the-minute furnishings and ancient wooden beams makes this small collection of rooms above a central restaurant a very cool option indeed. The elevator is an unexpected bonus for a building this old.

❤ HÔTEL L'ÉCRIN // HONFLEUR €€

☎ 02 31 14 43 45; www.honfleur.com/default-ecrin .htm; 19 rue Eugène Boudin; d €100-180, ste €220-250; P 🛜 🖥

The parlour and public spaces of this lavish manor house are dripping with gilt, art and antiques, recreating the opulence of times long past. The 30 rooms, which come with thoroughly modern bathrooms, retain touches of the 1800s – alongside TVs hung on the walls like paintings.

❤ LA MAISON DE LUCIE // HONFLEUR €€€

☎ 02 31 14 40 40; www.lamaisondelucie.com; 44 rue des Capucins; d €150-220, ste €315

Former home of the novelist Lucie Delarue Mardrus (1874–1945), this romantic hideaway is decorated with a mixture of antiques and contemporary *objects d'art*. Some of the bedrooms, panelled in oak, have Moroccan-tile bathrooms and boast fantastic views across the harbour to the Pont de Normandie.

SEINE-MARITIME & EURE

For details of camping options in these *départements*, see boxed text, p227.

LE HAVRE

❤ LE PETIT VATEL €

☎ 02 35 41 72 07; www.lepetitvatel.com; 86 rue Louis Brindeau; s €48-59, d €59-72, tw/tr/f €72/80/86; 🖥 🛜

A sunny welcome is matched by bright orange walls hung with African paintings in this central, family-run hotel. The 25 small but space-efficient rooms are a little less exuberant but no less smart and the double-glazing really works.

❤ LES VOILES €€

☎ 02 35 54 68 90; www.hotel-lesvoiles.com; 3 place Clemenceau; r €99-135; 🛜

If it's sea views you're after, this Ste-Adresse hotel above a busy pub and restaurant has them in abundance. The rooms are modern and comfortable, if a little scuffed in places. Expect to pay around €15 extra for a weekend stay.

☙ VENT D'OUEST €€

☎ 02 35 42 50 69; www.ventdouest.fr; 4 rue de Caligny; r €100-130, ste/apt/f €148/158/159; 💻 🛜

The 38-room West Wind is decorated in shipshape fashion, with nautical memorabilia scattered about the stylish sisal-floored rooms; ask for one with a balcony. Downstairs you can get snacks from a fashionable *salon de thé* (tearoom) or shoot some pool.

ÉTRETAT & FÉCAMP

☙ HÔTEL LA RÉSIDENCE // ÉTRETAT €

☎ 02 35 27 02 87; fax 02 35 27 17 07; 4 bd René Coty; r €36-120

This 14th-century half-wooden house with an appealingly dilapidated facade once belonged to an alchemist. Renovations have added modern bathrooms but left intact the creaky stairway and ancient beams. Rooms vary considerably in size and comfort; some share bathrooms.

☙ JARDIN GORBEAU // ÉTRETAT €€€

☎ 02 35 27 16 72; www.gorbeau.com; 27 rue Adolphe Boissaye; d/q €130/160; 🛜

Gay-friendly, family-friendly and straight-out friendly, this *chambre d'hôte* has five stylishly renovated minisuites in a cluster of 19th-century buildings opening onto a large private garden. Movie buffs can amuse themselves on rainy days with the DVD projector and large screen in the main house.

☙ HÔTEL NORMANDY // FÉCAMP €

☎ 02 35 29 55 11; www.normandy-fecamp.com; 4 av Gambetta; low season s/d/tr €47/56/64, high season s/d/tr €54/62/73; 🅿 🛜

In a smart fin-de-siècle building just up the hill from the train station, this solid option has 30 inconspicuously refurbished rooms – some quite spacious – with light yellow walls, baize-green carpets and lots of light.

☙ LE GRAND PAVOIS // FÉCAMP €€€

☎ 02 35 10 01 01; www.hotel-grand-pavois.com; 15 quai de la Vicomté; r €88-125, tr €150, ste €125-250; 🅿 💻

Thoroughly modern, this well-run hotel offers large, sleek, double-glazed rooms with safes, minibars and balconies; the pricier ones come with panoramic sea views. Expect to pay around €20 extra during peak season and on weekends.

DIEPPE & PAYS DE BRAY

☙ AU GRAND DUQUESNE // DIEPPE €

☎ 02 32 14 61 10; http://augranduquesne.free.fr; 15 place St-Jacques; d €42-63

Once you've lugged your suitcase up the small staircase and through the narrow corridors of this old-style building in the centre of town, you may be surprised to find modern little rooms awaiting you. Recent renovations have left them bright and comfortable.

☙ VILLA DES CAPUCINS // DIEPPE €€

☎ 02 35 82 16 52; www.villa-des-capucins.fr; 11 rue des Capucins; d/tr €75/95

Behind the high walls of this former friary (1820) is a tranquil garden where spring daffodils sprout around religious statues. Accommodation is in a brick terrace of mezzanine units facing the garden, and their ornamental garrets give them the appearance of a minichâteau.

♥ MANOIR DE GRAINCOURT // DIEPPE €€

☎ 02 35 84 12 88; www.manoir-de-graincourt.fr; 10 place Ludovic Panel, Derchigny-Graincourt; d €95-110; P

Built from flint, wood and brick, this 17th- to 19th-century manor abuts a pretty flint church and village green in a hamlet favoured by Renoir. Laze in your rustic bedroom or avail yourself of the billiard room, reading salon or gardens.

♥ FERME DE BRAY // SOMMERY €

☎ 02 35 90 57 27; http://ferme.de.bray.free.fr; D915; s/d/tr/q €38/45/55/65; P

The Perriers are the 18th generation to run this dairy farm, turning it into a combination museum-inn. The comfortable rooms are furnished in French country style with wooden furniture and Laura Ashley wallpaper.

LE TRÉPORT & EU

♥ LA VILLA MARINE // LE TRÉPORT €

☎ 02 35 86 02 22; www.hotel-lavillamarine.com; 1 place Sémard; r €45-95; 📶

Pebble-printed carpet, brightly painted rooms and a nautical theme enliven this moderately priced hotel near the station. You'll pay a little more for a bigger room with a sea view. Some of the beds are a little saggy.

♥ MANOIR DE BEAUMONT // EU €

☎ 02 35 50 91 91; www.demarquet.eu; rte de Beaumont; r €48-57; P

Relaxation is the raison d'être of this cottage on the edge of the forest, 2km southeast of Eu. Like the peaceful gardens, there's a rambling charm to the decor, including wall furnishings, curtains and bedspreads printed in matching pastoral scenes.

ROUEN

♥ HÔTEL ANDERSEN €

☎ 02 35 71 88 51; www.hotelandersen.com; 4 rue Pouchet; s €51-56, d €56; 📶

Ensconced in an early-19th-century mansion near the train station, this quiet gay-friendly hotel has an old-world atmosphere, classical music wafting through the lobby and 15 spare but cosy rooms. The friendly young owners are quick with helpful advice.

♥ HÔTEL DANDY €€

☎ 02 35 07 32 00; www.hotels-rouen.net; 93 rue Cauchoise; r €80-105; P

Comfortable digs on a quiet street with the convenience of a coffee-maker in each room make this a dandy option. The decor is an updated version of Old Normandy; some rooms have chandeliers, heavy drapes, gilded beds and chic wallpaper patterned with French pastoral scenes.

♥ HÔTEL DES CARMES €

☎ 02 35 71 92 31, www.hoteldescarmes.com; 33 place des Carmes; r €49-67; 📶

Occupying an elegant building with colourfully planted window boxes on a central square, this friendly hotel offers simple but pleasant rooms that are cheaper the higher you climb (there's no lift). The 12 rooms are decked out with patchwork quilts and vibrant colours.

♥ HÔTEL LE CARDINAL €

☎ 02 35 70 24 42; www.cardinal-hotel.fr; 1 place de la Cathédrale; s €54-68, d €64-86; P 📶

In a super-central spot facing the cathedral, this postwar hotel has 18 businesslike rooms with lots of natural light and spacious showers. The 4th-floor rooms have fantastic private terraces overlooking the square.

🌱 LE CLOS JOUVENET €€

☎ 02 35 89 80 66; www.leclosjouvenet.com; 42 rue Hyacinthe Langlois; r €92-98; Ⓟ

One of the mansions on the hill, this grand 19th-century house sits among large and lovely gardens surrounded by high walls. Four stylish B&B rooms are available with decor ranging from traditional to bright and modern. The smaller ones have city views.

🌱 LE VIEUX CARRÉ €

☎ 02 35 71 67 70; www.vieux-carre.fr; 34 rue Ganterie; r €58-65

Brimming with charm and good cheer, this quiet half-timbered hotel has a delightfully old-fashioned *salon de thé* and 13 smallish rooms set around a cute little garden courtyard.

AROUND ROUEN

🌱 LE CLOS DES FONTAINES // JUMIÈGES €€€

☎ 02 35 33 96 96; www.leclosdesfontaines.com; 191 rue des Fontaines; r €90-230; Ⓟ 🛜 🖲

Cleverly designed to echo traditional half-timber-and-brick architecture, the purpose-built four-room blocks of this chic boutique hotel combine modern luxury with a rustic ambience. The views of horses grazing in the fields help with the latter.

🌱 SWEET HOME (AUCRETERRE) // EPREVILLE €

☎ 02 35 23 76 05; http://jy.aucreterre.free.fr; 534 rue des Marronniers; d €52-90; Ⓟ 🛜

Life is indeed sweet in this wonderful B&B situated in a hamlet 16km east of Rouen. Each of the four rooms is quite different but even the cheapest is extremely charming. The hosts complete the charm offensive and serve a delicious breakfast.

PAYS D'OUCHE & RISLE-CHARENTONNE

🌱 AUBERGE DE L'ABBAYE // LE BEC-HELLOUIN €€

☎ 02 32 44 86 02; www.auberge-abbaye-bec-hel louin.com; 12 place Guillaume-le-Conquérant; s/d/ste €70/80/115

Rustic but extremely comfortable rooms are offered in this charming half-wooden building in the centre of peaceful Le Bec-Hellouin village. A recent renovation has left everything very spick and span.

🌱 LE CYGNE // CONCHES-EN-OUCHES €

☎ 02 32 30 20 60; www.lecygne.fr; 2 rue Paul Guilbaud; r €45-52; Ⓟ

Draped in wisteria, this rustic manor offers old-fashioned but pretty rooms where the look is more gran than élan. Think lace curtains and floral prints.

🌱 NORMANDY HÔTEL // ÉVREUX €€

☎ 02 32 33 14 40; www.normandyhotel.eu; 37 rue Édouard Feray; r €76-115; Ⓟ 🛜

Ivy clings to the walls and bright flowers fill the window boxes of this half-timbered hotel near the main square. Although the cheaper rooms are reasonably small, they're attractively decorated.

🌱 LA PLUIE DE ROSES // GIVERNY €€

☎ 02 32 51 10 67; ameliphi@club-internet.fr; 14 rue Claude Monet; r €110-120; Ⓟ

Two adorable spaniels patrol the huge gardens of this private home just down the road from Monet's. The lovely stone house has two charming rooms with en suites upstairs and a studio sleeping three downstairs. Breakfast is included in the rates.

♥ LES JARDINS D'HÉLÈNE //
GIVERNY €€

☎ 02 32 21 30 68; http://giverny-lesjardinsdhelene.com; 12 rue Claude Monet; r €80; 🛜

Monet's era comes alive in this chic *chambre d'hôte*, complete with antiques and cuttings from *belle époque* fashion magazines. If the crowds in Monet's garden get too much, you should be able to find a quiet corner in Hélène's.

NORTHEASTERN EURE

♥ LA CHAÎNE D'OR //
LES ANDELYS €€

☎ 02 32 54 00 31; www.hotel-lachainedor.com; 27 rue Grande; r €85-110, ste €125-135; 🅿 🖥 🛜

Rustically stylish without being twee, this boutique hotel offers spacious and romantic rooms in a charming 1751 building by the Seine. Its acclaimed **restaurant** (menus €46-59; ⏲ Mon-Tue) is the town's best.

♥ LE MOULIN DE CONNELLES //
CONNELLES €€€

☎ 02 32 59 53 33; www.moulin-de-connelles.fr; 40 rte d'Amfreville-sous-les-Monts; r €130-140, ste €200-310; 🅿 🏊

In a quiet village 14km west of Les Andelys, this turreted 19th-century mansion forms a bridge onto a sleepy island on the Seine. The 14 bedrooms are decorated in an antique style; some have Jacuzzis, balconies and river views.

♥ LE PRÉ SAINT GERMAIN //
LOUVIERS €€

☎ 02 32 40 48 48; www.le-pre-saint-germain.com; 7 rue St-Germain; s €78, d €95-110; 🅿 🖥 🛜

A peaceful stay is assured at this businesslike but welcoming hotel, set back from a quiet road leading off place Ernest Thorel. The rooms have all the modern conveniences and very comfy beds.

♥ HÔTEL DE LA LICORNE //
LYONS-LA-FORÊT €€

☎ 02 32 48 24 24; www.hotel-licorne.com; place Isaac Benserade; r €95-150; 🅿 🛜

This excellent hotel and **restaurant** (menus €25-33; ⏲ Wed-Sun) occupies a 400-year-old building with a lush garden terrace behind. Some rooms have views over the marketplace and one has a claw-foot bath in the centre of the bedroom.

♥ LES LIONS DE BEAUCLERC //
LYONS-LA-FORÊT €€

☎ 02 32 49 18 90; www.lionsdebeauclerc.com; 7 rue l'Hôtel de Ville; r €59-74; 🛜

There are six antique-filled rooms in this romantic ivy-covered place. Prices increase on the weekend but they're still terrific value for the ambience. Downstairs there's a justifiably popular *salon de thé* and **crêperie** (menus €15-28, ⏲ closed Tue).

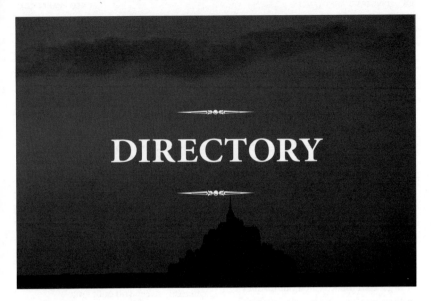

DIRECTORY

BUSINESS HOURS

French business hours are regulated by a maze of government regulations, including the 35-hour working week. Shop hours are usually 9am or 10am to 7pm or 8pm, often with a break from noon or 1pm to 2pm or 3pm. Most businesses are required to close on Sunday; exceptions include grocery stores, *boulangeries,* cake shops, florists and businesses catering exclusively to the tourist trade. Some shops close on Saturday afternoon and/or Monday. Most open-air markets start at between 6am to 8am and finish at 12.30pm or 1pm.

Banks are usually open from 8am or 9am to some time between 11.30am or 1pm and then from 1.30pm or 2pm to 4.30pm or 5pm, Monday to Friday or Tuesday to Saturday. Post offices generally open 8.30am or 9am to 5pm or 6pm on weekdays, usually with a two-hour break at midday, and Saturday mornings.

Most museums close at least one day of the week (usually Sunday, Monday or Tuesday) and they often close at lunchtime as well. Hours can vary widely month-to-month, and in July and August many museums open daily with extended closing hours and no lunch closure. The same is true of tourist offices.

As most sights and shops will be closed, you may as well make like a local and settle in for a lengthy lunch. Restaurants generally serve lunch from noon or 12.30pm to 2pm or 2.30pm and dinner from 7pm or 7.30pm until 9.30pm or 10pm; they are often closed one or two days of the week, according to the owner's whim. Cafés are usually open from early morning until around midnight. Many bars open in the early evening and close at 1am or 2am.

CUSTOMS REGULATIONS

Goods brought in and out of countries within the EU incur no additional taxes provided duty has been paid somewhere within the EU and the goods are for personal consumption. Duty-free shopping is available only if you're leaving the EU.

Coming from non-EU countries (including the Channel Islands), duty-free allowances (for adults) are 200 cigarettes (or 50 cigars), 1L of spirits, 4L of wine and other goods up to the value of €430 (€90 for under 15s). Higher limits apply if you're coming from Andorra. Anything over these limits must be declared. For details, see www.douane.gouv.fr, partly in English.

DANGERS & ANNOYANCES

Brittany and Normandy are generally safe places but sensible precautions should be taken to prevent opportunistic or organised theft. Watch out for pickpockets and bag-snatchers, particularly at airport, train, bus and ferry terminals.

Unfortunately, out-of-town, foreign or red-coloured purchase-repurchase license plates (along with rental-company stickers) easily identify your vehicle as belonging to a traveller – the equivalent of painting a bullseye on the side for a would-be car thief. Never leave anything irreplaceable in your car and avoid leaving anything visible that might attract the attention of an opportunist, who won't think twice about breaking a window to see if there's a camera hidden underneath an item of clothing.

Tides along the Brittany and Normandy coastline are among the biggest and most powerful in the world. If you plan to explore any low-tide area, or an island accessible only at low tide, make sure you know the tide times. Always check with the local tourist office. Don't go swimming from a beach unless you are sure it is safe – again, ask locally. Undertows and tidal currents can easily sweep you out to sea.

Although the rocky coasts look appealing, huge swells can roll in from the Atlantic – even when the weather is fine – and sweep unsuspecting hikers and anglers from rocks a few metres above the water level. Take care.

PRACTICALITIES

- ★ France uses the metric system for weights and measures.
- ★ Electrical plugs have two round pins, so visitors from English-speaking lands will need an adaptor; the electric current is 220V at 50Hz AC (you may need a transformer for 110V electrical appliances).
- ★ Videos in France work on the PAL system.
- ★ Locals read their news in centre-left, highly intellectual *Le Monde* (www.lemonde.fr), right-leaning *Le Figaro* (www.lefigaro.fr) or left-leaning *Libération* (www.liberation.fr). All are in French only.
- ★ For radio news, tune in to the French-language Radio France Info (105.5MHz or thereabouts in most areas), the multilanguage RFI (738kHz) or BBC World Service (648kHz) and BBC Radio 4 (198kHz).
- ★ In many areas, Autoroute Info (107.7MHz) has around-the-clock information on autoroute travel conditions.
- ★ Popular national FM music stations include NRJ (pronounced 'energy'; www.nrj.fr, in French), Skyrock (www.skyrock.fm, in French) and Nostalgie (www.nostalgie.fr, in French).

Hunting season runs from September to February. If you see signs reading *'chasseurs'* or *'chasse gardée'* strung up or tacked to trees, think twice about wandering into the area. As well as millions of wild animals, 25 French hunters die each year after being shot by other hunters.

See also Women Travellers, p314.

DISCOUNT CARDS

The **Normandie Pass** (www.normandiepass .com; €1) provides discounted admission to 40 regional attractions, particularly the smaller D-Day museums, and can be purchased from participating establishments or by the website.

Reduced admission prices are charged for people aged over 60 or 65 at most cultural centres, including museums, galleries and public theatres. SNCF issues the Carte Senior to those aged over 60, which gives reductions of 20% to 50% on train tickets.

An International Student Identity Card (ISIC; price varies in different countries) can easily pay for itself through half-price admissions and cheap meals in student cafeterias. Many places stipulate a maximum age, usually 24 or 25. For more details, check the website of the **International Student Travel Confederation** (ISTC; www.istc.org).

If you're under 26 but not a student, you can apply for an International Youth Travel Card (IYTC or Go25), also issued by ISTC, which entitles you to many of the same discounts as an ISIC. The **European Youth Card** (Euro<26 card; www .euro26.org) offers similar discounts across 41 European countries to anyone under 26.

FOOD & DRINK

The Food and Drink section, p279, has additional information about eating in Brittany and Normandy, while highlights of eating in France are presented, p16.

In this book's restaurant reviews, we always indicate the price of *menus* (two- or three-course set menus) where they're available, the quickie lunchtime version of which is also known as a *formule* (literally 'formula'). Ordering *à la carte* (choosing individual items from the menu) generally works out to be much more expensive. On 1 July 2009 the French government cut VAT in restaurants from 19.6% to 5.5% meaning, fingers crossed, a marginal drop in restaurant prices.

At eateries listed as 'budget', *menus* cost up to €20. At midrange places, with more atmosphere and seasonal specialities, *menus* go for €20 to €35. Top-end restaurants generally have impeccable service, outstanding cuisine and *menus* costing anything upwards of €35.

Vegetarians are a small minority in France and are not well catered for. Specialised vegetarian restaurants are few and far between, and very few restaurants list any vegetarian options on their menus, apart from lots of eggs and cheese. The best solution will often be shopping for fruit and vegetables, bread and cheese, and having a picnic.

WHERE TO EAT & DRINK

Restaurants usually only open for lunch and dinner and often specialise in a particular style of food, whereas brasseries and bistros tend to be more informal, serve standard fare and stay open throughout the day. In this book we've highlighted French eateries, particularly those with a strong regional focus.

Cafés concentrate on beverages (including alcoholic ones) and may serve light breakfasts. *Salons de thé* (tearooms) are trendy and often somewhat pricey establishments that usually offer quiches, salads, cakes, tarts, pies and pastries in addition to tea and coffee. Traditional *crêperies* are found all over Brittany and Normandy specialising in crêpes and galettes (see p280).

Most French people buy a good proportion of their food from small neighbourhood shops, each with its own speciality, including *boulangeries* (bakeries), *pâtisseries* (cake and pastry shops), *fromageries* (cheese shops), *marchands de fruits et légumes* (greengrocers), *boucheries* (butchers), *poissonneries* (fishmongers) and *épiceries* (small grocery stores). At first, having to go to four shops and stand in four queues to fill the fridge (or assemble a picnic) may seem rather a waste of time, but the whole ritual is an important part of the way many French people live their daily lives.

In most towns and cities, there are weekly markets where a wide variety of food is sold, usually more cheaply than in the stores, and the merchandise, especially fruit and vegetables, is generally fresher and of better quality.

GAY & LESBIAN TRAVELLERS

France is one of Europe's most liberal countries when it comes to homosexuality, in part because of a long tradition of tolerance towards people who choose not to live by conventional social codes. Predictably, attitudes towards homosexuality tend to be more conservative in the countryside than in the large cities.

Rouen has the biggest gay scene (see p243) but there are also gay venues in Caen, Évreux, Cherbourg, Alençon, Le Havre and Dieppe. An excellent resource for tracking them down is www.gaynor mandie.com (in French only). Rennes and Nantes have their own miniscenes.

Once you find a gay venue, pick up a copy of *Wag!*, a free gay magazine, in French, covering Brittany, Normandy and the Loire Valley. The same publishers produce the free *Wag! Map* covering the bigger cities. **Têtu** (www.tetu.com, in French) is a glossy monthly that bills itself as *le magazine des gais et des lesbiennes*, which is widely available from newsagents. The monthly national magazine *Lesbia* provides a run-down of what's happening in France's lesbian community.

HOLIDAYS

The following *jours fériés* (public holidays) are observed in France:
New Year's Day (Jour de l'An) 1 January.
Easter Sunday & Monday (Pâques & lundi de Pâques) Late March/April.
May Day (Fête du Travail) 1 May – traditional parades.
Victoire 1945 8 May – celebrates the Allied victory in Europe that ended WWII.
Ascension Thursday (Ascension) May – celebrated on the 40th day after Easter.
Pentecost/Whit Sunday & Whit Monday (Pentecôte & lundi de Pentecôte) Mid-May to mid-June – celebrated on the seventh Sunday after Easter.
Bastille Day/National Day (Fête Nationale) 14 July – *the* national holiday.
Assumption Day (Assomption) 15 August.
All Saints' Day (Toussaint) 1 November.
Remembrance Day (L'onze novembre) 11 November – marks the WWI armistice.
Christmas (Noël) 25 December.

INSURANCE

For car insurance, see p319.

TRAVEL INSURANCE

If you're an EU citizen, an **EHIC** (European Health Insurance Card; www.e111.org.uk) covers you for most medical care. EHIC, however, will not cover any nonemergencies or emergency repatriation to a home country. Non-EU citizens should find out if there is a reciprocal arrangement for free medical care between their home country and France. If you do need health insurance, be sure you get a policy that covers you for the worst possible scenario, such as an accident needing an ambulance or an emergency flight home. Find out in advance if your insurance will make payments directly to providers or reimburse you later. If you have to claim later, make sure you keep all documentation. Some policies require the holder to carry an EHIC if they are an EU citizen.

Getting travel insurance to cover theft, loss and medical problems is highly recommended. Some policies specifically exclude dangerous activities such as scuba diving, motorcycling and even trekking, so read the fine print.

Paying for your airline ticket with a credit card often provides limited travel accident insurance – ask your credit-card company what it's prepared to cover.

INTERNET ACCESS

Wireless (wi-fi) hot spots can now be found at major airports, in most hotels (often for free) and at lots of cafés. Internet cafés can be found in towns and cities countrywide. Prices range from €2 to €6 per hour. Public libraries *(bibliothèques or médiathèques)* often have free or inexpensive internet access, though hours are limited and you may have to fill in some forms. Some tourist offices also offer connections.

LEGAL MATTERS

French police have wide powers of search and seizure and can ask you to prove your identity at any time – whether or not there is 'probable cause'. Police have been known to search chartered coaches, cars and train passengers for drugs just because they're coming from Amsterdam.

Foreigners must be able to prove their legal status in France (eg passport, visa, residency permit) without delay. If the police stop you for any reason, be polite and remain calm. You may refuse to sign a police statement and have the right to ask for a copy. People who are arrested are considered innocent until proven guilty but can be held in custody until trial.

Because of the threat of terrorism, French police are very strict about security. Do not leave baggage unattended, especially at airports or train stations: suspicious objects may be summarily blown up.

The laws are very tough when it comes to drinking and driving. The legal blood-alcohol limit is 0.05% and drivers exceeding this amount face fines of up to €4500 plus up to two years in jail. Licences can be suspended immediately.

Ivresse (drunkenness) in public is punishable by an €150 fine.

MAPS

Road maps and city maps are available at *Maisons de la Presse* (large newsagents), found all over the region, as well as bookshops and even some newsstands. Check with the local tourist offices, which usually have free town maps, as well as maps that detail interesting itineraries in the vicinity.

A variety of *cartes routiéres* (road maps) are available, but a good bet is Michelin's yellow-orange 1:200,000-scale fold-out maps (€6.60) No 512 (Brittany) and No 513 (Normandy).

As well as road maps, **IGN** (www.ign
.fr) publishes the *Top 25* and *Série Bleue*
hiking maps and specialised *cyclocartes*
(cycle maps).

MONEY

France has adopted the euro although
franc notes can still be changed at banks
until 17 February 2012. Some shops still
list prices in both euros and francs. Euro
coins come in denominations of one,
two, five, 10, 20 and 50 cents, and €1 and
€2, while notes come in €5, €10, €20, €50,
€100, €200 and €500. Bills over €50 can
be difficult to change.

Exchange rates at publication time are
given on the inside of the front cover.

ATMS

Automated Teller Machines (ATMs) –
known as *distributeurs automatiques
de billets* (DAB) or *points d'argent* in
French – are the cheapest and most
convenient way to get money. ATMs
connected to international networks are
situated in all cities and towns and usually offer an excellent exchange rate.

CREDIT & DEBIT CARDS

Credit and debit cards are convenient,
relatively secure and usually offer a better
exchange rate than travellers cheques or
cash exchanges. Credit cards issued in
France have embedded chips – you have
to type in a PIN code to make a purchase –
and some places (eg 24-hour petrol stations, some autoroute toll machines) will
no longer accept traditional signature-
style cards. Otherwise cards are accepted
almost anywhere but it pays to enquire
first at smaller hotels and restaurants.

Cash advances are a supremely convenient way to stay stocked up with
euros. However, getting cash with a
credit card involves both fees (sometimes
US$10 or more) and interest – ask your
credit-card issuer for details. Debit-card
fees are usually much less.

TIPPING

By law, restaurant and bar prices are
service compris (include a 15% service
charge) so there's no expectation of a tip,
except in very upscale establishments
where 5% is the norm. Taxi drivers are
usually tipped 10%.

ORGANISED TOURS

Details of tours available in the region
are presented under the Getting Started
section of each of the regional chapters.

POST

French post offices are flagged with a yellow or brown sign reading 'La Poste' and
every town and most villages have one.
Since La Poste also has banking, finance
and bill-paying functions, queues can be
long but machines dispense stamps.

TELEPHONE

France has one of the most modern –
and overpriced – telecommunications
systems in the world. The mobile network
uses GSM 900/1800, compatible with the
rest of Europe and Australia but not with
the North American GSM 1900 or the
totally different system in Japan (though
some North Americans have tri-band
phones that work here). Check with your
service provider about roaming charges –
using a mobile phone outside your home
country can be hideously expensive. Local SIM cards are readily available and
prepaid recharge cards are sold at most
tabacs (tobacconists) and newsagents.

To get explanations in English and other languages on how to use a public telephone, push the button engraved with a two-flags icon. Emergency numbers (see inside front cover) can be dialled from public phones without a phonecard.

USEFUL NUMBERS & CODES

French telephone numbers have 10 digits, except for a few commercial access numbers that have four digits and some emergency numbers that have just two or three. France is divided into five telephone-dialling areas, signified by numbers starting with ☎ 01 to ☎ 05 (numbers in Brittany and Normandy start with ☎ 02), and you need to dial all the digits no matter where you are in France. Numbers beginning with ☎ 08 00 or ☎ 08 05 are free but other ☎ 08 numbers are not. Mobile numbers start with ☎ 06 and calls can be very expensive.

To dial a French number from overseas, dial your country's international access code, then 33 (France's country code), then the 10-digit local number *without* the initial 0.

* International access code ☎ 00
* International directory enquiries ☎ 118700 (€2 or €3) Has English-speaking operators available who may also help with local directory enquiries
* Local directory enquiries ☎ 118712 (€1.18 per call from a fixed-line phone)
* Rape crisis hotline ☎ 0800 05 95 95
* SOS Médecins (24hr house calls) ☎ 0820 33 24 24

TIME

France uses the 24-hour clock and is on Central European Time, which is one hour ahead of GMT/UTC. During daylight-saving time, which runs from the last Sunday in March to the last Sunday in October, France is two hours ahead of GMT/UTC.

TOILETS

Toilets in France are of the bog-standard sit-down variety. Public toilets are usually free but sometimes charge up to about €0.50. Restaurants, cafés and bars all have toilets for customers to use, as do some shopping centres.

TOURIST INFORMATION

Almost every city, town, village and hamlet has an *office de tourisme* (a tourist office, run by some unit of local government) or *syndicat d'initiative* (a tourist office run by an organisation of local merchants). Both are excellent resources and can supply you with local maps as well as details on accommodation, restaurants and activities. Many, but by no means all, have English-speaking staff and English-language resources. If you have a special interest such as hiking, cycling, architecture or food, ask about it. Many tourist offices make local hotel and B&B reservations, sometimes for a small fee. Some have limited currency-exchange services and internet access.

Details on tourist offices appear under Essential Information at the beginning of each major city, town or area listing. *Départemental* tourist-board websites are listed at under Getting Started in each regional chapter.

TRAVELLERS WITH DISABILITIES

France is not well equipped for *handicapés* (people with disabilities): cobblestone streets are a nightmare to navigate in a wheelchair; kerb ramps are often lacking; and older public facilities and

DIRECTORY

budget hotels frequently lack lifts. However things have been steadily improving and organisations exist to make visits easier.

Tourisme et Handicaps (☎ 01 44 11 10 41; www.tourisme-handicaps.org, in French) issues its label to tourist sites, restaurants and hotels that comply with strict accessibility and usability standards. Different symbols indicate the sort of access afforded to people with physical, mental, hearing and/or visual disabilities.

Details on rail access for people with disabilities appear in the SNCF's French-language booklet *Mobilité Réduite,* available at train stations. You can also contact **Accès Plus** (☎ 08 90 64 06 50, per minute €0.11; www.accessibilite.sncf.fr, in French), to check station accessibility, to arrange for a *fauteuil roulant* (wheelchair) or to receive help getting on or off a train.

The portal www.jaccede.com, in French, has loads of information and accessibility reviews of sights, hotels and restaurants. Michelin's *Guide Rouge* uses icons to indicate hotels with lifts and with facilities that make them at least partly accessible to people with disabilities, while the Gîtes de France (see p287) group can provide details on *gîtes ruraux* and *chambres d'hôtes* with 'disabled access' (this is one of their website's search criteria).

Specialised travel agencies abroad include UK-based **Access Travel** (☎ in UK 01942-888 844; www.access-travel.co.uk). **Tourism for All** (☎ in UK 0845-124 9971; www.tourismforall .info) is a UK-based group that provides tips and information for travellers with disabilities.

VISAS

For up-to-date details on visa requirements, see the website of the **French**

Foreign Affairs Ministry (www.diplomatie .gouv.fr) and click 'Going to France'.

EU nationals and citizens of Iceland, Norway and Switzerland need only a passport or a national identity card in order to enter France and stay in the country. Citizens of Australia, Canada, Israel, Hong Kong, Japan, Malaysia, New Zealand, Singapore, the USA and many Latin American countries do not need visas to visit France as tourists for up to 90 days.

Other people wishing to come to France as tourists have to apply for a Schengen Visa, named after the agreements that abolished passport controls between 25 European countries: Austria, Belgium, Czech Republic, Denmark, Estonia, Finland, France, Germany, Greece, Hungary, Iceland, Italy, Latvia, Lithuania, Luxembourg, Malta, the Netherlands, Norway, Poland, Portugal, Slovakia, Slovenia, Spain, Sweden and Switzerland. It allows unlimited travel throughout the entire zone for a 90-day period. Application should be made to the consulate of the country you are entering first, or that will be your main destination.

Among other things, all travellers will need travel and repatriation insurance and be able to show that you have sufficient funds to support yourself.

Tourist visas *cannot* be extended except in emergencies (such as medical problems). When your visa expires you'll need to leave and reapply from outside the EU.

WOMEN TRAVELLERS

Women tend to attract more unwanted attention than men but need not walk around in fear; people are rarely assaulted on the street, though it pays to take cautions, particularly at night. Be aware of your surroundings and of situations that could be dangerous: empty streets, lonely beaches, dark corners of large train stations. Using metros late at night is generally OK, as stations are rarely deserted.

In some places women may have to deal with what might be called low-intensity sexual harassment: 'playful' comments and invitations that can become overbearing or aggressive and which some women find threatening or offensive. Remain polite and keep your distance. Hearing a foreign accent may provoke further unwanted attention.

Be alert to vibes in cheap hotels, sometimes staffed by apparently unattached men who may pay far more attention to your comings and goings than you would like. Change hotels if you feel uncomfortable or allude to the imminent arrival of your husband (whether you have one or not).

On overnight trains, you may prefer to ask (when reserving) if there's a women's compartment available. If your compartment companions are overly attentive, don't hesitate to ask the conductor for a change of compartment. Sleeping cars, which have their own bathrooms, offer greater security than a couchette.

In an emergency, contact the **police** (☎ 17), who will take you to the hospital if you have been attacked or injured. You can reach France's national **rape crisis hotline** (☎ 08 00 05 95 95; ☯ 10am-7pm Mon-Fri) toll-free from any telephone without using a phonecard.

TRANSPORT

ARRIVAL & DEPARTURE
AIR

Although there are several airports in Brittany and Normandy, there are relatively few international flights. Most international visitors enter through Paris via either Charles de Gaulle or Orly airport. France is a heavily touristed destination, making it wise to book ahead, especially if you are travelling around Christmas, Easter or any time during the summer holiday period, when fares are

THINGS CHANGE...

The information in this chapter is particularly vulnerable to change. Check directly with the transport provider or a travel agent to make sure you understand how a fare (and the ticket you may buy) works, and be aware of the security requirements for international travel. The details given in this chapter should be regarded as pointers and are not a substitute for your own careful, up-to-date research.

likely to shoot up. If you are travelling from one of France's far-flung African *départements* or territories in the South Pacific, be aware that flights may be booked solid many months in advance.

AIRPORTS

France's main international gateway is Paris, with three airports – Charles de Gaulle, Orly and Beauvais-Tillé – although the latter is actually closer to Rouen than Paris. Airports at Rouen, Caen, Cherbourg and Le Havre serve Normandy and there are local airports at Brest, Dinard, Lannion, Lorient, Nantes, Quimper and St-Brieuc in Brittany.

Brest (code BES; ☎ 02 98 32 01 00; www.airport.cci -brest.fr) Year-round from Paris-CDG, Paris-Orly, Toulon, Lyon, Nice, Marseilles, Bordeaux, Ouessant; international flights from London-Luton and Manchester, with summer services from Southampton, Birmingham, Exeter, Dublin.

Caen-Carpiquet (code CFR; ☎ 02 31 71 20 10; www.caen.aeroport.fr, in French) Direct flights from Paris-Orly, Lyons and Nice.

Cherbourg-Maupertis (code CER; ☎ 02 33 88 57 60; www.aeroport-cherbourg.com) Paris-Orly and charter flights.

Dinard (code DNR; ☎ 08 25 08 35 09; www
.saint-malo.cci.fr/en/services/airport/) Flights from
London-Stansted, Bristol, Birmingham, East Midlands
and Guernsey.

Lannion (code LAI; ☎ 02 96 05 82 22; www.lannion
.aeroport.fr) Flights from Paris-Orly.

Le Havre (code LEH; ☎ 02 35 54 65 00; www.havre
.aeroport.fr) Lyons and Amsterdam.

Lorient (code LRT; www.lorient.aeroport.fr) Flights
from Paris-Orly, Lyons and Ireland.

Nantes-Atlantique (code NTE; ☎ 02 40 84 80
00; www.nantes.aeroport.fr) Western France's biggest
airport, welcoming flights from many European cities,
the Americas (including French Canada), French-
speaking Africa and all around France.

Paris-Beauvais-Tillé (code BVA; ☎ 03 44 11 19
82; www.aeroportbeauvais.com) This budget airline hub
is 85km due east of Rouen. It has direct flights from Marseilles, Scotland, Ireland, Portugal, Spain, Italy, Romania,
Hungary, Czech Republic, Poland and Sweden.

Paris–Charles de Gaulle (code CDG; ☎ 3950,
per minute €0.34; www.aeroportsdeparis.fr) France's
major hub with flights from all over the world.

Paris-Orly (code ORY; same contacts as CDG)
Another large international hub.

Quimper (code CFR; ☎ 02 98 94 30 30; www
.quimper.aeroport.fr) Flights from Paris-Orly.

Rennes (code RNS; ☎ 02 99 29 60 00; www.rennes
.aeroport.fr) Flights from the UK, Ireland and several
French cities.

Rouen (code URO; ☎ 02 35 79 41 00; www.rouen
.aeroport.fr) Lyons and Figari.

St-Brieuc (code SBK; ☎ 02 96 94 95 00; www
.st-brieuc.aeroport.fr) Flights to Newquay.

Many airlines fly to Paris but the following have regular flights to and from
Normandy and Brittany.

Aer Arann (airline code RE; ☎ in Ireland 353-818
210 210; www.aerarran.com) Flies from Cork to Lorient
and Nantes-Atlantique.

Aer Lingus (airline code EI; ☎ 01 70 20 00 72;
www.aerlingus.ie) Flies to Rennes from Ireland.

Air France (airline code AF; ☎ 3654; www.air
france.com) Flies from many French cities to Brest, Caen,
Lannion, Le Havre, Lorient, Nantes-Atlantique, Quimper,
Rennes and Rouen.

Air Transat (airline code TS; ☎ 08 25 12 02
48; www.airtransat.com) Flies from Canada to
Nantes-Atlantique.

Airlinair (airline code A5; ☎ 08 10 47 84 78; www
.airlinair.com) Flies from Paris or Bordeaux to Brest, Caen,
Cherbourg, Le Havre and Rennes.

Atlas-Blue (airline code 8A; ☎ 08 20 88 78
87; www.atlas-blue.com) Flies from Marrakesh to
Nantes-Atlantique.

Aurigny (airline code GR; ☎ 02 99 46 18 46; www
.aurigny.com) Flies from Guernsey to Dinard.

Corsairfly (airline code SS; ☎ 08 00 04 20 42 per
minute €0.12; www.corsairfly.com) Flies from Canada
and some other destinations to Nantes-Atlantique.

EasyJet (airline code U2; ☎ 08 25 08 25 08;
www.easyjet.com) Flies from Geneva or Lyon to
Nantes-Atlantique.

Flybe (airline code BE; ☎ in the UK 0871 70 0 0535;
www3.flybe.com) Flies to Brest and Rennes from UK
destinations.

Iberia (airline code IB; ☎ 08 25 80 09 65; www
.iberia.com) Flies to Nantes-Atlantique from Spain and
other destinations.

Jetairfly (airline code TB; ☎ in Belgium 32 70 22 00
00; www.jetairfly.com) Flies to Brest from Toulon.

Royal Air Maroc (airline code AT; www.royalair
maroc.com) Flies to Nantes-Atlantique.

Ryanair (airline code FR; ☎ 08 92 68 20 73; www
.ryanair.com) Flies from European cities to Brest, Dinard,
Nantes-Atlantique and Paris-Beauvais-Tillé.

Skybus (airline code 5Y; ☎ in UK 01736-334 224;
www.skybus.co.uk) Flies from Newquay to St-Brieuc.

Tunisair (airline code TU; ☎ in Tunisia 070-837 100;
www.tunisair.com) Flies to Nantes-Atlantique.

BUS

Europe's international buses are slower
and less comfortable than trains but are
considerably cheaper, especially if you
are under 26 or over 60, or get a promo-
tional fare.

Eurolines (☎ 08 92 89 90 91, per minute €0.34;
www.eurolines.eu) is a grouping of dozens

TRANSPORT

of long-haul coach operators that link 500 destinations all across Europe and in Morocco. Return fares are about 20% cheaper than two one-ways. In summer it's best to make reservations at least two working days in advance. Some international services, particularly from Britain, head directly to Brittany and Normandy but for many you'll need to connect through Paris.

From London, a one-way online fare to Rouen will cost around UK£42. Booked on the French site, the return journey starts at around €39; supplements sometimes apply. Channel crossings are by ferry.

CAR & MOTORCYCLE

Arriving in France by car is easy. At some border points you may be asked for a passport or EU national identity card (your driving licence will not be sufficient ID). Police searches are not uncommon for vehicles entering France, particularly from Spain and Belgium (as these are seen as the main routes used for smuggling drugs from Morocco or the Netherlands). See p324 for further details about driving in the region.

BRINGING YOUR OWN VEHICLE

A right-hand-drive vehicle brought to France from the UK or Ireland must have deflectors affixed to the headlights to avoid dazzling oncoming traffic.

A foreign motor vehicle entering France must display a sticker or licence plate identifying its country of registration. In the UK, information on driving in France is available from the **RAC** (☎ in UK 0800 550 055; www.rac.co.uk) and the **AA** (☎ in UK 0162-495 8945; www.theaa.com).

Try not to be on the roads when the French are involved in their massive seasonal shift from home to holiday spot.

ONLINE TICKET

Cheap Flights (www.cheapflights.com)
Ebookers (www.ebookers.com)
Expedia (www.expedia.com)
Flight Centre (www.flightcentre.com)
Kayak (www.kayak.com)
Last Minute (www.lastminute.com)
Mobissimo (www.mobissimo.com)
Orbitz (www.orbitz.com)
Priceline (www.priceline.com)
STA Travel (www.statravel.com)
Travelocity (www.travelocity.com)

On the first and last weekends of August roads can be completely clogged, and the weekend around 15 August is also a time of heavy traffic. Tune in to 107.7MHz FM, which gives traffic reports in English every 30 minutes during the summer.

DRIVING LICENCE & DOCUMENTATION

All drivers must carry at all times: an EU national ID card or passport; a valid driving licence (*permis de conduire;* most foreign licences can be used in France for up to a year); car-ownership papers, known as a *carte grise* (grey card); and proof of third-party liability *assurance* (insurance).

An International Driving Permit (IDP), valid only if accompanied by your original licence (an IDP is basically just a translation), is good for a year and can be issued by your local automobile association before you leave home. However, you shouldn't need to produce one.

EUROTUNNEL

The Channel Tunnel, inaugurated in 1994, is the first dry-land link between England and France since the last ice age. High-speed **Eurotunnel shuttle trains** (☎ in UK 0870 535 3535, in France 08 10 63 03 04; www.eurotunnel.com) whisk bicycles, motorcycles, cars and buses from Folkestone to Coquelles, 5km southwest of Calais, in air-conditioned and soundproofed comfort in just 35 minutes. Shuttles run 24 hours each day, with up to three departures an hour during peak periods. LPG and CNG tanks are not permitted, which eliminates gas-powered cars and many campervans and caravans.

Eurotunnel sets its fares the way budget airlines do: the longer in advance you book and the lower the demand for a particular crossing, the less you pay; same-day fares can cost a fortune.

Depending on the date and, especially, the time of day, one-way car fares range from UK£59 to UK£199 (€74 to €279), including all passengers, unlimited luggage and taxes. The fee for a bicycle, including its rider, is UK£16 one way;

cyclists must make advance reservations (☎ in UK 01303-282 201).

From Coquelles, count on a two-hour drive to Le Tréport, the northernmost town in Normandy.

INSURANCE

Third-party liability insurance *(assurance au tiers)* is compulsory for all vehicles in France, including cars brought in from abroad. Normally, cars registered and insured in other European countries can circulate freely in France, but it's a good idea to contact your insurance company before you leave home to make sure you've got coverage – and to check who to contact in case of a breakdown or accident.

If you get into a minor accident with no injuries, the easiest way for drivers

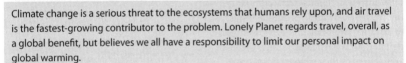

CLIMATE CHANGE & TRAVEL

Climate change is a serious threat to the ecosystems that humans rely upon, and air travel is the fastest-growing contributor to the problem. Lonely Planet regards travel, overall, as a global benefit, but believes we all have a responsibility to limit our personal impact on global warming.

Flying & Climate Change

Pretty much every form of motorised travel generates carbon dioxide (the main cause of human-induced climate change) but planes are far and away the worst offenders, not just because of the sheer distances they allow us to travel, but because they release greenhouse gases high into the atmosphere. The statistics are frightening: two people taking a return flight between Europe and the US will contribute as much to climate change as an average household's gas and electricity consumption over a whole year.

Carbon Offset Schemes

Climatecare.org and other websites use 'carbon calculators' that allow travellers to offset the level of greenhouse gases they are responsible for with financial contributions to sustainable travel schemes that reduce global warming – including projects in India, Honduras, Kazakhstan and Uganda.

Lonely Planet, together with Rough Guides and other concerned partners in the travel industry, support the carbon-offset scheme run by climatecare.org. Lonely Planet offsets all of its staff and author travel.

For more information check out our website, lonelyplanet.com.

to sort things out with their insurance companies is to fill out a *Constat Aimable d'Accident Automobile* (European Accident Statement), a standardised way of recording important details about what happened. In rental cars it's usually in the packet of documents in the glove compartment. Make sure the report includes any information that will help you prove that the accident was not your fault. Remember, if it was your fault you may be liable for a hefty insurance excess. Don't sign anything you don't fully understand. If problems crop up, call the **police** (☎ 17).

French-registered cars have details of their insurance company printed on a little green square affixed to their windscreens (from inside the car, in the lower right-hand corner).

SEA

Like Eurotunnel, most ferry companies set fares the way airlines do: the longer in advance you book and the lower the demand for a particular sailing, the less you pay, with the cheapest tickets costing just one-third of the priciest ones. Seasonal demand is a crucial factor (July and August are especially busy), as is the time of day (an early evening ferry can cost much more than one at 4am). On some routes, three- or five-day excursion (return) fares cost about the same as regular one-way tickets. Deals available in one country may not be available from another, even on the same route.

Tickets are available from most travel agencies in France and the countries served, though it's generally cheapest to book directly online. To get the best fare by comparing prices on various options, check out the booking service offered by **Ferry Savers** (☎ in UK 0844-371 8021; www .ferrysavers.com). Booking by phone incurs a UK£25 fee.

If you're travelling with a vehicle, for safety reasons you are usually denied access to it during the voyage. If you pay the foot-passenger fare, transporting a bicycle is often (but not always) free.

Except where noted, the prices given here are for last-minute one-way tickets; in some cases, return fares cost less than two one-way tickets. People under 25 and over 60 may qualify for discounts. Many companies charge a supplement if you book by phone.

CHANNEL ISLANDS

Year-round fast car ferries run by **Condor Ferries** (☎ in UK 0845-609 1024, in France 08 25 16 54 63; www.condorferries.com) link the Breton port of St-Malo with Jersey (1¼ hours, 18 weekly) and Guernsey (1¾ hours, 12 weekly). Tickets are cheaper with advance bookings, but last-minute passenger-only fares cost around £24, or with a small car between £73 and £113.

Compagnie Corsaire (☎ 08 25 13 81 00; www.compagniecorsaire.com) operates Jersey to St-Malo passenger services between April and September (€39, 80 minutes, daily).

Passenger ferries run by **Manche Îles Express** (☎ 08 25 13 30 50, per minute €0.15; www.manche-iles-express.com) link Normandy's west coast with Jersey, Guernsey (Guernesey), Alderney (Aurigny) and Sark (Sercq). Sailing are regular but less frequent outside of the peak April to September period. The main routes are Granville–Jersey (€50, 1¼ hours, nearly daily), Granville–Jersey-Sark (€56, two hours, one to seven weekly), Carteret–Jersey (€50, one hour, nearly daily), Carteret–Guernsey (€50, 80 minutes, 12 to 14 per month), Diélette–Guernsey (€50, 1¼ hours, 12 to 16 per month) and

Diélette–Alderney (€50, 45 minutes, one to five per month).

IRELAND

Irish Ferries (☎ in Ireland 0818-300 400, in France 08 10 00 13 57; www.irishferries.ie) has overnight services from Rosslare to either Cherbourg (17½ hours) or Roscoff (17½ hours, mid-May to September only) every other day (three times a week from October to May, except late December and January). Last-minute foot passengers pay €80 to €100, while a car with a driver costs from €180 to €340, not including a reserved seat (€16) or a cabin (from €120 to €175 for a two-berth cabin). Special fares can be as low as €59 (passenger only) to €99 with a car.

A mainly freight ship run by **Celtic Link** (☎ in Ireland 0402-38 084, in France 02 33 43 23 87; www.celticlinkferries.com) connects Rosslare with Cherbourg (18½ hours, two or three weekly except mid-December to mid-January). A car with a driver costs €100 to €230, not including a mandatory sleeping berth (€80 for two). Foot passengers are not accepted.

LD Lines (☎ in UK 0844-576 8836, in France 08 25 30 43 04, per minute €0.15; www.ldlines.com) sends two car ferries a week from Rosslare to Le Havre (from €99, 22 hours). From March to early November, **Brittany Ferries** (☎ in UK 0871-244 1400, per minute €0.10, in France 08 25 82 88 28; www.brittanyferries.com) runs a weekly car ferry from Cork (Ringaskiddy) to Roscoff (14 hours).

UK

Brittany Ferries (☎ in UK 0871-244 1400, per minute €0.10, in France 08 25 82 88 28; www.brittanyferries.com) links Plymouth with Roscoff (6½ hours by day, nine hours overnight,

TRANSPORT

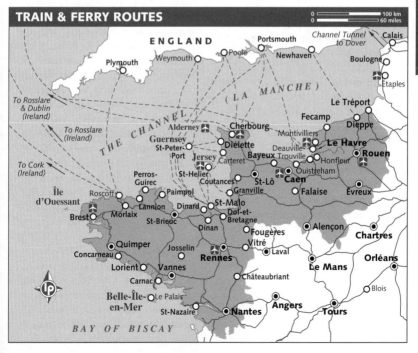

TRAIN & FERRY ROUTES

one to three daily from mid-March to mid-November, almost daily in winter); and Poole with Cherbourg (high-speed ferry 2¼ hours, regular ferry 4½ to 6½ hours, two or three daily). From Portsmouth they head to St-Malo (8¾ hours by day, 10¾ hours overnight, almost daily); Cherbourg (three hours, one or two daily); and Ouistreham (high-speed ferry 3¾ hours, regular ferry 5¾ to seven hours, two to four daily).

Condor Ferries (☎ in UK 0845-609 1024, in France 08 25 16 54 63; www.condorferries.com) runs car ferries from Poole to St-Malo (4½ hours), almost daily from late May to September; from Weymouth to St-Malo (5¼ hours), daily from late March to October and at least once a week in winter; and from Portsmouth to Cherbourg (five hours), weekly from late May to early September.

Year-round, **LD Lines** (☎ in UK 0844-576 8836, in France 08 25 30 43 04, per minute €0.15; www .ldlines.com), incorporating Transmanche Ferries, offers two daily sailings on weekdays between Portsmouth and Le Havre (5½ to eight hours) and one on Saturdays and Sundays. Last-minute one-way passage for a car and two adults costs up to UK£104. Car ferries also head twice-daily between Newhaven and Dieppe (four hours).

Regular ferries also link Dover with Calais and Boulogne. Travel by car from these cities to Normandy is straight-forward, but those who require public transport may find it quicker to travel via Paris; see www.voyages-sncf.com for possibilities.

ELSEWHERE

It's possible to travel as a passenger on a cargo ship from North America and East Asia to Le Havre; expect to pay from around US$135 per day. Such ves-sels typically carry five to 12 passengers (more than 12 would require a doctor on board). At the opposite extreme, luxury cruise liners are another option. Useful websites:

Cruise People (www.cruisepeople.co.uk) Based in London.

Freighter World Cruises (www.freighter world.com) Based in California.

TRAIN

Rail services link France with virtually every country in Europe. For details on train travel within Brittany and Normandy, see p328.

The fastest way into Brittany and Normandy by train is via SNCF's high-speed services, branded as **TGV** (Train à Grand Vitesse; www.tgv-europe.com). Pronounced teh zheh veh, they zip passengers along at speeds of up to 320km/h (200 mph). The network extends out of France to major cities in Belgium, the Netherlands, Germany, Switzerland, Italy, Spain and also the UK (London). In Brittany, stops on the TGV network include Auray, Brest, Dol-de-Bretagne, Guingamp, Lannion, Lorient, Morlaix, Nantes, Rennes, St-Brieuc, St-Malo, St-Nazaire, Quimper, Quimperlé and Vannes and Vitré. Another branch heads through Nantes to St-Nazaire and other stops in Loire-Atlantique. For Normandy, one TGV branch connects Paris to Le Havre via Rouen. Other types of trains also take you to Normandy from Paris; main stations on these routes include Alençon (change in Le Mans), Caen, Cherbourg, Dieppe, Granville and Le Tréport.

You can book tickets and get information from **Rail Europe** (☎ in UK 0844-848 4064; www.raileurope.com); phone bookings incur an €8 fee. In France ticketing is handled by the national rail operator **SNCF** (Société Nationale des Chemins de Fer Français;

☎ in France 3635, per minute €0.34, from abroad 08 92 35 35 35; www.sncf.com); telephone and internet bookings are possible but tickets can't be posted outside France. Several brands fall under the SNCF umbrella.

For more details on Europe's 200,000km rail network, see www.rail passenger.info, set up by a grouping of European rail companies. Information on 'seamless high-speed rail travel' is available from www.railteam.co.uk. Another very useful resource is the information-packed website the **Man in Seat 61** (www.seat61.com).

EUROSTAR

Thanks to the long-awaited high-speed track, the highly civilised **Eurostar** (☎ in UK 0870-518 6186, in France 08 92 35 35 39; www.euro star.com) whisks you between London and Paris in just 2¼ hours.

Eurostar offers a bewildering array of fares. A standard flexible one-way ticket from London to Paris costs a whopping UK£179, but super-discount returns go for as little as UK£59.

You'll get the best deals if you buy a return ticket, stay over a Saturday night, book well in advance (the cheapest fares sell out early) and don't mind nonexchangeability and nonrefundability. Special fares are also available if you're aged under 26 or over 60 on your departure date. Booking by phone incurs a UK£5 surcharge. Student travel agencies may have youth fares not available directly from Eurostar.

GETTING AROUND

Getting around Brittany and Normandy is a breeze, either with your own wheels or by taking advantage of the excellent public-transport network, which covers all the major centres. In addition to its environmental benefits, travelling by train, metro, tram and bus lets you experience France the way ordinary French people do, taking in the sights, encountering the unexpected and meeting locals at a pace set by the leisurely rhythm of day-to-day life.

The state-owned SNCF takes care of almost all land transport between *départements*. Transport within *départements* is handled by a combination of short-haul trains, SNCF buses and local bus companies that are either government-owned or government-contracted. The larger cities have their own urban transport services.

Flying within Brittany and Normandy isn't a practical option, possibly excepting the flights to the Ouessant Islands from Brest with **Finist'air** (☎ 02 98 84 64 87; www.finistair.fr).

BICYCLE

This region is generally a great place to cycle. Not only is much of the countryside drop-dead gorgeous but it has a growing number of urban and rural *pistes cyclables* (cycle paths and lanes), some linking one town to the next, and an extensive network of secondary and tertiary roads with relatively light traffic. One pitfall: back roads rarely have proper shoulders so wearing a fluorescent reflective vest is highly recommended. For ideas of where to go and how to organise some cycling, see Outdoors, p20. If you plan to do a lot of cycling, Lonely Planet's *Cycling in France* has a chapter devoted to these regions.

French law dictates that bicycles must have two functioning brakes, a bell, a red reflector on the back, and yellow reflectors on the pedals. After sunset and when visibility is poor, cyclists must turn on a white light at the front and a red

TRANSPORT

one at the rear. When being overtaken by a vehicle, cyclists are required to ride in single file. Towing children in a bike trailer is permitted.

The SNCF does its best to make travelling with a bicycle easy and even has a special website dealing with bikes and trains, www.velo.sncf.com (in French). Bicycles are not allowed on most local or intercity buses or on trams. On some of the regional trains you can take a bicycle free of charge, while others charge €10. On train timetables, a bicycle symbol indicates that bicycles are allowed on particular trains. On some regional trains, bikes have to be stored in the luggage van.

HIRE

Most cities and towns have at least one place that rents out *vélos tout terrains* (mountain bikes; generally €10 to €20 a day), popularly known as VTTs; more road-oriented *vélos tout chemin* (VTCs); or cheaper city bikes. You usually have to leave ID and/or a deposit (often a credit-card slip) that you forfeit if the bike is damaged or stolen. For details on rental options, see Getting Around under city and town listings throughout this book.

Rennes, Nantes, Rouen, Le Havre and Caen have automatic bike-rental systems, intended to encourage cycling as a form of urban transport, with computerised pick-up and drop-off sites all over town. In general, you have to sign up either short-term or long-term, providing credit-card details, and can then use the bikes for no charge for the first half-hour.

BUS

Each *département* within Normandy and Brittany has its own extensive network of buses linking the major cities and

towns, but schedules are mostly designed to accommodate the needs of students and workers. Some smaller villages in the interior are not served at all by bus links. Services are cut dramatically on Saturdays and are often nonexistent on Sundays. School holidays also involve a rearrangement of bus schedules. The bigger cities have their own urban bus services.

Buses are generally clean, comfortable, reliable and easy to use. Tickets are either time- or stage-based but you'll rarely have to pay more than €2 for a short trip, and some *départements* (such as Seine-Maritime and Eure) have capped all intra-*départemental* travel at €2, no matter the distance. You can usually buy a ticket directly from the driver but it's often cheaper to purchase a set of tickets or a multiday pass from the station. In either case you'll need to validate your ticket in the automatic machines when you start your journey.

SNCF has replaced some uneconomic train services with buses. Travellers can often (but not always) take advantage of any train pass they have when travelling on SNCF bus services.

CAR & MOTORCYCLE

Having your own wheels gives you lots of freedom and makes it easy to visit more remote parts of the region. Rural areas, such as Orne, have a surfeit of cute villages and picturesque country lanes that you would never experience if relying on public transport. Motorcyclists will find Normandy and Brittany great for touring, with good quality roads and lots of stunning scenery. Just make sure your wet-weather gear is up to scratch.

France (along with Belgium) has the densest highway network in Europe.

TRANSPORT

There are four types of intercity roads, which have alphanumeric designations:

Autoroutes (highway names beginning with A) Multilane divided highways, usually with tolls *(péages)*, that are generously outfitted with rest stops.
Routes Nationales (N, RN) National highways, often with sections with a divider strip.
Routes Départementales (D) Local roads.
Routes Communales (C, V) Minor rural roads.

Autoroute tolls can be expensive (you'll rake up €23.50 in 235km between Le Havre and Paris' Charles de Gaulle airport) but, unless you're in a huge rush, they can usually be avoided. Information on tolls, rest areas, traffic and weather is available from www.autoroutes.fr. The websites www.viamichelin.com and www.mappy.fr plot itineraries between your departure and arrival points.

FUEL & SPARE PARTS

Essence (petrol), also known as *carburant* (fuel), comes in regular *(ordinaire)* and 95 unleaded *(Sans Plomb 95* or SP95, usually available from a green pump). Diesel *(diesel, gazole, gasoil)* is usually distinguished by a yellow pump. Filling up *(faire le plein)* is most expensive at the rest stops along the autoroutes and often cheapest at hypermarkets.

Many small petrol stations close on Sunday afternoons and, even in cities, it can be hard to find a staffed station open late at night. In general, after-hours purchases (eg at hypermarkets' 24-hour stations) can only be made with a credit card that has an embedded PIN chip, so if all you've got is cash or a magnetic-strip credit card, you could be stuck.

If your car is *en panne* (breaks down), you'll have to find a garage that handles your *marque* (make of car). Peugeot, Renault and Citroën garages are common, but if you have a non-French car, you may have trouble finding someone to service it in more remote areas.

HIRE

To hire a car in France, you'll generally need to be over 21 years old, have had a driving licence for at least a year, and have an international credit card. Drivers aged under 25 usually have to pay a surcharge *(frais jeune conducteur)* of €25 to €35 per day.

Car-rental companies provide mandatory third-party liability insurance but things such as collision-damage waivers (CDW, or *assurance tous risques*) vary greatly from company to company. When comparing rates and conditions (ie the fine print), the most important thing to check is the *franchise* (excess), which for a small car is usually around €600 for damage and €800 for theft. With many companies, you can reduce the excess to zero (or at least to half) by paying a daily insurance supplement of €10 to €16. Your credit card may cover CDW if you use it to pay for the car rental but the rental company won't know anything about this – verify conditions and details with your credit-card issuer to be sure.

Arranging your car rental or fly/drive package before you leave home is usually considerably cheaper than a walk-in rental, but beware of website offers that don't include CDW or you may be liable for up to 100% of the car's value.

Major rental companies include the following:
ADA (☎ 08 25 16 91 69, per minute €0.15; www .ada.fr, in French)
Avis (☎ 08 20 05 05 05; www.avis.com) Has branches at many train stations.
Budget (☎ 08 25 00 35 64, per minute €0.15; www .budget.com)
Easycar (☎ in UK 08710-500 444; www.easycar .com)

TRANSPORT

DISTANCE CHART (KM)

Note: Distances between destinations are approximate

	Aleçon	Bayeux	Brest	Caen	Cherbourg-Octeville	Dieppe	Honfleur	Lorient	Mont St-Michel	Morlaix	Nantes	Quimper	Rouen	St-Brieuc
Bayeux	125													
Brest	383	367												
Caen	105	29	376											
Cherbourg-Octeville	224	95	399	124										
Dieppe	204	206	550	174	302									
Honfleur	130	86	415	58	182	121								
Lorient	293	338	135	321	352	495	379							
Mont St-Michel	134	119	256	132	157	302	181	207						
Morlaix	323	307	58	298	339	472	356	123	202					
Nantes	230	305	299	292	317	466	346	167	174	292				
Quimper	359	350	73	362	377	536	420	70	231	84	234			
Rouen	147	153	506	118	247	65	74	439	250	416	396	472		
St-Brieuc	237	221	145	212	248	386	270	422	111	91	204	129	343	
St-Malo	180	153	233	168	191	342	226	193	54	178	178	215	304	90

TRANSPORT

Europcar (☎ 08 25 35 83 58; www.europcar.com)
Hertz (☎ 01 39 38 38 38; www.hertz.com)
National-Citer (www.citer.fr)
Renault Rent (☎ 08 25 10 11 12, per minute €0.15; www.renault-rent.com, in French) Renault's new car-rental arm.
Sixt (☎ 08 20 00 74 98; www.sixt.fr, in French)

Deals can be found on the internet, with travel agencies or through companies such as **Auto Europe** (☎ in USA 1-888-223-5555; www.autoeurope.com) in the USA, **DriveAway Holidays** (☎ in Australia 1300 723 972; www.driveaway.com.au) in Australia and **Holiday Autos** (☎ in UK 0871-472 5229; www.holidayautos.co.uk) in the UK.

Note that rental cars with automatic transmission are very much the exception in France. You will usually need to order one well in advance, with a much smaller (and invariably costlier) range of models to choose from.

Hybrid-car hire is in its infancy but Hertz has a few Toyota Priuses available

in France and, despite the higher rental rates, more companies are sure to follow suit. For more information, see www.greencarsite.co.uk/green-car-hire.htm.

All rental cars registered in France have a distinctive number on the licence plate, making them easily identifiable – including to thieves, so *never* leave anything of value in a parked car, even in the boot.

PARKING

In city centres, most on-the-street parking places are *payant* (metered) from about 9am to 7pm (sometimes with a break from noon to 2pm) from Monday to Saturday, except for public holidays. Parking buildings are plentiful and clearly signposted. In many towns it's possible to find free street parking on the outskirts, without requiring too much of a walk or bus ride to the centre.

SPEED LIMITS

★ Built up areas 50km/h

★ Undivided highways 90km/h (80km/h if it's raining)

★ Non-autoroute divided highways 110km/h (100km/h if it's raining)

★ Autoroutes 130km/h (110km/h in the rain, 60km/h in icy conditions)

PURCHASE-REPURCHASE PLANS

If you'll be needing a car in France (or Europe) for one to six months, by far the cheapest option is to 'purchase' a brand-new one from **Citroën** (www.euro cartt.com, www.citroendriveeurope.com.au or www .citroentt.com), **Peugeot** (www.peugeot-open europe.com) or **Renault** (www.eurodrive.renault .com) and then 'sell' it back to them at the end of your trip. In reality, you pay only for the number of days you have the vehicle but the paperwork means that the car is registered under your name – and that the whole deal is exempt from all sorts of taxes. Eligibility is restricted to people who are not residents of the EU (citizens of EU countries are eligible if they live outside the EU). Pricing and special offers depend on your home country.

Prices include unlimited kilometres, 24-hour towing and breakdown service, and comprehensive insurance with – incredibly – no excess, so returning the car is totally hassle-free, even if it's damaged. Extending your contract is possible (using a credit card) but you'll end up paying about double the prepaid per-day rate.

These cars – which have special red licence plates – can be picked up at about three-dozen cities and airports all over France and dropped off at any other purchase-repurchase centre. You can also pick up or return your car in some cities outside France for a fee.

ROAD RULES

Enforcement of traffic laws has been stepped up in France in recent years and speed cameras are becoming ever more common.

French law requires that all passengers, including those in the back seat, wear seat belts. Babies weighing less than 13kg must travel in the rear in backward-facing child seats; children up to 18kg must ride in child seats. Children under 10 must sit in the back unless it's already occupied by other children under 10. North American drivers should remember that turning right on a red light is illegal in France.

Under the *priorité à droite* rule, any car entering an intersection (including a T-junction and a roundabout) from a road on your right has the right of way, unless the intersection is marked *vous n'avez pas la priorité* (you do not have right of way) or *cédez le passage* (give way). *Priorité à droite* is also suspended on priority roads, which are marked by an upended yellow square with a black square in the middle.

It is illegal to drive with a blood-alcohol concentration over 0.05% (0.5g per litre of blood) – the equivalent of two glasses of wine in the first hour for a 75kg adult. Police often conduct breathalyser tests at random and penalties can be severe, including imprisonment. Mobile phones may only be used when accompanied by a hands-free kit or speakerphone.

Since July 2008, all French vehicles must carry a reflective safety jacket and a reflective triangle; the fine for not carrying one/both is €90/135. Radar detectors are illegal.

TRANSPORT

Riders of any type of two-wheeled vehicle with a motor (except motor-assisted bicycles) must wear a helmet. No special licence is required to ride a motorbike that has an engine smaller than 50cc, which is why you often find places renting scooters rated at 49.9cc.

TAXI

All medium and large train stations – and many small ones – have a taxi stand out the front. In small cities and towns, where taxi drivers are unlikely to find another fare anywhere near where they let you off, one-way and return trips often cost the same. Tariffs are about 30% higher at night and on Sundays and holidays. Having a taxi wait for you costs about €18 an hour. There may be a surcharge for getting picked up at a train station or airport and a small additional fee for a fourth passenger and/or for suitcases.

TRAIN

Travelling by train is a comfortable and environmentally friendly way to get between the major (and many of the minor) towns in Brittany and Normandy. Since many train stations have car-rental agencies, it's easy to combine rail travel with rural exploration by car. The rail network is run by state-owned **SNCF** (☎ 3635; www.voyages-sncf.com), including TGV (high-speed trains), TER (regional trains), Corail Intercités (medium-haul routes) and Lunéa (overnight trains).

CLASSES & COSTS

Most French trains have both 1st- and 2nd-class sections. Full-fare tickets for the former cost 50% more than the latter. Full-fare return passage costs twice as much as one-way fares. By way of exam-ple, a full-fare 2nd-class one-way ticket from Rennes to Caen costs between €39 and €44. Children aged under four travel for free; those aged four to 11 pay half price.

Ticket prices for some trains, including most TGVs, reflect supply and demand and so are pricier during peak periods, eg during workday rush hours, on Friday evening and at the beginning and end of holiday periods.

The SNCF's most heavily discounted tickets are, oddly, known as Prem's. They can be booked on the internet, by phone, at ticket windows and from ticket machines a maximum of 90 days and a minimum of four days before your travel date, though the very cheapest seats often sell out early on. Once you buy a Prem's ticket, it's use it or lose it – getting your money back or changing the time is not allowed. At the other extreme of the planning spectrum, it's worth checking the SNCF website for last-minute fares (Prem's Dernière Minute), which offer up to 50% discounts on selected routes.

Corail fares that require neither a discount card nor advance purchase but get you 25% off include **Loisir Week-End** rates, good for return travel that includes a Saturday night at your destination or involves travel on a Saturday or Sunday; and **Découverte** fares, for low-demand 'blue-period' trains, which are available to young people aged 12 to 25, seniors and the adult travel companions of children under 12. **Mini-Groupe** tickets can save lots for three to six people travelling together, provided you spend a Saturday night at your destination.

TICKETS & RESERVATIONS

At stations you can buy tickets from the counter or a *billeterie automatique* (automatic ticket machine), which accept both cash and computer-chip credit cards. Push on the Union Jack for instructions in English.

Using a credit card, you can buy a ticket by phone or via the booking site of **SNCF** (www.voyages-sncf.com, in French) and either have it sent to you by post (if you have an address in France) or collect it from any SNCF ticket office or from train-station ticket machines.

Before boarding the train, you must validate *(composter)* your ticket by time-stamping it in a *composteur,* one of those yellow posts located on the way to the platform. If you forget (or don't have a ticket for some other reason), find a conductor on the train before they find you – otherwise you can be fined.

In Basse-Normandy there's a weekend pass, the *Carte Sillage Loisirs*, that offers a 50% reduction for the passholder and a second person and only a €0.15 charge for additional people. The journey must be completed on either Saturday or Sunday; the pass costs €7 and is valid for a year.

You cannot hope to recoup the cost of an **InterRail France Pass** (www.interrailnet .com) or any pass with **Eurail** (www.eurail .com) if travelling only or mostly around the region covered by this book.

TRANSPORT

LANGUAGE

French is the principal language of communication in both Brittany and Normandy. Some English is spoken, especially by young people.

The indigenous language of Brittany is Breton *(breiz)*, a Celtic language related to Cornish and Welsh and, more distantly, to Irish and Scottish Gaelic. See the Breton section, p337, for some basic words and greetings in Breton.

The Norman dialect died out several centuries ago and remains in only a few words that you may hear older people use. They may refer to a *cheval* (horse) as a *qu'va*, or a *coq* (rooster) as a *cô*. Unlike regions such as Brittany or Provence, there is no movement to revive the dialect.

FRENCH

· · · · · ·

Modern French developed from the *langue d'oïl*, a group of dialects spoken north of the River Loire that grew out of the vernacular Latin used during the late Gallo-Roman period. The *langue d'oïl* – particularly the Francien dialect

spoken in the Île de France – eventually displaced the *langue d'oc*, the dialects spoken in the south of the country, from which the Mediterranean region of Languedoc got its name.

Around 130 million people worldwide speak French as their first language. The French, rightly or wrongly, have a reputation for assuming that all human beings should speak French – until WWI it was *the* international language of culture and diplomacy – and you'll find that any attempt to communicate in French will be much appreciated. Your best bet is to approach people politely in French, even if the only sentence you know is '*Pardon, monsieur/madame/mademoiselle, parlez-vous anglais?*' (Excuse me, sir/madam/miss, do you speak English?).

For a more comprehensive guide to the language, pick up a copy of Lonely Planet's *French Phrasebook*.

PRONUNCIATION

Most letters in French are pronounced more or less the same as their English counterparts. Here are a few that may cause confusion:

j	as the 's' in 'leisure', eg *jour* (day)
c	before **e** and **i**, as the 's' in 'sit'; before **a**, **o** and **u**, it's pronounced as English 'k'. See also when underscored with a 'cedilla' below
ç	as the 's' in 'sit'
r	pronounced from the back of the throat while constricting the muscles to restrict the flow of air
n, m	where a syllable ends in a single **n** or **m**, these letters are not pronounced, but the preceding vowel is given a nasal pronunciation

BE POLITE

An important distinction is made in French between *tu* and *vous*, which both mean 'you'; *tu* is only used when addressing people you know well, children or animals. If you're addressing an adult who isn't a personal friend, *vous* should be used unless the person invites you to use *tu*. In general, younger people insist less on this distinction between polite and informal, and you will find that in many cases they use *tu* from the beginning of an acquaintance.

GRAMMAR

All nouns in French are either masculine or feminine and adjectives reflect the gender of the noun they modify. The feminine form of some nouns and adjectives is indicated by a silent **e** added to the masculine form, as in *ami* and *amie* (the masculine and feminine for 'friend'); other words undergo more complex changes.

In the following phrases both masculine and feminine forms have been

indicated where necessary (by 'm' and 'f' respectively). The gender of a noun is often indicated by a preceding article, eg *le/un* (m) and *la/une* (f), meaning 'the/ a'; or one of the possessive adjectives, eg *mon/ton/son* (m) and *ma/ta/sa* (f), meaning 'my/your/his, her'. French is unlike English in that the possessive adjective agrees in number and gender with the thing in question, eg 'his mother' and 'her mother' are both translated as *sa mère*.

ACCOMMODATION

I'm looking for a ...	*Je cherche ...*	zher shersh ...
camping ground	*un camping*	un kom·peeng
guest house	*une pension (de famille)*	ewn pon·syon (der fa·mee·yer)
hotel	*un hôtel*	un o·tel
youth hostel	*une auberge de jeunesse*	ewn o·berzh der zher·nes

Where is a cheap hotel?
Où est-ce qu'on peut oo es kon per
trouver un hôtel pas cher? troo·vay un o·tel pa shair
What is the address?
Quelle est l'adresse? kel ay la·dres
Could you write it down, please?
Est-ce que vous pourriez es ker voo poo·ryay
l'écrire, s'il vous plaît? lay·kreer seel voo play

How much is it ...?	*Quel est le prix ...?*	kel ay ler pree ...
per night	*par nuit*	par nwee
per person	*par personne*	par per·son

Do you have any rooms available?
Est-ce que vous avez des es ker voo za·vay day
chambres libres? shom·brer lee·brer
May I see the room?
Est-ce que je peux voir es ker zher per vwa
la chambre? la shom·brer
Where is the bathroom?
Où est la salle de bain? oo ay la sal der bun
Where is the toilet?
Où sont les toilettes? oo son lay twa·let

LANGUAGE

I'd like (a) ...	Je voudrais ...	zher voo·dray ...
single room	une chambre à un lit	ewn shom·brer a un lee
double-bed room	une chambre avec un grand lit	ewn shom·brer a·vek un gron lee
twin room (with two beds)	une chambre avec des lits jumeaux	ewn shom·brer a·vek day lee zhew·mo
room with a bathroom	une chambre avec une salle de bain	ewn shom·brer a·vek ewn sal der bun
to share a dorm	coucher dans un dortoir	koo·sher don zun dor·twa

I'm leaving today.

Je pars aujourd'hui. zher par o·zhoor·dwee

We're leaving today.

Nous partons aujourd'hui. noo par·ton o·zhoor·dwee

CONVERSATION & ESSENTIALS

Hello.	Bonjour.	bon·zhoor
Goodbye.	Au revoir.	o rer·vwa
Yes.	Oui.	wee
No.	Non.	non
Please.	S'il vous plaît.	seel voo play
Thank you.	Merci.	mair·see
You're welcome.	Je vous en prie.	zher voo zon pree
	De rien. (inf)	der ree·en
Excuse me.	Excusez-moi.	ek·skew·zay·mwa
Sorry. (forgive me)	Pardon.	par·don

What's your name?

| Comment vous appelez-vous? (pol) | kom·mon voo za·pay·lay voo |
| Comment tu t'appelles? (inf) | kom·mon tew ta·pel |

My name is ...

Je m'appelle ... zher ma·pel ...

I'd like to introduce you to ...

Je vous présente. zher voo pray·zont

I'm pleased to meet you.

Enchanté(e). (m/f) on·shon·tay

Where are you from?

| De quel pays êtes-vous? | der kel pay·ee et·voo |
| De quel pays es-tu? (inf) | der kel pay·ee ay·tew |

MAKING A RESERVATION

Use these expressions in letters, faxes and emails:

To ...	A l'attention de ...
From ...	De la part de ...
Date	Date
I'd like to book ...	Je voudrais réserver ...
in the name of ...	au nom de ...
from ... to ...	du ... au ...
credit card (...)	(...) carte de crédit
number	numéro de
expiry date	date d'expiration de la
Please confirm availability and price.	Veuillez confirmer la disponibilité et le prix.

I'm from ...

Je viens de ... zher vyen der ...

I like ...

J'aime ... zhem ...

I don't like ...

Je n'aime pas ... zher nem pa ...

Just a minute.

Une minute. ewn mee·newt

DIRECTIONS

Where is ...?

Où est ...? oo ay ...

Go straight ahead.

Continuez tout droit. kon·teen·way too drwa

Turn left.

Tournez à gauche. toor·nay a gosh

Turn right.

Tournez à droite. toor·nay a drwat

at the corner

au coin o kwun

at the traffic lights

aux feux o fer

behind	derrière	dair·ryair
in front of	devant	der·von
far (from)	loin (de)	lwun (der)
near (to)	près (de)	pray (der)
opposite	en face de	on fas der

SIGNS

Chambres Libres	Rooms Available
(Commissariat de) Police	Police Station
Complet	Full/No Vacancies
Entrée/Sortie	Entrance/Exit
Interdit	Prohibited
Ouvert/Fermé	Open/Closed
Renseignements	Information
Toilettes/WC	Toilets
Hommes	Men
Femmes	Women

beach	*la plage*	la plazh
bridge	*le pont*	ler pon
castle	*le château*	ler sha·to
cathedral	*la cathédrale*	la ka·tay·dral
church	*l'église*	lay·gleez
island	*l'île*	leel
lake	*le lac*	ler lak
main square	*la place centrale*	la plas son·tral
museum	*le musée*	ler mew·zay
old city (town)	*la vieille ville*	la vyay veel
palace	*le palais*	ler pa·lay
quay	*le quai*	ler kay
riverbank	*la rive*	la reev
ruins	*les ruines*	lay rween
sea	*la mer*	la mair
square	*la place*	la plas
tourist office	*l'office de tourisme*	lo·fees der too·rees·mer
tower	*la tour*	la toor

EATING OUT

I'd like ..., please.

Je voudrais ...,   zher voo·dray ...
s'il vous plaît.   seel voo play

That was delicious!

C'était délicieux!   say·tay day·lee·syer

Please bring the bill.

Apportez-moi l'addition,   a·por·tay·mwa la·dee·syon
s'il vous plaît.   seel voo play

I'm vegetarian.

Je suis   zher swee
végétarien(ne). (m/f)   vay·zhay·ta·ryun/ryen

I'm allergic to ...	*Je suis allergique ...*	zher swee za·lair·zheek ...
dairy produce	*aux produits laitiers*	o pro·dwee lay·tyay
eggs	*aux œufs*	o zer
nuts	*aux noix*	o nwa
seafood	*aux fruits de mer*	o frwee der mair

HEALTH

I'm ill.

Je suis malade.   zher swee ma·lad

It hurts here.

J'ai une douleur ici.   zhay ewn doo·ler ee·see

I'm ...	*Je suis ...*	zher swee ...
asthmatic	*asthmatique*	as·ma·teek
diabetic	*diabétique*	dee·a·bay·teek
epileptic	*épileptique*	ay·pee·lep·teek

I'm allergic to ...	*Je suis allergique ...*	zher swee za·lair·zheek ...
antibiotics	*aux antibiotiques*	o zon·tee·byo·teek
aspirin	*à l'aspirine*	a las·pee·reen
bees	*aux abeilles*	o za·bay·yer
penicillin	*à la pénicilline*	a la pay·nee·see·leen

antiseptic	*l'antiseptique*	lon·tee·sep·teek
aspirin	*l'aspirine*	las·pee·reen
condoms	*des préservatifs*	day pray·zair·va·teef
contraceptive	*le contraceptif*	ler kon·tra·sep·teef
diarrhoea	*la diarrhée*	la dya·ray
medicine	*le médicament*	ler may·dee·ka·mon
nausea	*la nausée*	la no·zay
sunblock cream	*la crème solaire*	la krem so·lair
tampons	*des tampons hygiéniques*	day tom·pon ee·zhen·eek

LANGUAGE DIFFICULTIES

Do you speak English?

Parlez-vous anglais?   par·lay·voo ong·glay

Does anyone here speak English?

Y a-t-il quelqu'un qui   ee a·teel kel·kung kee
parle anglais?   parl ong·glay

LANGUAGE

How do you say ... in French?

Comment est-ce qu'on   kom·mon es kon
dit ... en français?   dee ... on fron·say
What does ... mean?

Que veut dire ...?   ker ver deer ...
I (don't) understand.

Je (ne) comprends (pas).   zher (ner) kom·pron (pa)
Could you write it down, please?

Est-ce que vous pouvez   es ker voo poo·vay
l'écrire?   lay·kreer
Can you show me (on the map)?

Pouvez-vous m'indiquer   poo·vay·voo mun·dee·kay
(sur la carte)?   (sewr la kart)

NUMBERS

0	*zéro*	zay·ro
1	*un*	un
2	*deux*	der
3	*trois*	trwa
4	*quatre*	ka·trer
5	*cinq*	sungk
6	*six*	sees
7	*sept*	set
8	*huit*	weet
9	*neuf*	nerf
10	*dix*	dees
11	*onze*	onz
12	*douze*	dooz
13	*treize*	trez
14	*quatorze*	ka·torz
15	*quinze*	kunz
16	*seize*	sez
17	*dix-sept*	dee·set
18	*dix-huit*	dee·zweet
19	*dix-neuf*	deez·nerf
20	*vingt*	vung
21	*vingt et un*	vung tay un
22	*vingt-deux*	vung·der
30	*trente*	tront
40	*quarante*	ka·ront
50	*cinquante*	sung·kont
60	*soixante*	swa·sont
70	*soixante-dix*	swa·son·dees
80	*quatre-vingts*	ka·trer·vung
90	*quatre-vingt-dix*	ka·trer·vung·dees
100	*cent*	son
1000	*mille*	meel

EMERGENCIES

Help!

Au secours!   o skoor
There's been an accident!

Il y a eu un accident!   eel ee a ew un ak·see·don
I'm lost.

Je me suis égaré(e). (m/f)   zhe me swee zay·ga·ray
Leave me alone!

Fichez-moi la paix!   fee·shay·mwa la pay

Call ...!	*Appelez ...!*	a·play ...
a doctor	*un médecin*	un mayd·sun
the police	*la police*	la po·lees

PAPERWORK

name	*nom*	nom
nationality	*nationalité*	na·syo·na·lee·tay
date/place	*date/place*	dat/plas
of birth	*de naissance*	der nay·sons
sex/gender	*sexe*	seks
passport	*passeport*	pas·por
visa	*visa*	vee·za

QUESTION WORDS

Who?	*Qui?*	kee
What?	*Quoi?*	kwa
What is it?	*Qu'est-ce que c'est?*	kes ker say
When?	*Quand?*	kon
Where?	*Où?*	oo
Which?	*Quel(le)? (m/f)*	kel
Why?	*Pourquoi?*	poor·kwa
How?	*Comment?*	kom·mon

SHOPPING & SERVICES

I'd like to buy ...

Je voudrais acheter ...   zher voo·dray ash·tay ...
How much is it?

C'est combien?   say kom·byun
I don't like it.

Cela ne me plaît pas.   ser·la ner mer play pa
I'm just looking.

Je regarde.   zher rer·gard

May I look at it?

Est-ce que je peux   es ker zher per

le/la voir? (m/f)   ler/la vwar

It's too expensive.

C'est trop cher.   say tro shair

I'll take it.

Je le/la prends. (m/f)   zher ler/la pron

Can I pay by …?	*Est-ce que je peux*	es ker zher per
	payer avec …?	pay-yay a-vek …
credit card	*ma carte de*	ma kart der
	crédit	kray-dee
travellers	*des chèques*	day shek
cheques	*de voyage*	der vwa-yazh

more	*plus*	plews
less	*moins*	mwun
smaller	*plus petit*	plew per-tee
bigger	*plus grand*	plew gron

I'm looking for …	*Je cherche …*	zhe shersh …
a bank	*une banque*	ewn bonk
the (…) embassy	*l'ambassade (de …)*	lam-ba-sahd (der …)
the hospital	*l'hôpital*	lo-pee-tal
the market	*le marché*	ler mar-shay
the police	*la police*	la po-lees
the post office	*le bureau de poste*	ler bew-ro der post
a public phone	*une cabine téléphonique*	ewn ka-been tay-lay-fo-neek
a public toilet	*les toilettes*	lay twa-let

TIME & DATES

What time is it?

Quelle heure est-il?   kel er ay til

It's (eight) o'clock.

Il est (huit) heures.   il ay (weet) er

It's half past (…)

Il est (…) heures et   il ay (…) er ay

demie.   der-mee

in the morning	*du matin*	dew ma-tun
in the afternoon	*de l'après-midi*	der la-pray-mee-dee
in the evening	*du soir*	dew swar

today	*aujourd'hui*	o-zhoor-dwee
tomorrow	*demain*	der-mun
yesterday	*hier*	yair

Monday	*lundi*	lun-dee
Tuesday	*mardi*	mar-dee
Wednesday	*mercredi*	mair-krer-dee
Thursday	*jeudi*	zher-dee
Friday	*vendredi*	von-drer-dee
Saturday	*samedi*	sam-dee
Sunday	*dimanche*	dee-monsh

January	*janvier*	zhon-vyay
February	*février*	fayv-ryay
March	*mars*	mars
April	*avril*	a-vreel
May	*mai*	may
June	*juin*	zhwun
July	*juillet*	zhwee-yay
August	*août*	oot
September	*septembre*	sep-tom-brer
October	*octobre*	ok-to-brer
November	*novembre*	no-vom-brer
December	*décembre*	day-som-brer

TRANSPORT

PUBLIC TRANSPORT

What time does … leave/arrive?	*À quelle heure part/arrive …?*	a kel er par/a-reev …
boat	*le bateau*	ler ba-to
bus	*le bus*	ler bews
plane	*l'avion*	la-vyon
train	*le train*	ler trun

I want to go to …

Je voudrais aller à …   zher voo-dray a-lay a …

I'd like a … ticket.	*Je voudrais un billet …*	zher voo-dray un bee-yay …
1st class	*de première classe*	der prem-yair klas
2nd class	*de deuxième classe*	der der-zyem klas
one-way	*simple*	sum-pler
return	*aller et retour*	a-lay ay rer-toor

The train has been delayed.
Le train est en retard. ler trun ay ton rer·tar
The train has been cancelled.
Le train a été annulé. ler trun a ay·tay a·new·lay

the first	*le premier* (m)	ler prer·myay
	la première (f)	la prer·myair
the last	*le dernier* (m)	ler dair·nyay
	la dernière (f)	la dair·nyair
platform number	*le numéro de quai*	ler new·may·ro der kay
ticket office	*le guichet*	ler gee·shay
timetable	*l'horaire*	lo·rair
train station	*la gare*	la gar

PRIVATE TRANSPORT

I'd like to hire a/an…	*Je voudrais louer …*	zher voo·dray loo·way …
4WD	*un quatre-quatre*	un kat·kat
bicycle	*un vélo*	un vay·lo
car	*une voiture*	ewn vwa·tewr
motorbike	*une moto*	ewn mo·to

petrol/gas	*essence*	ay·sons
unleaded	*sans plomb*	son plom
leaded	*au plomb*	o plom
diesel	*diesel*	dyay·zel

Is this the road to …?
C'est la route pour … ? say la root poor …
Where's a service station?
Où est-ce qu'il y a une station-service? oo es keel ee a ewn sta·syon·ser·vees
Please fill it up.
Le plein, s'il vous plaît. ler plun seel voo play
I'd like … litres.
Je voudrais … litres. zher voo·dray … lee·trer
(How long) Can I park here?
(Combien de temps) Est-ce que je peux stationner ici? (kom·byun der ton) es ker zher per sta·syo·nay ee·see?
I need a mechanic.
J'ai besoin d'un mécanicien. zhay ber·zwun dun may·ka·nee·syun
The car/motorbike has broken down (at …).
La voiture/moto est tombée en panne (à …). la vwa·tewr/mo·to ay tom·bay on pan (a …)

ROAD SIGNS

Cédez la Priorité	Give Way
Danger	Danger
Défense de Stationner	No Parking
Entrée	Entrance
Interdiction de Doubler	No Overtaking
Péage	Toll
Ralentissez	Slow Down
Sens Interdit	No Entry
Sens Unique	One-Way
Sortie	Exit

The car/motorbike won't start.
La voiture/moto ne veut pas démarrer. la vwa·tewr/mo·to ner ver pa day·ma·ray
I have a flat tyre.
Mon pneu est à plat. mom pner ay ta pla
I've run out of petrol.
Je suis en panne d'essence. zher swee zon pan day·sons
I had an accident.
J'ai eu un accident. zhay ew un ak·see·don

TRAVEL WITH CHILDREN

Is there …?
Y a-t-il …? ee a·teel …
I need …
J'ai besoin de … zhay ber·zwun der…

baby change room	*un endroit pour changer le bébé*	un on·drwa poor shon·zhay ler bay·bay
car baby seat	*un siège-enfant*	un syezh·on·fon
child-minding service	*une garderie*	ewn gar·dree
children's menu	*un menu pour enfant*	un mer·new poor on·fon
disposable nappies/diapers	*couches-culottes*	koosh·kew·lot
(English-speaking) babysitter	*une baby-sitter (qui parle anglais)*	ewn ba·bee·see·ter (kee parl ong·glay)
formula	*lait maternisé*	lay ma·ter·nee·zay
highchair	*une chaise haute*	ewn shayz ot
potty	*un pot de bébé*	un po der bay·bay
stroller	*une poussette*	ewn poo·set

Do you mind if I breastfeed here?

Je peux allaiter mon bébé ici?   zher per a·lay·tay mon bay·bay ee·see

Are children allowed?

Les enfants sont permis?   lay zon·fon son pair·mee

BRETON

· · · · · ·

Hello.	*Demad./Demat.*
Welcome.	*Degememat.*
Goodbye.	*Kenavo.*
See you again.	*D'ur wech all.*
Thank you.	*Trugarez.*
Cheers.	*Yehed mad/Yec'hed mat.*

The following are some Breton words you may come across, especially in place names. Note that the spelling may vary.

aber	river mouth
ar	the
aven	river
bae	bay
bed	world, land
bihan	little
braz	big
coz	old
deiz	day
dol	table
dour	water
du	black
enez	island
fao, faou	beech tree
fest-noz	night festival
gall	French
gwenn	white
hir	long, tall
-ig, -ic	diminutive suffix
iliz	church
kastell	castle
kember, kemper	confluence
koad, goat	forest
koan	dinner
kromm, crom	curved
lam, lan	monastery
loc	hermitage
men/mein	stone
menez	mountain
mor	sea
nant	valley
plou-, plo-, ple-	parish (used only as a prefix in place names)
poull	pond
pred	lunch
raz	strait
roc'h	rock, pointed hill
roz, ros	hillock, mound
ster, stêr, steir	river
stif, stivell	spring
tann	oak tree
telenn	Celtic harp
ti, ty	house
trev, tre, treo	parish division
trez	sand
uhel	high

LANGUAGE

Also available from Lonely Planet:
French Phrasebook

GLOSSARY

For a glossary of food and drink terms, see p284. For more useful words and phrases, see the Language chapter, p330. Below, (m) indicates masculine gender, (f) feminine gender and (pl) plural.

aber (m) – coastal inlet formed by a retreating glacier
accueil (m) – reception
alignements (m, pl) – series of standing stones, or *menhirs*, in straight lines
allée (f) – alley
AOC (m) – *appelation d'origine contrôlée*, the French equivalent of a trademark for food, wines, drinks and other products produced in a certain area
auberge de jeunesse (f) – youth hostel

baie (f) – bay
belon (m) – flat oyster harvested from the Bélon river
billet (m) – ticket
billet jumelé (m) – combination ticket, good for more than one site, museum etc
billeterie (f) – ticket office or counter
biniou kozh – double-reed bagpipe, specific to Brittany

bois (m) – wood
boisson comprise (f) – drink included
boîte (f) – nightclub, literally box
bombarde (f) – Breton version of the shawm, a precursor of the oboe
boucherie (f) – butcher
boulangerie (f) – bakery, bread shop
brasserie (f) – restaurant usually serving food all day
bureau de poste (m) or *poste* (f) – post office

cairn (m) – heap of dry stones, usually covering a burial chamber
canard (m) – duck
carnet (m) – a book of five or 10 bus, tram or metro tickets sold at a reduced rate
carrefour (m) – crossroads
carte (f) – card; menu; map
cave (f) – wine cellar
chambre (f) – room
chambre d'hôte (f) – B&B accommodation/guest house
charcuterie (f) – pork butcher's shop and delicatessen
château (m) – castle
chaumière (f) – thatched cottage

col (m) – pass; lowest point on a ridge between two peaks

colombier (m) – pigeon house, or dovecote

commissariat de police (m) – police station

confiserie (f) – chocolate/sweet shop

côte (m) – coast

couchette (f) – sleeping berth on a train or ferry

crêperie (f) – pancake restaurant

creuse (f) – Pacific oyster

criée (f) – fish market

cromlech (m) – circle of standing stones

Cyberposte (f) – the post office's internet access service

débarquement (m) – literally 'debarkation' – a French term for the D-Day landings

déjeuner (m) – lunch

demi-pension (f) – half-board (B&B with either lunch or dinner)

dentelle (f) – lace

département (m) – department, administrative division of France

dîner (m) – dinner

dolmen (m) – from the Breton *dol men* (stone table); horizontal stone slab supported by two vertical slabs set on edge to create a chamber

douane (f) – customs

église (f) – church

embarcadère (m) – pier, jetty

enclos paroissiaux (m) – parish enclosures

épicerie (f) – small grocery store

équitation (f) – horse riding

faïence (f) – ceramics

fauteuil (m) – seat on trains, ferries or at the theatre

fest-noz (pl *festoù-noz*) – literally, 'night festival'

fête (f) – festival, party

foire (f) – fair

fôret (f) – forest

forfait (m) – fixed-price deal at camping grounds

formule (f) – similar to a *menu* but allows choice of whichever two of three courses you want (eg starter and main course or main course and dessert)

fromagerie (f) – cheese shop

galerie (f) – covered shopping centre or arcade

gare (f) – railway station

gare interurbaine (f) – intercity bus station

gare maritime (f) – ferry terminal

gendarmerie (f) – police station; police force

gîte d'étape (m) – walkers' accommodation, usually in a village

golfe (m) – gulf

GR (f) – *grande randonnée* (long-distance hiking trail)

halles (f, pl) – covered market, central food market

horaire (m) – timetable or schedule

hôtel de ville (m) – city or town hall

hôtes payants (m, pl) or *hébergement chez l'habitant* (m) – homestays

interdit – prohibited

jardin (m) – garden

jours fériés (m, pl) – public holidays

lande (f) – moor, heath

langoustier (m) – traditional langoustine fishing boat

laverie (f) or **lavomatique** (m) – laundrette

mairie (f) – city or town hall

maison de la presse (f) – newsagent

maison du parc (f) – a national park's headquarters and/or visitors centre
marché (m) – market
marché couvert (m) – covered market
menhir (m) – from the Breton *men hir* (standing stone); a single upright stone
menu (m) – fixed-price meal with two or more courses
musée (m) – museum

navette (f) – shuttle bus, train or boat
nettoyage à sec – dry cleaning

office du tourisme (m) – tourist office

palais de justice (m) – law courts
parc (m) – park
parc naturel régional (m) – regional natural park
pardon (m) – traditional Breton religious festival in honour of a patron saint
pâtisserie (f) – cake and pastry shop
petit déjeuner (m) – breakfast
phare (m) – lighthouse
pharmacie de garde (f) – pharmacy on weekend/night duty
place (f) – square, plaza
plage (f) – beach
plan (m) – city map
plat du jour (m) – daily special meal
poissonnier (m) – fishmonger
pont (m) – bridge
port (m) – harbour, port
port de plaisance (m) – marina or pleasure-boat harbour
porte (f) – door, gate in a city wall
pourboire (m) – tip
presqu'île (f) – peninsula

quai (f) – quay, railway platform
quartier (m) – quarter, district

rive (f) – riverbank
rond point (m) – roundabout
rue (f) – street

salon de thé (m) – tearoom
SAMU – Service d'Aide Médicale d'Urgence (emergency medical aid service)
sentier (m) – trail
sentier des douaniers (m) – customs officers' trail
service des urgences (m) – hospital accident and emergency department
SNCF – Société Nationale des Chemins de Fer (state-owned railway company)
soirée étape – half-board
sortie (f) – exit
square (m) – public garden
stations balnéaires (pl) – seaside resorts
supermarché (m) – supermarket
syndicat d'initiative (m) – tourist office

tabac (m) – tobacconist (also sells bus tickets, phonecards)
télécarte (f) – phonecard
TGV – *train à grande vitesse* (high-speed train, bullet train)
toilettes (f, pl) – public toilets
tour (f) – tower
TTC – *toutes taxes comprises* (all taxes included)
tumulus (m) – mound of stone and/or earth covering a burial chamber
TVA – value added tax

vallée (f) – valley
vedette (f) – ferry
venelle (f) – alley
vente (f) – sale, or the selling rate when changing money
vin (m) – wine
V.O. (f) – *version originale*; a nondubbed film with French subtitles
voie (f) – train platform
VTT (m) – *vélo tout terrain*; mountain bike

BEHIND THE SCENES

THIS BOOK

The 1st edition of *Brittany & Normandy* was written by Jeanne Oliver and Miles Roddis. This 2nd edition was researched and written by Oliver Berry and Peter Dragicevich. It was commissioned in Lonely Planet's London office and produced by the following people:

Commissioning Editor Clifton Wilkinson
Coordinating Editor Evan Jones
Coordinating Cartographer Alex Leung
Coordinating Layout Designer Cara Smith
Managing Layout Designer Laura Jane
Managing Editors Brigitte Ellemor, Lauren Hunt

Managing Cartographers Adrian Persoglia, Herman So
Language Content Robyn Loughnane
Assisting Editors Sarah Bailey, Helen Koehne, Anne Mulvaney, Kirsten Rawlings
Assisting Cartographer Ross Butler
Cover Marika Mercer, lonelyplanet images.com
Internal Image Research Aude Vauconsant, lonelyplanetimages.com
Project Managers Glenn van der Knijff, Michelle Lewis
Thanks to Mark Adams, Imogen Bannister, Lucy Birchley, Yvonne Bischofberger, Sally Darmody, Janine Eberle, Owen Eszeki, Mark Germanchis, Michelle Glynn, Imogen Hall, James

THE LONELY PLANET STORY

Fresh from an epic journey across Europe, Asia and Australia in 1972, Tony and Maureen Wheeler sat at their kitchen table stapling together notes. The first Lonely Planet guidebook, *Across Asia on the Cheap,* was born.

Travellers snapped up the guides. Inspired by their success, the Wheelers began publishing books to Southeast Asia, India and beyond. Demand was prodigious, and the Wheelers expanded the business rapidly to keep up. Over the years, Lonely Planet extended its coverage to every country and into the virtual world via lonelyplanet.com and the Thorn Tree message board.

As Lonely Planet became a globally loved brand, Tony and Maureen received several offers for the company. But it wasn't until 2007 that they found a partner whom they trusted to remain true to the company's principles of travelling widely, treading lightly and giving sustainably. In October of that year, BBC Worldwide acquired a 75% share in the company, pledging to uphold Lonely Planet's commitment to independent travel, trustworthy advice and editorial independence.

Today, Lonely Planet has offices in Melbourne, London and Oakland, with over 500 staff members and 300 authors. Tony and Maureen are still actively involved with Lonely Planet. They're travelling more often than ever, and they're devoting their spare time to charitable projects. And the company is still driven by the philosophy of *Across Asia on the Cheap*: 'All you've got to do is decide to go and the hardest part is over. So go!'

BEHIND THE SCENES

Hardy, Paula Hardy, Rachel Imeson,
Nic Lehman, John Mazzocchi, Annelies
Mertens, Lucy Monie, Wayne Murphy,
Darren O'Connell, Julie Sheridan, John
Taufa, Juan Winata

THANKS

OLIVER BERRY

On the road, my thanks go out to
Philippe, Sylvie, Jerôme, Jean-Christophe
and, of course, to Peter Dragicevich
for braving the perils of a Norman diet
and doing such a stirling job across the
border. At the Planet, a special thanks
to Cliff Wilkinson and everyone on the
Regionals team for dreaming up the
ideas and providing guidance when all
other lights went out. Over in Kernow,
thanks to the Stig, TSP, the Hobo,
Arbuckle, o-region and Susie Berry.

PETER DRAGICEVICH

First and foremost, thanks are due
to my ever helpful Commissioning
Editor, Cliff Wilkinson, and my talented
Coordinating Author, Olly Berry –
it's been a pleasure. Thanks also to
everyone involved in the Regionals
relaunch, especially Imogen Hall and
Paula Hardy. *Merci beaucoup* to those
who harboured this itinerant writer:
Tim Benzie, Sue Ostler, Ed Lee, Vanessa
Irvine, Paul Sajewicz, Kerri Tyler and
Bob Dragicevich.

OUR READERS

**Many thanks to the travellers who
used the last edition and wrote to us
with helpful hints, useful advice and
interesting anecdotes:**
Jon Barnsley, Susan Cartwright, Lena
M Coen, Tania Durt, Frances Higgins,
Dan Leach, Clare Macdonald, Janet
Pennington, Patrick Young

SEND US YOUR FEEDBACK

We love to hear from travellers – your
comments keep us on our toes and help
make our books better. Our well-trav-
elled team reads every word on what
you loved or loathed about this book.
Although we cannot reply individually to
postal submissions, we always guarantee
that your feedback goes straight to the
appropriate authors, in time for the next
edition. Each person who sends us information is thanked in the next edition –
and the most useful submissions are
rewarded with a free book.

To send us your updates – and
find out about Lonely Planet events,
newsletters and travel news – visit our
award-winning website: **lonelyplanet
.com/contact**.

Note: We may edit, reproduce and
incorporate your comments in Lonely
Planet products such as guidebooks,
websites and digital products, so let us
know if you don't want your comments
reproduced or your name acknowl-
edged. For a copy of our privacy policy
visit lonelyplanet.com/privacy.

ACKNOWLEDGMENTS

All images are the copyright of the pho-
tographers unless otherwise indicated.
Many of the images in this guide are
available for licensing from Lonely
Planet Images: lonelyplanetimages.com.

INDEX

INDEX

INDEX

INDEX

INDEX